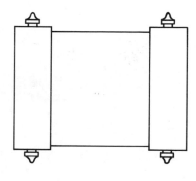

# A COMPANION TO YOUR STUDY OF THE OLD TESTAMENT

Daniel H. Ludlow

Deseret Book Company
Salt Lake City, Utah
1981

**Library of Congress Cataloging-in-Publication Data**

Ludlow, Daniel H
    A companion to your study of the Old Testament.

    1. Bible. O.T.—Criticism, interpretation, etc.
2. Bible. O.T.—Study.   I. Title.
BS1171.2.L83     221.5'2038        80-28088
ISBN 0-87747-853-8

Printed in the United States of America

10   9   8

# CONTENTS

# PREFACE

The Old Testament is considered by most people to be the book of scripture most difficult to understand and appreciate. Yet it was essentially the Old Testament that was available when Jesus Christ counseled that the scriptures should be searched diligently because they testified of him. It was also of this scripture and its companion, the New Testament, that Brigham Young stated:

"In all my teachings, I have taught the Gospel from the Old and New Testaments. I found therein every doctrine, and the proof of every doctrine, the Latter-day Saints believe in. . . . There may be some doctrines about which little is said in the Bible, but they are all couched therein." (JD 16:73.)

Of the Bible and its companion scripture, the Book of Mormon, the Lord said to a latter-day prophet: "And again, the elders, priests and teachers of this church shall teach the principles of my gospel . . . in the Bible and the Book of Mormon." (D&C 42:12.)

Many reasons have been given by people as to why they do not study the Old Testament more diligently—it is too long, it was written too many years ago and does not apply today, there are too many voids in the record and some overlapping and duplication, it is not always presented chronologically, it contains too much history and too many "endless genealogies," and so on.

One purpose of this book is to help you appreciate and understand the Old Testament. To help achieve this objective, several study and teaching features have been included in this book.

Part I contains a brief historical overview of the major families in the Old Testament, including their most important beliefs, customs, traditions, and practices, and their routes of travel and places of residence. Old Testament prophecies related to three major time periods are then listed and thoroughly documented: prophecies fulfilled within the period of the Old Testament, prophecies fulfilled in New Testament times, and prophecies to be fulfilled in the latter days.

Next are selected quotations from presidents of the Church

on the major Old Testament prophecies to be fulfilled in the latter days, including such topics as the gathering of Israel (Judah, the dispersed of Israel, and the ten "lost" tribes), the building up and redemption of Israel, events preceding and associated with the second coming of Jesus Christ, and the Millennium.

The concluding segments in Part I include excerpts from four documents related to Old Testament topics:

1. "A Review of God's Concerns with the Children of Abraham," by Anthony W. Ivins.

2. Dedicatory prayer pertaining to the return of Judah's descendants, by Orson Hyde.

3. The "Proclamation of 1845" addressed to the leaders of the earth and to all the inhabitants thereof, issued by the Twelve Apostles of The Church of Jesus Christ of Latter-day Saints.

4. "A Message to Judah from Joseph," by Ezra Taft Benson.

To assist in subsequent referencing, major topics and sections of Part I are indicated by numbers in the margins of the pages.

Part II, which comprises the bulk of the book, consists of observations, definitions, and explanations of topics, expressions, and words that might be hard to understand. These are identified by book, chapter, and verse, and are often supplemented by quotations, usually by General Authorities of the Church.

The Appendix contains hundreds of words and terms from the King James text, listed alphabetically, that might be hard to understand because of changes in meaning or problems of translation, or because they are idioms or parts of difficult expressions. Explanations, definitions, and alternate readings from the Hebrew and other sources are provided for these items.

This book has been planned to supplement the Latter-day Saint edition of the King James Bible, with its many excellent aids including: extensive cross-references to all the standard works; comprehensive footnotes from the Hebrew, Greek, Joseph Smith Translation, and other versions and editions of the Bible; thorough chapter headings; Topical Guide and Bible Dictionary entries; and gazetteer and maps. I feel that this special edition of the Bible is the most important biblical publication since 1611, when the first edition of the King James Bible was printed. I also believe that the LDS edition of the

King James Bible, together with the other scriptures and the inspired teachings and commentaries of modern prophets, seers,
and revelators, is sufficient for a thorough study and understanding of the Old Testament. *A Companion to Your Study of
the Old Testament* encourages the use of the new Bible and is
designed to augment the instructional aids in that superb edition.

I have frequently quoted: "One of the best ways to learn
something is to *teach* it." I will now add another expression:
"One of the best ways to learn something is to *write* about it."
The past few months of intense research, thought, and writing
on the Old Testament have brought with them a greater love,
appreciation, and understanding of this sublime scripture. If
this present book will help you experience these same feelings,
then one of my hopes will have been realized.

# ACKNOWLEDGMENTS

Many persons have assisted in the preparation and publication of this book. Special thanks and appreciation are extended to—

Luene, an ideal wife for all reasons and seasons, for her constant help and encouragement.

Kathy, the one of our eight daughters who was at the right maturity, spirituality, and availability for months of able and dedicated assistance.

Victor L. Ludlow, a son who teaches Old Testament courses at BYU, and a son-in-law, Nate LeRoy Pierce, who has taught Old Testament on the college level, for reading the manuscript and making perceptive suggestions.

Gary Gillespie, a friend, confidant, and fellow traveler in Israel for six months, for his wise assistance and strengthening encouragement.

Ellis Rasmussen, a friend and fellow teacher of many years, for his insights and enthusiasm for the Old Testament.

Merle Romer and Diane Chrysler, for typing and retyping and retyping portions of the manuscript.

Eleanor Knowles and Jack Lyon, editors at Deseret Book, for their warm, friendly, yet efficient and effective editorial assistance.

And special and eternal thanks to our Heavenly Father and to his divine Son, known by many honored and appropriate titles, including Jehovah and Jesus Christ, for making the sublime scripture of the Old Testament available to us, and for encouraging us to search it diligently so we might *know* and then to follow their teachings so we will also *do*. My prayer is that this book might serve in some small way to encourage people to read and ponder the Old Testament, thus demonstrating willingness to receive the word They have already given, so They might give more for our eternal benefit.

# KEY TO ABBREVIATIONS

| | |
|---|---|
| AF | *Articles of Faith,* James E. Talmage |
| AGQ | *Answers to Gospel Questions,* Joseph Fielding Smith |
| APPP | *Autobiography of Parley P. Pratt* |
| ASIF | Address to Seminary and Institute Faculty |
| BE | *Biographical Encyclopedia,* Andrew Jenson |
| BYUSY | *Brigham Young University Speeches of the Year* |
| CBM | *A Companion to Your Study of the Book of Mormon,* Daniel H. Ludlow |
| CDC | *A Companion to Your Study of the Doctrine and Covenants,* Daniel H. Ludlow |
| CDG | *A Compendium of the Doctrines of the Gospel,* Franklin D. Richards and James A. Little |
| CHC | *A Comprehensive History of the Church,* B. H. Roberts |
| CHMR | *Church History and Modern Revelation,* Joseph Fielding Smith |
| CR | Conference Report |
| CN | *Church News* |
| DBY | *Discourses of Brigham Young* |
| DCC | *Doctrine and Covenants Commentary,* Hyrum M. Smith and Janne M. Sjodahl |
| DNTC | *Doctrinal New Testament Commentary,* Bruce R. McConkie |
| DS | *Doctrines of Salvation,* Joseph Fielding Smith |
| DWB | *Discovering the World of the Bible,* LaMar C. Berrett |
| ECH | *Essentials in Church History,* Joseph Fielding Smith |
| E | *Ensign* |
| ER | *Evidences and Reconciliations,* John A. Widtsoe |
| FPM | *Faith Precedes the Miracle,* Spencer W. Kimball |
| GD | *Gospel Doctrine,* Joseph F. Smith |
| GG | *Government of God,* John Taylor |
| GI | *Gospel Interpretations,* John A. Widtsoe |
| GK | *Gospel Kingdom,* John Taylor |
| GSI | *Gospel Ideals,* David O. McKay |
| HC | *History of the Church,* Joseph Smith |
| IDYK | *Israel! Do You Know?,* LeGrand Richards |
| IE | *Improvement Era* |

| | |
|---|---|
| IOT | *An Introduction to the Old Testament and Its Teachings,* Ellis T. Rasmussen |
| IP | *Items on Priesthood,* John Taylor |
| JC | *Jesus the Christ,* James E. Talmage |
| JD | *Journal of Discourses* |
| JH | *Journal History* |
| JI | *Juvenile Instructor* |
| JST | *Joseph Smith's "New Translation" of the Bible* |
| JS | *Joseph Smith,* John A. Widtsoe |
| KT | *Key to the Science of Theology,* Parley P. Pratt |
| LDPS | *Latter-day Prophets Speak,* Daniel H. Ludlow |
| LHCK | *Life of Heber C. Kimball,* Orson F. Whitney |
| LJS | *Life of Joseph Smith the Prophet,* George Q. Cannon |
| MA | *Mediation and Atonement,* John Taylor |
| MD | *Mormon Doctrine,* 1966 ed., Bruce R. McConkie |
| MDC | *The Message of the Doctrine and Covenants,* John A. Widtsoe |
| MDOP | *Masterful Discourses of Orson Pratt* |
| MF | *The Miracle of Forgiveness,* Spencer W. Kimball |
| MFP | *Messages of the First Presidency,* compiled by James R. Clark |
| MS | *Millennial Star* |
| MWW | *A Marvelous Work and a Wonder,* LeGrand Richards |
| NE | *New Era* |
| OVBC | *One Volume Bible Commentary,* J. R. Dummelow |
| PC | *Program of The Church of Jesus Christ of Latter-day Saints* |
| RT | *The Restoration of All Things,* Joseph Fielding Smith |
| SHP | *Stand Ye in Holy Places,* Harold B. Lee |
| SMJB | *Sermons and Missionary Services of Melvin J. Ballard,* Bryant S. Hinckley |
| SNT | *Saturday Night Thoughts,* Orson F. Whitney |
| ST | *Signs of the Times,* Joseph Fielding Smith |
| TMH | *Temples of the Most High,* compiled by N.B. Lundwall |
| TPJS | *Teachings of the Prophet Joseph Smith,* compiled by Joseph Fielding Smith |
| VM | *The Vitality of Mormonism,* James E. Talmage |
| VW | *Voice of Warning,* Parley P. Pratt |
| WP | *The Way to Perfection,* Joseph Fielding Smith |
| WW | *Wilford Woodruff,* Matthias F. Cowley |
| YFY | *Your Faith and You,* Mark E. Petersen |
| YWJ | *Young Women's Journal* |

# PART I
# AN OVERVIEW OF
# THE OLD TESTAMENT
# AND ITS PROPHECIES

# TEACHINGS FROM THE OLD TESTAMENT

(Note: This book has been written for use with the LDS edition of the King James Version of the Bible published in 1979 by The Church of Jesus Christ of Latter-day Saints. All references to chapter headings, footnotes, and entries in the Topical Guide and Bible Dictionary pertain to that edition of the Bible.

The abbreviation TG refers to the Topical Guide; BD refers to the Bible Dictionary.

The numbers in the margin of each page in Part I indicate major segments; these numbers are used with the designation "Part I" for ease in reference. For example, the commentary for Micah 4:7 says that additional information on that verse appears in Part I 204, meaning segment 204 of Part I, found on page 84.)

# BELIEFS, CUSTOMS, AND TRADITIONS OF PRINCIPAL OLD TESTAMENT FAMILIES

The Old Testament is primarily a record of a series of families. In order to understand and appreciate the Old Testament, you will need to understand the major events, beliefs, customs, and traditions of the families discussed. **1**

The family of Adam is introduced first, but by chapter six of the first book (Genesis), the family of Noah appears. In only six more chapters (Genesis 12), the family of Abraham is featured, next Isaac (whose birth is recorded in chapter 21), and then Jacob (Israel), whose story begins in chapter 25 and whose descendants dominate the remainder of the Old Testament. Thus, of the 929 chapters in the thirty-nine books in the Old Testament, only 24 chapters do not deal directly with Jacob and his descendants, and these first 24 chapters provide the background for the coming forth of the family of Israel.

The last part of the Old Testament is primarily concerned with a specific segment of Jacob's family—the Jews, descendants of Jacob's fourth son (Judah), and also citizens of the kingdom of Judah. Thus, sometimes the entire Old Testament is referred to as the "record of the Jews."

Other titles associated with the heads of major families might be used to indicate that the Old Testament is also the record of— **2**

1. The Semites (descendants of Shem, the son of Noah).
2. The Hebrews (descendants of Abraham).
3. The Israelites (descendants of Jacob/Israel).

The problem of using these terms to refer to the major peoples of the Bible is that the terms are not synonymous—thus, the speaker must be certain he is using each term correctly. All Jews (descendants of Judah) are Israelites (descendants of Jacob/Israel), but not all Israelites are Jews. (There are many descendants of the other sons of Jacob who are not descendants of Judah.)

All Israelites (descendants of Jacob/Israel) are Hebrews (descendants of Abraham), but not all Hebrews are Israelites.

(The descendants of Ishmael and of the six sons of Abraham through Keturah are Hebrews, but they are not descendants of Jacob.)

All Hebrews (descendants of Abraham) are Semites (descendants of Shem), but not all Semites are Hebrews.

One reason the world is confused about these terms is that essentially the only Israelites the world has known about for over 2,700 years (from 722 B.C., when the ten tribes were taken captive, to the present) are the Jews. Most people, therefore, think the terms *Jew* and *Israelite* are synonymous, but they are not.

Some of the principal beliefs, customs, and traditions of these major families will be discussed in an effort to provide background for an understanding of the Old Testament.

### The Family of Adam

**3**     The King James version of the Old Testament provides only five chapters pertaining to the family of Adam before the family of Noah is introduced. Considerable information is provided in these few brief chapters, however, as is indicated by noting some of the chapter headings in the LDS edition of the King James Bible:

Chapter 2: *"Creation completed—God rests on the seventh day—Prior spirit creation explained—Adam and Eve placed in Garden of Eden—They are forbidden to eat of the tree of knowledge of good and evil—Adam names every living creature—Adam and Eve are married by the Lord."*

Chapter 3: *"The Serpent (Lucifer) deceives Eve—She and then Adam partake of the forbidden fruit—Her Seed (Christ) shall bruise the Serpent's head—Role of woman, and of man—Adam and Eve cast out of the Garden of Eden—Adam presides—Eve becomes the mother of all living."*

Chapter 4: *"Eve bears Cain and Abel—They offer sacrifices—Cain slays Abel and is cursed by the Lord, who also sets a mark upon him—The children of men multiply, etc."*

**4**     However, the Joseph Smith Translation of this same period adds a great deal of additional information, including the following:

1. Two great personages were directly involved in the creation of the world and of man, one of whom was the "Only Begotten" of the Father "from the beginning." (Gen. 1:27.)

2. All things were created spiritually before they appeared naturally upon the earth. (Gen. 2:5-11.)

3. Free agency was given to man, allowing him the privilege of choosing what he would do. (Gen. 2:21.)

4. Lucifer (Satan or the devil) influenced the serpent to tempt Eve and also influenced Cain to offer an unworthy sacrifice and to kill Abel. (Gen. 3:1-7; 5:6-26.)

5. The offering of sacrifice was instituted in the very beginning of the earth as "a similitude of the sacrifice of the Only Begotten of the Father, which is full of grace and truth." (Gen. 4:5-8.)

6. The Holy Ghost was active with Adam to "bear record of the Father and the Son." (Gen. 4:9.)

The Joseph Smith Translation includes almost two chapters **5** of additional information pertaining to Enoch and his people, indicating that the essentials of the gospel of Jesus Christ were upon the earth from earliest times, including faith in the Lord Jesus Christ, repentance, baptism by immersion for the remission of sins, and the laying on of hands for the gift of the Holy Ghost. (See Gen. 6:26-71; 7:1-85.)

The truth that baptism was introduced on the earth during the days of Adam and has continued except for periods of almost complete apostasy may be surprising to some theologians because the words *baptize* and *baptism* do not appear in the King James version of the Old Testament. However, some writings of Jewish scholars and recent discoveries such as the Dead Sea Scrolls indicate that groups of Israelites were performing baptisms hundreds of years before the time of Christ. Also the fact that Jesus Christ was not criticized by the Pharisees, Sadducees, and scribes in sanctioning baptism is evidence the practice must have then been current, for these groups were very quick to denounce Christ whenever he deviated from their customs and practices.

Some scholars have suggested that the reason the word **6** *baptize* does not appear in the Old Testament is that the word is of Greek derivation, not Hebrew. A more plausible explanation of the absence of baptism in the standard versions of the Old Testament is that this was one of the changes brought about by "designing and corrupt priests" either from Judaism or from Christianity who wanted to separate their particular theology from that of the other group. (See TPJS, p. 327.)

Some scholars may also be surprised to learn that the Holy Ghost and its gifts were operative from earliest times. This truth should be implicit from the teaching that God is the same yesterday, today, and forever. Also, the Holy Ghost is an integral component of the gospel of Jesus Christ, and the New Testament teaches that "the gospel" of Jesus Christ was preached "unto them [Old Testament peoples]" as well as "unto us." (Heb. 4:2.)

### The Family of Noah

**7**     Noah is first mentioned in Genesis 5:29, and his immediate family is emphasized in the following five chapters. Selected chapter headings from the Bible illustrate some of the beliefs and practices of these people:

Chapter 6: *"God establishes his covenant with Noah, who builds an ark to save his family and divers living things."*

Chapter 7: *"The flood comes and water covers the whole earth."*

Chapter 8: *"He [Noah] offers sacrifices."*

Chapter 9: *"Noah and his sons commanded to multiply and fill the earth—They are given dominion over all forms of life— Death penalty decreed for murder—God shall not again destroy the earth by a flood."*

The Joseph Smith Translation adds the following information concerning the period of Noah:

1. Noah taught the gospel to the people of his day, but they sought "to take away his life." (Gen. 8:3-9.)

2. In the last days the "city of Enoch which I [the Lord] have caught up unto myself . . . shall come down out of heaven" as will the "general assembly of the church of the first-born . . . and possess the earth." (Gen. 9:21-25.)

3. Noah and his descendants fulfill the promise of the Lord to Enoch that Enoch's seed which remained on the earth should not all be destroyed at the time of the flood. (Gen. 8:23; 9:14-15.)

### The Family of Abraham

**8**     Abraham (Abram) is first mentioned in Genesis 11:26, and his family (the Hebrews) is featured until his death in chapter 25. The chapter headings in the Bible provide a quick overview of the major events in the life of Abraham and should be studied carefully although they are not listed here. A full appreciation of this great man is possible, however, only through understanding the following beliefs, customs, traditions, and practices of the time in which he lived:

**9**     1. The Hebrews were governed through a patriarchal order

—that is, the right of ruling (presiding) in the family went from father to son.

From the time of Adam to well over two thousand years evidently the people were largely governed by patriarchal order, which means the right of governorship went from father to son. This is in contrast to matriarchy (where the right of rulership goes from mother to daughter), which was not practiced by the peoples of the Bible.

The basic meaning of the English word *patriarch* is *father,* coming from Latin and French. Some of the current usages of the word are: "one of the scriptural fathers of the human race or of the Hebrew people"; "the oldest member or representative of a group"; "a Mormon of the Melchizedek Priesthood empowered to perform the ordinances of the church and pronounce blessings within a stake or other prescribed jurisdiction." (*Webster's New Collegiate Dictionary* [Springfield, Mass.: G&C Merriam Co., 1979], p. 833.)

When seeing or hearing the term *patriarchs of the Bible,* many people would immediately think of Abraham, Isaac, and Jacob; these men were indeed "fathers" of most of the peoples discussed in the Bible.

(TG: Patriarch, pp. 359-60. BD: Patriarch, Patriarchs, p. 742.)

2. The Hebrews believed in primogeniture to determine **10** which son should succeed the father as the presiding head of the family.

The two basic parts of the word *primogeniture* have to do with *first* ("prime") and *birth* ("geniture"). The dictionary defines the word as "the state of being the firstborn of the children of the same parents" and "an exclusive right of inheritance belonging to the eldest son." (*Webster's,* p. 907.)

It is clear that at least by the time of Abraham the peoples of the Bible had adopted the custom or practice of primogeniture to determine which son would succeed the father as the head of the family upon the death of the father. The "firstborn" or eldest son would become the new leader of the family so long as he was qualified and worthy.

(TG: Birthright, p. 30; Firstborn, p. 149; Inheritance, p. 228. BD: Birthright, p. 625; Firstborn, p. 675; Inheritance, pp. 706-7.)

3. The Hebrews followed the law "of the birthright son." **11**
The law of the birthright pertained to the rights a son might

have because of his order of birth. Although daughters might also participate in the inheritance of their father, when the daughters married they were considered to belong to the family of their husbands so far as major inheritances were concerned.

The son to succeed the father as head of the family by right of his birth was entitled to a double portion of the father's inheritance. He was entitled to one portion as a son; then he received a second portion as the new head of the family. The second portion was to be used in taking care of any debts of the family, in caring for minor children or unmarried sisters, and so on.

Thus when a father who had four sons died, his inheritance would be divided into five portions—each son would receive one portion and the birthright son would receive a second portion. The birthright son would receive a double portion, twice as much as any one of the other sons; this law does not mean that the birthright son would receive twice as much as all the other sons combined.

(TG: Birthright, p. 30; Firstborn, p. 149; Inheritance, p. 228. BD: Birthright, p. 625; Firstborn, p. 675; Inheritance, pp. 706-7.)

**12**    4. The Hebrews practiced polygyny.

At least by the time of Abraham, some of the religious leaders of that time were practicing polygyny, which is defined as "the state or practice of having more than one wife or female mate at one time." (*Webster's,* p. 885.) This practice is in contrast to polyandry, which was not followed by these people —"the state or practice of having more than one husband or male mate at one time." (*Webster's,* p. 884.) Both polygyny and polyandry are forms of polygamy—"marriage in which a spouse of either sex may have more than one mate at the same time." (*Webster's,* p. 884.)

It is obvious from the Bible the practice of polygyny is not evil in and of itself, for some of the greatest religious leaders in the Bible (such as Abraham and Jacob) were polygynists. In the Book of Mormon the Lord makes it clear that polygyny is acceptable if he commands it to "raise up seed" unto him; otherwise the commandment is one wife per husband at one time.

(TG: Marriage, Plural, p. 311. Jacob 2:30; D&C 132:52, 61-62.)

**13**

5. At least some of the Hebrews had concubines among their wives.

The biblical definition and usage of the word *concubine* is not the same as current dictionary usage. A current dictionary defines a concubine as "a woman living in a socially recognized state of concubinage" and then defines concubinage as "co-habitation of persons not legally married." (*Webster's,* p. 232.) In biblical times, a concubine was a legally married wife, usually of a second class status either because of social order, economic position, race, or nationality (a foreigner). Concubines had legal status and rights as wives, although not always of the same order or magnitude as the rights of "first wives."

It should be remembered that concubines in Old Testament times were part of polygynous marriages, where the husband could legally have more than one wife at the same time. (TG: Concubine, p. 70; Marriage, Plural, p. 311.)

*Implications of These Customs of the Hebrews*

**14**

Because the Hebrews followed the custom of primogeniture and practiced polygyny at the same time, some students of the Bible have become confused as to which of the "firstborn" sons of the various wives and concubines was really the "birthright" son. If the father had only one wife at any one time during his life, then it would be immediately evident which son would be the "firstborn" son. However, if the father had been a polygynist with two or more wives at the same time, the problem of successorship could be more difficult since each of the wives could have a firstborn son.

The Hebrews were not confused on this matter, however, as they had developed the custom that the order of the marriage of the wives would be given first consideration in determining the order of the son to succeed the father as head of the family. Thus, the firstborn son of the first wife became the birthright son, if worthy. If the firstborn son of the first wife proved unworthy and if the father had sons from more than one wife, then the firstborn son of the second wife became the new birth-right son, and so on.

**15**

These practices and customs help explain why Ishmael was first considered to be the birthright son of Abraham: he was the eldest son of Abraham and was the firstborn son of the second wife (Hagar). However, when Isaac was born, he became the new birthright son by the order of primogeniture because he was the firstborn son of the first wife (Sarah).

The law or practice of primogeniture also helps explain how Joseph eventually became the head of the house or family of Israel, even though Joseph was the eleventh of the twelve sons of Jacob. Reuben was the initial birthright son of Jacob and was first in line to succeed his father, since he was the firstborn son of the first wife (Leah). However, Reuben lost the right to the birthright when he committed adultery with one of his father's wives (Bilhah). Through application of the law of primogeniture, Joseph then became the new birthright son because he was the firstborn son of the second wife (Rachel).

**16**     In polygynous marriages, all of the firstborn sons of the various wives would be considered as the new leader before any of the secondborn or other sons. Only in monogamous marriages would the secondborn son be immediately considered as the potential new leader if the firstborn son proved unworthy. The Bible is not exactly clear as to why Jacob (the secondborn son) succeeded Esau (the firstborn son) as the head of Isaac's family, although it does mention that Isaac and Rebekah were sorely displeased and of "a grief of mind" because Esau had married wives of the Hittites (Gen. 26:34–35). Isaac also specifically forbade Jacob to "take a wife of the daughters of Canaan" (Gen. 28:1), and Rebekah lamented "if Jacob take a wife of the daughters of Heth, such as these which are of the daughters of the land, what good shall my life do me?" (Gen. 27:46.) Evidently the poor marriage choices of Esau disqualified him as the new leader of the house of Isaac, as well as the selling of his birthright for a mess of pottage. (Gen. 25:29–34.)

The Bible is even less clear as to why Ephraim (the secondborn) replaces Manasseh (the firstborn) as the birthright son of Joseph. Evidently Jacob received a vision or revelation from the Lord concerning the fact that Ephraim was to have the birthright. (Gen. 48:8–20.) This is not only substantiated by the Joseph Smith Translation account of this episode, but the Lord himself declared later in the biblical account, "For I am Father to Israel, and Ephraim is my firstborn." (Jer. 31:9.)

### The Family of Isaac

**17**     The brief account of the family of Isaac (Gen. 24–26) adds little to an understanding of the peoples of his day. Isaac evidently followed the customs and practices of his father,

Abraham, which included the belief that the sons should marry
from among the Hebrew (or at least the Semitic) women. Thus
Abraham had sent back to Haran ("unto the city of Nahor"—
Gen. 24:10) to obtain a wife (Rebekah) for Isaac. (Gen.
24:1-67.) Later Isaac followed this same pattern in encouraging
his son Jacob to marry from among the "covenant" women.

### The Family of Jacob/Israel

Jacob's birth is recorded in Genesis 25:23-26, and within a **18**
few chapters his family becomes the dominant family for the
remainder of the Old Testament. When his name was changed
to Israel, his descendants became known as Israelites, or as the
house of Israel.

The Israelites continued with many of the beliefs, customs,
practices, and traditions of the Hebrews, but they also added
many new ones. Some of these were derived from the law and
commandments received from the Lord through Moses and
known as the "law of Moses" (also sometimes called the law of
carnal [fleshly] commandments). Others were added because of
subsequent interpretations of these commandments.

Other scriptural sources (the Joseph Smith Translation of
both Old and New Testaments, the Book of Mormon, the
Doctrine and Covenants, and the Pearl of Great Price) make it
abundantly clear that many of these practices were symbols of
the coming of the Anointed One (the Messiah) and were to be
performed only until he came and "fulfilled the law." Other
practices were eternal in nature, however, and were to be
performed "forever, from generation to generation."

In order to understand the Old Testament, the reader must
understand some of these customs and practices of Judaism,
including the following (scriptures in italics have commentaries
in Part II):

### Dietary Restrictions

1. No flesh to be eaten from animals unless the animal has a **19**
cloven foot and chews its cud (hence, no pork).
(TG: Law of Moses, pp. 279-80. BD: Clean and Unclean,
pp. 646-47; Kosher, p. 722. *Lev. 11:1-8;* Deut. 14:3-8.)

2. No flesh from the sea unless it has scales. **20**
(TG: Fish, p. 149; Law of Moses, pp. 279-80. BD: Kosher,
p. 722. *Lev. 11:9-10;* Deut. 14:9-10.)

**21**    3. No consumption of blood nor any blood products.

(TG: Blood, Eating of, p. 35; Blood, Symbolism of, p. 35; Law of Moses, pp. 279-80. BD: Blood, p. 626; Kosher, p. 722. *Lev. 17:10-16;* 19:26; Deut. 12:16, 23-25; 15:23.)

**22**    4. No meat to be consumed unless the animal has been killed in a certain way, with the blood properly drained.

(TG: Blood, Eating of, p. 35; Law of Moses, pp. 279-80. BD: Blood, p. 626; Kosher, p. 722. *Lev. 11:13-21;* Deut. 14:21.)

**23**    5. No dairy products and meat products to be eaten at the same meal. (Statements in the Old Testament do not specifically forbid the eating of meat products and dairy products together, but over the centuries the religious leaders of Judaism have placed that interpretation on the command "Thou shalt not seethe a kid [baby goat] in his mother's milk"—*Ex. 23:19;* 34:26; Deut. 14:21.)

(TG: Law of Moses, pp. 279-80. BD: Kosher, p. 722.)

*Dress and Grooming Standards*

**24**    1. Men not to be close shaven on their faces.

(TG: Israel, Judah, People of, p. 235; Shave, Shaved, Shaven, p. 469. *Lev. 19:27;* 21:5.)

**25**    2. Men not to cut the hair at the corners of the head.

(TG: Hair, p. 195; Head, p. 200; Israel, Judah, People of, p. 235. *Lev. 19:27;* 21:5; Ezek. 44:20.)

**26**    3. Fringes on the garments of men.

(TG: Fringe, p. 160; Garment, p. 163; Israel, Judah, People of, p. 235. *Num. 15:38-39;* Deut. 22:12.)

**27**    4. Head of married women to be shaved.

(TG: Israel, Judah, People of, p. 235; Shave, Shaved, Shaven, p. 469. *Deut. 21:12.)*

**28**    5. Women not to wear things appertaining to a man, and vice versa.

(TG: Garment, p. 163; Israel, Judah, People of, p. 235. *Deut. 22:5.)*

*Purification Procedures*

**29**    1. Purification rites for women after menstrual periods or giving birth.

(TG: Purification, Purify, Purifying, p. 403. BD: Purification, p. 756. *Lev. 12:1-8.)*

2. Purification rites after touching diseased persons or dead **30** bodies.

(TG: Purification, Purify, Purifying, p. 403. BD: Purification, p. 756. Lev. 11:8; 21:1-4, 11 [*Lev. 21:11];* 22:4-7; *Deut. 21:22-23.)*

### Sabbath Regulations

1. The Sabbath to be from sundown Friday to sundown **31** Saturday.

(TG: Israel, Judah, People of, p. 235; Sabbath, p. 441. BD: Sabbath, pp. 764-65. *Lev. 23:26-32.)*

2. No work to be performed on the Sabbath, including no **32** harvesting of food.

(TG: Israel, Judah, People of, p. 235; Sabbath, p. 441. BD: Sabbath, pp. 764-65. Ex. 12:16; 16:26; *20:8-11;* 34:21; 35:2; Lev. 23:7-8, 21; Jer. 17:21.)

3. No fire to be lit on the Sabbath. **33**

(TG: Israel, Judah, People of, p. 235; Sabbath, p. 441. BD: Sabbath, pp. 764-65. *Ex. 16:23;* 35:3.)

4. Only a certain distance to be walked on the Sabbath (a **34** Sabbath day's journey).

(TG: Israel, Judah, People of, p. 235; Sabbath, p. 441. BD: Sabbath, pp. 764-65; Sabbath Day's Journey, p. 765. *Ex. 16:29;* Josh. 3:4.)

5. The concept of a sabbatical year, including the belief the **35** land is to lie fallow every seven years.

(TG: Sabbatical Year, p. 441. BD: Sabbatical Year, p. 765. Ex. 21:2; 23:11; Lev. 25:20-22; *Deut. 15:1-6.)*

6. The concept of a sabbatical of Sabbath years, or Jubilee **36** every fifty years (7 x 7 plus 1), when slaves to be freed, lands to be restored, etc.

(TG: Sabbath, p. 441; Sabbatical Year, p. 441. BD: Jubilee, Year of, p. 718; Sabbath, pp. 764-65; Sabbatical Year, p. 765. *Lev. 25:8-16, 23-55;* 27:16-25.)

### Religious Symbols

1. Wearing of phylacteries on the forehead and left arm. **37**

(TG: Phylactery, p. 368. BD: Phylacteries, p. 751; Front-lets, p. 676. *Ex. 13:9;* Deut. 6:8; 11:18.)

**38**    2. Use of mezzuzahs (messuvot) on the right side of gate posts, doorways, etc. (Note: The word *mezzuzah* does not appear in the King James Version of the Old Testament, but the practice of placing words of the scriptures in certain places is implied in *Deut. 6:9* and 11:20. See also Isa. 57:8.)

**39**    3. Menorahs (the symbol and use of the seven-stemmed candelabrum or Sabbath candles).
(TG: Candlestick, p. 50. BD: Candlestick, pp. 629-30. *Ex. 25:31-37;* Num. 8:1-5.)

*Feasts and Festivals*

**40**    1. Passover.
(TG: Passover, p. 358. BD: Feasts, pp. 672-74; Firstfruits, p. 675; Wave Offering, p. 788. *Ex. 12:11-27;* 13-15; Lev. 23:10-14.)

**41**    2. Yom Kippur or "Day of Atonement."
(TG: [somewhat related topic is Feast, p. 143]. BD: Fasts, p. 671 [somewhat related topics are Feasts, pp. 672-74; Firstfruits, p. 675]. *Lev. 16:29-34;* 23:26-32.)

**42**    3. Feast of Pentecost (Shavuot); also called Feast of Weeks.
(TG: Feast, p. 143; Pentecost, p. 363. BD: Feasts, pp. 672-74; Firstfruits, p. 675. *Ex. 23:16;* Lev. 23:16; Deut. 16:10.)

**43**    4. Feast of the Tabernacles (Sukkot).
(TG: Feast, p. 143. BD: Feasts, pp. 672-74; Firstfruits, p. 675. Lev. 23:34; *1 Kgs. 8:54-66.*)

**44**    5. Purim (Lots).
(TG: Feast, p. 143. BD: Feasts, pp. 672-74; Firstfruits, p. 675; Purim, p. 756. *Esth. 9:20-32.*)

**45**    6. Feast of Dedication (Hanukkah).
(TG: Dedication, Dedicate, p. 93; Feast, p. 143. BD: Feasts, pp. 672-74; Firstfruits, p. 675.) (Note: This feast was instituted *after* the close of the Old Testament, in the days of Judas Maccabaeus.)

# OLD TESTAMENT PROPHECIES FULFILLED IN THE OLD TESTAMENT

In addition to knowing the beliefs, customs, and practices of **46** the Israelites, one must be acquainted with the major events, groupings, travels, and places of residence of these people in order to understand fully the Old Testament story.

For several hundred years after the time of Jacob (Israel), the Old Testament is concerned with the descendants of all of Jacob's twelve sons. This period covers the time of bondage in Egypt and of the exodus (covered in the books of Exodus, Leviticus, Numbers, and Deuteronomy), the era of the judges in the promised land (covered in Joshua, Judges, Ruth and 1 Samuel 1-9), and the time of the united kingdom under kings Saul, David, and Solomon (covered in 1 Samuel 9-31, 2 Samuel, 1 Kings 1-11, 1 Chronicles, and 2 Chronicles 1-10). **47**

Upon the death of Solomon and the beginning of the divided kingdom, the record then alternates between two major groups: (1) the northern kingdom (kingdom of Israel), led primarily by descendants of Joseph, with headquarters in the middle section of the land—Shechem and Samaria, and (2) the southern kingdom (kingdom of Judah), led by descendants of Judah, with headquarters at Jerusalem (covered in 1 Kings 12-22, 2 Kings 1-15, and 2 Chronicles 11-32).

About 722 B.C. the Assyrians swept out of the north, **48** captured the northern kingdom, and took many of the peoples of that kingdom captive into Assyria. The next year (721 B.C.) these captive Israelites, representing approximately ten of the twelve tribes of Israel, were lost to history; throughout the remainder of the record and of history they are referred to simply as the "ten lost tribes of Israel."

The remainder of the historical record is concerned almost **49** exclusively with the history of the kingdom of Judah, inhabitants of which are primarily from the tribe of Judah, the neighboring tribes of Simeon (to the south) and Benjamin (to the north), and remnants of all the tribes whose ancestors had immigrated to the kingdom of Judah earlier—especially members of the tribes of Ephraim and Manasseh, who "fell . . . out of Israel in abundance" during a time of spiritual famine in the north. (See 2 Chronicles 15:9.)

**50**    The biblical record catalogs the fall of the peoples of Judah into almost complete apostasy, follows them into captivity in Babylon, returns with them to the promised land after Cyrus of Persia conquers Babylonia, and remains with them during the rebuilding of the temple to the end of their written biblical record. The historical sections concerned almost exclusively with the peoples of the kingdom of Judah are 2 Kings 16–25 and 2 Chronicles 33–36; the "prophetic" books concerned with this period of Judah's history include parts of Amos, Isaiah, Hosea, and Micah and all of Nahum, Jeremiah, Obadiah, Zephaniah, Habakkuk, Daniel, Ezekiel, Haggai, Zechariah, and Malachi.

**51**    The prophecies of Old Testament prophets concerning these early scatterings, captivities, and gatherings of segments of the house of Israel were fulfilled in Old Testament times—that is, both the prophecies and accounts of fulfillment of the prophecies are contained within the present Old Testament. These include the following events:

**52**    1. The descendants of Abraham and of Jacob in bondage in Egypt.

(TG: Israel, Bondage of, in Egypt, p. 233. BD: Abraham, Covenant of, p. 602; Captivities of the Israelites, p. 631.)

**53**    2. The deliverance of the house of Israel from Egypt to the promised land, where tribal inheritances were assigned.

(TG: Israel, Deliverance of, pp. 233-34; Israel, Land of, pp. 235-36. BD: Exodus, Book of, p. 668; Moses, pp. 734-35; Wilderness of the Exodus, p. 789.)

**54**    3. The captivity and dispersion of the ten tribes comprising the northern kingdom of Israel.

(TG: Israel, Bondage of, in Other Lands, p. 233; Israel, Ten Lost Tribes of, pp. 237-38. BD: Israel, Kingdom of, p. 708.)

**55**    4. The scattering of "remnants of Israel" or of the "dispersed of Israel" to various parts of the earth.

(TG: Israel, Bondage of, in Other Lands, p. 233. BD: Diaspora, p. 657; Dispersion, p. 658.)

**56**    5. The captivity of the kingdom of Judah by the Babylonians in sixth century B.C.

(TG: Israel, Bondage of, in Other Lands, p. 233; Israel, Judah, People of, p. 235; Israel, Scattering of, p. 237. BD: Assyria and Babylonia, pp. 615-16.)

6. The return of the Jewish exiles from the Babylonian captivity to the promised land.    **57**

(TG: Israel, Deliverance of, pp. 233-34; Israel, Gathering of, p. 234; Israel, Restoration of, pp. 236-37. BD: Assyria and Babylonia, pp. 615-16.)

The Old Testament prophets also foresaw the eventual dispersion of virtually the entire house of Israel among the nations of the earth, but the fulfillment of this prophecy was not completed until New Testament times when the Jews were scattered by the Romans in the days of Nero, Vespasian, and Titus.    **58**

(TG: Israel, Bondage of, in Other Lands, p. 233; Israel, Scattering of, p. 237.)

# OLD TESTAMENT PROPHECIES FULFILLED IN NEW TESTAMENT TIMES

**59**     Other prophecies of Old Testament prophets were not fulfilled until New Testament times. In fact, one purpose of the New Testament is to witness and testify concerning the fulfillment of Old Testament prophecies. This procedure is consistent with the principle "in the mouth of two or three witnesses shall every word [or truth] be established." (See Deut. 19:15; Matt. 18:16; 2 Cor. 13:1.)

    Many of the Old Testament prophecies fulfilled in New Testament times pertained to the birth, life, teachings, mission, atonement, and resurrection of "the Anointed One" (Jesus Christ, the Messiah). As examples, Old Testament prophets knew the Savior would—

**60**     1. Be of the loins of David.

    (TG: Jesus Christ, Davidic Descent of, p. 245. BD: Jesse, p. 713; Shiloh, p. 773. 2 Sam. 7:13; Ps. 89:4; 132:17; Isa. 9:7; 11:1; Jer. 23:5; 33:15.)

**61**     2. Be born of a virgin.

    (TG: Jesus Christ, Birth of, pp. 243-44. BD: Christ, Names of, pp. 633-35. Isa. 7:14.)

**62**     3. Be born in Bethlehem of Judea.

    (TG: Jesus Christ, Birth of, pp. 243-44; Jesus Christ, Messiah, p. 250; Jesus Christ, Prophecies about, pp. 252-53. BD: Bethlehem, p. 621; Messiah, p. 731. Micah 5:2.)

**63**     4. Come forth out of Egypt.

    (Hosea 11:1.)

    5. Be reared in the tribal lands assigned to Zebulun and Naphtali (which include Nazareth and the Galilee), where a light

**64** would break forth.

    (TG: Jesus Christ, Messiah, p. 250; Jesus Christ, Prophecies about, pp. 252-53. BD: Galilee, p. 677; Messiah, p. 731;

Naphtali, p. 737; Nazareth, p. 737; Zebulun, p. 791. Isa. 9:1-2.)

6. Have power over the physical elements of the earth.    **65**

(TG: Jesus Christ, Messiah, p. 250; Jesus Christ, Power of, pp. 251-52; Jesus Christ, Prophecies about, pp. 252-53. BD: Messiah, p. 731. Isa. 42:5.)

7. Have power over the physical body, healing the sick,    **66**
causing the blind to see, etc.

(TG: Jesus Christ, Messiah, p. 250; Jesus Christ, Mission of, pp. 250-51; Jesus Christ, Power of, pp. 251-52; Jesus Christ, Prophecies about, pp. 252-53. BD: Messiah, p. 731. Isa. 42:7.)

8. Ride into Jerusalem seated on the foal of an ass.    **67**

(TG: Ass, p. 18; Foal, p. 152; Jesus Christ, Messiah, p. 250; Jesus Christ, Prophecies about, pp. 252-53. BD: Messiah, p. 731. Zech. 9:9.)

9. Be betrayed for thirty pieces of silver.    **68**

(TG: Jesus Christ, Betrayal of, p. 243; Jesus Christ, Messiah, p. 250; Silver, p. 474. BD: Messiah, p. 731. Zech. 11:12-13.)

10. Bear the sin of the world and the iniquities and trans-    **69**
gressions of many.

(TG: Iniquity, pp. 228-29; Jesus Christ, Atonement through, p. 242; Jesus Christ, Messiah, p. 250; Jesus Christ, Mission of, pp. 250-51; Jesus Christ, Prophecies about, pp. 252-53; Jesus Christ, Savior, pp. 254-55; Sin, pp. 475-76; Transgress, Transgression, p. 534. BD: Christ, Names of, pp. 633-35; Messiah, p. 731. Isa. 50:6; 53:4-6.)

11. Be "lifted up on a tree" (crucified) and have hands and    **70**
feet pierced.

(TG: Jesus Christ, Crucifixion of, pp. 244-45; Jesus Christ, Death of, p. 245. BD: Crucifixion, p. 651. Ps. 22:16; Zech. 12:10; 13:6.)

12. Be with the wicked in his death.    **71**

(TG: Jesus Christ, Death of, p. 245; Jesus Christ, Messiah, p. 250; Jesus Christ, Prophecies about, pp. 252-53; Wickedness, Wicked, pp. 574-75. BD: Messiah, p. 731. Isa. 53:9.)

13. Be with the rich in his grave.    **72**

(TG: Grave, pp. 190-91; Jesus Christ, Death of, p. 245; Jesus Christ, Messiah, p. 250; Jesus Christ, Prophecies about, pp. 252-53; Rich, p. 431. BD: Death, p. 655; Messiah, p. 731. Isa. 53:9.)

**73**    14. Be resurrected from the dead and provide for resurrection of all mankind.

(TG: Jesus Christ, Death of, p. 245; Jesus Christ, Messiah, p. 250; Jesus Christ, Prophecies about, pp. 252-52; Jesus Christ, Resurrection, p. 254; Resurrection, pp. 426-27. BD: Death, p. 655; Messiah, p. 731; Resurrection, p. 761. Job 19:25; Isa. 25:8; 26:19; 53:12; Ezek. 37:12; Hosea 13:14.)

**74**    15. Be called by many titles, including sacred title "Son of Man," meaning "Son of Man of Holiness" or "Son of God."

(TG: Jesus Christ, Divine Sonship, pp. 245-46; Jesus Christ, Messiah, p. 250; Jesus Christ, Prophecies about, pp. 252-53; Jesus Christ, Son of Man, p. 256. BD: Christ, Names of, pp. 633-35; God, pp. 681-82; Holy One of Israel, p. 704; Jehovah, pp. 710-11; Messiah, p. 731; Seed of Abraham, p. 771. Gen. 49:24; Ex. 3:14; Num. 24:17; 1 Sam. 12:12; Ps. 24:7; Isa. 9:6; 43:15; 49:26; Dan. 7:13.)

# OLD TESTAMENT PROPHECIES PERTAINING TO THE LATTER DAYS, INCLUDING THE SECOND COMING AND THE BEGINNING OF THE MILLENNIUM

**75** Still other Old Testament prophecies pertained to events in the last days ("the dispensation of the fulness of times"), when there would be a restoration or restitution of all things. Many of these prophecies were concerned with the restoration of the gospel and the true Church; others with the restoration of priesthood authority and keys; others with events which would help prepare the earth and peoples of the earth for the coming of the Messiah in power and great glory (the second coming of Jesus Christ); still others pertained specifically to the second coming.

Following are some of the many Old Testament prophecies concerning these great events of the last days with sources of additional information, including selected references from other scriptures. The numbers following the scripture references refer to section numbers printed in the margins of Part I.

**76** 1. The reestablishment of the true Church upon the earth with legitimate priesthood power and appropriate ordinances.

(TG: Dispensations, p. 105. BD: Restitution; Restoration, p. 761. Jer. 31:31; Ezek. 37:26; Dan. 2:44; Acts 3:21; Eph. 1:10; Rev. 14:6; 2 Ne. 9:2; D&C 13:1; 27:6; 65:2; 110:16. Part I 76, 103-4, 202-3, 221, 229-30.)

**77** 2. Elijah the prophet to return to the earth before the coming of the great and dreadful day of the Lord.

(TG: Elijah, p. 120; Jesus Christ, Second Coming, pp. 255-56; Last Days, pp. 277-78; Millennium, p. 320. BD: Elijah, p. 664; Prophet, p. 754. Mal. 4:5-6; 3 Ne. 24-25; D&C 110:13-16; 133:64; JS-H 1:36-39. Part I 77, 147.)

**78** 3. The "dispersed of Israel" (including descendants of Joseph and Ephraim) to be gathered to the lands of their inheritance, there to become a "mighty" and covenant people.

(TG: Israel, Gathering of, p. 234; Israel, Joseph, People of, pp. 234-35; Israel, Remnant of, p. 236; Israel, Restoration of, pp. 236-37. BD: Ephraim, p. 666. Ps. 107:3; Isa. 10:22; 11:11; 51:11; 56:8; Jer. 23:3; Joel 2:32; 2 Ne. 20:22; 3 Ne. 5:23-26; 20:13, 21, 29-33. Part I 78, 116-19, 204, 214-19, 233-38.)

**79**    4. The descendants of the ten lost tribes of Israel to come out of the lands of the north to receive their "inheritance with Judah, never to be separated again."

(TG: Israel, Gathering of, p. 234; Israel, Ten Lost Tribes of, pp. 237-38. BD: Israel, Kingdom of, p. 708. Isa. 43:6; 49:12; Jer. 3:12, 18; 16:15; 23:8; 31:8; 2 Ne. 29:13-14; 3 Ne. 16:1-3; 17:4; 21:26; Eth. 13:11; D&C 110:11; 133:26-34. Part I 79, 120-23, 224.)

**80**    5. Descendants of Judah to gather to the land of their inheritance, which is the "land of Jerusalem."

(TG: Israel, Gathering of, p. 234; Israel, Judah, People of, p. 235; Israel, Restoration of, pp. 236-37; Jerusalem, p. 239; Lands of Inheritance, p. 276. BD: Captivities of the Israelites, p. 631; Jerusalem, pp. 712-13; Jew, p. 713; Judah, Stick of, p. 719. Isa. 11:12; Zech. 10:6-9, 12; 1 Ne. 19:13-17; 2 Ne. 6:11; 9:2; 10:7-8; Jacob 6:2; Ether 13:11-12; D&C 110:11. Part I 80-95, 105-15, 177-91, 193-97, 205-13, 223, 228-32, 239-50.)

**81**    6. Gold and silver to come from the nations of the earth to help rebuild the nation of Israel and reclaim the land.

(TG: Gold, p. 184; Israel, Land of, pp. 235-36; Last Days, pp. 277-78; Silver, p. 474. BD: Gold, p. 682; Israel, p. 708. Isa. 60:9, 14; Jer. 32:41, 43-44; Zech. 14:14. Part I 81, 108.)

**82**    7. Land of Jerusalem to become abundantly fruitful—"the land that was desolate will become as the Garden of Eden."

(TG: Desolate, p. 97; Fruitful, p. 161; Israel, Land of, pp. 235-36; Jerusalem, p. 239. BD: Eden, Garden of, pp. 659-60; Israel, p. 708; Jerusalem, pp. 712-13. Isa. 35:1-2, 5-7, 10; Ezek. 36:33-36; Amos 9:14-15; 2 Ne. 27:28. Part I 82, 195.)

**83**    8. Descendants of Judah to be attacked by larger forces but will be delivered from them.

(TG: Israel, Deliverance of, pp. 233-34; Israel, Judah, People of, p. 235. BD: Jew, p. 713; Judah, Kingdom of, pp. 718-19. Isa. 14:1-2; 54:15, 17; Jer. 23:5-8; 46:28; Zech. 12:6-9; 2 Ne. 6:8; 24:1-2; 3 Ne. 22:15-17. Part I 83.)

9. Jerusalem to come under the control of Israel and to  **84**
serve as the capital of Israel.

(TG: Israel, Land of, pp. 235-36; Jerusalem, p. 239; Last
Days, pp. 277-78. BD: Israel, p. 708; Jerusalem, pp. 712-13.
Zech. 2:11-12; 12:6-8; 3 Ne. 20:29, 33-34. Part I 84.)

10. The Jewish people will begin to believe in Jesus Christ;  **85**
then the time will come when the fulness of the gospel will be
preached to them.

(TG: Israel, Judah, People of, p. 235; Israelite, p. 238;
Restoration of the Gospel, pp. 425-26. BD: Jew, p. 713;
Messiah, p. 731. Deut. 4:25-31; Jer. 31:31-34; Dan. 2:44-45;
Matt. 24:14; 1 Ne. 10:14, 15-16; 2 Ne. 30:7; 3 Ne. 20:29-31, 46;
Morm. 5:12-14; D&C 133:8. Part I 85, 110-11.)

11. A new temple will be built in Jerusalem before the  **86**
coming of the Messiah in power and great glory (the second
coming of Jesus Christ.)

(TG: Jerusalem, p. 239; Jesus Christ, Messiah, p. 250; Jesus
Christ, Prophecies of, pp. 252-53; Jesus Christ, Second
Coming, pp. 255-56; Last Days, pp. 277-78; Millennium, p.
320; Temple, House of the Lord, pp. 519-20. BD: Jerusalem,
pp. 712-13; Messiah, p. 731. Isa. 2:1-5; Ezek. 40-48; Micah 4:1-
7; Zech. 8:7-9; D&C 124:36-37; 133:13. Part I 86, 112.)

12. Water will come out from under the foundation of the  **87**
temple in Jerusalem—this water will become a river within a
relatively short distance.

(TG: Jerusalem, p. 239; Last Days, pp. 277-78; Millennium,
p. 320; Temple, House of the Lord, pp. 519-20; Water, p. 565.
BD: Jerusalem, pp. 712-13. Ezek. 47:1-8; Joel 3:18; Zech. 14:8;
Rev. 22:1. Part I 87.)

13. The waters of the Dead Sea will be healed; "fish of the  **88**
great sea" will be caught in the Dead Sea.

(TG: Fish, p. 149; Last Days, pp. 277-78; Sea, p. 454;
Water, p. 565. BD: Dead Sea, p. 654; Fish, p. 675. Ezek. 47:8-
11. Part I 88.)

14. A leader named David, from the loins of ancient King  **89**
David, will be a great leader in Israel.

(TG: Israel, Deliverance of, pp. 233-34; Kings, Earthly, pp.
269-70; Last Days, pp. 277-78. Israel, p. 708. Isa. 55:3-4; Jer.
23:3-8; 30:3-9; Ezek. 34:23-24, 28; 37:21-25; Hosea 3:4-5; Zech.
3:8-9; 6:11-13; D&C 113:4, 6. Part I 89.)

**90**     15. The nations of the earth will gather to battle against Israel; Judah will be smitten and part of Jerusalem will be captured.

(TG: Israel, Judah, People of, p. 235; Israel, Land of, pp. 235-36; Jerusalem, p. 239; Last Days, pp. 277-78. BD: Israel, p. 708; Jerusalem, pp. 712-13; Judah, Kingdom of, pp. 718-19. Ezek. 36; Dan. 7:25; 12:1; Joel 2:2-3; Zech. 14:1-2; Rev. 11:1-13; 16:14-21; 2 Ne. 25:16; D&C 45:26-27; 133:35. Part I 90, 113, 206-13.)

**91**     16. Two prophets to be raised up to the Jewish nation in the last days, after they have gathered home and rebuilt their city; these two prophets are the "two witnesses" of the eleventh chapter of Revelation.

(TG: Israel, Judah, People of, p. 235; Last Days, pp. 277-78; Millennium, Preparing a People for, p. 320. BD: Jew, p. 713; Prophet, p. 754. JST Isa. 51:19. Zech. 4:11-14; Rev. 11:6-12; 2 Ne. 8:18-20; D&C 77:15. Part I 91.)

**92**     17. The Lord "shall suddenly come to his temple." (This prophecy of Malachi was at least partially fulfilled when Jesus Christ appeared in the Kirtland Temple April 3, 1836. Many prophecies have multiple fulfillments, however, and Jesus Christ may well come "suddenly" [quickly, without time for further preparation] to other temples, including the ones to be built in Jerusalem and in Zion [Jackson County, Missouri].)

(TG: Day of the Lord, p. 87; Last Days, pp. 277-78; Temple, House of the Lord, pp. 519-20. Mal. 3:1; D&C 36:8, 42:36. Part I 92.)

**93**     18. The Messiah (the resurrected Jesus Christ) will come to the Mount of Olives and show himself to the Jewish people, who will then recognize and acknowledge him as their deliverer.

(TG: Day of the Lord, p. 87; Israel, Judah, People of, p. 235; Jesus Christ, Messiah, p. 250; Jesus Christ, Prophecies about, pp. 252-53; Jesus Christ, Resurrection, p. 254; Jesus Christ, Savior, pp. 254-55; Last Days, pp. 277-78. BD: Messiah, p. 731. Zech. 12:10; 13:6; 14:9; D&C 45:51-53; 133:20-21. Part I 93, 114-15, 210.)

**94**     19. Under the direction of the Messiah (the resurrected Jesus Christ), the army of Israel will be victorious over the combined armies of the nations of the earth.

(TG: Israel, Deliverance of, pp. 233-34; Jesus Christ, Messiah, p. 250; Jesus Christ, Resurrection, p. 254; Last Days, pp. 277-78. Joel 3:1-17; Zech. 14:2-3, 9; Rev. 16:16; D&C 133:41-42. Part I 94.)

20. Two great capital cities will be prepared for the coming **95** of the Messiah (the second coming of Jesus Christ)—Jerusalem in Israel and Zion (a New Jerusalem) in America.

(TG: Day of the Lord, p. 87; Jerusalem, p. 239; Jerusalem, New, p. 239; Zion, Sion, pp. 597-98. BD: Jerusalem, pp. 712-13; Zion, pp. 792-93. Isa. 2:2-3; Heb. 12:22; Rev. 3:12; 3 Ne. 20:22; 21:20-25; Ether 13:4-11; D&C 45:66-67; 57:1-3; 58:3-4; 84:2-5; 97:19-20; D&C 133:19-25. Part I 95, 132-33.)

21. Great physical changes in the earth will occur at about **96** the time of the second coming of Jesus Christ in power and glory.

(TG: Day of the Lord, p. 87; Earth, Renewal of, p. 116; Jesus Christ, Second Coming, pp. 255-56. Isa. 24:20; Joel 2:11, 30-31; 3:15-16; Amos 5:18; Hag. 2:6; Mal. 3:2; 4:1. Part I 96, 148-54.)

22. The earth shall be cleansed through burning at the **97** second coming of Jesus Christ in power and great glory; the resurrected Savior to judge the people; the earth to be "renewed and receive its paradisiacal glory." (Mal. 4:1.)

(TG: Burn, Burned, Burnt, p. 47; Day of the Lord, p. 87; Earth, Cleansing of, pp. 114-15; Earth, Renewal of, p. 116; Jesus Christ, Second Coming, pp. 255-56. Ps. 21:8-10; Isa. 24:6; 66:16; Amos 4:11-12; Mal. 4:1. Part I 97, 154.)

23. The city of Enoch will return to the earth, and the city **98** of Zion on earth will be caught up to meet this city and the resurrected Jesus Christ.

(Part I 98, 134-36.)

24. The Messiah (the resurrected Jesus Christ) will reign on **99** the earth for 1,000 years as King of kings and Lord of lords.

(TG: Jesus Christ, King, pp. 248-49; Jesus Christ, Lord, pp. 249-50; Jesus Christ, Messiah, p. 250; Jesus Christ, Millennial Reign, p. 250; Jesus Christ, Prophecies about, pp. 262-53; Jesus Christ, Resurrection, p. 254; Millennium, p. 320. BD: Messiah, p. 731. Ps. 102:16; Isa. 24:23; 40:10; Micah 4:7; Zech. 14:9, 20, 21; Matt. 16:27; 25:31-46; Mark 13:26-37; Luke 21:26-30; 1 Thes. 3:13; 4:16; 2 Thes. 1:7; Jude 1:14-15; Rev. 5:10; 1 Ne. 22:24-26; 3 Ne. 26:3; D&C 29:11; 45:44, 59; 65:5; Moses 7:60-65; A of F 10. Part I 99, 155-65, 225.)

**100**

    25. Righteousness will prevail upon the earth during the Millennium, and all enmity will cease between beasts and beasts, beasts and men, and men and men.

    (TG: Beast, p. 24; Men, p. 316; Millennium, p. 320; Righteousness, p. 434. BD: Kingdom of Heaven or Kingdom of God, p. 721. Isa. 11:6-9; 65:25; Ezek. 34:25; Hosea 2:18; Micah 4:3; Rev. 20:1-7; 1 Ne. 22:26; 2 Ne. 12:14; D&C 29:11; 43:30-35; Moses 7:64-65. Part I 100, 155-65.)

# STATEMENTS FROM MODERN PROPHETS CONCERNING THE LAST DAYS

(Note: This book has been written for use with the LDS edition of the King James Version of the Bible published in 1979 by The Church of Jesus Christ of Latter-day Saints. All references to chapter headings, footnotes, and entries in the Topical Guide and Bible Dictionary pertain to that edition of the Bible.

The abbreviation TG refers to the Topical Guide; BD refers to the Bible Dictionary.

The numbers in the margin of each page in Part I indicate major segments; these numbers are used with the designation "Part I" for ease in reference. For example, the commentary for Micah 4:7 says that additional information on that verse appears in Part I 204, meaning segment 204 of Part I, found on page 84.)

# THE PRINCIPLE OF GATHERING

### Prophets Have Testified Concerning the Gathering

**101** "All that the prophets that have written, from the days of righteous Abel, down to the last man that has left any testimony on record for our consideration, in speaking of the salvation of Israel in the last days, goes directly to show that it consists in the work of the gathering." (Joseph Smith, HC 2:260.)

"The gathering . . . is as necessary to be observed by believers, as faith, repentance, baptism, or any other ordinance. It is an essential part of the Gospel of this dispensation, as much so, as the necessity of building an ark by Noah, for his deliverance, was a part of the Gospel of his dispensation." (Joseph F. Smith, JD 19:192.)

"One of the most important points in the faith of the Church of the Latter-day Saints, through the fullness of the everlasting Gospel, is the gathering of Israel (of whom the Lamanites constitute a part)—that happy time when Jacob shall go up to the house of the Lord, to worship Him in spirit and in truth, to live in holiness; when the Lord will restore His judges as at the first, and His counselors as at the beginning; when every man may sit under his own vine and fig tree, and there will be none to molest or make afraid; when He will turn to them a pure language, and the earth will be filled with sacred knowledge, as the waters cover the great deep; when it shall no longer be said, the Lord lives that brought up the children of Israel out of the land of Egypt, but the Lord lives that brought up the children of Israel from the land of the north, and from all the lands whither He has driven them. That day is one, all important to all men." (Joseph Smith, HC 2:357.)

### The Keys of Gathering Have Been Restored

**102** "Six years after the Church was organized, the keys of gathering were committed to Joseph Smith and Oliver Cowdery in the Kirtland Temple. The record of that marvelous restoration is given in these words: [D&C 110:11, quoted.] The spirit of gathering has been with the Church from the days of that restoration. Those who are of the blood of Israel, have a righteous desire after they are baptized, to gather together with the body of the Saints at the designated place. . . .

"Thus, clearly, the Lord has placed the responsibility for directing the work of gathering in the hands of the leaders of the Church to whom he will reveal his will where and when such gatherings would take place in the future." (Harold B. Lee, CR, Apr. 1948, p. 55.)

"It was the design of the councils of heaven before the world was, that the principles and laws of the priesthood should be predicated upon the gathering of the people in every age of the world. . . .

"It is for the same purpose that God gathers together His people in the last days, to build unto the Lord a house to prepare them for the ordinances and endowments, washings and anointings, etc." (Joseph Smith, HC 5:423-24.)

### The Gospel Includes the Spirit of Gathering

**103**    "When the Lord restored the Gospel the spirit of gathering came with it. The Lord commanded the people to gather together, and that they should not only be organized as a Church, but that they should be organized under the laws of the land, so that they might not be helpless and dependent and without influence or power; but that by means of united effort and faith they should become a power for the accomplishment of righteousness in the earth." (Joseph F. Smith, CR, Apr. 1900, p. 47.)

"The Spirit of the Lord Jesus Christ is a gathering spirit. Its tendency is to gather the virtuous and good, the honest and meek of the earth, and, in fine, the Saints of God. The time has come when the Lord is determined to fulfill his purposes. . . .

"The Lord does not require every soul to leave his home. . . . But He *does* require them to hearken to counsel, and follow that course which He points out, whether to gather or stay to do some other work. . . .

"Perhaps some of you are ready to ask, 'Cannot the Lord save us as well where we are as to gather together?' Yes, if the Lord says so. But if He commands us to come out and gather together, He will not save us by staying at home." (Brigham Young, HC 6:12.)

### The Church Believes in and Practices Gathering

"Why is it that you are here to-day? and what brought you here? Because the keys of the gathering of Israel from the four quarters of the earth have been committed to Joseph Smith, and he has conferred those keys upon others that the gathering of Israel may be accomplished, and in due time the same thing will be performed to the tribes in the land of the north. It is on this account, and through the unlocking of this principle, and through those means, that you are brought together as you are to-day." (John Taylor, JD 25:179.)

"The gathering of Israel is one of the important doctrines taught by the Church of Jesus Christ of Latter-day Saints, and is presumptive evidence of the divine mission of Joseph Smith. The Church must not only teach this doctrine of the gathering, but must also practice it. The Church of Jesus Christ of Latter-day Saints stands alone among the Christian churches teaching and practicing the gathering of its members, in fulfilment of the ancient prophets." (Joseph Fielding Smith, RT, p. 139.)

**104**

# THE GATHERING OF JUDAH TO THE "LAND OF JERUSALEM"

### *Jews to Return and Govern in Their Own Land*

**105**
"The Lord has decreed that the Jews should be gathered from all the Gentile nations where they have been driven, into their own land, in fulfillment of the words of Moses their law-giver." (Wilford Woodruff, WW, p. 509.)

"The God of Abraham, of Isaac, and of Jacob, has set His hand again the second time to recover the remnants of his people." (Joseph Smith, HC 1:313.)

"By the authority of the Holy Priesthood of God, that has again been restored to the earth, . . . Apostles of the Lord Jesus Christ have been to the Holy Land and have dedicated that country for the return of the Jews; and we believe that in the due time of the Lord they shall be in the favor of God again." (Heber J. Grant, CR, Apr. 1921, p. 124.)

"The descendants of Abraham . . . expect to see [the] promise fulfilled, when his descendants will again inherit that land of promise, and when all things spoken of by the mouth of the Prophets will be accomplished. The measuring line will yet go forth again in Jerusalem, and Jerusalem will yet be inhabited on its own place, even in Jerusalem." (John Taylor, JD 18:325.)

### *Judah Remembered in Dedicatory Prayers of Temples*

**106**
"O Lord . . . have mercy upon the children of Jacob, that Jerusalem, from this hour, may begin to be redeemed;

"And the yoke of bondage may begin to be broken off from the house of David;

"And the children of Judah may begin to return to the lands which thou didst give to Abraham, their father." (Joseph Smith, D&C 109:60-64.)

"Wilt thou show unto [the sons of Judah] mercy, . . . They have been trampled under foot of the Gentiles and have been made a hiss and a byword in the fulfillment of the words of

Moses, their law giver, and of Jesus of Nazareth. We pray Thee, O Thou great Eloheim, that their past sufferings may suffice. Inspire their hearts to return home to Jerusalem, the land of their fathers, and to rebuilt their city and temple. Prepare them for the coming of Shiloh, their king." (Wilford Woodruff, WW, p. 493.)

"Have thou mercy upon Judah and Jerusalem; hasten the going forth of this sacred record [the Book of Mormon] to the Hebrews of all nations; raise up men and means to carry the glad tidings of thy returning favor to that afflicted people. Wilt thou hear and answer the prayers of thy servants and turn away the barrenness of their land? Make it very fertile as in days of old; turn the hearts of the exiles to thy promises made to their fathers, and let the land of Jerusalem become inhabited as towns without walls for the multitude of men and cattle therein, that they may rebuild their city and temple, that the glory of the latter house may be greater than that of the former house." (Lorenzo Snow, MS 50:390.)

**107**

"We thank thee, O God, our Eternal Father, that the land of Palestine, the land where our Savior and Redeemer ministered in the flesh, where he gave to the world the plan of life and salvation, is now redeemed from . . . thralldom. . . . We acknowledge thy hand, O God, in the wonderful events which have led up to the partial redemption of the land of Judah, and we beseech thee, O Father, that the Jews may, at no far distant date, be gathered home to the land of their fathers." (Heber J. Grant, IE 26:1077.)

"Wilt thou, O Lord, have in remembrance the promises made by thee to Judah in his stricken and scattered condition. Hasten the time when he shall be restored to the land of his inheritance. Remove from him thy displeasure, and may the days of his tribulation soon cease, and Jerusalem rejoice, and Judah be made glad. . . .

"Wilt thou, O gracious Father, in thy wisdom and mercy, speedily fulfil thy promises unto Israel and cause that they may again be gathered and hearken unto the voice of thy servants, the prophets, and thereby merit the rich blessings thou hast promised them when they acknowledge Jesus Christ, thy Beloved Son, as their Redeemer." (George Albert Smith, IE 48:562–65.)

"Wilt thou, O Lord, remember thy covenants with

Abraham, Isaac, and Jacob concerning their seed. . . .

"And hasten the day, O Lord of Hosts, when the scattered remnants of Judah, after their pain, shall be sanctified in holiness before thee and shall build again the waste places of Jerusalem, that they may once again be numbered with thy people; that the promises may be fulfilled, 'for out of Zion shall go forth the law, and the word of the Lord from Jerusalem.' " (Harold B. Lee, E, Mar. 1972, p. 10.)

### Gold and Silver to Help Reclaim the Land

**108**    "These fleeing Jews [will] take back their gold and silver to Jerusalem and re-build their city and temple . . . as the Lord lives. Then the gentiles will say, 'Come let us go up to Jerusalem; let us go up and spoil her. The Jews have taken our gold and silver from the nations of the earth—come let us go up and fight against Jerusalem.' " (Wilford Woodruff, JD 22:173.)

"The time is not far distant when the rich men among the Jews may be called upon to use their abundant wealth to gather the dispersed of Judah, and purchase the ancient dwelling places of their fathers in and about Jerusalem, and rebuild the holy city and temple. . . . The Lord has decreed that the Jews should be gathered from all the Gentile nations where they have been driven, into their own land, in fulfillment of the words of Moses their law-giver." (Wilford Woodruff, MS 41:244.)

### Judah to Be Redeemed

**109**    "The day of the return is here. . . . Judah is to be redeemed from all his rebellion and will once more occupy the lands of his inheritance. Nations may oppose it; Arabs may fight it; but every opposition in the due time of the Lord will melt away and Israel will again possess the land northward and southward, and eastward and westward, for all this land was given to Abraham and Israel by the Lord, for an everlasting possession." (Joseph Fielding Smith, ST, p. 234.)

"The Israelites of the Kingdom of Judah were carried into Babylon about 130 years later [after the captivity of the ten tribes] and when they returned they were known as Jews. It seems a little strange that in this present time, when again the government of the Jews is established, that they call it Israel instead of Judah. In doing so, perhaps they have built better than they knew, for eventually this land is to be inhabited by those of the other tribes of Israel and it will not be a kingdom just of Jews. . . . That . . . is the fulfillment of prophecy." (Joseph Fielding Smith, ST, p. 234.)

"After the Jews are gathered to Palestine in sufficient numbers and have built cities, cultivated farms and orchards, formed their government and executed their laws, they will have taken only the preparatory steps towards their redemption and the redemption of their land." (Joseph Fielding Smith, ST, p. 236.)

### The Gospel to Be Preached to the Jews in Their Own Land

**110**

"The promise is . . . made to the Jews that they shall be gathered again, after their pain and suffering. They will gather as predicted by Zechariah and by the Lord in . . . revelation (D&C 45) in their unbelief. They will begin to believe in Christ but will not be ready to accept him in his full right as their Deliverer and as the Son of God. (See 2 Nephi 30:5-8.) In this state they shall gather to Jerusalem and its vicinity." (Joseph Fielding Smith, CHMR 1:265.)

"The Jews have got to gather to their own land in unbelief. . . . They do not believe in Jesus of Nazareth now, nor ever will until he comes and sets his foot on Mount Olivet and it cleaves in twain, one part going towards the east, and the other towards the west. Then, when they behold the wounds in his hands and in his feet, they will say, 'Where did you get them?' And he will reply, 'I am Jesus of Nazareth, King of the Jews, your Shiloh, him whom you crucified.' Then, for the first time will the eyes of Judah be opened. They will remain in unbelief until that day." (Wilford Woodruff, JD 15:277-78.)

"When the Gentiles reject the Gospel it will be taken from them, and go to the house of Israel, to that long suffering people that are now scattered abroad through all the nations upon the earth, and they will be gathered home by thousands, and by hundreds of thousands, and they will re-build Jerusalem their ancient city, and make it more glorious than at the beginning, and they will have a leader in Israel with them, a man that is full of the power of God and the gift of the Holy Ghost." (Wilford Woodruff, JD 2:200.)

**111**     "The time has at last arrived when the God of Abraham, of Isaac, and of Jacob, has set His hand . . . to . . . establish that covenant with them, which was promised when their sins should be taken away." (Joseph Smith, HC 1:313.)

"The restored gospel of Jesus Christ is to be preached to the gathered Jews, and the Saints are glad to behold the signs of the coming day." (Joseph F. Smith, IE 21:261.)

"The time is rapidly approaching when [the gospel] will be preached to the Jews, who are to gather in from their long dispersion, upon the land of their inheritance. Palestine is to be inhabited as a city without walls and the glory of the Lord will rest upon his chosen people, when they repent of their sins and turn unto him." (George Albert Smith, MS 83:2.)

"So it is not a far distant day . . . when that great race of people that has done so much for us, the people beloved of the Lord, they of whom He spoke so tenderly and affectionately upon many occasions, . . . will . . . rejoice in the knowledge that God is our Father, that He is a personal being, that Jesus Christ, His Son, was the manifestation of God in the flesh, the Redeemer of the world, and that He is our elder brother." (George Albert Smith, *Liahona,* Vol. 5, pt. 2, p. 838.)

### A Temple to Be Built in Jerusalem

**112**     "What was the object of gathering the Jews, or the people of God in any age of the world? . . .

"The main object was to build unto the Lord a house whereby He could reveal unto His people the ordinances of His house and the glories of His kingdom, and teach the people the way of salvation; for there are certain ordinances and principles that, when they are taught and practiced, must be done in a place or house built for that purpose. . . .

"It is for the same purpose that God gathers together His people in the last days, to build unto the Lord a house to prepare them for the ordinances and endowments, washings and anointings, etc." (Joseph Smith, HC 5:423–24.)

"I remember, some time ago, having a conversation with Baron Rothschild, a Jew. I was showing him the Temple here, and said he—'Elder Taylor, what do you mean by this Temple? What is the object of it? Why are you building it?' Said I, . . . 'You will build a Temple, for the Lord has shown us, among other things, that you Jews have quite a role to perform in the latter days, and that all the things spoken by your old prophets will be fulfilled, that you will be gathered to old Jerusalem, and that you will build a Temple there; and when you build that Temple, and the time has arrived, "the Lord whom you seek will suddenly come to this temple." ' " (John Taylor, JD 18:199-200.)

### Nations of the Earth to Fight Against Jerusalem

"O house of Judah. . . . it is true that after you return and **113** gather your nation home, and rebuild your City and Temple, that the Gentiles may gather together their armies to go against you to battle, to take you a prey and to take you as a spoil, which they will do, for the words of your prophets must be fulfilled; but when this affliction comes, the living God, that led Moses through the wilderness, will deliver you, and your Shiloh will come and stand in your midst and will fight your battles; and you will know him, and the afflictions of the Jews will be at an end, while the destruction of the Gentiles will be so great that it will take the whole house of Israel who are gathered about Jerusalem, seven months to bury the dead of their enemies, and the weapons of war will last them seven years for fuel, so that they need not go to any forest for wood. These are tremendous sayings—who can bear them? Nevertheless they are true, and will be fulfilled, according to the sayings of Ezekiel, Zechariah, and other prophets. Though the heavens and the earth pass away, not one jot or tittle will fall unfulfilled." (Wilford Woodruff, WW, pp. 509-10.)

### Resurrected Jesus Christ to Appear to the Jews

"At [the coming of the Savior] the Mount of Olives will **114** cleave in twain and the besieged Jews will flee for safety into the valley thus created. Then the Savior will come and they will see the wounds in his hands and in his feet and in the spirit of deep sorrow and remorse they will bow down and acknowledge him as their long-expected Messiah. They will be forgiven and in sincere repentance will acknowledge him as their King. Then shall they be cleansed, and the sanctuary of the Lord will be established among them forever. The nations of the earth will come to their end; the wicked will be destroyed, and Christ will be proclaimed as 'King over all the earth, and his name one.' " (Compare D&C 45.) (Joseph Fielding Smith, ST, p. 238.)

"We have a great desire for their [Jews] welfare, and are looking for the time soon to come when they will gather to Jerusalem, build up the city and the land of Palestine, and prepare for the coming of the Messiah. When he comes again, he will not come as he did when the Jews rejected him. . . .

"When the Savior visits Jerusalem, and the Jews look upon him, and see the wounds in his hands and in his side and in his feet, they will then know that they have persecuted and put to death the true Messiah, and then they will acknowledge him, but not till then. They have confounded his first and second coming, expecting his first coming to be as a mighty prince instead of as a servant. They will go back by and by to Jerusalem and own their Lord and Master. [D&C 109:62–64; 110:11.]" (Brigham Young, JD 11:279.)

**115**    "When [the Jews'] enemies come upon them and part of the city is taken, there shall come a great earthquake and the mount of Olives shall cleave in twain forming a valley into which the Jews shall flee for safety. At that time Christ will appear to them and show them his hands and his feet, and they shall fall down and acknowledge him as their King and Redeemer." (Joseph Fielding Smith, CHMR 1:265.)

"This is the will of your great Elohim, O house of Judah, and whenever you shall be called upon to perform this work, the God of Israel will help you. You have a great future and destiny before you and you cannot avoid fulfilling it; you are the royal chosen seed, and the God of your father's house has kept you distinct as a nation for eighteen hundred years, under all the oppression of the whole Gentile world. You may not wait until you believe on Jesus of Nazareth, but when you meet with Shiloh your king, you will know him; your destiny is marked out, you cannot avoid it." (Wilford Woodruff, WW, p. 509.)

# THE GATHERING OF THE DISPERSED OF ISRAEL, INCLUDING LAMANITES

(Note: Various terms have been used to denote this aspect of the gathering—"dispersed of Israel," "remnants of Israel," "seed of Joseph," "Ephraim," "seed or descendants of Lehi," "Lamanites," etc.)

### The "Dispersed of Israel" Includes the Lamanites

**116** "I am looking for the fulfillment of all things that the Lord has spoken, and they will come to pass as the Lord God lives. Zion is bound to rise and flourish. The Lamanites will blossom as the rose on the mountains. . . . Every word that God has ever said of them will have its fulfillment, and they, by and by, will receive the Gospel. It will be a day of God's power among them. . . . Their chiefs will be filled with the power of God and receive the Gospel, and they will go forth and build the new Jerusalem, and we shall help them. They are branches of the house of Israel." (Wilford Woodruff, JD 15:282.)

"[From the Book of Mormon] we learn that our western tribes of Indians are descendants from that Joseph who was sold into Egypt, and that the land of America is a promised land unto them, and unto it all the tribes of Israel will come, with as many of the Gentiles as shall comply with the requisitions of the new covenant." (Joseph Smith, TPJS, p. 17.)

**117** "The Book of Mormon has made known who Israel is, upon this continent. And while we behold the government of the United States gathering the Indians, and locating them upon lands to be their own, how sweet it is to think that they may one day be gathered by the Gospel!" (Joseph Smith, HC 2:358.)

"We pray . . . our Lord Thou wilt make bare Thine arm in the preservation and salvation of the small remnants of the Lamanites that are left in the land. Deliver them, we pray Thee, from the hands of the Gentiles who are bringing about their threatened anihilation from off the earth. Inspire their hearts with Thy spirit, that they may receive the Gospel of the Son of God, that they may be prepared to build up Zion, and to fulfill the covenants and promises made to them by their forefathers who inherited this land." (Wilford Woodruff, WW, p. 493.)

**118**    "We beseech thee, O Lord, that thou wilt stay the hand of the destroyer among the descendants of Lehi who reside in this land and give unto them increasing virility and more abundant health, that they may not perish as a people but that from this time forth they may increase in numbers and in strength and in influence, that all the great and glorious promises made concerning the descendants of Lehi may be fulfilled in them; that they may grow in vigor of body and of mind, and above all love for Thee and Thy Son, and increase in diligence and in faithfulness in keeping the commandments which have come to them through the gospel of Jesus Christ." (Heber J. Grant, TMH, p. 177.)

"Wilt thou, O Lord, remember thy covenants with . . . Lehi and Nephi and thy 'other sheep' on the American continent; that their descendants should have the blessings of the gospel, 'which are the blessings of salvation, even of life eternal.' Cause that the scattered remnants of thine ancient chosen people may open their hearts to the message of those living prophets whom thou dost now send to them." (Harold B. Lee, E, Mar. 1972, p. 10.)

### The Day of the Lamanite Is Here

**119**    "The day of the Lamanite is here and the gospel brings opportunity. . . . They must have the emancipating gospel. . . . They must hear the compelling truths. Millions through North America are deprived, untrained, and achieving less than their potential. They must have the enlightening gospel. It will break their fetters, stir their ambition, increase their vision, and open new worlds of opportunity to them. Their captivity will be at an end—the captivity of misconceptions, illiteracy, superstition, fear. 'The clouds of error disappear before the rays of truth divine.'

"The brighter day has dawned. The scattering has been accomplished—the gathering in process. May the Lord bless us all as we become nursing parents unto our Lamanite brethren and hasten the fulfillment of the great promises made to them." (Spencer W. Kimball, FPM, p. 358.)

"The day of the Lamanite is surely here and we are God's instrument in helping to bring to pass the prophecies of renewed vitality, acceptance of the gospel, and resumption of a favored place as part of God's chosen people. The promises of the Lord will all come to pass; we could not thwart them if we would. But we do have it in our power to hasten or delay the process by our energetic or neglectful fulfillment of our responsibilities." (Spencer W. Kimball, FPM, p. 349.)

# RETURN OF THE
# TEN LOST TRIBES

### Prophecies Concerning the Lost Tribes
### Will Be Fulfilled

**120**     "All that God has said with regard to the ten tribes of Israel, strange as it may appear, will come to pass. They will, as has been said concerning them, smite the rock, and the mountains of ice will flow before them, and a great highway will be cast up, and their enemies will become a prey to them; and their records, and other choice treasures they will bring with them to Zion. These things are as true as God lives." (Wilford Woodruff, JD 21:301.)

"We know nothing about them [the ten tribes of Israel] only what the Lord has said by His Prophets. There are Prophets among them, and by and by they will come along, and they will smite the rocks, and the mountains of ice will flow down at their presence, and a highway will be cast up before them, and they will come to Zion, receive their endowments, and be crowned under the hands of the children of Ephraim." (Wilford Woodruff, JD 4:231-32.)

"Remember, O Lord, Thy covenant people in the north country; hasten the day when they shall come in remembrance before Thee, when their prophets shall smite the rocks and the mountains of ice shall flow down before them. May the highways speedily be cast up in the midst of the great deep, that they may come over dry shod. May the everlasting hills tremble at their presence and their enemies disappear before them. May they come forth unto Zion and bow the knee, that they may be crowned under the hands of Ephraim, Thy servant." (Wilford Woodruff, WW, p. 493.)

### Some of Lost Tribes Together in a Group

**121**     "In the scattering of Israel the descendants of Jacob were driven into all lands and climes and have mingled among all nations. There is, however, a body of these tribes hidden away, where they are we do not know, but the Lord says they shall come from the North. Isaiah has spoken of them (Chap. 43:15-21), and Jeremiah speaking of their return has said: [Quoted Jeremiah 16:14, 15.] Here the Lord says that these people have prophets among them, and Joseph Smith at a conference of the Church held in June, 1831, said: 'John the Revelator was then among the ten tribes of Israel who had been led away by Shalmaneser, King of Assyria, to prepare them for their return from their long dispersion.' This is the mission given to John portrayed in the symbol of the little book which he was given to eat, in the tenth chapter of Revelation. (See Sec. 77:14.)

"When these Israelites come to Zion they will bring their rich treasures to the children of Ephraim, and the children of Ephraim will give unto them the blessings of the fulness of the Gospel. This also is according to the predictions. Ephraim received the birthright in Israel and in these last days he stands in his place at the head of the tribes of Israel. It will be his duty, therefore, to crown the tribes of Israel, when they come to Zion. We are also promised that their enemies will be a prey to them when the Lord brings them on their journey. An highway will be thrown up in the midst of the great deep. Barren deserts shall then become fruitful with springs of water, and the parched ground shall not longer be a thirsty land." (Joseph Fielding Smith, CHMR 1:265.)

**122**

"Notwithstanding all that has been written, there are many members of the Church who think that these 'lost tribes' were scattered among the nations and are now being gathered out and are found through all the stakes and branches of the Church. They reach this conclusion because the general opinion is that these tribes went into the North, and it is the northern countries from whence most of gathered Israel has been found. . . .

"Speaking of this, Elder Orson F. Whitney has said:

" 'It is maintained by some that the lost tribes of Israel— those carried into captivity about 725 B.C.—are no longer a distinct people; that they exist only in a scattered condition, mixed with the nations among which they were taken by their captors, the conquering Assyrians. If this be true, and those tribes were not intact at the time Joseph and Oliver received the keys of the gathering why did they make so pointed a reference to ''the leading of the ten tribes from the land of the north''? . . . What need to particularize as to the Ten Tribes, if they were no longer a distinct people? And why do our Articles of Faith give these tribes a special mention?' (See SNT, p. 174.)

". . . The Savior also bore witness that these tribes were in a body like the Nephites and he would visit them. [3 Ne. 15:20 and 16:1-4.]" (Joseph Fielding Smith, ST, pp. 185-88.)

### Ten Tribes to Come from the North

**123**    "Whether these tribes are in the north or not, I am not prepared to say. As I said before, they are 'lost' and until the Lord wishes it, they will not be found. All that I know about it is what the Lord has revealed, and He declares that they will come from the North. He has also made it very clear and definite that these lost people are separate and apart from the scattered Israelites now being gathered out. If this be not true, then the commission of Moses to the Prophet Joseph Smith is without meaning. [Quoted D&C 110:11.] The statement that the tribes are to be led from the north harmonizes perfectly with the words of Jeremiah (Jer. 16:14-15) and Section 133, verses 26 to 34. Surely there must be a time when this great body of people will come to the children of Ephraim to receive their blessings." (Joseph Fielding Smith, ST, p. 186.)

# ZION (THE NEW JERUSALEM) TO BE BUILT AND REDEEMED

*We Believe "that Zion (the New Jerusalem) Will Be Built upon the American Continent." (Joseph Smith, A of F 10.)*

"The building up of Zion is a cause that has interested the people of God in every age; it is a theme upon which prophets, priests and kings have dwelt with peculiar delight; they have looked forward with joyful anticipation to the day in which we live; and fired with heavenly and joyful anticipations they have sung and written and prophesied of this our day; but they died without the sight; we are the favored people that God has made choice of to bring about the Latter-day glory." (Joseph Smith, HC 4:609–10.)

**124**

"In regard to the building up of Zion, it has to be done by the counsel of Jehovah, by the revelations of heaven; and we should feel to say, 'If the Lord go not with us, carry us not up hence.' " (Joseph Smith, HC 5:65.)

"Men and angels are to be co-workers in bringing to pass this great work, and Zion is to be prepared, even a new Jerusalem, for the elect that are to be gathered from the four quarters of the earth, and to be established an holy city, for the tabernacle of the Lord shall be with them." (Joseph Smith, HC 2:260.)

**125**

"The city of Zion spoken of by David, in the one hundred and second Psalm, will be built upon the land of America." (Joseph Smith, HC 1:315.)

"There will be a literal Zion, or gathering of the Saints to Zion, as well as a gathering of the Jews to Jerusalem." (John Taylor, GG, p. 104.)

"Without Zion, and a place of deliverance, we must fall; because the time is near when the sun will be darkened, and the moon turn to blood, and the stars fall from heaven, and the earth reel to and fro. Then, if this is the case, and if we are not sanctified and gathered to the places God has appointed . . . we cannot stand; we cannot be saved; for God will gather out His Saints from the Gentiles, and then comes desolation and destruction, and none can escape except the pure in heart who are gathered." (Joseph Smith, HC 2:52.)

## What and Where Is Zion?

**126**    "And what is Zion? In one sense Zion is the pure in heart. But is there a land that ever will be called Zion? Yes, brethren. What land is it? It is the land that the Lord gave to Jacob, who bequeathed it to his son Joseph, and his posterity, and they inhabit it, and that land is North and South America. That is Zion, as to land, as to Territory, and location. . . .

"As to the spirit of Zion, it is in the hearts of the Saints, of those who love and serve the Lord with all their might, mind, and strength." (Brigham Young, JD 2:253.)

*"The whole of America is Zion itself from north to south, and is described by the Prophets, who declare that it is the Zion where the mountain of the Lord should be, and that it should be in the center of the land.* When elders shall take up and examine the old prophecies in the Bible, they will see it." (Joseph Smith, HC 6:318-19.)

**127**    "This American continent will be Zion; for it is so spoken of by the prophets. Jerusalem will be rebuilt and will be the place of gathering, and the tribe of Judah will gather there; but this continent of America is the land of Zion." (Brigham Young, JD 5:4.)

"Zion will extend, eventually, all over this earth. There will be no nook or corner upon the earth but what will be in Zion. It will all be Zion." (Brigham Young, JD 9:138.)

## Center Place of Zion

**128**    "I received, by a heavenly vision, a commandment in June following, to take my journey to the western boundaries of the State of Missouri, and there designate the very spot which was to be the central place for the commencement of the gathering together of those who embrace the fullness of the everlasting gospel. Accordingly I undertook the journey, with certain ones of my brethren, and after a long and tedious journey, suffering many privations and hardships, arrived in Jackson County, Missouri, and after viewing the country, seeking diligently at the hand of God, he manifested Himself unto us, and designated, to me and others, the very spot upon which He designed to commence the work of the gathering, and the upbuilding of an 'holy city,' which should be called Zion—Zion, because it is a place of righteousness, and all who build thereon are to worship the true and living God, and all believe in one doctrine, even the doctrine of our Lord and Savior Jesus Christ.'' (Joseph Smith, HC 2:254.)

"This is the land of Zion; but we are not yet prepared to go and establish the Centre Stake of Zion. The Lord tried this in the first place. He called the people together to the place where the New Jerusalem and the great temple will be built, and where He will prepare for the City of Enoch. And He gave revelation after revelation; but the people could not abide them, and the Church was scattered. . . . Now, it is for you and me to prepare to return back again . . . to build up the Centre Stake of Zion. We are not prepared to do this now, but we are here to learn until we are of one heart and of one mind in the things of this life." (Brigham Young, JD 11:324.)

### Zion to Be Built Up and Redeemed

**129**

"I know that Zion, in the due time of the Lord, will be redeemed; but how many will be the days of her purification, tribulation, and affliction, the Lord has kept hid from my eyes; and when I inquire concerning this subject, the voice of the Lord is: Be still, and know that I am God! all those who suffer for my name shall reign with me, and he that layeth down his life for my sake shall find it again.

"Now, there are two things of which I am ignorant; and the Lord will not show them unto me . . . Why God has suffered so great a calamity to come upon Zion, and what the great moving cause of this great affliction is; and again, by what means He will return her back to her inheritance, with songs of everlasting joy upon her head." (Joseph Smith, HC 1:453–54.)

"Jesus will never receive the Zion of God unless its people are united according to celestial law, for all who go into the presence of God have to go there by this law. Enoch had to practice this law, and we shall have to do the same if we are ever accepted of God as he was. It has been promised that the New Jerusalem will be built up in our day and generation, and it will have to be done by the United Order of Zion and according to celestial law." (Wilford Woodruff, JD 17:250.)

**130**     "We will have to go to work and get the gold out of the mountains to lay down, if we ever walk in streets paved with gold. . . . When we enjoy a Zion in its beauty and glory, it will be when we have built it. If we enjoy the Zion that we now anticipate, it will be after we redeem and prepare it." (Brigham Young, JD 8:354–55.)

"When will Zion be redeemed? . . . Just as soon as the Latter-day Saints are ready and prepared to return to Independence, Jackson County, in the State of Missouri, North America, just so soon will the voice of the Lord be heard, 'Arise now, Israel, and make your way to the centre Stake of Zion.' " (Brigham Young, JD 9:137.)

**131**     "When Zion is established in her beauty and honour and glory, the kings and princes of the earth will come, in order that they may get information and teach the same to their people. They will come as they came to learn the wisdom of Solomon." (John Taylor, JD 6:169.)

"The day will come when it will be said of our children, as the old Prophets have prophesied, that such and such a one was born in Zion. It will be considered a great blessing and one of the greatest honors that could have been inherited by our children to have been born in Zion among the people of God." (John Taylor, JD 22:317.)

### Two World Capitals to Be Established on Earth

**132**     "Jerusalem of old, after the Jews have been cleansed and sanctified from all their sin, shall become a holy city where the Lord shall dwell and from whence he shall send forth his word unto all people. Likewise, on this continent, the city of Zion, New Jerusalem—shall be built, and from it the law of God shall also go forth. [D&C 45:66, 67; 84:2.] There will be no conflict, for each city shall be headquarters for the Redeemer of the world, and from each he shall send forth his proclamations as occasion may require. Jerusalem shall be the gathering place of Judah and his fellows of the house of Israel, and Zion shall be the gathering place of Ephraim and his fellows, upon whose heads shall be conferred 'the richer blessings.' " [D&C 133:34.] (Joseph Fielding Smith, IE, July, 1919, pp. 815-16.)

"America and Jerusalem are set forth as two places of

gathering for the nations, that they may escape the judgements about to overtake the world, as the prophets have testified, that in Mount Zion and in Jerusalem shall be deliverance." (Wilford Woodruff, MS 6:136.)

**133**

"Now many will feel disposed to say, that this New Jerusalem spoken of, is the Jerusalem that was built by the Jews on the eastern continent. But you will see, from Revelation xxi:2, there was a New Jerusalem coming down from God out of heaven, adorned as a bride for her husband; that after this, the Revelator was caught away in the Spirit, to a great and high mountain, and saw the great and holy city descending out of heaven from God. Now there are two cities spoken of here. . . . There is a New Jerusalem to be established on this continent, and also Jerusalem shall be rebuilt on the eastern continent (see Book of Mormon, Ether xiii: 1-12). Behold, Ether saw the days of Christ, and he spake also concerning the house of Israel, and the Jerusalem from whence Lehi should come; after it should be destroyed, it should be built up again, a holy city unto the Lord, wherefore it could not be a New Jerusalem, for it had been in a time of old.' " (Joseph Smith, TPJS, p. 86.)

### Zion on Earth to Meet Zion in Heaven

**134**

"We have no business here other than to build up and establish the Zion of God. It must be done according to the will and law of God, after that pattern and order by which Enoch built up and perfected the former-day Zion, which was taken away to heaven, hence the saying went abroad that Zion had fled. By and by it will come back again, and as Enoch prepared his people to be worthy of translation, so we through our faithfulness must prepare ourselves to meet Zion from above when it shall return to earth, and to abide the brightness and glory of its coming." (Brigham Young, JD 18:356.)

"Did Enoch build up a Zion? So we are doing. What is it? The Zion of God. What does it mean? The pure in heart in the first place. In the second place those who are governed by the law of God—the pure in heart who are governed by the law of God . . . they built up a similar thing before the flood; and the Elders went forth in those days as they now go forth; and they baptized people and laid hands upon them, and gathered them to Zion; and after a while that Zion was caught up from the earth. And we will build up a Zion. . . . And that Zion also, when the time comes, will ascend to meet the Zion from above, which will descend, and both, we are told, will fall on each other's necks and kiss each other." (John Taylor, JD 26:109-10.)

**135**     "When Zion descends from above, Zion will also ascend from beneath, and be prepared to associate with those from above. The people will be so perfected and purified, ennobled, exalted, and dignified in their feelings and so truly humble and most worthy, virtuous and intelligent that they will be fit, when caught up, to asociate with that Zion that shall come down from God out of heaven." (John Taylor, JD 10:147.)

"In regard to the work in which we are engaged. Will it go on? I tell you it will. Will Zion be built up? I tell you it will. Will the Zion that Enoch built up, descend? It most assuredly will, and this that we are building up will ascend, and the two will meet and the peoples thereof will fall on each other's necks and embrace each other. So says the word of God to us." (John Taylor, JD 26:37.)

**136**     "We will build up our Zion after the pattern that God will show us, and we will be governed by his law and submit to his authority and be governed by the holy priesthood and by the word and will of God. And then when the time comes that these calamities we read of, shall overtake the earth, those that are prepared will have the power of translation, as they had in former times, and the city will be translated. And Zion that is on the earth will rise, and the Zion above will descend, as we are told, and we will meet and fall on each other's necks and embrace and kiss each other. And thus the purposes of God to a certain extent will then be fulfilled." (John Taylor, JD 21:253.)

# EVENTS AND CONDITIONS PRECEDING THE SECOND COMING

### Signs of the Second Coming Have Commenced

"I will prophesy that the signs of the coming of the Son of **137** Man are already commenced. One pestilence will desolate after another. We shall soon have war and bloodshed. The moon will be turned into blood. I testify of these things and that the coming of the Son of Man is nigh, even at your doors." (Joseph Smith, HC 3:390.)

"When I contemplate the rapidity with which the great and glorious day of the coming of the Son of Man advances, when He shall come to receive His Saints unto Himself, where they shall dwell in His presence, and be crowned with glory and immortality; when I consider that soon the heavens are to be shaken, and the earth tremble and reel to and fro; and that the heavens are to be unfolded as a scroll when it is rolled up; and that every mountain and island are to flee away, I cry out in my heart. What manner of persons ought we to be in all holy conversation and godliness!" (Joseph Smith, HC 1:442.)

### Wars and Calamities

"The time is soon coming, when no man will have any peace **138** but in Zion and her stakes.

"I saw men hunting the lives of their own sons, and brother murdering brother, women killing their own daughters, and daughters seeking the lives of their mothers. I saw armies arrayed against armies. I saw blood, desolation, fires. The Son of Man has said that the mother shall be against the daughter, and the daughter against the mother. These things are at our doors. They will follow the Saints of God from city to city. Satan will rage, and the spirit of the devil is now enraged. I know not how soon these things will take place; but with a view of them, shall I cry peace? No! I will lift up my voice and testify of them." (Joseph Smith, HC 3:391.)

"We see nations rising against nations; we hear of the

pestilence destroying its thousands in one place and its tens of thousands in another; the plague consuming all before it, and we witness this terror that reigns in the hearts of the wicked, and we are ready to exclaim, 'The Lord is certainly about bringing the world to an account of its iniquity.' Let us reflect, then, in the last days, that there was to be great tribulations; for the Saviour says, nation shall rise against nation, kingdom against kingdom, and there shall be famine, pestilence, and earthquakes in divers places, and the prophets have declared that the valleys should rise; that the mountains should be laid low; that a great earthquake should be, in which the sun should become black as sackcloth of hair, and the moon turn into blood; yea, the Eternal God hath declared that the great deep shall roll back into the north countries and that the land of Zion and the land of Jerusalem shall be joined together, as they were before they were divided in the days of Peleg. No wonder the mind starts at the sound of the last days." (Joseph Smith, *Inspired Prophetic Warnings*, Lundwall, pp. 41-42.)

**139**     "The servants of God will not have gone over the nations of the Gentiles, with a warning voice, until the destroying angel will commence to waste the inhabitants of the earth, and as the prophet hath said, 'It shall be a vexation to hear the report.' I speak thus because I feel for my fellow men; I do it in the name of the Lord, being moved upon by the Holy Spirit. Oh, that I could snatch them from the vortex of misery, into which I behold them plunging themselves, by their sins; that I might be enabled by the warning voice, to be an instrument of bringing them to unfeigned repentance, that they might have faith to stand in the evil day!" (Joseph Smith, HC 2:263.)

"When the testimony of the Elders ceases to be given, and the Lord says to them, 'Come home; I will now preach my own sermons to the nations of the earth,' all you now know can scarcely be called a preface to the sermon that will be preached with fire and sword, tempests, earthquakes, hail, rain, thunders and lightnings, and fearful destruction. . . . You will hear of magnificent cities, now idolized by the people, sinking in the earth, entombing the inhabitants. The sea will heave itself beyond its bounds, engulphing mighty cities. Famine will spread over the nations, and nation will rise up against nation, kingdom against kingdom, and states against states, in our own country and in foreign lands; and they will destroy each other, caring not for the blood and lives of their neighbours, of their families, or for their own lives." (Brigham Young, JD 8:123.)

"You will see worse things than [the Civil War], for God will lay his hand upon this nation, and they will feel it more terribly than ever they have done before; there will be more bloodshed, more ruin, more devastation than ever they have seen before. . . . There is yet to come a sound of war, trouble and distress, in which brother will be arrayed against brother, father against son, son against father, a scene of desolation and destruction that will permeate our land until it will be a vexation to hear the report thereof." (John Taylor, JD 20:318.)

**140**

### Wickedness to Increase

"My testimony is this unto all men and nations, that . . . you live in the age in which God will bring to pass the fulfillment of that word of prophecy and prediction which has been spoken by all the prophets since the world began. . . .

"Thrones will be cast down, nations will be overturned, anarchy will reign, all legal barriers will be broken down, and the laws will be trampled in the dust. You are about to be visited with war, the sword, famine, pestilence, plague, earthquakes, whirlwinds, tempests, and with the flame of devouring fire, by fire and with the sword will God plead with all flesh, and the slain of the Lord will be many. The anger of the Lord is kindled and his sword is bathed in heaven, and is about to fall upon Idumea, or the world. . . . The fig trees are leafing, and the signs of all heaven and earth indicate the coming of the Son of Man. The seals are about to be opened; the plagues to be poured forth. Your rivers and seas will be turned to blood and to gall. And the inhabitants of the earth will die of plagues. . . . The question may be asked why these judgments are coming upon the world in the last days? I answer because of the wickedness of the inhabitants thereof . . . the whole earth is filled with murders, whoredoms, blasphemies, and every crime in the black catalogue that was manifest in the antideluvian world, or Sodom and Gomorrah, until the whole earth groans under its abominations, and the heavens weep, and all eternity is pained, and the angels are waiting the great command to go forth and reap down the earth. This testimony I bear to all nations under heaven, and I know it is true by the inspiration of Almighty God." (Wilford Woodruff, MS 41:241, 245–46.)

**141**

**142**    "Consider for a moment, brethren, the fulfillment of the words of the prophet; for we behold that darkness covers the earth, and gross darkness the minds of the inhabitants thereof —that crimes of every description are increasing among men— vices of great enormity are practiced—the rising generation growing up in the fullness of pride and arrogance—the aged losing every sense of conviction, and seemingly banishing every thought of a day of retribution—intemperance, immorality, extravagance, pride, bindness of heart, idolatry, the loss of natural affection; the love of this world, and indifference toward the things of eternity increasing among those who profess a belief in the religion of heaven, and infidelity spreading itself in consequence of the same—men giving themselves up to commit acts of the foulest kind, and deeds of the blackest dye, blaspheming, defrauding, blasting the reputation of neighbors, stealing, robbing, murdering; advocating error and opposing the truth, forsaking the covenant of heaven, and denying the faith of Jesus—and in the midst of all this, the day of the Lord fast approaching when none except those who have won the wedding garment will be permitted to eat and drink in the presence of the Bridegroom, the Prince of Peace!" (Joseph Smith, HC 2:5.)

**143**    "The Lord is withdrawing His Spirit from the nations of the earth, and the power of the devil is gaining dominion over the children of men. See how crime is increasing. What will the end be? Death, destruction, whirlwinds, pestilence, famine and the judgments of God will be poured out upon the wicked; for the Lord has withheld these judgments until the world is fully warned." (Wilford Woodruff, JD 22:175.)

### God Will Prevail and Rule

**144**    "If your eyes were opened, you would see his hand in the midst of the nations of the earth in the setting up of governments and in the downfall of kingdoms—in the revolutions, wars, famine, distress, and wretchedness among the inhabitants of the earth. In these manifestations you would discern the footsteps of the Almighty just as plainly as you may see the footsteps of your children upon the soft earth." (Brigham Young, JD 7:144.)

"The judgments will begin at the house of God. We have to pass through some of these things, but it will only be a very little compared with the terrible destruction, the misery and suffering that will overtake the world who are doomed to suffer the wrath of God. It behooves us, as the Saints of God, to stand firm and faithful in the observance of his laws, that we may be worthy of his preserving care and blessing." (John Taylor, JD 21:100.)

"We read in the Scriptures of a time that is coming when **145** there will be a howling among the merchants in Babylon, for men will not be found to buy their merchandise. This is in accordance with the prediction of John the Revelator. And the gold and the silver and the fine linen, etc., in Babylon will be of no avail. But before that time comes, we as a people must prepare for those events, that we may be able to live and sustain ourselves when in the midst of convulsions that by and by will overtake the nations of the earth, and among others, this nation. The time that is spoken of is not very far distant." (John Taylor, JD 21:33.)

"God has held the angels of destruction for many years, lest **146** they should reap down the wheat with the tares. But I want to tell you now, that those angels have left the portals of heaven, and they stand over this people and this nation now, and are hovering over the earth waiting to pour out the judgments. And from this very day they shall be poured out." (Wilford Woodruff, YWJ 5:512.)

"We are living in a period of time when upheavals in the world are daily, almost momentary. Marvelous things are occurring. The map of the world is changing. The order of government is being modified. In our own nation we are almost helpless before the problems that confront us, notwithstanding we are probably the wealthiest and most powerful nation in all the world. What is our difficulty, brethren and sisters? It is that men refuse to hear what the Lord has said. They refuse to pay attention to his wise counsel. They absolutely neglect to give credence to the things that he teaches us, and *he will not be mocked.* He gives us the advice and the counsel that we need, but he will not compel us. But if we refuse we lose our opportunity, and it passes away from us, in many cases to return again no more forever." (George Albert Smith, CR, Apr. 1933, p. 71.)

### Elijah the Prophet to Return

"There is a custom among the Jews, described by Alfred **147** Edersheim, in his book, 'The Temple,' in which it is said at the feast of the passover the Jews look for the return of Elijah. I will let Mr. Edersheim tell the story: . . . 'Jewish tradition has this curious conceit: That the most important events in Israel's history were connected with the Paschal season. . . . Hence to this day, in every Jewish home, at a certain part of the Paschal service—just after the "third cup" or the "cup of blessing," has been drunk—the door is opened to admit Elijah the prophet as forerunner of the Messiah, while appropriate passages are at the same time read which foretell the destruction of all heathen nations.'—pp. 196-97.

"At the very time, on the third day of April, 1836, when Elijah appeared and committed his dispensation to Joseph Smith and Oliver Cowdery, the Jews were celebrating the Paschal feast and opening their doors to receive Elijah. He came, but not to the Jewish homes, but to two humble youths in the house of the Lord in Kirtland." (Joseph Fielding Smith, RT, pp. 170–71.) (Note: See commentary for Mal. 4:5.)

# THE SECOND COMING OF JESUS CHRIST

### Jesus Christ Will Descend from Heaven

"The coming of the Son of Man never will be—never can be **148** till the judgments spoken of for this hour are poured out: which judgments are commenced. . . .

"Judah must return, Jerusalem must be rebuilt, and the temple, and water come out from under the temple, and the waters of the Dead Sea be healed. It will take some time to rebuild the walls of the city and the temple, etc.; and all this must be done before the Son of Man will make His appearance. There will be wars and rumors of wars, signs in the heavens above and on the earth beneath, the sun turned into darkness and the moon to blood, earthquakes in divers places, the seas heaving beyond their bounds; then will appear one grand sign of the Son of Man in heaven. But what will the world do? They will say it is a planet, a comet, etc. But the Son of Man will come as the sign of the coming of the Son of Man, which will be as the light of the morning cometh out of the East." (Joseph Smith, HC 5:336-37.)

"The Lord Jesus Christ is coming to reign on earth. The world may say that he delays his coming until the end of the earth. But they know neither the thoughts nor the ways of the Lord. The Lord will not delay his coming because of their unbelief, and the signs both in heaven and earth indicate that it is near. The fig trees are leafing in sight of all the nations of the earth, and if they had the Spirit of God they could see and understand them." (Wilford Woodruff, JD 16:35.)

"Do you know that it is the eleventh hour of the reign of **149** Satan on the earth? Jesus is coming to reign, and all you who fear and tremble because of your enemies, cease to fear them, and learn to fear to offend God, fear to transgress his laws, fear to do any evil to your brother, or to any being upon the earth, and do not fear Satan and his power, nor those who have only power to slay the body, for God will preserve his people." (Brigham Young, JD 10:250.)

"[The Savior] will never come until the Jews are gathered home and have re-built their Temple and city, and the Gentiles have gone up there to battle against them. He will never come until his Saints have built up Zion, and have fulfilled the revelations which have been spoken concerning it. He will never come until the Gentiles throughout the whole Christian world have been warned by the inspired elders of Israel." (Wilford Woodruff, JD 18:111.)

**150**    "You and I live in a day in which the Lord our God has set his hand for the last time, to gather out the righteous and to prepare a people to reign on this earth,—a people who will be purified by good works, who will abide the faith of the living God and be ready to meet the Bridegroom when he comes to reign over the earth, even Jesus Christ . . . and be prepared for that glorious event—the coming of the Son of Man." (Joseph F. Smith, MS 36:220.)

"We believe that Jesus Christ will descend from heaven to earth again even as He ascended into heaven. 'Behold, He cometh with clouds, and every eye shall see Him, and they also which pierced Him: and all kindreds of the earth shall wail because of Him.' He will come to receive His own, and rule and reign king of nations as He does king of saints; 'For He must reign, till He hath put all enemies under His feet. The last enemy that shall be destroyed is death.' He will banish sin from the earth and its dreadful consequences, tears shall be wiped from every eye and there shall be nothing to hurt or destroy in all God's holy mountain." (Brigham Young, JD 11:123–24.)

### Generation Known, but Not Day nor Hour

**151**    "I will take the responsibility upon myself to prophesy in the name of the Lord, that Christ will not come this year, . . . and I also prophesy, in the name of the Lord, that Christ will not come in forty years; and if God ever spoke by my mouth, He will not come in that length of time. Brethren, when you go home, write this down, that it may be remembered.

"Jesus Christ never did reveal to any man the precise time that He would come. Go and read the Scriptures, and you cannot find anything that specifies the exact hour He would come; and all that say so are false teachers." (Joseph Smith, HC 6:254.)

"I have asked of the Lord concerning His coming; and while

asking the Lord, He gave a sign and said, 'In the days of Noah I set a bow in the heavens as a sign and token that in any year that the bow should be seen the Lord would not come; but there should be seed time and harvest during that year: but whenever you see the bow withdrawn, it shall be a token that there shall be famine, pestilence, and great distress among the nations, and that the coming of the Messiah is not far distant.' " (Joseph Smith, HC 6:254.)

"No man knows the day or the hour when Christ will come, **152** yet the generation has been pointed out by Jesus himself. . . . The Savior, when speaking to his disciples of his second coming and the establishment of his kingdom on the earth, said the Jews should be scattered and trodden under foot until the times of the Gentiles were fulfilled. But, said he, when you see light breaking forth among the Gentiles, referring to the preaching of his Gospel amongst them; when you see salvation offered to the Gentiles, and the Jews—the seed of Israel—passed by, the last first and the first last; when you see this you may know that the time of my second coming is at hand as surely as you know that summer is nigh when the fig tree puts forth its leaves; and when these things commence that generation shall not pass away until all are fulfilled.

"We are living in the dispensation and generation to which Jesus referred." (Wilford Woodruff, JD 14:5.)

"The hour and day of the Lord's future advent is withheld from the knowledge of both men and angels; yet the signs, so definitely specified as harbingers of His coming, are multiplying apace. The prevailing unrest among men and nations, the fury of the elements, widespread destruction by land and sea, the frequency and intensity of volcanic and earthquake disturbances —all tell to the well-tuned and listening ear that the gladsome yet terrible day of the Lord is nigh—aye, even at the doors!

"A sure indication of the great event, as specified by the Lord Himself, was and is that the Gospel of the kingdom shall be preached in all the world. The missionary service of the Church of Jesus Christ of Latter-day Saints attests the progressive fulfilment of this prediction." (Heber J. Grant, MS 91:34.)

"There is something also to be looked to in the future. The **153** Son of God has again to figure in the grand drama of the world . . . when he will go forth as a man of war and tread down the people in his anger and trample them in his fury, when blood should be on his garments and the day of vengeance in his heart, when he would rule the nations with an iron rod and break them to pieces like a potter's vessel. . . .

"When he comes again he comes to take vengeance on the ungodly and to bring deliverance unto his Saints; 'For the day of vengeance,' it is said, 'is in mine heart, and the year of my redeemed is come.' (Isaiah 63:4) . . . When the Son of God shall come the second time with all the holy angels with him, arrayed in power and great glory to take vengeance on them that know not God and obey not the Gospel, or when he shall come in flaming fire, [hopefully] we shall be among that number who shall be ready to meet him with gladness in our hearts and hail him as our great Deliverer and friend." (John Taylor, JD 10:115–16.)

### Earth to Be Burned at His Coming

**154**    "Now, when Christ comes, we will get a new heaven and a new earth and all of these corruptible things will be removed. They will be consumed by fire; and somebody said, 'Brother Smith, do you mean to say that it is going to be literal fire?' I said, 'Oh, no, it will not be literal fire any more than it was literal water that covered the earth in the flood.' . . .

"To my great astonishment this has been misunderstood by some, who failed to recognize the irony of this remark. For the benefit of such I will say I do not know of any other kind of water except *literal* water—$H_2O$, the kind we drink, bathe in, and which makes floods and drowns people. I think fire which consumes will also be literal when it comes." (Joseph Fielding Smith, ST, p. 41.)

"It is not a figure of speech that is meaningless, or one not to be taken literally when the Lord speaks of the burning. All through the scriptures we have the word of the Lord that at his coming the wicked and the rebellious will be as stubble and will be consumed. Isaiah has so prophesied. . . . Surely the words of the Lord are not to be received lightly or considered meaningless." (Joseph Fielding Smith, CHMR 1:238.)

# THE MILLENNIUM

### The Millennium Is Near

"The millennium is dawning upon the world, we are at the **155** end of the sixth thousand years, and the great day of rest, the Millennium of which the Lord has spoken, will soon dawn and the Savior will come in the clouds of heaven to reign over his people on the earth one thousand years." (Wilford Woodruff, JD 18:113.)

"We are living at the commencement of the Millennium, and near the close of the 6,000th year of the world's history. Tremendous events await this generation." (Wilford Woodruff, JD 25:10.)

"The world has had a fair trial for six thousand years; the Lord will try the seventh thousand Himself. . . . Satan will be bound, and the works of darkness destroyed; righteousness will be put to the line and judgment to the plummet, and 'he that fears the Lord will alone be exalted in that day.' " (Joseph Smith, HC 5:64–65.)

### The Church Will Help Prepare for Christ's Coming

"We believe this Church will prepare the way for the coming **156** of Christ to reign as King, and that this Church will then develop into the kingdom of God, which all Christians pray will come; that the will of God may be done on earth as it is in heaven. We believe in the full and free agency of man, and that when that kingdom is established there will be perfect liberty on earth, civil, political and religious." (Wilford Woodruff, MS 52:162.)

"It startles men when they hear the Elders of Israel tell about the kingdoms of this world becoming the kingdom of our God and His Christ. They say it is treason for men to teach that the kingdom Daniel saw is going to be set up, and bear rule over the whole earth. Is it treason for God Almighty to govern the earth? Who made it? God, did He not? Who made you? God, if you have any eternal Father. Well, whose right is it to rule and reign over you and the earth? It does not belong to the devil, nor to men. It has never been given to men yet; it has never been given to the nations. It belongs solely to God and He is coming to rule and reign over it.'' (Wilford Woodruff, JD 13:164.)

### Jesus Christ Will Reign Personally

**157**    "It has been the design of Jehovah, from the commencement of the world, and is His purpose now, to regulate the affairs of the world in His own time, to stand as a head of the universe, and take the reins of government in His own hand. When that is done, judgment will be administered in righteousness; anarchy and confusion will be destroyed, and 'nations will learn war no more.' It is for want of this great governing principle, that all this confusion has existed; 'for it is not in man that walketh, to direct his steps;' this we have fully shown." (Joseph Smith, HC 5:63.)

"Christ and the resurrected Saints will reign over the earth during the thousand years. They will not probably dwell upon the earth, but will visit it when they please, or when it is necessary to govern it. There will be wicked men on the earth during the thousand years. The heathen nations who will not come up to worship will be visited with the judgments of God, and must eventually be destroyed from the earth." (Joseph Smith, HC 5:212.)

**158**    "When Jesus comes to rule and reign King of Nations as he now does King of Saints, the veil of the covering will be taken from all nations, that all flesh may see his glory together, but that will not make them all Saints. Seeing the Lord does not make a man a Saint, seeing an Angel does not make a man a Saint by any means. A man may see the finger of the Lord, and not thereby become a Saint; the veil of the covering may be taken from before the nations, and all flesh see His glory together, and at the same time declare they will not serve Him." (Brigham Young, JD 2:316.)

"When the will of God is done on earth as it is in heaven, that Priesthood will be the only legitimate ruling power under the whole heavens; for every other power and influence will be subject to it. When the millennium . . . is introduced, all potentates, powers, and authorities—every man, woman, and child will be in subjection to the kingdom of God; they will be under the power and dominion of the Priesthood of God; then the will of God will be done on the earth as it is done in heaven." (John Taylor, JD 6:25.)

### Nonmembers on Earth During Millennium

**159** "If the Latter-day Saints think, when the kingdom of God is established on the earth, that all the inhabitants of the earth will join the church called Latter-day Saints, they are egregiously mistaken. I presume there will be as many sects and parties then as now. Still, when the kingdom of God triumphs, every knee shall bow and every tongue confess that Jesus is the Christ, to the glory of the Father. Even the Jews will do it then; but will the Jews and Gentiles be obliged to belong to the Church of Jesus Christ of Latter-day Saints? No; not by any means. . . . They will cease their persecutions against the Church of Jesus Christ, and they will be willing to acknowledge that the Lord is God, and that Jesus is the Savior of the World." (Brigham Young, JD 11:275.)

**160** "The order of society will be as it is when Christ comes to reign a thousand years; there will be every sort of sect and party, and every individual following what he supposes to be the best in religion, and in everything else, similar to what it is now." (Brigham Young, JD 2:316.)

"In the millennium men will have the privilege of being Presbyterians, Methodists or Infidels, but they will not have the privilege of treating the name and character of Deity as they have done heretofore. No, but every knee shall bow and every tongue confess to the glory of God the Father that Jesus is the Christ." (Brigham Young, JD 12:274.)

### Restoration of Earth to Be Accomplished

**161** "The great change which shall come when Christ our Savior begins his Millennial reign, is to be a restoration to the conditions which prevailed before the fall of man. The tenth article of faith of the Church of Jesus Christ of Latter-day Saints teaches us that Christ will reign personally upon the earth, and that the earth will be renewed, or restored, and receive its paradisiacal glory when that day comes.

"This new heaven and earth which will come into existence when our Lord comes to reign, is this same earth with its heavens renewed or restored to its primitive condition and beauty. Everything is to be brought back as nearly as it is possible to its position as it was in the beginning. The mountains, we are informed, are to be thrown down, the valleys are to be exalted, and 'the earth shall be like as it was in the days before it was divided.' " (Joseph Fielding Smith, RT, pp. 294–95.)

### Satan Will Be Bound

**162**    "The millennium consists in this—every heart in the Church and Kingdom of God being united in one; the Kingdom increasing to the overcoming of everything opposed to the economy of heaven, and Satan being bound, and having a seal set upon him." (Brigham Young, JD 1:203.)

"Satan will be bound for a thousand years, and during that time we will have a chance to build temples and to be baptized for the dead, and to do a work pertaining to the world that has been, as well as to the world that now is, and to operate under the direction of the Almighty in bringing to pass those designs which He contemplated from the foundation of the world." (John Taylor, JD 24:235.)

### Purposes of the Millennium

**163**    "Do you know what the Millennium is for, and what work will have to be done during that period? . . . To build temples. . . . . What are we going to do in these temples? . . . In these temples we will officiate in the ordinances of the Gospel of Jesus Christ for our friends, for no man can enter the kingdom of God without being born of the water and of the Spirit. We will officiate for them who are in the spirit world, where Jesus went to preach to the spirits, as Peter has written in the third chapter, verses 18, 19, 20, of his first epistle. . . .

"We will also have hands laid on us for the reception of the Holy Ghost; and then we will receive the washings and anointings for and in their behalf, preparatory to their becoming heirs of God and joint-heirs with Christ." (Brigham Young, JD 13:329.)

**164**    "In the millennium, when the kingdom of God is established on the earth in power, glory and perfection, and the reign of wickedness that has so long prevailed is subdued, the Saints of God will have the privilege of building their temples, and of entering into them. . . . And we will have revelations to know our forefathers clear back to Father Adam and Mother

Eve, and we will enter into the temples of God and officiate for them. Then man will be sealed to man until the chain is made perfect back to Adam, so that there will be a perfect chain of priesthood from Adam to the winding-up scene.

"This will be the work of the Latter-day Saints in the millennium." (Brigham Young, JD 15:138-39.)

"The great work of the Millennium shall be the work in the temples for the redemption of the dead; and then, we hope to enjoy the benefits of revelation through the Urim and Thummim, or by such means as the Lord may reveal concerning those for whom the work shall be done, so that we may not work by chance, or by faith alone, without knowledge, but with the actual knowledge revealed unto us." (Joseph F. Smith, IE 5:146-47.)

**165**

"When the Savior comes, a thousand years will be devoted to this work of redemption; and Temples will appear all over this land of Joseph,—North and South America—and also in Europe and elsewhere; and all the descendants of Shem, Ham, and Japheth who received not the Gospel in the flesh, must be officiated for in the Temples of God, before the Savior, can present the kingdom to the Father, saying, 'It is finished.' " (Wilford Woodruff, JD 19:230.)

# SELECTED READINGS

(Note: This book has been written for use with the LDS edition of the King James Version of the Bible published in 1979 by The Church of Jesus Christ of Latter-day Saints. All references to chapter headings, footnotes, and entries in the Topical Guide and Bible Dictionary pertain to that edition of the Bible.

The abbreviation TG refers to the Topical Guide; BD refers to the Bible Dictionary.

The numbers in the margin of each page in Part I indicate major segments; these numbers are used with the designation "Part I" for ease in reference. For example, the commentary for Micah 4:7 says that additional information on that verse appears in Part I 204, meaning segment 204 of Part I, found on page 84.)

# "A REVIEW OF GOD'S CONCERNS WITH THE CHILDREN OF ABRAHAM," BY ANTHONY W. IVINS

(Note: The following excerpts are from a talk by Anthony W. Ivins of the First Presidency, presented at the general conference of the Church on April 5, 1925.)

To properly comprehend the great plan of human **166** redemption, designed by the Father for the blessing of his children, it is necessary that we be familiar with his hand-dealings with the people of the world, from the beginning of time, as we count it, until the present. It is not sufficient that we familiarize ourselves alone with the dispensation in which we live, important though that be. We must know something of the past, as history has written it, the present as we see and understand it, and the future as the prophets have declared it. Without this grouping of the past, the present and the future, our vision will be restricted, and incomplete.

### Looking Back Four Thousand Years

I desire . . . to take you back more than four thousand years, to a period of time when an event occurred which was of transcendent importance to us, when a promise was made by the Lord which has not yet been fully fulfilled, but toward the fulfilment of which we are rapidly moving.

### The Promise to Abraham

It was about 122 years after the deluge that the Lord called **167** Abram, who at that time was seventy-five years of age, and a direct descendant of Shem, the chosen son of Noah, commanding him to go out from the country of his kindred, and from his father's house, into a land which he promised to give him, and to his posterity after him, for an ever-lasting inheritance. In obedience to the word of the Lord, Abram went from Haran, to which place he had been taken by his father, from Ur of Chaldea, and pitched his tent in the land of Canaan. Twenty-four years later the Lord spoke to him as follows: [Quoted Gen. 17:1-6.]

### God's Promise Never Fails

**168**    We have here a promise made by the Lord, which, judged by human standards, was impossible of fulfilment. Abraham was an hundred years old, and his wife, Sarah, ninety years of age, a supposedly barren woman, but the Lord had spoken, and his word never fails. Isaac was born, and the Lord repeated to him the promise made to his father. Isaac in turn, became the father of Jacob, through whose lineage, and the twelve sons who were born to him, the foundation was laid for the twelve tribes of Israel, the progenitors of a mighty nation.

### The History of Israel and the Story of Joseph

**169**    To follow the history of this interesting people from that time to the present in detail, would be impossible in the short time which is at my disposal. You who are familiar with the story know that twelve sons were born to Jacob, six of whom, Reuben, Simeon, Levi, Judah, Issachar and Zebulon, were the sons of Leah, his first wife. Joseph and Benjamin the sons of Rachel; Dan and Naphtali the sons of Bilha, the handmaid of Rachel; and Gad and Asher, the sons of Zilpah, the handmaid of Leah.

You are familiar with the story of Joseph, who was sold by his brethren to passing Ishmaelites who carried the boy into Egypt, and sold him to Potiphar, a captain of the king's guard. How he was cast into prison, and finally released and made the vice-regent of the king, the most powerful personage, except the Pharaoh, in all Egypt. You know how famine came to the land, which made it necessary for Jacob to send his sons to Egypt to procure food, where these men discovered that the governor of all the land was their younger brother, whom they had sold into slavery, and after returning to Canaan brought down their father and all of their possessions into Egypt, and were established in the land of Goshen, where they became a numerous people.

**170**    But Egypt was not the heritage of Israel. Naturally they would have remained there and been absorbed by the Egyptians, but the Lord had decreed otherwise. He had given them Palestine as the land of their inheritance, and their return to that land was inevitable, even though it were against their will.

After remaining in Egypt more than two hundred years, some chronologists say four hundred, the Lord delivered them from the bondage of the Egyptians, through his servant Moses, and under the leadership of Joshua they again entered and took possession of the promised land, a great people. From the seventy souls who went into Goshen with Jacob, there went out 603,500 men more than twenty years of age, men able to bear arms, probably not less than three millions of people in all.

**171**

The history of the Israelitish people, from the time they crossed the river Jordan, under Joshua, and subdued Jericho, until the establishment of the kingdom, under Saul, about four hundred years, is one of almost constant war and contention, which resulted in the subjugation of neighboring kingdoms and peoples, until Israel, under David became the possessors of Palestine from Dan on the north to Beersheba on the south.

It was under Solomon that Israel reached the zenith of her power and glory as a nation and kingdom. One hundred and twenty years had elapsed from the establishment of the kingdom, under Saul, until the division of the nation, which occurred during the reign of Rehoboam, the son of Solomon. Five hundred years in all, since the return from Egypt. Years of conflict among themselves and with other peoples, years of faithlessness on the part of Israel, and suffering because of their transgression and indifference to the words of the prophets whom the Lord sent among them to call them back into the old way of righteousness, but they said, we will not walk therein. When the watchmen whom the Lord placed on the towers of Zion sounded the warning trumpet they said, we will not hearken.

### The Day of the Prophets

**172**

It was the day of Isaiah, Jeremiah, Ezekiel and others of the prophets of old, through whom the Lord strove to keep the people in the path of righteousness and justice, the only road that leads to ultimate success, for final triumph has never been achieved and never will be, by a nation which denies the living God, and departs from the path which he has marked out for us to follow. In their pride of conquest Israel saw, in the glory which had come to them, fulfilment of the promise made by the Lord to Abraham. He had given them the land of promise, from north to south, and east to west, they were in possession of it, and in their pride believed themselves strong enough to hold it forever.

### The Dissolution of Israel

**173**    The dissolution of Israel, as a great nation, commenced when the ten tribes, under the leadership of Jeroboam, the son of Nebat, broke away from Judah and Benjamin and established the kingdom of Israel, with Samaria as its capital city, while Judah and Benjamin, with a part, at least, of the tribes of Simeon and Dan retained Jerusalem as the capital city of their kingdom.

Both nations rapidly relapsed into idolatry, Israel to the worship of the golden calf of the Egyptians, while Judah, to a great extent, turned to the worship of Bel of the Babylonians, and the idolatrous gods of the nations with which they were surrounded.

In this condition Israel continued until about seven hundred years before Christ, when the Assyrian armies, under Sennacherib overcame the Israelitish armies, captured Samaria, carried the Ten Tribes captive into Assyria, at the head of the Euphrates, and brought people from their own country whom they established in the cities of northern Palestine, and the identity of Israel as a distinct people, was lost to the world.

**174**    Judah continued to maintain a semblance of power for more than one hundred years after the fall of Israel, when they suffered the same fate. Judea was overrun by the Babylonian armies under Nebuchadnezzar, Jerusalem taken, the temple desecrated, and despoiled of its wealth, and Judah carried captive into Babylon, as their brethren had been carried into Assyria.

### The Christian Era Ushered In

This hasty and imperfect review brings us to the ushering in of the Christian Era.

**175**    After the fall of the Babylonian kingdom to the armies of Media and Persia, King Cyrus permitted the Jews to return from Babylon to Palestine and rebuild their city and temple which had been destroyed by Nebuchadnezzar. With great enthusiasm this work was undertaken, and it appears that the Jews who returned from the Babylonian captivity showed greater faith in the God of their fathers than had been manifested before they were carried [a]way.

### The Fate of the House of Israel Foretold

**176**    The fate which befell the House of Israel had been plainly outlined by the prophets whom the Lord had sent to warn them that the penalty of disobedience would be the dissolution of the nation, and that they would be taken from the land of their inheritance, and scattered among the strange and unbelieving nations of the world. A final fulfilment of this prophecy occurred when, about one hundred years after the birth of the Redeemer, Judea was trodden down by the Roman armies under Vespasian and his son Titus, Jerusalem taken, the temple destroyed, and the Jews scattered among the nations of the world, where they have remained until the present day.

The prophets Zechariah and Ezekiel had declared that the shepherds would neglect the flock, and that the sheep would be scattered, and become the prey of strange nations. To all human appearance, judged by every law of human reasoning, the promise made to Abraham had failed, he had been promised that Palestine should be the everlasting heritage of his children, and now they held dominion over no part of it. The end, it appeared, had come, the words of the prophets had been literally fulfilled, the promise made by the Lord if ever to be realized was still future.

### Israel Not Forsaken of the Lord
### Shall Be Gathered Again

Notwithstanding the fact that the Israelitish people had been **177** scattered and lost to the world, to become the prey of strange and unbelieving nations, the Lord had not forgotten nor forsaken them. He remembered the covenant made with their father Abraham, and decreed that it should be verified. The prophet Jeremiah, six hundred years before the birth of Christ, speaking upon this subject, declared that the Lord who scattered Israel would gather him again, in these words: [Quoted Jer. 31:10–12.]

Isaiah, seven hundred years before the birth of the Redeemer, referring to this same matter, said: [Quoted Isa. 11:10–13.]

### Christ's Promise to Israel Prior
### to His Crucifixion

During his ministry among the Nephite people, upon this **178** continent, after his resurrection from the dead, the Redeemer of the world, referring to this matter used the following language: [Quoted 3 Ne. 20:29–31.]

More definite and direct on this subject than any other, and to which I desire more particularly to call your attention, are the words of the Redeemer, just prior to his crucifixion. He called his disciples together, and in answer to questions which they propounded, spoke as follows: [Quoted D&C 45:18-20.]

This was literally fulfilled at the time of the taking of Jerusalem by Titus, the son of Vespasian. [Quoted D&C 45:21-30.]

That the final destiny of Judah was different to that of Joseph is plainly indicated by the blessing pronounced upon him by his father.

### The Blessings of Jacob

**179**    Just before his death, Jacob called his sons to him and gave to each his last blessing. Upon Judah he pronounced the blessing of leadership, declaring that the scepter of power should not depart from his house until the coming of Shiloh, to whom the Jews looked forward as their final king.

When he laid his hands upon the head of Joseph, he said:

"Joseph is a fruitful bough, even a fruitful bough by a well, whose branches run over the wall. The blessings of thy father have prevailed above the blessings of my progenitors, unto the utmost bounds of the everlasting hills. They shall be upon the head of him who was separated from his brethren."

The promise made to Abraham gave to him and his posterity after him the land of Canaan, which was to be the land of his inheritance, and this promise was renewed to Isaac, and to Jacob, and the Lord, through the latter, enlarged this promise to Joseph, his heritage, like a fruitful bough by a well, whose roots are well watered, ran over the wall, and extended beyond the heritage of Judah to the utmost bounds of the Everlasting hills, to America, where the Zion of our God is to be established.

### The Destiny of Israel Plainly Indicated

**180**    The scripture which I have just read indicates plainly the unchangeable decree of the Lord regarding the destiny of the Israelitish people. Scattered and lost to the world as they have been, they are not lost to the Lord, nor has he forgotten the covenant which he made with their father Abraham, and which was reconfirmed upon the heads of Isaac and Jacob.

### The Work Begun in This Dispensation

**181**    With the opening of the present gospel dispensation, . . .

the Lord commenced the work which is destined to result in the establishment of Ephraim, and other descendants of Joseph upon this continent, where the Zion of our God is to be established, and the restoration of the Jews to Palestine, the land of their fathers.

With the organization of the Church the Lord made plain the duty of its members. Men holding the restored priesthood, with its keys of authority, were sent into every country where they were permitted to go, proclaiming the opening of a new gospel dispensation, calling the people to repentance, and bearing witness that the mountain of the Lord's House was to be established in the tops of the mountains, and to be exalted above the hills, where we are today and that people from all nations should flow unto it, in order that they might be taught the way of the Lord, and learn to walk in his paths.

### The Jews to Be Restored to the
### Promised Land

The promise made by the Lord, regarding the restoration of **182** the Jews to the Promised Land was not overlooked. At the conference of the Church, held on the 6th of April, 1840, . . . Orson Hyde, a member of the Council of the Twelve, and John E. Page were called to go on a special mission to Jerusalem, for the purpose of dedicating the Holy Land for the latter-day gathering of the remnant of Judah. John E. Page failed in the accomplishment of the mission which was assigned him, but Orson Hyde, after surmounting many difficulties, a year and a half later knelt upon the Mount of Olives, and dedicated Palestine as the gathering place of the scattered remnant of Judah, and this servant of the Lord, moved upon by the spirit of prophecy, declared that inasmuch as it was by political power and influence that the Jews were scattered, it would be by political power and influence that they would be gathered, and that England was destined to be the nation which would take the leading part in the work of restoration.

More than seventy-five years had elapsed, almost a **183** generation, as the scripture counts time, since the light of the gospel had broken forth among those who sat in darkness, since Orson Hyde dedicated the land of Palestine for the latter-day gathering of scattered Judah, and the Holy Land still remained under the dominion of the Turk, the star and crescent still floated from the minaret of a Moslem Mosque, where the temple of Solomon once stood.

### The Great War and British Protectorate

**184**    Then came the great world war, and final peace at Versailles when Great Britain was given the responsibility of establishing and maintaining a protectorate over the Holy Land. The British armies, it is true, had already occupied Jerusalem, but it was with the signing of the treaty of Versailles that the first definite step was taken looking to the fulfilment of the words of the prophets, who had declared the redemption of Israel, and the restoration of Judah to the lands of their fathers, thousands of years ago.

### Interest of the Jews in the Restoration

**185**    The interest manifested by the Jewish people in the restoration of Palestine has few parallels in the history of the world. One is reminded of the zeal which their fathers showed as they returned from Babylon to Jerusalem to rebuild their city and temple, when women as well as men worked, and gave lavishly of their most cherished possessions that the task might be accomplished.

Jewish societies have been organized in various parts of the world, having for their purpose the creation of a publicly recognized, legally acquired home in Palestine, and the building up of the Jewish homeland in the Canaan of their fathers. Many millions of dollars have been subscribed by Jews throughout the world, to be used in the purchase of land, and the development of the dormant resources of the country. . . .

**186**    A movement such as this cannot fail to excite the interest and admiration of the civilized world. The Hebrew people have suffered during the past centuries as no other people have ever suffered, so far as my study and observation entitle me to judge. They have been scattered among strangers, where they have been denied the right of citizenship, and participation in the commercial and industrial activities of the people. They have been ruthlessly robbed of that which they have honestly acquired by the labor of their own hands. Worse than all, pogroms have been declared against them, when the protection of the law has been officially declared to be inoperative, and permission given to wicked men and women to despoil them of their goods, and even deprive them of life itself.

### The Movement Must Elicit Praise and Sympathy

**187**    The wonder is that they have survived and maintained their nationality during all these centuries of affliction, and now that they are undertaking to establish a home in the land of their fathers, where they may live in peace, and be a blessing to the non-progressive people who have so long dominated it, they certainly must elicit the praise and sympathy of all right thinking people.

### The Hand of the Lord in It

From a human point of view it is a movement of great **188** interest, but to me the one outstanding feature is the manifest hand-dealing of the Lord, which I see in it, and which they themselves do not fully realize. It will come in a natural way, it may be England, it may be some other nation, but it will be the Lord who will direct.

### The Lord Will Use the Nations to
### Accomplish His Purpose

When Cyrus led the victorious Medio-Persian army to the **189** overthrow of the great Babylonian kingdom he was not aware that he was fulfilling the words of the prophets who had lived long before, but he did so in wondrous detail. When Alexander of Macedon halted his army, after he had crossed the Dardanelles and won the battle of Granicus, and notwithstanding the protest of his generals delayed his campaign against Persia, in order that he might besiege and finally destroy Tyre, he had no knowledge of the fact that the prophets had declared that the greatest maritime city of the world should be destroyed in just that manner, but it was nevertheless true.

So will the Lord continue to use the nations for the accom-**190** plishment of his purposes, until the words of his servants the prophets have all been fulfilled, until Zion is established, Judea redeemed, and his will done upon earth, as it is done in heaven. **191**

God bless the Jews in this important work. May the eyes of their understanding be opened, and the time soon come when Shiloh, to whose coming they have so long looked forward, shall stand upon the Mount of Olives, and they recognize in him, Jesus of Nazareth, the Redeemer of the world, whom their fathers rejected. And may we, Latter-day Saints, we people who are of Ephraim, appreciate the part we are playing in this great latter-day drama, the like of which was never played before, and never will be again.

# DEDICATORY PRAYER OF ORSON HYDE

(Note: The following excerpts are from a prayer dedicating the land of Jerusalem for the gathering of Judah, offered October 24, 1841 by Orson Hyde, an Apostle of the Church [HC 4:456–459].)

**192** O Thou! who art from everlasting to everlasting, eternally and unchangeably the same, even the God who rules in the heavens above, and controls the destinies of men on the earth, wilt Thou not condescend, through thine infinite goodness and royal favor, to listen to the prayer of Thy servant which he this day offers up unto Thee in the name of Thy holy child Jesus, upon this land, where the Sun of Righteousness set in blood, and thine Anointed One expired. . . .

**193** Now, O Lord! Thy servant has been obedient to the heavenly vision which Thou gavest him in his native land; and under the shadow of Thine outstretched arm, he has safely arrived in this place to dedicate and consecrate this land unto Thee, for the gathering together of Judah's scattered remnants, according to the predictions of the holy Prophets—for the building up of Jerusalem again after it has been trodden down by the Gentiles so long, and for rearing a Temple in honor of Thy name. . . .

**194** O Thou, Who didst covenant with Abraham, Thy friend, and Who didst renew that covenant with Isaac, and confirm the same with Jacob with an oath, that Thou wouldst not only give them this land for an everlasting inheritance, but that Thou wouldst also remember their seed forever. Abraham, Isaac, and Jacob have long since closed their eyes in death, and made the grave their mansion. Their children are scattered and dispersed abroad among the nations of the Gentiles like sheep that have no shepherd, and are still looking forward for the fulfillment of those promises which Thou didst make concerning them; and even this land, which once poured forth nature's richest bounty, and flowed, as it were, with milk and honey, has, to a certain extent, been smitten with barrenness and sterility since it drank from murderous hands the blood of Him who never sinned.

Grant, therefore, O Lord, in the name of Thy well-beloved **195**
Son, Jesus Christ, to remove the barrenness and sterility of this
land, and let springs of living water break forth to water its
thirsty soil. Let the vine and olive produce in their strength, and
the fig-tree bloom and flourish. Let the land become
abundantly fruitful when possessed by its rightful heirs; let it
again flow with plenty to feed the returning prodigals who come
home with a spirit of grace and supplication; upon it let the
clouds distil virtue and richness, and let the fields smile with
plenty. Let the flocks and the herds greatly increase and
multiply upon the mountains and the hills; and let Thy great
kindness conquer and subdue the unbelief of Thy people. Do
Thou take from them their stony heart, and give them a heart of
flesh; and may the Sun of Thy favor dispel the cold mists of
darkness which have beclouded their atmosphere. Incline them
to gather in upon this land according to Thy word. Let them
come like clouds and like doves to their windows. Let the large
ships of the nations bring them from the distant isles; and let
kings become their nursing fathers, and queens with motherly
fondness wipe the tear of sorrow from their eyes.

Thou, O Lord, did once move upon the heart of Cyrus to **196**
show favor unto Jerusalem and her children. Do Thou now also
be pleased to inspire the hearts of kings and the powers of the
earth to look with a friendly eye towards this place, and with a
desire to see Thy righteous purposes executed in relation
thereto. Let them know that it is Thy good pleasure to restore
the kingdom unto Israel—raise up Jerusalem as its capital, and
constitute her people a distinct nation and government, with
David Thy servant, even a descendant from the loins of ancient
David to be their king.

Let that nation or that people who shall take an active part **197**
in behalf of Abraham's children, and in the raising up of
Jerusalem, find favor in Thy sight. Let not their enemies prevail
against them, neither let pestilence or famine overcome them,
but let the glory of Israel overshadow them, and the power of
the Highest protect them; while that nation or kingdom that will
not serve Thee in this glorious work must perish, according to
Thy word—'Yea, those nations shall be utterly wasted.' . . . **198**

O my Father in Heaven! I now ask Thee in the name of
Jesus to remember Zion, with all her Stakes, and with all her
assemblies. She has been grievously afflicted and smitten; she
has mourned; she has wept; her enemies have triumphed, and
have said, "Ah, where is thy God?" Her Priests and Prophets

have groaned in chains and fetters within the gloomy walls of prisons, while many were slain, and now sleep in the arms of death. How long, O Lord, shall iniquity triumph, and sin go unpunished?

**199**     Do Thou arise in the majesty of Thy strength, and make bare Thine arm in behalf of Thy people. Redress their wrongs, and turn their sorrow into joy. Pour the spirit of light and knowledge, grace and wisdom, into the hearts of her Prophets, and clothe her Priests with salvation. Let light and knowledge march forth through the empire of darkness, and may the honest in heart flow to their standard, and join in the march to go forth to meet the Bridegroom.

**200**     Let a peculiar blessing rest upon the Presidency of Thy Church, for at them are the arrows of the enemy directed. Be Thou to them a sun and a shield, their strong tower and hiding place; and in the time of distress or danger be Thou near to deliver. Also the quorum of the Twelve, do Thou be pleased to stand by them for Thou knowest the obstacles which they have to encounter, the temptations to which they are exposed, and the privations which they must suffer. Give us (the Twelve) therefore, strength according to our day, and help us to bear a faithful testimony of Jesus and His Gospel, to finish with fidelity and honor the work which Thou hast given us to do, and then give us a place in Thy glorious kingdom. And let this blessing rest upon every faithful officer and member in Thy Church. And all the glory and honor will we ascribe unto God and the Lamb forever and ever. Amen.

# EXCERPTS FROM THE "PROCLAMATION OF 1845," BY THE TWELVE APOSTLES

(Note: The following excerpts are from a proclamation of **201** the Twelve Apostles of The Church of Jesus Christ of Latter-day Saints issued to the world April 6, 1845. It is believed by some that this proclamation had been prepared in response to the following revelation received by the Prophet Joseph Smith:

"You are now called immediately to make a solemn proclamation of my gospel . . .

"This proclamation shall be made to all the kings of the world, to the four corners thereof, to the honorable president-elect, and the high-minded governors of the nation in which you live, and to all the nations of the earth scattered abroad.

"Let it be written in the spirit of meekness and by the power of the Holy Ghost, which shall be in you at the time of the writing of the same;

"For it shall be given you by the Holy Ghost to know my will concerning those kings and authorities, even what shall befall them in a time to come." [D&C 124:2-5.])

PROCLAMATION *of the Twelve Apostles of the Church of Jesus Christ of Latter-day Saints.*

*To all the Kings of the World;*
*To the President of the United States of America;*
*To the Governors of the several States;*
*And to the Rulers and People of all Nations:*
GREETING:

KNOW YE:—

That the kingdom of God has come: as has been predicted **202** by ancient prophets, and prayed for in all ages; even that kingdom which shall fill the whole earth, and shall stand for ever. . . .

Being established in these last days for the restoration of all **203** things spoken by the prophets since the world began; and in order to prepare the way for the coming of the Son of Man.

And we now bear witness that his coming is near at hand; and not many years hence, the nations and their kings shall see him coming in the clouds of heaven with power and great glory.

In order to meet this great event there must needs be a preparation. . . .

We testify that the . . . gospel of Jesus Christ, in its fulness . . . is the only true, everlasting, and unchangeable gospel; and the only plan revealed on earth whereby man can be saved.

**204**

We also bear testimony that the *"Indians"* (so called) of North and South America are a remnant of the tribes of Israel; as is now made manifest by the discovery and revelation of their ancient oracles and records.

And that they are about to be gathered, civilized, and made *one nation* in this glorious land.

They will also come to the knowledge of their forefathers, and of the fulness of the gospel; and they will embrace it, and become a righteous branch of the house of Israel.

And we further testify that the Lord has appointed a holy city and temple to be built on this continent for the endowment and ordinances pertaining to the priesthood; and for the Gentiles, and the remnant of Israel to resort unto, in order to worship the Lord; and to be taught in his ways and walk in his paths: in short, to finish their preparations for the coming of the Lord.

**205**

And we further testify, that the Jews among all nations are hereby commanded, in the name of the Messiah, to prepare, to return to Jerusalem in Palestine; and to rebuild that city and temple unto the Lord:

And also to organize and establish their own political government, under their own rulers, judges, and governors in that country.

For be it known unto them that *we* now hold the keys of the priesthood and kingdom which is soon to be restored unto them. . . .

**206**

There is also another consideration of vast importance to all the rulers and people of the world, in regard to this matter. It is this: As this work progresses in its onward course, and becomes more and more an object of political and religious interest and excitement, no king, ruler, or subject, no community or individual, will stand *neutral*. All will at length be influenced by one spirit or the other; and will take sides either for or against the kingdom of God, and the fulfilment of the prophets, in the great restoration and return of his long dispersed covenant people.

Some will act the part of the venerable Jethro, the father-in-law of Moses; or the noble Cyrus; and will aid and bless the people of God; or like Ruth, the Moabitess, will forsake their people and their kindred and country, and will say to the Saints, or to Israel: *"This people shall be my people, and their God my God."* While others will walk in the footsteps of a Pharaoh, or a Balak, and will harden their hearts, and fight against God, and seek to destroy his people. These will commune with priests and prophets who love the wages of unrighteousness; and who, like Balaam, will seek to curse, or to find enchantments against Israel.

**207**

You cannot therefore stand as idle and disinterested spectators of the scenes and events which are calculated in their very nature to reduce all nations and creeds to *one* political and religious *standard*, and thus put an end to Babel forms and names, and to strife and war. You will, therefore, either be led by the good Spirit to cast in your lot, and to take a lively interest with the Saints of the Most High, and the covenant people of the Lord, or on the other hand, you will become their inveterate enemy, and oppose them by every means in your power.

**208**

To such an extreme will this great division finally extend, that the nations of the old world will combine to oppose these things by military force. They will send a great army to Palestine, against the Jews; and they will besiege their city, and will reduce the inhabitants of Jerusalem to the greatest extreme of distress and misery.

**209**

Then will commence a struggle in which the fate of nations and empires will be suspended on a single battle.

In this battle the governors and people of Judah distinguish themselves for their bravery and warlike achievements. The weak among them will be like David, and the strong among them will be like God; or like the angel of the Lord.

In that day the Lord will pour upon the inhabitants of Jerusalem the spirit of grace and supplication, and they shall look upon the Messiah whom they have pierced.

**210**

For lo! he will descend from heaven, as the defender of the Jews: and to complete their victory. His feet will stand in that day upon the Mount of Olives, which shall cleave in sunder at his presence, and remove one half to the north, and the other to the south; thus forming a great valley where the mountain now stands.

The earth will quake around him, while storm and tempest,

**211**

hail and plague, are mingled with the clash of arms, the roar of artillery, the shouts of victory, and the groans of the wounded and dying.

In that day all who are in the siege, both against Judea and against Jerusalem, shall be cut in pieces; though all the people of the earth should be gathered together against it.

This signal victory on the part of the Jews, so unlooked for by the nations, and attended with the personal advent of Messiah, and the accompanying events, will change the whole order of things in Europe and Asia, in regard to political and religious organization, and government.

**212**

The Jews as a nation become holy from that day forward; and their city and sanctuary becomes holy. There also the Messiah establishes his throne, and seat of government.

Jerusalem then becomes the seat of empire, and the great centre and capital of the old world.

All the families of the land shall then go up to Jerusalem once a year, to worship the King, the Lord of Hosts, and to keep the feast of Tabernacles.

**213**

Those who refuse to go up, shall have no rain, but shall be smitten with dearth and famine. And if the family of Egypt go not up (as it never rains there) they shall be smitten with the plague. And thus all things shall be fulfilled according to the words of the holy prophets of old, and the word of the Lord which is now revealed, to confirm and fulfil them.

In short the kings, rulers, priests and people of Europe, and of the old world, shall know this once that there is a God in Israel, who, as in days of old, can utter his voice, and it shall be obeyed. . . .

**214**

While these great events are rolling on the wheels of time, and being fulfilled in the old world, the Western Continent will present a scene of grandeur, greatness, and glory, far surpassing the scene just described.

The Lord will make her that halted a remnant; and gather her that was driven out and afflicted; and make her who was cast afar off, a strong nation; and will reign over *them* in Mount Zion from that time forth and for ever.

Or, in other words, He will assemble the Natives, the remnants of Joseph in America; and make of them a great, and strong, and powerful nation: and he will civilize and enlighten them, and will establish a holy city, and temple, and seat of government among them, which shall be called Zion.

And there shall be his tabernacle, his sanctuary, his throne, and seat of government for the whole continent of North and South America for ever.

In short, it will be to the western hemisphere what Jerusalem will be to the eastern.

And there the Messiah will visit them in person; and the old Saints, who will then have been raised from the dead, will be with him. And he will establish his kingdom and laws over all the land.

**215**

To this city, and to its several branches or stakes, shall the Gentiles seek, as to a standard of light and knowledge. Yea, the nations, and their kings and nobles, shall say, Come and let us go up to the Mount Zion, and to the temple of the Lord; where his holy priesthood stand to minister continually before the Lord; and where we may be instructed more fully, and receive the ordinances of remission, and of sanctification, and re-demption; and thus be adopted into the family of Israel, and identified in the same covenants of promise.

**216**

The despised and degraded son of the forest, who has wandered in dejection and sorrow, and suffered reproach, shall then drop his disguise, and stand forth in manly dignity, and exclaim to the Gentiles who have envied and sold him: *"I am Joseph: does my father yet live?"* Or, in other words: I am a descendant of that Joseph who was sold into Egypt. You have hated *me*, and sold *me*, and thought *I* was dead. But lo! I live, and am heir to the inheritance, titles, honors, priesthood, sceptre, crown, throne, and eternal life and dignity of my fathers, who live for evermore.

He shall then be ordained, washed, anointed with holy oil, and arrayed in fine linen, even in the glorious and beautiful garments and royal robes of the high priesthood, which is after the order of the Son of God; and shall enter into the congregation of the Lord, even into the Holy of Holies, there to be crowned with authority and power which shall never end.

The Spirit of the Lord shall then descend upon him, like the dew upon the mountains of Hermon, and like refreshing showers of rain upon the flowers of Paradise.

His heart shall expand with knowledge, wide as eternity; and his mind shall comprehend the vast creations of his God, and His eternal purpose of redemption, glory, and exaltation, which was devised in heaven before the worlds were organized; but made manifest in these last days, for the fulness of the Gentiles, and for the exaltation of Israel.

He shall also behold his Redeemer and be filled with his

**217** presence, while the cloud of his glory shall be seen in his temple.

The city of Zion, with its sanctuary and priesthood, and the glorious fulness of the gospel, will constitute a *standard* which will put an end to jarring creeds and political wranglings, by uniting the republics, states, provinces, territories, nations, tribes, kindred, tongues, people, and sects of North and South America in one great and common bond of brotherhood.

While truth and knowledge shall make them free, and love cement their union. The Lord also shall be their king and their lawgiver; while wars shall cease and peace prevail for a thousand years.

**218** Thus shall American rulers, statesmen, citizens, and savages know, *"this once,"* that there is a God in Israel, who can utter his voice, and it shall be fulfilled.

Americans! This mighty and strange work has been commenced in your midst, and must roll on in fulfilment.

You are now invited, and earnestly intreated, to investigate it thoroughly, and to aid and participate in its accomplishment. . . .

**219** The Lord has spoken, and who can disannul it? He has uttered his voice, and who can gainsay it? He has stretched out his arm, and who can turn it back? . . .

**220** We would now make a solemn appeal to our rulers and other fellow-citizens, whether it is treason to *know?* or even to publish what we *know?* If it is, then strike the murderous blow, but listen to what we say.

We say, then, in life or in death, in bonds or free, that the great God has spoken in this age.—*And we know it.*

**221** He has given us the Holy Priesthood and Apostleship, and the keys of the kingdom of God, to bring about the restoration of all things as promised by the holy prophets of old.—*And we know it.*

He has revealed the origin and the Records of the aboriginal tribes of America, and their future destiny.—*And we know it.*

He has revealed the fulness of the gospel, with its gifts, blessings, and ordinances.—*And we know it.*

He has commanded *us* to bear witness of it, first to the Gentiles, and then to the remnants of Israel and the Jews.—*And we know it.*

**222** He has commanded us to gather together his Saints on this Continent, and build up holy cities and sanctuaries.—*And we know it.*

He has said, that the Gentiles should come into the same

gospel and covenant; and be numbered with the house of Israel; and be a blessed people upon this good land for ever, if they would repent and embrace it.—*And we know it.*

He has also said that, if they do not repent, and come to the knowledge of the truth, and cease to fight against Zion, and also put away all murder, lying, pride, priestcraft, whoredom, and secret abomination, they shall soon perish from the earth, and be cast down to hell.—*And we know it.*

He has said, that the time is at hand for the Jews to be gathered to Jerusalem.—*And we know it.*

**223**

**224**

He has said, that the Ten Tribes of Israel should also be revealed in the North country, together with their oracles and records, preparatory to their return, and to their union with Judah, no more to be separated.—*And we know it.*

He has said, that when these preparations were made, both in this country and in Jerusalem, and the gospel in all its fulness preached to all nations for a witness and testimony, He will come, and all the Saints with him, to reign on the earth one thousand years.—*And we know it.*

**225**

He has said that he will not come in his glory and destroy the wicked, till these warnings were given and these preparations were made for his reception.—*And we know it.*

Now, fellow-citizens, if this knowledge, or the publishing of it, is *treason or crime,* we refuse not to die.

**226**

But be ye sure of this, that whether we live or die, the words of the testimony of this proclamation which we now send unto you, shall all be fulfilled.

Heaven and earth shall pass away, but not one jot or tittle of his revealed word shall fail to be fulfilled.

Therefore, again we say to all people, Repent, and be baptized in the name of Jesus Christ, for remission of sins; and you shall receive the Holy Spirit, and shall know the truth, and be numbered with the House of Israel.

And we once more invite all the kings, presidents, governors, rulers, judges, and people of the earth, to aid us, the Latter-day Saints; and also, the Jews, and all the remnants of Israel, by your influence and protection, and by your silver and gold, that we may build the cities of Zion and Jerusalem, and the temples and sanctuaries of our God; and may accomplish the great restoration of all things, and bring in the latter-day glory.

**227**

That knowledge, truth, light, love, peace, union, honor, glory, and power, may fill the earth with eternal life and joy.

That death, bondage, oppression, wars, mourning, sorrow, and pain, may be done away for ever, and all tears be wiped from every eye. (MFP 1:252-64.)

# "A MESSAGE TO JUDAH FROM JOSEPH," BY EZRA TAFT BENSON

(Note: The following excerpts are from a talk given to Mormons, non-Mormons, and Jews May 2, 1976, by President Ezra Taft Benson of the Council of Twelve Apostles, at Calgary, Alberta, Canada.)

Our affinity toward modern Judah . . . is prompted out of a knowledge of our peculiar relationships together—relationships which claim a common heritage. Jeremiah has prophesied that in the latter times "the house of Judah shall walk with the house of Israel, and they shall come together." (Jeremiah 3:18.)

**228**

### Kindred Doctrines of the Mormons and the Jews

Among the kindred doctrines of the Mormons and the Jews is our mutual belief in Jehovah, a God of revelation. We share a common belief in the Messiah who will come. We further hold reciprocal beliefs in prophets. We hold a common commitment to the return of the Jews to the "land of Jerusalem," in fulfillment of the words of the ancient prophets. There are many other doctrinal and social similarities.

### Foundation of the Church Known as "the Mormons"

The foundation of the Church which is sometimes referred to by nonmembers as the "Mormon" Church, is a belief in revelation—modern revelation by God of his purposes and directions to living prophets.

**229**

We believe as Amos declared: "Surely the Lord God will do nothing, but he revealeth his secret unto his servants the prophets." (Amos 3:7.)

We declare that secrets long since hidden through the ages have been revealed again through a prophet by the revelation of "a new and everlasting covenant" to Israel. That prophet's name was Joseph Smith. . . .

### The Mormons' Interest in the Jews

**230**     From the very inception of this latter-day work, which claims to be a restoration of the covenants given by God to Abraham, Isaac, and Jacob, this church has had a deep interest in the remnant of the house of Israel, the descendants of Judah.

In 1836, the Mormons completed their first temple at Kirtland, Ohio. In the dedicatory prayer which was offered on that occasion, Joseph Smith petitioned the "Lord God of Israel":

"O Lord . . . thou knowest that thou hast a great love for the children of Jacob, who have been scattered upon the mountains for a long time. . . .

"We therefore ask thee to have mercy upon the children of Jacob, that Jerusalem, from this hour, may begin to be redeemed;

"And the yoke of bondage may begin to be broken off from the house of David;

"And the children of Judah may begin to return to the lands which thou didst give to Abraham, their father." (Doctrine and Covenants 109:60-64.)

This was said during the Passover season, March 27, 1836.

### The Orson Hyde Expedition to Israel

**231**     Before Joseph Smith was killed, he dispatched an apostle by the name of Orson Hyde to dedicate the land of Palestine for the return of the Jews. This concern for a homeless people and the sending of this apostle was done at a time when the Mormons themselves were virtually homeless, having been dispossessed of their lands and possessions in Missouri.

Orson Hyde left on his assignment in the fall of 1840. He arrived in Palestine in October 1841. On October 24, 1841, he ascended the Mount of Olives all alone, built an altar to the Lord, and offered a dedicatory prayer. [Quoted portions of that prayer; see Part I 192-200.]

### The Mormon Interest in the Jews
### Is Based on Kinship

**232**     Historically, we must recognize that this interest in the restoration of the Jews to their homeland is older than modern Zionism and the great work of Theodor Herzl and others. There were a number of Christian sects in the nineteenth century which held millennial views and saw the return of the Jews to their homeland as a "sign of the times" which would precede the second advent of Jesus Christ. The Mormon interest was and is more than this. Our concern and interest is a kinship to our Jewish brothers.

Our common heritage goes back to Abraham, Isaac, and Jacob. God reiterated to Jacob the same promises which were given to Abraham, and then gave Jacob the new name of Israel. His posterity—*all those* who descended through his twelve sons —were known by this designation. They were variously referred to as the "house of Israel," "children of Israel," or "tribes of Israel." I emphasize that *all of his posterity* received the family name designation through the twelve sons. Today it has become common practice to identify only one of his twelve sons, Judah, with the family designation "Israelite" because they have maintained their separate identity.

### Israel's Blessing to Joseph

**233**

As you carefully read the forty-ninth chapter of Genesis, you will find that Jacob, or Israel, pronounced blessings on *all* his twelve sons. Each was given a peculiar and distinctive blessing. Time will only permit a consideration of the blessings of two of these sons, whose blessings were preeminent above the blessings of the others. I refer to the blessings pronounced on Judah and Joseph. May I read first the blessing pronounced on Joseph:

"Joseph is a fruitful bough, even a fruitful bough by a well; whose branches run over the wall:

"The archers have sorely grieved him, and shot at him, and hated him:

"But his bow abode in strength, and the arms of his hands were made strong by the hands of the mighty God of Jacob; (from thence is the shepherd, the stone of Israel:)

"Even by the God of thy father, who shall help thee; and by the Almighty, who shall bless thee with blessings of heaven above, blessings of the deep that lieth under, blessings of the breasts, and of the womb:

"The blessings of thy father have prevailed above the blessings of my progenitors unto the utmost bound of the everlasting hills: they shall be on the head of Joseph, and on the crown of the head of him that was separate from his brethren." (Genesis 49:22–26.)

**234**

There are several points which we should note carefully about this blessing:

1. Joseph's posterity would be numerous; that is, he would be a "fruitful bough."

2. His posterity or "branches" would "run over the wall."

3. His descendants would be sorely persecuted, which is the meaning of the phraseology "the archers have sorely grieved him, and shot at him, and hated him."

4. The blessings on Joseph's posterity were to prevail "above the blessings of my progenitors unto the utmost bound of the everlasting hills."

Later I shall comment on the interpretation of this blessing as it affects the relationships of the present-day Mormons and Jews; but first it will be instructive to review the history of the descendants of Israel after they came into the land promised to Abraham as "the land of Canaan . . . an everlasting possession." (Genesis 17:8.)

### The Scattering of Israel

**235**  For a time the confederated tribes were a united monarchy under Saul, David, and Solomon, but ultimately they divided into two major kingdoms. The kingdom to the north—which comprised 10½ tribes, including the descendants of Joseph—retained the designation *Israel*. The kingdom to the south—made up primarily of the tribe of Judah—adopted the name of *Judah*. (See 1 Kings 11:31-32; 12:19-24.)

Prophets were raised up among these two nations to call them to repentance because of their idolatry and wickedness. The prophet Amos predicted the results of this disobedience to God.

"Now shall they [Israel] go captive with the first that go captive." (Amos 6:7.)

"I will sift the house of Israel among all nations, like as corn is sifted in a sieve, yet shall not the least grain fall upon the earth." (Amos 9:9.)

**236**  The northern kingdom, Israel, was subsequently taken into captivity by the Assyrians 721 years B.C.E., or Before Common Era. The Old Testament contains no history of Israel, nor of Joseph's descendants after this date. Are we to believe that God's promises to Joseph were for naught, that the prophecy of his posterity being numerous, "running over the wall," being sorely persecuted, and going to the "utmost bound of the everlasting hills" would not be fulfilled?

### Separate Records to Be Kept

Because of the division which occurred between the two **237** kingdoms, the Lord made special provision that separate records were kept. The prophet Ezekiel spoke of these records in these words: [Quoted Ezek. 37:15–20.]

From this commandment from God to the prophet Ezekiel, these provisions should be noted:

1. That a stick or record was to be kept for Judah, and that a stick or record was to be kept for Joseph;

2. That the two records were to be joined together into "one stick," or record, in the hands of that prophet.

Where is the fulfillment of this important commandment? Who claims to have the record of Joseph today?

### The Book of Mormon Fulfills
### Joseph's Prophecy

The record of Joseph has been brought forth in this day to **238** Joseph Smith by a messenger sent from God. That record is called the Book of Mormon, named after one of the seed of Joseph who abridged the records of his people. The record tells the account of a colony of Israelites, descended from Joseph, who left Jerusalem before its great destruction during the Babylonian siege under King Nebuchadnezzar. It tells how these descendants of Joseph came "over the wall"—a metaphoric expression which denoted a barrier to them. That barrier was the great ocean between the continents of Asia and the Americas. This record tells how they were guided by the hand of the Lord to the land of America, a land of promise to Joseph and his descendants, a land "of everlasting hills." It tells how Joseph's posterity became very numerous upon the land until they filled it with a mighty nation. All this was in fulfillment of Joseph's blessing! The Book of Mormon further records the destruction of this mighty civilization because of their departure from the commandments of the God of Israel.

The records of these people lay buried in the earth for centuries. Then in 1827, a heavenly messenger turned them over to Joseph Smith. They were subsequently translated from their ancient reformed Egyptian writing into the English language and were published to the world in the year 1830.

The Judean prophet Ezekiel had declared that these records were to be "one in thine hand." I witness before you the fulfillment of that prophecy—the record of Judah in one hand, the record of Joseph in the other—one in our hands today.

### Judah's Scattering and Persecution

**239**    But what about the prophecies that pertain to the house of Judah? The northern tribes of Israel were not the only ones to be dispersed according to prophecy. Judah, the southern kingdom, was also to be scattered:

"And the Lord said, I will remove Judah *also* out of my sight, as I have removed Israel, and will cast off this city Jerusalem which I have chosen, and the house of which I said, My name shall be there." (2 Kings 23:27; italics added.)

The history of the scattering of the nation Judah is so well known as to be regarded proverbial. Under the seizure of Babylon, the nation was taken into exile. A remnant returned to rebuild Jerusalem and the temple after the Persians came into power. Since that time, except for a short period of independence under the Maccabees, Judah has been under the yoke of foreign domination: the Macedonian Empire; the tripartite government rule by Egypt, Syria, and Macedonia; Syrian domination; then the Roman rule, and a final dispersion among all nations.

Time will not permit extensive comment about the depth of the suffering and their persecution among many nations. Some of the most evil of those deeds were perpetrated upon the remaining Jews in Palestine in the name of Christianity during the Crusades. Will Durrant has correctly written of this sad chapter of human suffering, "No other people has ever known so long an exile, or so hard a fate." . . . Yes, the prophecies regarding the dispersion and suffering of Judah have been fulfilled. But the gathering and reestablishment of the Jews was also clearly predicted.

### Prophecies Concerning the Gathering of Israel and the Jews

**240**    This predicted gathering has three phases: the gathering of Israel to the land of Zion, the American hemisphere; the return of the Ten Tribes from the north countries; and the reestablishment of the Jews in Palestine which had been long ago predicted by the prophets in these words: [Quoted Isa. 11:11-12; Jer. 30:3; 31:31; Zech. 10:6, 8; 2 Ne. 10:8-9; 25:15-17; Isa. 29:14.]

In 1950, I said, "There has been much confusion over the **241** Palestine question—much talk of division of the land, of quotas, import restrictions—but out of it all I cannot help feeling that we will see a complete fulfilment of the prophecies which have been made regarding this people. These prophecies are in rapid course of fulfilment before our very eyes today." (*Conference Report,* April 1950, p. 77.)

Since that time, the nation of Israel has fought three wars, regained Jerusalem and the western wall (Wailing Wall), and added the Golan Heights and much of the Sinai Peninsula to its territory.

### The Blessing of Israel Pronounced on Judah

We previously considered the blessing that Jacob, or Israel, **242** pronounced on Joseph. Let us now consider the blessing pronounced on Judah:

"Judah, thou art he whom thy brethren shall praise: thy hand shall be in the neck of thine enemies; thy father's children shall bow down before thee.

"Judah is a lion's whelp: from the prey, my son, thou art gone up: he stooped down, he couched as a lion, and as an old lion; who shall rouse him up?

*"The sceptre shall not depart from Judah, nor a lawgiver from between his feet, until Shiloh come; and unto him shall the gathering of the people be.*

"Binding his foal unto the vine, and his ass's colt unto the choice vine; he washed his garments in wine, and his clothes in the blood of grapes:

"His eyes shall be red with wine, and his teeth white with milk." (Genesis 49:8–12.)

The great blessing to Judah is that it contemplated the **243** coming of Shiloh who would gather his people to him. This prophecy concerning Shiloh has been subject to several rabbinic and Christian interpretations and the object of considerable controversy. The interpretation given this passage by the Mormon Church is one based on revelation to modern prophets, not on scholarly commentary. It was revealed to Joseph Smith that Shiloh is the Messiah. . . . (See Genesis 50:24, Inspired Version.)

"The sceptre shall not depart from Judah, nor a lawgiver from between his feet, until Shiloh come." (Genesis 49:10.) We see the fulfillment of the Shiloh prophecy this way: Judah came to power when David was exalted to the throne. Even after the division of the northern and southern kingdoms, the kings of Judah sat on the throne. Following the Babylonian captivity, "lawgivers" were provided to the Jewish remnant who returned to Jerusalem. Zerubbabel, Ezra, and Nehemiah are examples. Subsequently, the Sanhedrin was established, and it continued as the ruling body of the Jews until the destruction of Jerusalem and the scattering of the Jews. From that time, the Jews had no lawgiver to whom they could turn. Shiloh had come. He was Jesus of Nazareth, who was later crucified as "King of the Jews."

**244**     Christian history has emphasized the point that the Jews as a nation rejected their Messiah. Overlooked has been the fact that many Jews did believe him to be the Messiah. Among those Jews who did so were his twelve apostles and thousand of other Jews who were converted by their ministry. We declare that after his ministry in Palestine, the resurrected Messiah personally visited the house of Joseph in this land of America, taught them, blessed them, and renewed the everlasting covenant with them. His ministry to America is recorded in the Book of Mormon.

### The Story of Joseph Revisited

**245**     You will recall the episode of Joseph and his brethren in the Old Testament, and how he was sold into Egypt. You will remember that, because of a famine in the land of Canaan, his brethren were compelled to go to Egypt to purchase corn from the granaries. Joseph had risen to the position of governor over the land, and was in charge of those granaries. One of the most touching scenes recorded in the Torah is when Joseph made himself known to his brethren: "I am Joseph your brother . . ." (Genesis 45:4.)

To you, our friends of modern Judah, we declare, "We are Joseph, your brothers." We claim kinship with you as descendants from our fathers, Abraham, Isaac, and Jacob. We belong to the same family. We, too, are the house of Israel.

There is yet another parallel to this story of Joseph.

**246**     The brethren of Joseph in times past came to him during a famine for physical sustenance. Today there is another famine in the land, "not a famine of bread, nor a thirst of water, but of hearing the words of the Lord." (Amos 8:11.)

Has not the Lord God said through Isaiah, "Every one that thirsteth, come ye to the waters. . . .

"[I will] satisfy thy soul in drought, and make fat thy bones: and thou shalt be like a watered garden, and like a spring of water, whose waters fail not." (Isaiah 55:1; 58:11.)

We are also cognizant of God's charge to Judah through his prophet Jeremiah:

"For my people have committed two evils; they have forsaken me the fountain of living waters, and hewed them out cisterns, broken cisterns, that can hold no water." (Jeremiah 2:13.)

Of far greater value than the physical sustenance that Joseph of old provided his brethren is the sustenance that modern Joseph has to offer modern Judah today. We offer freely bread to eat and water to drink. I repeat, our interest in Judah is one of kinship, for we are your brothers. We come with a message and say, "We have 'living water' from its true source and well, which, if a man will drink it, 'shall be in him a well of living water, springing up unto everlasting life.' " (D&C 63:23.)

**247**

In Jacob's blessing to Judah, he declared: "Judah is . . . as an old lion; *who shall rouse him up?*" (Genesis 49:9; italics added.) We come as messengers bearing the legitimate authority to arouse Judah to her promises. We do not ask Judah to forsake her heritage. We are not asking her to leave father, mother, or family. We bring a message that Judah does not possess. That message constitutes "living water" from the Fountain of living water.

Our prophet, Joseph Smith, was given a commandment by the Lord to turn "the hearts of the Jews unto the prophets, and the prophets unto the Jews." (D&C 98:17.) We are presently sending our messengers to every land and people whose ideology permits us entrance. We have been gathering Joseph's descendants for 146 years. We hope you, who are of Judah, will not think it an intrusion for us to present our message to you. You are welcome to come to our meetings. We display no crosses. We collect no offerings. We honor your commitment to your unique heritage and your individuality. We approach you in a different way than any other Christian church because we represent the restored covenant to the entire house of Israel.

Yes, we understand the Jews, . . . because we belong to the same house of Israel. We are your brothers—Joseph. We look forward to the day of fulfillment of God's promise when "the house of Judah shall walk with the house of Israel." (Jeremiah 3:18.)

### *A Blessing on Judah*

As one who, by special assignment, has been given authority in the house of Israel today, I ask the God of Abraham, Isaac, and Jacob to bless my brethren of Judah and have mercy on them; that the land to which Judah has returned after a long night of dispersion shall be fruitful, prosperous, and become the envy to her neighbors; that the nation Israel shall be delivered from all her oppressors and enemies; that Judah will "draw water out of the wells of salvation" (Isaiah 12:3) and fulfill all those prophecies that God declared through his prophets Isaiah, Ezekiel, and Jeremiah, even that prophecy through Zechariah that "the Lord shall inherit Judah his portion in the holy land, and shall choose Jerusalem again" (Zechariah 2:12).

I witness to you, my brothers and sisters of all the house of Israel, that I know that the God of heaven presides over the destinies of all his children. I witness that he has set his hand *a second time* to recover his people from the four corners of the earth to the lands of their inheritance. I testify that *he* has restored his new covenant with Israel. I know the Book of Mormon is a truthful account of God's dealings with the house of Joseph, that its testimony is true, and that it is the word of the Lord to the Gentiles, Jews, and all the house of Israel. I further witness that Joseph Smith was what he represented himself to be, a prophet of the living God and a messenger of the new covenant to Israel. I would urge all to give heed to the message given by God through him.

# PART II
# A COMPANION TO
# YOUR STUDY OF
# THE OLD TESTAMENT

# GENESIS

*Genesis* is a Greek word meaning origin or beginning. The book of Genesis serves as an introduction to the remainder of the Bible. For background on the book of Genesis, see "Genesis" in the Bible Dictionary, pages 678-79.

**1-6** The Joseph Smith Translation of the Bible makes a tremendous contribution to the first six chapters of Genesis. As the Lord had foretold to Moses when the book of Genesis was first written, by the time of Joseph Smith the "children of men" would have taken many truths from the original book and would esteem the words of the Lord "as naught." (See Moses 1:40-41.)

A careful comparison of the King James text of Genesis chapters one through six, verse thirteen, with the corresponding materials of the Joseph Smith Translation reveals that the Joseph Smith Translation contains over twice as many verses as the King James Version.

**1-2** Although many scholars and students, both religious and nonreligious, have offered many theories and explanations on the creation of the earth, it is still not certain *exactly* what processes were followed by God in its creation.

Mankind will probably not know the precise details of the creation of the earth until Jesus Christ comes on the earth to reign himself, for he has stated that when he comes he "shall reveal . . . things which no man knew, things of the earth, by which it was made." (D&C 101:32-33.)

The following statement concerning the creation has been provided by the first president of the Church in this dispensation:

> This earth was organized or formed out of other planets which were broken up and remodeled and made into one on which we live. The elements are eternal. . . . In the translation "without form and void," it should read, "empty and desolate." The word *created* should be "formed or organized." (Joseph Smith, CDG, p. 271.)

**1:1** The Hebrew word translated "create" by the King James translators means "organize," "fashion," or "form."

Joseph Smith has provided the following commentary on this point:

You ask the learned doctors why they say the world was made out of nothing; and they will answer, "Doesn't the Bible say He *created* the world?" And they infer, from the word create, that it must have been made out of nothing. Now, the word create came from the word *Baurau* which does not mean to create out of nothing; it means to organize; the same as a man would organize materials and build a ship. Hence, we infer that God had materials to organize the world out of chaos— chaotic matter, which is element, and in which dwells all the glory. Element had an existence from the time he had. The pure principles of element are principles which can never be destroyed; they may be organized and re-organized, but not destroyed. They had no beginning, and can have no end. (TPJS, pp. 350-52.)

**1:1**    Joseph Smith has analyzed the very first Hebrew word of the Bible, and the first sentence:

I shall comment on the very first Hebrew word in the Bible; I will make a comment on the very first sentence of the history of creation in the Bible—*Berosheit.* I want to analyze the word. *Baith*—in, by, through, and everything else. *Rosh*—the head. *Sheit*—grammatical termination. When the inspired man wrote it, he did not put the *baith* there. An old Jew without any authority added the word; he thought it too bad to begin to talk about the head! It read first, "The head one of the Gods brought forth the Gods." That is the true meaning of the words. *Baurau* signifies to bring forth. . . . *Thus the head God brought forth the Gods in the grand council.*

I will transpose and simplify it in the English language. . . . The head God called together the Gods and sat in grand council to bring forth the world. The grand councilors sat at the head in yonder heavens and contemplated the creation of the world which were created at the time. (TPJS, pp. 348-49.)

**1:1**    *God* is a title, not a name. As a title, it could refer to several different personages. The "God" who created this earth was Jesus Christ (the pre-earthly Jehovah), as is made clear in this statement by Joseph Fielding Smith:

Under the direction of his Father, *Jesus Christ created this earth.* No doubt *others helped him,* but it was Jesus Christ, our Redeemer, who, under the direction of his Father, came down and organized matter and made this planet, so that it might be inhabited by the children of God. . . .

. . . We know that Jesus our Savior was a Spirit when this great work was done. He did all of these mighty works before he tabernacled in the flesh. (DS 1:74-75.)

**1:3** According to Brigham Young, "light" came to the earth when the earth was moved near the sun:

When the Lord said—"Let there be light," there was light, for the earth was brought near the sun that it might reflect upon it so as to give us light by day, and the moon to give us light by night. This is the glory the earth came from, and when it is glorified it will return again unto the presence of the Father, and it will dwell there, and these intelligent beings that I am looking at, if they live worthy of it, will dwell upon this earth. (JD 17:143.)

**1:24-25** Animals have spirits and will be resurrected, according to Joseph Fielding Smith:

Animals do have spirits and . . . through the redemption made by our Savior they will come forth in the resurrection to enjoy the blessing of immortal life. The Bible as it has come to us through numerous translations and copies does not contain the information concerning the immortality of the animal world in the clearness which, without any doubt, it was invested with the pure inspiration of the revelations of the Lord. However, there are some passages which still remain bearing witness to the eternal nature of the animal world. (AGQ 2:48.)

**1:26** The plural pronouns in this indicate very clearly that God was talking to someone else: "Let *us* make man in *our* image." (Italics added.) The question has been asked, "To whom was God speaking on this occasion?" The answer has been provided by God himself in another scripture:

"And I, God, said unto mine Only Begotten, which was with me from the beginning: Let us make man in our image, after our likeness." (Moses 2:26.)

The "Only Begotten" of God was the pre-earthly Jehovah, who came to earth as Jesus Christ. Thus, God the Father was speaking to Jesus Christ on that occasion.

**1:26-27** The terms "in our image" and "after our likeness" indicate that God had bodily parts just as man does. This truth has been taught by Joseph Smith.

God himself was once as we are now, and is an exalted man, and sits enthroned in yonder heavens! That is the great secret. . . . If you were to see him today, you would see him like a man in form—like yourselves in all the person, image, and very form as a man; for Adam was created in the very fashion, image and likeness of God, and received instruction from, and walked, talked and conversed with him, as one man talks and communes with another. (TPJS, p. 345.)

**1:26-28** When God gave power to Adam to "have

dominion" over the cattle (v. 26), to "have dominion" over the fish and fowl (v. 28), to "subdue the earth," and "to multiply and replenish [fill] the earth," he was bestowing priesthood authority upon Adam. Joseph Smith taught that since that time the priesthood has always been bestowed or revealed under Adam's authority:

> The Priesthood was first given to Adam; he obtained the First Presidency, and held the keys of it from generation to generation. He obtained it in the Creation, before the world was formed, as in Gen. 1:26, 27, 28. He had dominion given him over every living creature. He is Michael the Archangel, spoken of in the Scriptures. Then to Noah, who is Gabriel; he stands next in authority to Adam in the Priesthood; he was called of God to this office, and was the father of all living in his day, and to him was given the dominion. These men held keys first on earth, and then in heaven.
>
> The Priesthood is an everlasting principle, and existed with God from eternity, and will to eternity, without beginning of days or end of years. The keys have to be brought from heaven whenever the Gospel is sent. When they are revealed from heaven, it is by Adam's authority. . . . The Priesthood is everlasting. (HC 3:385-87.)

**1:28**  The fact that God *spoke* to Adam and Eve indicates that they had a language common to each other. Joseph Fielding Smith has commented concerning this "Adamic" language:

> When Adam was in the Garden of Eden he lived in the presence of God. . . . He was taught His language, and so Adam had a perfect language. It was not a bow-wow language, as some will tell you. It was the Lord's language. (ST, p. 40.)

Wilford Woodruff related the following experience in regard to "the pure language" of Adam:

> I read over several of the old sermons of Joseph [Smith] that were not recorded anywhere except in my journal. We passed a pleasant evening together, and before they left they sang in tongues in the pure language which Adam and Eve spoke in the Garden of Eden. This gift was obtained in the Kirtland Temple through a promise of the Prophet Joseph Smith. He told Sister Whitney if she would rise upon her feet she should have the pure language. She did so, and immediately began to sing in tongues. It was nearer to heavenly music than anything I ever heard. (Wilford Woodruff, WW, p. 355.)

The footnote for this verse in the Bible suggests that "replenish" might better have been translated as "fill." Joseph Fielding Smith explains why:

*Replenish,* however, is incorrectly used in the King James translation. The Hebrew verb is Mole meaning fill, to fill, or make full. This word *Mole* is the same word which is translated *fill* in Genesis 1:22, in the King James Bible, wherein reference is made to the fish, fowl, and beasts of the earth. (AGQ 1:208-9.)

Spencer W. Kimball has indicated that the commandment to fill the earth was to be carried out only after Adam and Eve were married by the Lord:

The first commandment recorded seems to have been "Multiply and replenish the earth." Let no one ever think that the command came to have children without marriage. No such suggestion could ever have foundation. When God had created the woman, he brought her unto the man and gave her to him as his wife, and commanded, "Therefore shall a man leave his father and his mother, and shall cleave unto his wife: and they shall be one flesh." (Gen. 2:24.) (BYUSY, Sept. 1973, p. 262.)

**1:29** Many things that were created by God for the good of man have been used by man in a detrimental way. Spencer W. Kimball has stated:

These plants were made expressly for man, since he is the supreme creation with divine potential. But through the ages, man has corrupted the use of many of the products and used them for his downfall; corn, barley, dates, grapes, and other crops have been diverted from "food" channels for which they were created into destructive, death-dealing liquor. And that which was good for man has become destructive and bad for him. (CR, Oct. 1967, p. 29.)

**2:1-25** The Joseph Smith Translation makes several significant changes in this chapter. Perhaps its most important contribution is that "all things" were created "spiritually, before they were naturally upon the face of the earth" (v. 5); . . . "for in heaven created I them" (v. 6).

Another contribution from the Joseph Smith Translation is that when God commanded Adam and Eve not to partake of the fruit of the tree of the knowledge of good and evil, he added: "Nevertheless, thou mayest choose for thyself, for it is given unto thee; but remember that I forbid it." (Gen. 2:21.)

**2:1** Joseph Fielding Smith has observed concerning this verse:

It is reasonable to believe that in the beginning, before the earth was prepared, the Lord would have all things organized from the beginning to the end of time. . . . [Quoted Gen. 2:1.] This is equivalent to the Lord's saying that everything was in preparation to be placed on the earth in its due course when mankind should be placed upon it. (AGQ 5:182.)

### 2:2-3   Laws concerning the Sabbath have been on the earth since the very beginning, as is clarified by Spencer W. Kimball.

Moses came down from the quaking, smoking Mount Sinai and brought to the wandering children of Israel the Ten Commandments. This was not the origin of these specific laws, for Adam and his posterity knew the gospel and had been commanded to live them. This spectacular experience was neither the beginning nor the end. The laws of God were premortal. They were part of the test for mortals spoken of in the council in heaven.

The law of the Sabbath, as with other laws, antedated earth life and has been reiterated through the dispensations to that of the Fulness of Times. It distinguished the early Israelites from pagans. (*The Ten Commandments Today,* p. 54.)

### 2:4-8   Joseph Fielding Smith has contributed the following commentaries on the spiritual and physical creations of the earth:

There is no *account* of the creation of man or other forms of life when they were created as spirits. There is just the simple statement that they were so created *before* the physical creation. The statements in Moses 3:5 and Genesis 2:5 are *interpolations* thrown into the account of the physical creation, explaining that all things were first created in the spirit existence in heaven before they were placed upon this earth. (DS 1:75-76.)

While it is true that all things were created spiritually, or as spirits, before they were naturally upon the face of the earth, this creation, we are informed, was in heaven. This applies to animals of all descriptions and also to plant life, before there was flesh upon the earth, or in the water, or in the air. *The account of the creation of the earth as given in Genesis, and the Book of Moses, and as given in the temple, is the creation of the physical earth, and of physical animals and plants.* I think the temple account, which was given by revelation, is the clearest of all of these. *These physical creations were made out of the natural elements.* (DS 1:75.)

### 2:7   Concerning this "creation" of man, the Pearl of Great Price indicates: "And man [Adam] became a living soul, the first flesh upon the earth, the first man also." (Moses 3:7.) Although the exact details of the birth of Adam are not given, it is clear (1) he did not evolve from lower animals (he was the "first flesh" upon the earth), and (2) there were no pre-Adamic men (Adam was the "first man also").

It is held by some that Adam was not the first man upon this earth, and that the original human being was a development from lower orders of the animal creation. These, however, are the theories of men. The word of the Lord declares that Adam was "the first man of all men" [Moses 1:34], and we are therefore in duty bound to regard him as the primal parent of our race. (First Presidency, IE, Nov. 1909, p. 80.)

**2:7** Concerning the process of becoming "a living soul," Joseph Smith has stated:

The 7th verse of 2nd chapter of Genesis ought to read—God breathed into Adam his spirit [i.e. Adam's spirit] or breath of life. (HC 5:392-93.)

We say that God himself is a self-existent being. . . . God made a tabernacle and put a spirit into it, and it became a living soul. [Referred to the old Bible.] How does it read in the Hebrew? It does not say in the Hebrew that God created the spirit of man. It says, "God made man out of the earth, and put into him Adam's spirit, and so became a living body." (JD 6:6.)

The spirit of man is not a created being; it existed from eternity, and will exist to eternity. Anything created cannot be eternal; and earth, water, etc., had their existence in an elementary state, from eternity. (HC 3:387.)

Joseph Fielding Smith also taught that life and matter are eternal:

The scriptures plainly and repeatedly affirm that God is the Creator of the earth and the heavens and all things that in them are. In the sense so expressed the Creator is an Organizer. God created the earth as an organized sphere; but He certainly did not create, in the sense of bringing into primal existence, the ultimate elements of the materials of which the earth consists, for "the elements are eternal."

So also life is eternal, and not created; but life, or the vital force, may be infused into organized matter, though the details of the process have not been revealed unto man. (First Presidency, MFP 5:26.)

**2:8-14** The exact location of the Garden of Eden has been a matter of dispute by biblical scholars. The problem is complicated by (1) the occurrence of the flood (which would probably have obliterated evidences of the Garden of Eden), (2) the reasonable inference that Noah and his ark did not land at the exact spot from which it had started, and (3) the fact that the continents did not have their present relationship to each other until after the earth was divided in the days of Peleg, who lived *after* Noah.

Latter-day Saint leaders have offered the following commentaries on the location of the Garden of Eden:

In the beginning, after this earth was prepared for man, the Lord commenced his work upon what is now called the American continent, where the Garden of Eden was made. In the days of Noah, in the days of the floating of the ark, he took the people to another part of the earth; the earth was divided, and there he set up his kingdom. (Brigham Young, JD 8:195.)

There *were not* an Eastern and a Western Hemisphere at the time of Adam. (Joseph Fielding Smith, AGQ 4:21.)

It is an error to say that the Bible states that the Garden of Eden was on the Eastern Hemisphere. The fact is that there is no place that can be definitely pointed out where the Garden of Eden was. There have been great changes on the face of the earth since the days of Adam. The Latter-day Saints would not know if the Lord had not revealed it to them. Such knowledge is beyond the skill of mortal man to discover without the revelation from the Lord. (Joseph Fielding Smith, AGQ 4:19.)

Joseph, the Prophet, told me that the Garden of Eden was in Jackson County, Missouri. When Adam was driven out he went to the place we now call Adam-ondi-Ahman, Daviess County, Missouri. There he built an altar and offered sacrifices. (Quoted in WW, p. 481.)

You have been both to Jerusalem and Zion, and seen both, I have not seen either, for I have never been in Jackson County, now it is a pleasant thing to think of and to know where the Garden of Eden was. Did you ever think of it? I do not think many do, for in Jackson County was the garden of Eden. Joseph has declared this, and I am as much bound to believe that as to believe that Joseph was a prophet of God. (Brigham Young, JH, Mar. 15, 1857, p. 1.)

**2:15**    Spencer W. Kimball has observed concerning this verse:

It seems this landlord-tenant relationship is fair—the Lord, the owner, furnishes the land, the air, the water, the sunshine, and all the elements to make it fruitful. The tenant gives his labor. (CR, Apr. 1968, p. 75.)

**2:17**    There was no death of any kind in the Garden of Eden, as is explained by Joseph Fielding Smith:

When Adam and Eve were placed in the Garden of Eden, there was no death. It was by the violation of a commandment that brought mortality and death upon them. (CR, Apr. 1956, p. 125.)

The disobedience of Adam and Eve to God's commandment resulted in spiritual death, and the later consequence of that disobedience was the introduction of physical death (also called temporal death), as explained in these commentaries:

When Adam, our first parent, partook of the forbidden fruit, transgressed the law of God, and became subject unto Satan, he was banished from the presence of God, and was thrust out into outer spiritual darkness. This was the first death. Yet living, he was dead—dead to God, dead to light and truth, dead spiritually; cast out from the presence of God; communication between the Father and the son was cut off. He was as absolutely thrust out from the presence of God as was Satan and the hosts that followed him. That was spiritual death. But the Lord said that he would not suffer Adam nor his posterity to come to the temporal death until they should have the means by which they might be redeemed from the first death, which is spiritual. Therefore angels were sent unto Adam, who taught him the gospel, and revealed to him the principle by which he could be redeemed from the first death, . . . and was thus given a chance to be redeemed from the spiritual death before he should die the temporal death. (Joseph F. Smith, GD, pp. 432-33.)

Spiritual death is defined as a state of *spiritual alienation* from God—the eternal separation from the Supreme Being; condemnation to everlasting punishment is also called the second death. In other words, the second or spiritual death, which is the final judgment passed upon the wicked, is the same as the first death, banishment from the presence of the Lord. (Joseph Fielding Smith, DS 2:217.)

Because of Adam's transgression, a spiritual death—banishment from the presence of the Lord—as well as the temporal death, were pronounced upon him. The spiritual death came at the time of the fall and banishment; and the seeds of the temporal death were also sown at that same time; that is, a physical change came over Adam and Eve, who became mortal, and were thus subject to the ills of the flesh which resulted in their gradual decline to old age and finally the separation of the spirit from the body.

Before this temporal death took place the Lord, by his own voice and the visitation and ministration of angels, taught Adam the principles of the gospel and administered unto him the saving ordinances, through which he was again restored to the favor of the Lord and to his presence. Also, through the atonement, not only Adam, but all his posterity were redeemed from the temporal effects of the fall, and shall come forth in the resurrection to receive immortality. (Joseph Fielding Smith, DS 1:111-12.)

**2:18-24** The first marriage on this earth (of Adam and Eve) was obviously meant to be eternal because there was no death of any kind on the earth at that time. Also, the marriage was performed by God, who is eternal and whose power can seal on earth as it can seal in heaven. (Matt. 16:19; see also heading for Gen. 2.)

Because marriage was intended to be eternal and marriage partners have been commanded "to multiply," the power of procreation (power to beget children) is also eternal if the marriage has been performed by the power of God.

The first marriage on record appertaining to this earth, was solemnized by the Almighty. The first couple married were immortal beings—Adam and Eve, our first parents—before they had partaken of the forbidden fruit, and became subject to the penalty of death. Marriage, as then understood, could not have been what it is now popularly supposed to be by the so-called Christian world. Then the marriage vow was made, and the ceremony was performed by immortal or celestial beings, with no reference to death or to a time when that sacred and holy union should cease. (Joseph F. Smith, MS 36:312.)

When Eve was given to Adam, it was not "until death doth you part," but it was a perpetual union.

The Prophet Joseph Smith taught that "marriage is an institution of heaven, instituted in the garden of Eden, and that it should be solemnized by the authority of the everlasting priesthood." Except a man and his wife enter into an everlasting covenant and be married for eternity, while in this probation, by the power and authority of the Holy Priesthood, "they will cease to increase when they die; that is, they will not have any children after the resurrection. But those who are married by the power and authority of the priesthood in this life, and continue without committing the sin against the Holy Ghost, will continue to increase and have children in the celestial glory." [TPJS, pp. 300-301.] (Joseph Fielding Smith, RT, pp. 242-43.)

Before there was any mortal death, the Lord declared: . . . "It is not good that the man should be alone; I will make him an help meet for him." [Gen. 2:18.]

Therefore Eve was given to Adam, and it is clear from this scripture that the intention was that marriage between the man and his wife was to endure forever, for death had not at that time come upon the earth. (Joseph Fielding Smith, AGQ 4:144-45.)

**2:19** The word in the Hebrew translated as "Adam" means "man." In his pre-earthly existence the man Adam was known as Michael, which is said to have meant "Who is as God." (D&C 27:11; 128:21; "Adam," BD, p. 604.)

**2:24** The basic meaning of "cleave" has been given by Spencer W. Kimball:

To cleave is to adhere closely, to cling; and the Lord gave as the purpose for their cleaving, the peopling of the earth, the replenishing of the earth, the subduing of the earth, the dominion over the earth. There was high purpose in the creation and in the proper associations of husband and wife, but intimacies could never be defended outside of marriage. (BYUSY, Jan. 1965, p. 15.)

**3:1-24** The Joseph Smith Translation changes in this chapter are so numerous and significant that the versions should be compared verse by verse. If a Joseph Smith Translation is not readily available, Moses chapter 4 might be used.

The important contributions of the Joseph Smith Translation chapter 3 include the following:

1. Satan offered himself as the possible savior in the pre-earthly council; he then rebelled against God and became the adversary to God's plans.

2. Satan is "the father of all lies"; he seeks to destroy the free agency of man and to lead men captive at his will.

3. Satan "put it into the heart of the serpent . . . to beguile Eve, for he knew not the mind of God; wherefore, he sought to destroy the world."

4. Jesus Christ, the "beloved Son," was "beloved and chosen from the beginning" to come to earth as the Savior and Redeemer.

These are exactly the type of omissions the devil would want in the scriptures if he could have any influence over them or their preservation.

Concerning the importance of free agency in this life, David O. McKay has stated:

> Next to the bestowal of life itself, the right to direct that life is God's greatest gift to man. Among the immediate obligations and duties resting upon members of the Church today, and one of the most urgent and pressing for attention and action of all liberty-loving people is the preservation of individual liberty. Freedom of choice is more to be treasured than any possession earth can give. It is inherent in the spirit of man. It is a divine gift to every normal being. Whether born in abject poverty or shackled at birth by inherited riches, everyone has this most precious of all life's endowments—the gift of free agency; man's inherited and inalienable right.
>
> Free agency is the impelling source of the soul's progress. It is the purpose of the Lord that man become like him. In order for man to achieve this it was necessary for the Creator first to make him free. (CR, Apr. 1950, p. 32.)

**3:16** Spencer W. Kimball has provided some thoughts on the term "rule over thee":

> And unto the woman the voice of the Lord was saying, "In sorrow [or pain or distress or waiting] thou shalt bring forth children; and thy desire shall be to thy husband, and he shall rule over thee" (Gen. 3:16)—or, I like the term "preside over thee." (BYUSY, Sept. 1974, p. 237.)

**3:16-19** See "Fall of Adam" in the Bible Dictionary,

p. 670. The "fall" of Adam and Eve is one of the most misunderstood events that has been recorded in the scriptures. Most Christians have been taught that the fall was an evil, unnecessary act, and Adam and Eve became eternally damned because of their actions. This same fallacious reasoning says that every child born on the earth "inherits," and thus in a sense is responsible for, the fall of Adam and Eve. This error is followed by the teaching that everyone must be baptized in order to have the responsibility for the fall removed from them.

An analysis of the status of Adam and Eve before and after the fall may help to clarify this matter.

A correct concept of the fall of Adam is necessary to an understanding of the basic claims of Christianity. The churches of the world, however, have largely lost sight of the essential differences in the status of Adam and Eve before and after the fall. The general conditions of Adam and Eve before the fall are listed on the left side of the chart which follows; the corresponding general conditions of Adam and Eve after the fall are listed on the right side of the chart.

| *Status of Adam and Eve before the fall* | *Status of Adam and Eve after the fall* |
|---|---|
| 1. They were in the presence of God. | 1. They were cast out of the presence of God—that is, they suffered a spiritual death. |
| 2. They were not mortal—that is, they were not subject to physical death. (2 Nephi 2:22.) | 2. They became mortal (subject to to physical death). |
| 3. They were in a state of innocence —that is, they did not know the difference between good and evil. (2 Nephi 2:23.) | 3. They knew good from evil. |
| 4. They "would have had no children." (2 Nephi 2:23.) | 4. They had children. |

Thus, . . . two major conclusions [can be reached] from these teachings: (1) the fall was necessary in order for "men to be"—that is, in order for Adam and Eve to have children. (2) A major purpose of man's existence is for him to have "joy." True joy was not possible for Adam and Eve before the fall.

These truths are stated clearly . . . in 2 Nephi 2:22-23: "And now, behold, if Adam had not transgressed he would not have fallen . . . and they (Adam and Eve) *would have had no children;* wherefore they would have remained in a state of innocence, *having no joy,* for they knew no misery; doing no good, for they knew no sin." (Italics added.) (CBM, pp. 126-27.)

**3:23-24** Read the material under "Fall of Adam" on page 670 of the Bible Dictionary.

**4:1-26** The Joseph Smith Translation adds a complete chapter (4) of thirteen verses between chapters 3 and 4 of the King James Version. The major contents of these inspired additional verses are:

1. Adam and Eve had many children after they were driven out of the Garden of Eden *before* Cain and Abel were born to them. These children intermarried and "begat sons and daughters."

2. Adam was commanded to "offer sacrifices unto the Lord" which he immediately did. Later, an angel explained "This thing is a similitude of the sacrifice of the Only Begotten of the Father . . . thou shalt repent, and call upon God, in the name of the Son for evermore."

3. The "Holy Ghost fell upon Adam, which beareth record of the Father and the Son."

4. Filled with the Holy Ghost, Adam began to prophesy.

5. Adam and Eve came to know that their transgression in the Garden of Eden was necessary for them (a) to have seed, (b) to know good from evil, (c) to know the joy of their redemption, and (d) to know "eternal life."

6. Satan tried to deceive the children of Adam and Eve and was successful in having some of them follow him. "And man began from that time forth to be carnal, sensual and devilish."

Chapter 5 of the Joseph Smith Translation corresponds roughly to chapter 4 of the King James version. Again, the Joseph Smith Translation makes several very significant changes or additions, including the following:

1. God called upon men to repent, and the Holy Ghost started to work with them.

2. Cain loved Satan more than God. Satan influenced Cain to offer an unacceptable offering to the Lord, and "it pleased" Satan.

3. Satan influenced Cain to murder and get gain and promised to deliver Abel into Cain's hands.

4. Cain "gloried" in his killing of Abel.

5. As punishment, Cain was driven out "from the face of the Lord" (not "from the face of the *earth*" as recorded in the King James Version).

6. Several generations of wicked men are listed, including Lamech, who also "entered into a covenant with Satan."

7. "The gospel began to be preached from the beginning, being declared by holy angels sent forth from the presence of God, by his own voice, and by the gift of the Holy Ghost."

A careful analysis of the changes and additions in the Joseph Smith Translation reveals that these deletions are exactly the type of information Satan would want to have deleted from the scriptural account: (1) the knowledge that he is the devil and that he seeks to have all men become evil; (2) the knowledge that the gospel has been on the earth from the beginning, made efficacious through the foreordaining of Jesus Christ as the Savior and Redeemer; and (3) the realization that the Holy Ghost is available to any person who is worthy and seeks after his guidance.

**4:3-5**   The Joseph Smith Translation provides additional vital information on the sacrifices offered by Cain and Abel. (Gen. 5:1-8.) The Prophet Joseph Smith has provided the following commentary:

> By faith in this atonement or plan of redemption, Abel offered to God a sacrifice that was accepted, which was the firstlings of the flock. Cain offered of the fruit of the ground, and was not accepted, because he could not do it in faith, he could have no faith, or could not exercise faith contrary to the plan of heaven. It must be shedding the blood of the Only Begotten to atone for man; for this was the plan of redemption; and without the shedding of blood was no remission; and as the sacrifice was instituted for a type, by which man was to discern the great Sacrifice which God had prepared; to offer a sacrifice contrary to that, no faith could be exercised, because redemption was not purchased in that way, nor the power of atonement instituted after that order; consequently Cain could have no faith; and whatsoever is not of faith, is sin. But Abel offered an acceptable sacrifice, by which he obtained witness that he was righteous, God Himself testifying of his gifts. Certainly, the shedding of the blood of a beast could be beneficial to no man, except it was done in imitation, or as a type, or explanation of what was to be offered through the gift of God Himself; and this performance done with an eye looking forward in faith on the power of that great Sacrifice for a remission of sins. (TPJS, p. 58.)

**4:7**   The laws underlying the statement "if thou doest not well, sin lieth at the door" have been explained by Spencer W. Kimball:

Should there be readers who think of the Lord as an angry, cruel God who brings vengeance on people for not complying with his laws, let them think again. He organized a plan which was natural—a cause-and-effect program. It is inconceivable that God would desire to punish or to see his children in suffering or pain or distress. He is a God of peace and tranquility. He offers joy and growth and happiness and peace. . . .

But however he tries, a man cannot escape the consequences of sin. They follow as the night follows the day. Sometimes the penalties are delayed in coming, but they are as sure as life itself. Remorse and agony come. Even ignorance of the law does not prevent, though it may mitigate, the punishment. (MF, pp. 140-41.)

**4:9-13** Cain brought this punishment upon himself because of disobedience to divine law, as explained by Spencer W. Kimball:

After looking down at the crumpled body at his feet, and especially after the torments of hell began to persecute him and the ghost of his brother began to follow him, Cain must have wished that he would give Abel's life back. The Lord did not curse Cain; it was Cain who, breaking eternal law, cursed himself. (BYUSY, Jan. 1965, p. 14.)

**5:1-32** The Joseph Smith Translation adds over one hundred verses of new material for the time period covered by chapter 5 of the King James Version. Most of these verses are concerned with the life and translation of Enoch and should be inserted between verses 21 and 22 of the King James Version. This new section provides a wealth of information on the way God works with his prophets, on the purposes of life on the earth, on the necessity of the basic ordinances such as baptism and receiving the Holy Ghost, and on how a people can prepare themselves to be translated to a higher plane (terrestrial instead of telestial) of existence. The new verses also provide new insights into the personality and characteristics of God and, on the opposite end, new information on the devil and some of the nefarious methods he employs to deceive men. The role of the pre-earthly Jesus Christ (Jehovah) is also clarified.

If possible, Genesis 6:26-7:81 of the Joseph Smith Translation should be carefully analyzed; these verses are similar to Moses 6:26-8:1 in the Pearl of Great Price.

Other significant additions in chapter 6 of the Joseph Smith Translation are:

1. The people in Adam's day had a "pure and undefiled" language.

2. Adam kept a "book of remembrance . . . in the which

was recorded . . . the language of Adam.''

**5:18-24**　Joseph Fielding Smith has written concerning Enoch:

> Very little is known by the world concerning the great prophet Enoch, who is mentioned in the Bible only in Genesis 4 and 5 of the Old Testament and Luke 3:37, Hebrews 11:5, and Jude 1:14 of the New Testament. However, the writers of both the Old Testament and New Testament indicate that Enoch was so righteous that he was translated (transfigured).
>
> Modern scriptures and revelations provide much additional information on this great man, including some of his writings. His life and teachings are of particular importance to Latter-day Saints, because Enoch was able to prepare a people who became so righteous they were actually taken off the telestial earth so they could live a terrestrial order. In a somewhat similar manner, a people must be prepared in these latter days to be worthy to live at least a terrestrial order so they will be able to live with Jesus Christ when he comes on the earth to rule in power and great glory. (CHMR 1:81.)

**5:21-27**　This Methuselah is mentioned in the Old Testament only in this chapter of Genesis, but is referred to several times in other scriptures. (See D&C 107:50-53; Moses 6:25; 8:2-7.) He is generally considered to have lived longer on the earth (without translation) than any other man—969 years.

Doctrine and Covenants 107:50 indicates ''Methuselah was one hundred years old when he was ordained under the hand of Adam.'' Doctrine and Covenants 107:53 mentions that the high priest Methuselah was present when Adam called his righteous posterity ''into the valley of Adam-ondi-Ahman.''

The Joseph Smith Translation mentions specifically that Methuselah was left on the earth at the time of the translation of Enoch and his city ''that the covenants of the Lord might be fulfilled which he made to Enoch; for he truly covenanted with Enoch, that Noah should be of the fruit of his loins.'' (Gen. 7:79.)

**5:24**　Joseph Smith has provided the following additional information on the translation of Enoch:

> ''And Enoch walked with God after he begat Methuselah 300 years, and begat sons and daughters, and all the days of Enoch were 365 years; and Enoch walked with God, and he was not, for God took him.'' (Gen. 5th chap., 22nd ver.) Now this Enoch God reserved unto Himself, that he should not die at that time, and appointed unto him a ministry unto terrestrial bodies, of whom there has been but little revealed. . . . He is a ministering angel, to minister to those who shall be heirs of salvation, and appeared unto Jude as Abel did unto Paul; therefore Jude spoke of him

(14, 15 verses). And Enoch, the seventh from Adam, revealed these sayings: "Behold, the Lord cometh with ten thousand of His Saints."

Paul was also acquainted with this character, and received instructions from him. "By faith Enoch was translated, that he should not see death, and was not found, because God had translated him; for before his translation he had this testimony, that he pleased God; but without faith, it is impossible to please Him, for he that cometh to God must believe that He is, and that he is a revealer to those who diligently seek him." [Hebrews 11:5.]

Now the doctrine of translation is a power which belongs to this Priesthood. There are many things which belong to the powers of the Priesthood and the keys thereof, that have been kept hid from before the foundation of the world; they are hid from the wise and prudent to be revealed in the last times.

Many have supposed that the doctrine of translation was a doctrine whereby men were taken immediately into the presence of God, and into an eternal fullness, but this is a mistaken idea. Their place of habitation is that of the terrestrial order, and a place prepared for such characters He held in reserve to be ministering angels unto many planets, and who as yet have not entered into so great a fullness as those who are resurrected from the dead. "Others were tortured, not accepting deliverance, that they might obtain a better resurrection." (See Heb. 11th chap., part of the 35th verse.)

Now it was evident that there was a better resurrection, or else God would not have revealed it unto Paul. Wherein then, can it be said a better resurrection. This distinction is made between the doctrine of the actual resurrection and translation: translation obtains deliverance from the tortures and sufferings of the body, but their existence will prolong as to the labors and toils of the ministry, before they can enter into so great a rest and glory. (HC 4:209-10.)

**5:29**   In the pre-earthly existence Noah was known as Gabriel, and after he was born on the earth, proved faithful to the Lord, and survived the flood, he was placed "next in authority to Adam in the Priesthood; he was called of God . . . and was the father of all living in this day, and to him was given the dominion." (Joseph Smith, TPJS, p. 157.)

**6:2**   The "sons *of God*" were offspring of people who believed in God, while the "daughters *of men*" were offspring of people who believed in following the ways of the world. The significance of these terms is explained by Joseph Fielding Smith:

Because the daughters of Noah married the sons of men contrary to the teachings of the Lord, his anger was kindled, and this offense was one cause that brought to pass the universal flood. You will see that the condition appears reversed in the Book of Moses. It was the daughters of the sons of God who were marrying the sons of men, which was displeasing unto the

Lord. The fact was, as we see it revealed, that the daughters who had been born, evidently under the covenant, and were the daughters of the sons of God, that is to say of those who held the priesthood, were transgressing the commandment of the Lord and were marrying *out of the Church*. Thus they were cutting themselves off from the blessings of the priesthood contrary to the teachings of Noah and the will of God.

The Lord has revealed to us in this dispensation that those who obey his will, will be called the sons of God. (AGQ 1:136-37.)

**6:6** The Joseph Smith Translation reads: "And it repented Noah, and his heart was pained, that the Lord had made man on the earth, and it grieved him at his heart." (Gen. 8:13.)

**6:7** The last clause of the King James Version has been revised in the Joseph Smith Translation: "For it repenteth Noah that I have created them, and that I have made them; and he hath called upon me, for they have sought his life." (Gen. 8:15.)

**6:14** This is the only reference in the Bible to "gopher wood." Scholars have speculated that it was a species of cypress or cedar.

**7:11** John Taylor has provided the following commentary on how the earth was covered with water at the time of the flood:

How they could manage to get enough water out of the seas, and out of the oceans, and out of the rivers, and out of the clouds, to cover the tops of these mountains and fifteen cubits above, and let that spread all over the earth? I would like to know by what known law the immersion of the globe could be accomplished. It is explained here in a few words: "The windows of heaven were opened"—that is, the waters that exist throughout the space surrounding the earth from whence come these clouds from which the rain descends. That was one cause. Another cause was "the fountains of the great deep were broken up"—that is something beyond the oceans, something outside of the seas, some reservoirs of which we have no knowledge, were made to contribute to this event, and the waters were let loose by the hand and by the power of God; for God said He would bring a flood upon the earth and He brought it, but He had to let loose the fountains of the great deep, and pour out the waters from there, and when the flood commenced to subside, we are told "that the fountains also of the deep and the windows of heaven were stopped, and the rain from heaven was restrained, and the waters returned from off the earth." Where did they go to? From whence they came. [The Bible] simply tells us that "all the high hills that were under the whole heaven were covered. Fifteen cubits upwards did the waters prevail; and the mountains were covered." That is, the earth was immersed. It was a period of baptism. (JD 26:74-75.)

**7:19-20** The complete immersion of the earth at the time of the flood was the "baptism of the earth by water" as taught by several modern prophets, including Brigham Young and John A. Widtsoe:

The earth . . . has been baptized with water, and will, in the future be baptized with fire and the Holy Ghost, to be prepared to go back into the celestial presence of God. (Brigham Young, DBY, p. 393.)

Latter-day Saints . . . look upon the flood as a baptism of the earth, symbolizing a cleansing of the impurities of the past, and the beginning of a new life. This has been repeatedly taught by the leaders of the Church. The deluge was an immersion of the earth in water. (John A. Widtsoe, ER 1:111.)

**8:4** According to Joseph Fielding Smith the "mountains of Ararat" could be a considerable distance from the area where Noah lived before the flood:

Without any question a considerable distance separated the point where the Ark commenced the journey and where it landed. There can be no question to contradict the fact that during the flood great changes were made on the face of the earth. The land surface was in the process of division into continents. The rivers mentioned in Genesis were rivers that existed in the garden of Eden long before the land was divided into continents and islands. (AGQ 2:94.)

**8:20-22** The Joseph Smith Translation makes significant changes in these verses. (See Gen. 9:4-6, Bible Appendix, p. 797.)

**9:4-7** The Joseph Smith Translation makes significant changes in these verses. (See Gen. 9:10-14, Bible Appendix, p. 797.)

**9:16-7** The Joseph Smith Translation contributes to an understanding of "the bow." (See Gen. 9:21-25, Bible Appendix, p. 797.)

Joseph Smith has added the following commentary:

The Lord hath set the bow in the cloud for a sign that while it shall be seen, seed time and harvest, summer and winter shall not fail; but when it shall disappear, woe to that generation, for behold the end cometh quickly. (TPJS, p. 305.)

**10:5** This verse contains the first reference in the Bible to the word *gentile*. The basic meaning of the Hebrew word (*goyim*) frequently translated as "gentile" is "nations" or "peoples." However, in time *gentile* came to mean "stranger" or "foreigner." Thus, to a member of a particular group, a gentile is any person who does not belong to that group. To a

Hebrew (a descendant of Abraham), a gentile is a person who is not a Hebrew. To an Israelite (a descendant of Jacob or Israel), a gentile is a person who is not an Israelite. To a Jew (a descendant of Judah, a citizen of the kingdom of Judah, or a descendant of such a citizen), a gentile is a non-Jew.

The word *Hebrew* is first used in the Bible in Genesis 14, the word *Israel* in Genesis 32, and the word *Jews* in 2 Kings 16. Most of the Bible was written after these terms were in rather common usage. The word *gentile,* then, refers either to non-Hebrew, non-Israelite, or non-Jew, depending on the time and the situation of the usage.

**10:25**    Joseph Fielding Smith has contributed a commentary on the dividing of the earth's land masses:

The dividing of the earth was not an act of division by the inhabitants of the earth by tribes and peoples, but a breaking asunder of the continents, thus dividing the land surface and creating the Eastern Hemisphere and Western Hemisphere. By looking at a wall map of the world, you will discover how the land surface along the northern and southern coast of the American Hemisphere and Europe and Africa has the appearance of having been together at one time. Of course, there have been many changes on the earth's surface since the beginning. We are informed by revelation that the time will come when this condition will be changed and that the land surface of the earth will come back as it was in the beginning and all be in one place. (AGQ 5:73-74.)

The notion prevails quite generally that the dividing of the earth in the days of Peleg was a division politically among the people, but from this word of the Lord we gain the idea that the earth itself was divided and that when Christ comes it will again be brought back to the same conditions physically as prevailed before this division took place. The sea is to be driven back into the north. The land is to be brought back as it was originally and the lands of Zion (America) and Jerusalem (Palestine and all the land pertaining unto it) will be restored to their own place as they were in the beginning. (CHMR 1:264.)

**11:6**    The Joseph Smith Translation equivalent verse reads: "And the Lord said, Behold, the people are the *same,* and they all have the *same* language; and this tower they begin to build, and now, nothing will be restrained from them, which they have imagined, *except I, the Lord* confound their language." (Gen. 11:5. Italics added.)

**11:9**    After "because," the Joseph Smith Translation adds the clause "the Lord was displeased with their works." (Gen. 11:6.)

**12:1-3** Some of the ways in which Abraham and his descendants have blessed "all the families of the earth" have been listed by Joseph Fielding Smith:

When the Lord called Abraham out of Ur, the land of his fathers, he made certain covenants with him because of his faithfulness. One promise was that through him and his seed after him all nations of the earth should be blessed. [Gen. 12:1-3.] This blessing is accomplished in several ways.

1. Through Jesus Christ who came through the lineage of Abraham;

2. Through the priesthood which was conferred upon Abraham and his descendants;

3. Through the scattering of Israel among all nations by which the blood of Israel was sprinkled among the nations, and thus the nations partake of the leaven of righteousness, on condition of their repentance, and are entitled to the promises made to the children of Abraham; and

4. In the fact that the Lord covenanted with Abraham that after his time all who embraced the gospel should be called by his name, or, should be numbered among his seed, and should receive the Holy Ghost. (DS 3:246.)

Orson F. Whitney has provided the following background on Abraham:

Abraham was a dweller in Ur of the Chaldees, a city of Mesopotamia, which means, "between the rivers." The rivers in question were the Tigris and the Euphrates. God said to Abraham: [Quoted Gen. 12:1-3.] The land referred to was Canaan, now Palestine. Abraham, in order to reach that land, had to pass over the river, Euphrates. Hence he was called by the Canaanites a "hebrew," which signifies, "one from beyond the river."

What was the purpose of Abraham's call? Why was he taken out of his own country and from his father's house and promised that he should become a great nation? It was because Mesopotamia was steeped in the sin of idolatry, and the time had arrived for the founding of the lineage through which the Lord Jesus Christ, the Savior, would come into the world. Abraham was required to separate himself from his idolatrous surroundings, that he might establish such a lineage. The strict laws given to Israel, Abraham's descendants, had as their object the preservation in purity of the lineage of our Lord, the "Lamb without spot or blemish." (MS 86:641-42.)

**12:3** John Taylor has provided the following insights on how the seed of Abraham has blessed "all families of the earth."

We go to the promise made to Abraham, which was that in him and in his seed all the families of the earth should be blessed. Moses, as I have said was of his seed, and he was the deliverer of the whole of that nation. And who were the prophets that existed among ancient Israel? They were descendants of Abraham; and to them came the word of God and the light of revelation. Who was Jesus? After the flesh of the seed of Abraham. Who were his Twelve Apostles? Of the seed of Abraham. Who were the people that came to this continent—Lehi and his family, about 600 years B.C.? Of the seed of Abraham. Who were the Apostles they had among them that spread forth among the millions that then lived upon this continent? Of the seed of Abraham. Who was Joseph Smith? Of the seed of Abraham. (JD 20:224.)

**12:15**   The phrase "and commended her before Pharaoh" is changed in the Joseph Smith Translation to "and commanded her to be brought before Pharaoh."

**13:15**   The term "for ever" suggests that much of this blessing will be realized in the future, as explained by Joseph Fielding Smith:

This expression "forever" in some texts has reference to this mortal existence, but in the case of this promise to Abraham, it had no such meaning, and when the Lord said he would multiply him and make his seed as numerous "as the stars of heaven, and as the sand which is upon the sea shore," that also was a promise extending beyond the bounds of mortality and time, for his blessing of increase was to extend forever. (CHMR 1:216.)

**14:13**   After the word "Hebrew," the Joseph Smith Translation adds "the man of God."

**14:18**   Notice the impact of the additional words in the Joseph Smith Translation: "And he break bread and blest it; and he blest the wine, he being the priest of the most high God. And he gave to Abram." (Gen. 14:17-18.) Evidently the prophets had the sacrament before the time of Jesus Christ upon the earth.

The Joseph Smith Translation adds several very significant verses at the end of this chapter, providing information on the man Melchizedek and on the priesthood be held. Also, these additional verses indicate "Abram paid" tithes unto Melchizedek. (See Gen. 14:25-40, Bible Appendix, pp. 791-98.)

**14:20**   This is the first mention of tithes in the Old Testament, although the principle of sacrifice (and perhaps specifically of tithing) had been on earth since the very beginning. Brigham Young has declared: "The Lord instituted tithing, it was practiced in the days of Abraham, and Enoch and Adam." (JD 15:163.)

Joseph Smith left the following account of the beginning of tithing in this dispensation:

On the evening of the 29th of November, I united in prayer with

Brother Oliver for the continuance of blessings. After giving thanks for the relief which the Lord had lately sent us . . . we agreed to enter into the following covenant with the Lord, viz:

That if the Lord will prosper us in our business and open the way before us that we may obtain means to pay our debts, that we be not troubled nor brought into disrepute before the world, nor His people; after that, of all that He shall give unto us, we will give a tenth to be bestowed upon the poor in His Church, or as He shall command; and that we will be faithful over that which he has entrusted to our care, that we may obtain much; and that our children after us shall remember to observe this sacred and holy covenant; and that our children, and our children's children, may know of the same, we have subscribed our names with our own hands. (TPJS, p. 70.)

### Joseph F. Smith indicated tithing is a test of faith:

By this principle (tithing) the loyalty of the people of this Church shall be put to the test. By this principle it shall be known who is for the kingdom of God and who is against it. By this principle it shall be seen whose hearts are set on doing the will of God and keeping his commandments, thereby sanctifying the land of Zion unto God, and who are opposed to this principle and have cut themselves off from the blessings of Zion. There is a great deal of importance connected with this principle, for by it it shall be known whether we are faithful or unfaithful. In this respect it is as essential as faith in God, as repentance of sin, as baptism for the remission of sin, or as the laying on of hands for the gift of the Holy Ghost. (GD, p. 225.)

### According to Spencer W. Kimball, all true believers in the Bible should pay tithing:

Does not the law of tithing apply to all the children of men, regardless of church or creed? All who believe the Bible really must believe that this is a law of God.

There echo again and again the words of the Master: "Render therefore unto Caesar the things which are Caesar's, and unto God the things that are God's." The Lord will bless all those who love and live this law. (FPM, p. 290.)

**14:21-23** Spencer W. Kimball has commented on the integrity of Abraham in this instance:

The king of Sodom knew nothing about Abraham's covenant with the Lord; Abraham could have made himself rich by receiving of the king's generosity. But he had made an oath which he would not violate. Oh, that all of God's children could be so true! (E, June 1975, p. 6.)

**15:5-6** The Joseph Smith Translation adds several significant verses, indicating Abram "looked forth and saw the days of the Son of Man." (See Gen. 15:9-12, Bible Appendix, p. 798.)

**15:16** The term "iniquity . . . is not yet full" is explained by John Taylor:

There were times when the iniquity of these people was not yet full. In Abraham's day the Lord told that Patriarch that he should go to his fathers in peace, but in the fourth generation his posterity should "come hither again: for the iniquity of the Amorites is not yet full:" by the days of Moses they appear to have filled the cup of their iniquity, for he enjoined upon the Israelites, "thou shalt utterly destroy them, as the Lord thy God hath commanded thee." . . . Thus men and nations are adjudged by the Almighty, according to the infinite and eternal laws and principles which exist in the heavens, and with a reference to eternal duration and not according to the finite, erratic and limited ideas of men. (JD 26:36.)

**16:10** The word "I" is replaced with the words "the Lord" in the Joseph Smith Translation. (Gen. 16:11.)

**16:13** The Joseph Smith Translation clarifies this verse: "And she called the name of the angel of the Lord. And he spake unto her, saying, Knowest thou that God seest thee? And she said, I know that God seest me, for I have also here looked after him." (Gen. 16:14-16.)

**17:1** The significance of the Lord's commandment to Abraham "be thou perfect" is explained by Lorenzo Snow:

We learn that the Lord appeared to Abraham and made him very great promises, and that before he was prepared to receive them a certain requirement was made of him, that he should become perfect before the Lord. And the same requirement was made by the Savior of his disciples, that they should become perfect, even as he and his Father in heaven were perfect. . . .

When the Lord made this requirement of Abraham, He gave him the means by which he could become qualified to obey that law and come up fully to the requirement. He had the privilege of the Holy Spirit, as we are told the Gospel was preached to Abraham, and through that Gospel he could obtain that divine aid which would enable him to understand the things of God, and without it no man could arrive at a state of perfection before the Lord. (JD 20:187-88.)

The formula for Abraham's becoming perfect has been given by the Lord: "Abraham received all things, whatsoever he received, by revelation and commandment . . . Abraham . . . did none other things than that which [he was] commanded" therefore he has "entered into [his] exaltation." (D&C 132:29, 37.)

**17:3-4** See Joseph Smith Translation Genesis 17:3-7 on

page 798 of the Bible Appendix for information concerning baptism, which was taught to the Hebrews.

**17:3-7**    Concerning the covenant God made with Abraham, see the commentary for Genesis 12:1-3 and Genesis 12:3.

**17:7-14**    The Joseph Smith Translation makes it clear that circumcision is "a covenant with" God that men may know forever "that children are not accountable before [the Lord] until they are eight years old." (See Gen. 17:11-12, Bible Appendix, p. 798.)

The ordinance of circumcision was thus connected at least symbolically with the ordinance of baptism; however, Joseph Smith taught: "Circumcision is not baptism, neither was baptism instituted in the place of circumcision." (TPJS, p. 314.)

Joseph Smith also taught:

> The covenant of circumcision made with Abraham, and practiced steadily up to the departing of Israel out of Egypt, was abandoned in the wilderness, forty years—and renewed by Joshua after he passed over Jordan, and encamped at Gilgal, where he made sharp knives and circumcised the whole male portion of the church. (TPJS, p. 264.)

**18:14**    The second clause has been enlarged and clarified in the Joseph Smith Translation: "At the time appointed, behold, I will return unto thee from my journey, which the Lord hath sent me; and according to the time of life thou mayest know that Sarah shall have a son."

**18:18**    The fact that God knew beforehand that "Abraham shall surely become a great and mighty nation" has been explained by Brigham Young and Willard Richards:

> This includes the general principle of election, i.e. that God chose, elected, or ordained Jesus Christ, His Son, to be the creator, governor, savior, and judge of the world; and Abraham to be the father of the faithful, on account of His foreknowledge of their obedience to His will and commandments, which agrees with the saying in 2 Tim. 2:21, "If a man therefore purge himself from these [i.e. iniquities], he shall be a vessel unto honor, sanctified, and meet for the master's use, and prepared unto every good work."
>
> Thus it appears that God has chosen or elected certain individuals to certain blessings, or to the performance of certain works. (HC 4:258.)

**18:20-33**    Spencer W. Kimball has provided the following commentary on these verses:

> Abraham knew that the cities of the plains—Sodom and Gomorrah

and other places—were wicked cities, housing wicked, godless people, saying with Cain, "Who is the Lord that I should know him?" (Moses 5:16.) He was aware that destruction of those cities was imminent; but in his compassion for his fellowman, he begged and pleaded with the Lord, "Peradventure there be fifty righteous within the city," will you spare the others of the city? (See Gen. 18:24.) That pleading being granted, came Abraham again and prayed that the cities would be saved if 45 were found, or 40 or 30 or 20 or down to ten, but apparently there could not be found even ten, in those vicious cities, who were righteous. (See Gen. 18:24-32.)

The evil continued. The sin was too well entrenched. They had laughed and joked about a destruction. The transgressions for which Sodom had apparently been renowned continued on. In fact, the people wanted to take advantage of the pure angel men they had seen come into the city. The vicious men pressed and would have broken down the doors to get to them. (See Gen. 19:4-11.)

Everything was done that could be done by Abraham to save the city, but it had become so depraved and wanton that to save it was impossible. (CR, Apr. 1975, p. 161.)

**19:4-5** One of the most grievous sins of Sodom and Gomorrah was homosexuality. Spencer W. Kimball has forcefully condemned this practice:

We hear more and more each day about the sins of adultery, homosexuality, and lesbianism. Homosexuality is an ugly sin, but because of its prevalence, the need to warn the uninitiated, and the desire to help those who may already be involved with it, it must be brought into the open.

It is the sin of the ages. It was present in Israel's wandering as well as after and before. It was tolerated by the Greeks. It was prevalent in decaying Rome. The ancient cities of Sodom and Gomorrah are symbols of wretched wickedness more especially related to this perversion, as the incident of Lot's visitors indicates.

There is today a strong clamor to make such practices legal by passing legislation. Some would also legislate to legalize prostitution. They have legalized abortion, seeking to remove from this heinous crime the stigma of sin. . . .

"But let us emphasize that right and wrong, righteousness and sin, are not dependent upon man's interpretations, conventions and attitudes. Social acceptance does not change the status of an act, making wrong into right. If all the people in the world were to accept homosexuality, . . . the practice would still be a deep, dark sin." (CR, Oct. 1977, pp. 6-7.)

**19:9-11** The Joseph Smith Translation additions to these verses indicate that (1) Lot did *not* offer his daughters to the wicked men of Sodom and (2) the evil men "could not find" the door after they were stricken with blindness. (See Gen. 19:9-15, Bible Appendix, p. 798.)

**19:31** According to the Joseph Smith Translation, the

firstborn daughter "dealt wickedly" and said unto the younger: "Our father has become old, and we have not a man on the earth to come in unto us, *to live with us* after the manner of all that live on the earth." (Italics added.)

**20:7** This is the first of hundreds of times the word *prophet* is used in the Bible. Spencer W. Kimball has written concerning a prophet:

> To be a prophet of the Lord, one does not need to "be everything to all men." He does not need to be youthful and athletic, an industrialist, a financier, or an agriculturist; he does not need to be a musician, a poet, an entertainer, a banker, a physician, a college president, a military general, or a scientist.
>
> He does not need to be a linguist and speak French and Japanese, German and Spanish, but he must understand the divine language and be able to receive messages from heaven.
>
> He need not be an orator, for God can make his own. The Lord can present his divine messages through weak men made strong. He substituted a strong voice for the quiet, timid one of Moses, and he gave to the young man Enoch power that made men tremble in his presence, for Enoch walked with God as Moses walked with God.
>
> The Lord said: ". . . whether by mine own voice or by the voice of my servants, it is the same." (D&C 1:38.)
>
> What the world needs is a prophet-leader who gives example—clean, full of faith, godlike in his attributes with an untarnished name, a beloved husband, a true father.
>
> A prophet needs to be more than a priest or a minister or an elder. His voice becomes the voice of God to reveal new programs, new truths, new solutions. I make no claim of personal infallibility for him, but he does need to be recognized of God, to be an authoritative person. He is no pretender, as numerous persons are who presumptuously assume position without appointment and authority. He must speak like his Lord: "as one having authority, and not as the scribes." (Matthew 7:29.)
>
> He must be bold enough to speak truth even against popular clamor for lessening restrictions. He must be certain of his divine appointment, of his celestial ordination, and of his authority to call to service, to ordain, to pass keys that fit eternal locks. (FPM, pp. 318-19.)

**20:16** The clause "he is to thee a covering of the eyes" reads in the Joseph Smith Translation "he shall *give unto* thee a covering of the eyes." (Italics added.)

**21:1-2** The miracle of aged Sarah giving birth has drawn comments from both New Testament and modern prophets:

> Paul said again:
>
> "Through faith also Sara herself received strength to conceive seed, and was delivered of a child when she was past age, because she judged him faithful who had promised.

"Therefore sprang there even of one, and him as good as dead, so many as the stars of the sky in multitude, and as the sand which is by the sea shore innumerable." (Hebrews 11:11-12.)

So absurd it was to be told that children could be born of centenarians that even Sarah doubted at first. But the faith of a noble pair prevailed, and the miracle son was born to father multitudes of nations. (Spencer W. Kimball, FPM, p. 6.)

**21:21**    The clause "his mother took him a wife" has been changed to "he took him a wife," in the Joseph Smith Translation.

**22:2**    Many students of the Bible consider the supreme test of Abraham to be when the Lord commanded Abraham to offer his son Isaac. Concerning this event, Spencer W. Kimball has written:

Exceeding faith was shown by Abraham when the superhuman test was applied to him. His young "child of promise," destined to be the father of empires, must now be offered upon the sacrificial altar. It was God's command, but it seemed so contradictory! How could his son, Isaac, be the father of an uncountable posterity if in his youth his mortal life was to be terminated? Why should he, Abraham, be called upon to do this revolting deed? It was irreconcilable, impossible! And yet he believed God. His undaunted faith carried him with breaking heart toward the land of Moriah with this young son who little suspected the agonies through which his father must have been passing. . . .

Father Abraham and Mother Sarah knew—knew the promise would be fulfilled. *How*—they did not know and did not demand to know. Isaac positively would live to be the father of a numerous posterity. They knew he would, even though he might need to die. They knew he could still be raised from the dead to fulfil the promise, and faith here preceded the miracle. (CR, Oct. 1952, pp. 48-49.)

The Lord has commented on his command to Abraham in these words:

"Abraham was commanded to offer his son Isaac; nevertheless, it was written: Thou shalt not kill. Abraham, however, did not refuse, and it was accounted unto him for righteousness." (D&C 132:36.)

**22:6-14**    Spencer W. Kimball has reviewed the critical part of Abraham's test in these words:

The place was reached, the altar built, the fire kindled, and the lad now surely knowing, but trusting and believing, was upon the altar. The father's raised hand was stopped in mid-air by a commanding voice:

". . . Lay not thine hand upon the lad. . . ."

And as the near perfect prophet found the ram in the thicket and offered it upon the altar, he heard the voice of God again speaking:

"And in thy seed shall all the nations of the earth be blessed; because thou hast obeyed my voice." [Gen. 22:18.] . . .

Father Abraham and Mother Sarah knew—knew the promise would be fulfilled. *How*—they did not know and did not demand to know. (CR, Oct. 1952, pp. 48-49.)

**22:6** Abraham, not Isaac, carried the wood, according to the Joseph Smith Translation.

**22:16** The words "thine only son" are changed to "thine only Isaac" in the Joseph Smith Translation. Ishmael was also a son of Abraham.

**24:28** The Joseph Smith Translation reads: "And the damsel ran to the house, and *told her mother* these things." (Italics added.)

**25:23** Brigham Young and Willard Richards have explained that the Lord knew beforehand that the elder would serve the younger.

And the Lord said unto her, (Rebecca, Gen. xxv: 23) "The elder shall serve the younger." And why? Because that Isaac, the father of Esau and Jacob, the husband of Rebecca, and the son of promise to Abraham, was the heir; and as Esau was the elder son of his father Isaac, he had a legal claim to the heirship; but through unbelief, hardness of heart, and hunger, he sold his birthright to his younger brother Jacob (Gen. xxv: 33); and God knowing beforehand that he [Esau] would do this of his own free will and choice . . . said to his mother, "The elder shall serve the younger;" for as the elder son Esau, has sold his birthright, and by that means lost all claim to the blessings promised to Abraham; those blessings and promises must have failed, if they had not descended with the purchased birthright unto the younger son, Jacob, for there was no other heir in Abraham's family; and if those blessings had failed, the purposes of God according to election must have failed in relation to the posterity of Israel, and the oath of Jehovah would have been broken, which could not be though heaven and earth were to pass away. (HC 4:261-62.)

**28:22** The Joseph Smith Translation reads: "And *the place* of this stone which I have set for a pillar, shall be *the place* of God's house." (Italics added.)

**29:21** The Joseph Smith Translation reads: "And Jacob said unto Laban, Give unto me my wife, that I may go and *take her,* for my days *of serving thee* are fulfilled." (Italics added.)

**32:28** This is the first time the word *Israel* appears in the Bible. James E. Talmage commented concerning this title and name:

Israel—The combined name and title, *Israel,* in the original sense of the word, expressed the thought of one who had succeeded in his supplication before the Lord; "soldier of God," "one who contends with God," "a prince of God," are among the common English equivalents. The name first appears in sacred writ as a title conferred upon Jacob, when the latter prevailed in his determination to secure a blessing from his heavenly visitor in the wilderness, receiving the promise: [Quoted Gen. 32:28; 35:9-10.]

But the name-title thus bestowed under conditions of solemn dignity acquired a wider application, and came to represent the posterity of Abraham, through Isaac and Jacob [1 Sam. 25:1; Isa. 48:1; Rom. 9:4; 11:1], with each of whom the Lord had covenanted that through his descendants should all nations of the earth be blessed. The name of the individual patriarch thus grew into the designation of a people, including the twelve tribes, who delighted in the title Israelites, or children of Israel. (AF, p. 314.)

See Part I 2.

**37:2** Joseph Fielding Smith taught that Joseph, the son of Jacob, must have received the priesthood before he was seventeen years old.

There is ample evidence that boys were called and ordained [to the priesthood] in ancient times. In antediluvian times, when the lives of men were greatly prolonged, some were called to act at comparatively tender years. Enoch was but twenty-five when he was ordained by Adam; Lamech was but thirty-two; and Noah received the priesthood when he was but ten years of age. How old Joseph, son of Israel, was when he received the priesthood is not recorded; but it must have been when he was very young. He was sold by his brethren when he was only seventeen, and he must have had the priesthood before that time, for he exercised it in the land of Egypt. (AGQ 2:9.)

**38:8-9** The Joseph Smith Translation records the command as follows: "Go and marry thy brother's wife, and raise up seed unto thy brother." Although Onan married his brother's wife "*he would not lie with her,* lest he should raise up seed unto his brother." (Italics added.)

**39:7-9** Joseph's faithfulness in the face of this temptation has been extolled by Harold B. Lee:

Oh, the majesty of Joseph sold into Egypt, who shamed the beautiful but apparently unloved wife of Potiphar, when she would have tempted him to a serious sin, and he said, "My master trusts me, and thou art his wife. How can I do this great wickedness and sin against God?" (See Gen. 39:8.) He, too, felt his great responsibility in being a true witness of the divine truths which he professed to believe. (CR, Apr. 1951, p. 34.)

**39:7-20** The situation of Potiphar's wife is discussed in this insightful commentary by Spencer W. Kimball.

The case of Potiphar's wife is an example of the creeping tentacles of sin. Even though this scheming woman did not succeed in defiling Joseph, her sin was most grievous. The intent was there and the desire and the lust and the coveting. She had "already committed adultery with him in her heart and mind . . ." as she "cast her eyes upon Joseph day by day." This woman's transgression did not begin when she ripped the clothes from the body of this fleeing stalwart. Her perfidy had been born and nurtured in her mind and heart in the "day by day" of wanting him, teasing him, desiring him, lusting for him, and coveting him. Her sin was a progressive thing. So, for all the numerous people, who, like this seductive woman, carry in their hearts and minds designs or desires or covetings, deep sin lieth already at their doors.

"For as he thinketh in his heart, so is he: . . ." (Prov. 23:7.) Nothing justifies evil. Two wrongs do not make one right. Spouses are sometimes inconsiderate, unkind, and difficult, and they must share the blame for broken homes, but this never justifies the other spouse's covetousness and unfaithfulness and infidelity. (IE, Dec. 1962, p. 929.)

**42:23**   Ezra Taft Benson has indicated this verse means that Joseph's descendants "would be sorely persecuted." (See Part I 233-34, 245-48.)

**48:5-6**   The six extra verses of the Joseph Smith Translation provide an additional blessing of Jacob for Joseph. Also, they make clear that Ephraim and Manasseh did not replace Reuben and Simeon, but were to be considered as sons of Jacob just as Reuben and Simeon were also sons. (See Gen. 48:5-11, Bible Appendix, pp. 798-99.)

**48:10**   The King James text indicates Jacob "could not see"; the Joseph Smith Translation states Jacob "could not see *well*." (Italics added.)

**48:13-19**   The significance of Jacob's placing his right hand upon the head of Ephraim while pronouncing the blessing has been explained by Joseph Fielding Smith:

The performing of ordinances with the right hand in preference to the left is a well-established custom universally and is not confined to the Church. In various governments where oaths are administered, the candidate for office is asked to raise his right hand. There are occasions when he is sworn to give truthful testimony by placing his right hand on a copy of the Bible. This custom has come down from the beginning, and from many scriptural passages we gather that it has always received divine sanction. When Abraham sent his servant to his kindred to find a wife for Isaac, he had the servant place his right hand under Abraham's thigh and swear to him that he would accomplish this mission. . . . (AGQ 1:154-55.)

There are numerous passages in the scriptures referring to the right hand, indicating that it is a symbol of righteousness and was used in the making of covenants. . . . (AGQ 1:154-55, 57. See Isa. 41:10; Ps. 110:1.)

It is the custom to extend the right hand in token of fellowship. The right hand is called the *dexter*, and the left, the *sinister;* dexter means *right* and sinister means *left*. Dexter, or right, means *favorable* or *propitious*. Sinister is associated with evil, rather than good. Sinister means *perverse*.

We take the sacrament with the right hand. We sustain the authorities with the right hand. We make acknowledgment with the right hand raised. (DS 3:108.)

**49:10**    B. H. Roberts has provided the following commentary on this verse:

This passage by the Jews, in ancient times, who believed in the coming of the Messiah at all, was allowed to have reference to the coming of their Messiah, and as in some way fixing the time and circumstances of his coming.

It is evident that by "Judah" is meant, not the person, but the tribe, and by "Sceptre" and "lawgiver" are obviously intended the legislative and ruling power. In the course of time this commenced in David, and for centuries afterwards was continued in his descendants. Whatever variety the form of government assumed the law and polity were the same. . . .

The Jewish Targums paraphrase the passage thus: "The Sceptre shall not depart from Judah until the King Messiah comes, to whom it belongeth."

This prediction of Genesis 49:10, all the older Jewish commentators, referred to as Messiah. Ben Uzzel, whose Commentaries are among the most ancient Targums, renders the passage: "Until the time when the King Messiah shall come." The Targum of Onkelos speaks of it to the same effect, and the Targum of Jerusalem paraphrases it thus: "Kings shall not cease, from the House of Judah, nor doctors that teach the law from his children until that the King, Messiah, do come, whose the kingdom is: and all nations of the earth shall be subject unto him."

For modern Jewish commentators, these admissions represent tremendous consequences. If the integrity of the prophecy be regarded, then, since the Sceptre—symbol of the legislative and ruling power—has departed from Judah, the Messiah must have come, and long since come, for Judah has not held legislative authority, nor the Sceptre of power for two thousand years! The last trace of legislative power in the Sanhedrin, and all administrative authority departed from Judah with the coming of Jesus, the Christ, and with the destruction of the temple and Jerusalem under the Romans, 70 A.D. (*Rasha the Jew,* pp. 40-41.)

See Part I 179-80.

**49:22-26**    The Church of Jesus Christ of Latter-day Saints maintains that some of the descendants of Joseph who was sold into Egypt were led by the Lord about 600 B.C. to the lands now known as the Americas. Their descendants became much of the native stock of the later Mayan, Incan, and Aztec civilizations. The first 1,000 years of the history of these Josephites is recorded in the Book of Mormon.

Joseph Fielding Smith has stated that the preservation of the peoples in the Americas was a result of Jacob's promises to Joseph that he would be "a fruitful bough . . . whose branches run over the wall."

> Most of those who are receiving the gospel are of the tribe of Ephraim. The Lamanites, as we learn from the Book of Mormon, are descendants of both Ephraim and Manasseh. The record obtained by Lehi when he sent his sons back to Jerusalem declared that he was a descendant of Manasseh. We have been informed by revelation given to the Prophet Joseph Smith that the daughters of Ishmael who married the sons of Lehi were descendants of Ephraim. Therefore the prophecy of Jacob upon the head of Joseph was fulfilled. (AGQ 5:70.)

See Part I 233-34.

**50:24-26**   The Joseph Smith Translation adds twelve very significant verses to the account in the King James Version. (See Gen. 50:24-38, Bible Appendix, pp. 799-800.)

The following important concepts are discussed in these additional verses:

1. A righteous branch of Israel would be raised up out of the loins of Joseph who was sold into Egypt.

2. The Messiah (called Shiloh) would *not* be from Joseph.

3. Moses would be raised up to deliver the children of Israel from Egypt.

4. A "choice seer . . . like unto" Moses would be raised up from the loins of Joseph in the last days—"his name shall be called Joseph, and it shall be after the name of his father." (Latter-day Saints believe this choice seer was Joseph Smith, Jr.).

5. The descendants of Judah would keep a record (the Bible) and the descendants of Joseph would write (the Book of Mormon). In the last days these two records would "grow together unto the confounding of false doctrines . . . and bringing . . . a knowledge of my covenants, saith the Lord."

6. The house of Israel shall be restored "in the last days."

The following commentaries substantiate the claim that Joseph Smith, Jr., was the "choice seer" of the last days as revealed to Joseph who was sold into Egypt.

It was decreed in the counsels of eternity, long before the foundations of the earth were laid, that [Joseph Smith] should be the man, in the last dispensation of this world, to bring forth the word of God to the people, and receive the fulness of the keys and power of the Priesthood of the Son of God. The Lord had his eye upon him, and upon his father, and upon his father's father, and upon their progenitors clear back to Abraham, and from Abraham to the flood, from the flood to Enoch, and from Enoch to Adam. . . . He was foreordained in eternity to preside over this last dispensation. (Brigham Young, JD 7:289-90.)

God called [Joseph Smith] to occupy the position that he did . . . thousands of years ago before this world was formed. The Prophets prophesied about his coming, that a man should arise whose name should be Joseph, and that his father's name should be Joseph, and also that he should be a descendant of that Joseph who was sold into Egypt. (John Taylor, JD 26:106.)

# EXODUS

See "Exodus, Book of," in the Bible Dictionary, page 668.

**1:5**   The "seventy souls . . . that came out of the loins of Jacob" and went into Egypt obviously did not include the wives of the sons, grandsons, and so on. Genesis 46:8-27 included a listing of "threescore and ten" (70) with the notation "besides Jacob's sons' wives." Also Moses recorded that Jacob took into Egypt "his daughters, and his sons' daughters" (Gen. 46:7), yet only two women are mentioned by name as possibly being among the group (Dinah and Serah), and one of them (Dinah) is not included in the thirty-three who are descendants of Leah even though Genesis 34:25 indicates that Leah was Dinah's mother.

Most Bible scholars estimate that the number of Israelites who migrated into Egypt totaled several hundred. Jacob was 130 years old at the time (Gen. 47:9), his sons would have been at least 60 years of age, and many of his grandsons were mature men with children of their own.

**1:8-14**   The exact length of the enslavement of the Israelites is not given in this part of the Old Testament although Exodus 12:40 indicates "the sojourning of the children of Israel, who dwelt in Egypt, was four hundred and thirty years."

Evidently this figure includes Jacob's coming down into Egypt, and some scholars believe this reckoning must have started from Joseph's arrival in Egypt or even from Abraham's visit there.

Ellis Rasmussen has provided the following commentary on this question.

How long the slavery had lasted is difficult to know. Paul (in Galatians 3:17) accepts a Septuagint statement in Exodus 12:40 that there were 430 years from the time of Abraham's reception of the promise until the giving of the Mosaic Law. This would leave some 215 years for Israel in Egypt, and since the clan lived there in peace for some 71 years of Joseph's life after Jacob and the family all came in, there would remain some 144 years, some part of which would have been under the Pharaohs of Joseph's time and the remainder under the Pharaohs "who knew not Joseph." Though the date of the overthrow of the Hyksos is fairly well established (1540 BC), it is not known for sure which of the following Pharaohs was the Pharaoh of the Exodus. The phrase "land of Rameses" used (anachronistically?) in

Genesis 47:11 can hardly mean that Israel *entered* in the days of Pharaoh Rameses; but still the name of the treasure cities "Pithom and Raamses" (Exodus 1:11) is sometimes taken as evidence that the Israelites' slave labor was used in construction work which took place during the administration of Rameses II. Obviously, the internal evidences are insufficient, and conclusive external evidences are yet needed. So far, the circumstantial evidence pointing to confirmation of the general historical truthfulness of Exodus is becoming impressive. (IOT 1:72-73.)

**1:8**   The "new king" (Pharaoh) who "knew not Joseph" also "dealt subtilly" with the Israelites in Egypt according to the writer of Acts. (See Acts 7:18-19.) The idiomatic expression "knew not Joseph" obviously does not mean the Pharaoh was not acquainted with the Israelites; rather it indicates he was opposed to the Israelites and sought to do evil toward them.

**2:10**   The name *Moses* was already well known in the Egyptian court. Although scholars do not always agree as to the exact dating of Moses in Egypt, several Pharaohs had already borne names with the root Moses—e.g. Ramose (or Rameses) and Thutmose (or Thothmes).

In his writings, Josephus refers to a legend among the Egyptians, dating far earlier than Moses, that a leader by that particular name would someday come to great power in Egypt. The legend might well account for the frequency of names containing a form of *Moses*.

The Book of Mormon indicates that, at least from the time of Joseph, a group of Israelites might have known the exact name of the great deliverer who was to lead them from bondage. The Lord told Joseph, "Moses will I raise up, to deliver thy people out of the land of Egypt." (2 Ne. 3:10.)

The name *Moses* seems to be especially appropriate for the child drawn from the ark of bulrushes in the river by Pharaoh's daughter who claimed him as a son; it derives from a Hebrew word meaning "to draw out" of the water and from an Egyptian root "to beget a child."

**2:11**   The word *Hebrew* (which earlier meant "descendant of Abraham") is frequently used to refer to the Israelites during this period of biblical history. (See Part I 2.) Israelites are Hebrews, of course, but not all Hebrews are Israelites.

After the Lord tells Moses, "Israel is my son, even my first-born" (Ex. 4:22), the terms *Israel, children of Israel,* and *Israelites* are often used to designate the descendants of Jacob.

**2:11-15**   Ellis Rasmussen has provided the following

commentary on the killing of the Egyptian taskmaster by Moses:

His hour of decision came when Moses "went out unto his brethren, and looked on their burdens" and smote a taskmaster who was smiting one of them. The same verb is used to tell what both the taskmaster and Moses did: "Smote" and "slew" in King James English are both translated from Hebrew *nakhah,* meaning "to beat down"; it is the word used in describing the action taken by soldiers in combat against each other. It would be correct to say that Moses *slew* a man who was *slaying* another, or took a life in saving a life. His looking "this way and that" before doing so, simply indicates that he was aware that the Egyptians would not condone his defense of a slave. It is doubtless from this action, and from his attempt to settle strife between two Hebrews the following day who rejected and rebuffed him, that Stephen says Moses "supposed his brethren would have understood how that God by his hand would deliver them: but they understood not" (Acts 7:25). Naturally he had to flee from Egypt and find refuge elsewhere from that time on. (IOT 1:74.)

**2:18** The father-in-law of Moses is given two different names within a few verses: "Reuel" in Exodus 2:18 and "Jethro" as in Exodus 3:1. It is not unusual for Semites to have more than one name, as evidenced in Abraham (Abram) and Israel (Jacob). However, some scholars want to apply other names to the father-in-law of Moses, including *Raguel* (Num. 10:29) and *Hobab* (Judg. 4:11). A careful reading and comparison of the wording and punctuation of Numbers 10:29 and Judges 4:11 indicates that Raguel was the father of Hobab, and that Hobab (not Raguel) might be the only additional name for the father-in-law of Moses. If Moses had only one father-in-law, this still leaves at least three different names to refer to one man.

A possible solution to this difficulty is that Moses had several "wives and concubines" and thus might have had several different fathers-in-law. (See D&C 132:38.) This revealed fact still does not rule out the possibility that Reuel and Jethro are different names for the same man.

The Bible indicates Moses had at least one other wife in addition to Zipporah: "And Miriam and Aaron spake against Moses because of the Ethiopian woman whom he had married: for he had married an Ethiopian woman." (Num. 12:1.)

No further information is given in the Bible concerning the names of this Ethiopian wife or her father. Furthermore, the fact she was from Ethiopia does not necessarily indicate her lineage. Many Semites had undoubtedly settled in Ethiopia during early migrations into northern Africa.

**2:22** Two possible meanings have been given to the name *Gershom,* from the Hebrew *ger* (a sojourner) and *sham* (there) or from the verb *garash* (to expel). Either derivation suggests that Moses was thinking of his kindred back in Egypt when he named his firstborn son. A later son of Moses and Zipporah is named Eliezer (God is help). (See Ex. 18:4.)

**3:1** "Midian" was the name of one of the sons of Abraham and Keturah. (Gen. 25:2.) In Exodus 2:15, "Midian" refers to a land. Most scholars have assumed (1) that the Midianites were descendants of Midian the son of Abraham and (2) that the land where the Midianites lived was given the same name. If these suppositions are true, Jethro, "the priest of Midian" and father-in-law of Moses to whom he gave the "holy priesthood" (D&C 84:6), would have been a descendant of Abraham, and thus both a Semite and a Hebrew.

**3:5** Some of the most holy places on earth today are the temples (houses of the Lord), where the presence of the Lord can be felt by many. Here, also, the counsel is to remove shoes worn in the world "for the place whereon thou standest is holy ground."

**3:12** The mountain where Moses encountered the burning bush was given the name "Horeb" in Exodus 3:1. In verse 12, the Lord indicated that the children of Israel should be given the opportunity to "serve God upon this mountain." In Exodus 19:11 the name "mount Sinai" is given to the place where the Lord spoke to Moses and was heard by the Israelites. Thus, many biblical scholars believe Horeb and Sinai are the same mountain. It may be that *Horeb* refers to the mountain range whereas *Sinai* is the name of a particular mountain or peak within that range.

**3:14** The Lord has identified himself on several occasions by the sacred title I AM. To the Jews, Jesus said: "Before Abraham was, I am" (John 8:58), which, according to a modern apostle was the same as saying "Before Abraham was I Jehovah." (DNTC 1:464.) To Joseph Smith, the Lord declared: "Listen to the voice of Jesus Christ, your Redeemer, the Great I AM, whose arm of mercy hath atoned for your sins" (D&C 29:1); "Hearken and listen to the voice of him who is from all eternity to all eternity, the Great I AM, even Jesus Christ." (D&C 39:1; see also 38:1.)

Ellis Rasmussen has written the following explanation of the relationship of *I AM* to *Jehovah:*

On the identity of Him who calls Himself "I AM," study the implications in Exodus 6:3, John 8:58, I Corinthians 10:1-4, and then turn to the direct statements identifying the God of Moses with Jesus the Savior in III Nephi 15:4; I Nephi 19:10; Isaiah 63:7-14 and 49:26. Recall also Hebrews 1:1-3 and John 1:1-3 on the relationship of the Son to the Father in the creation of the earth.

In Hebrew, it is evident that the name *Jehovah* is composed from the verb which in its active form means "He is" and in its causative form means "He causes to be" (i.e., "He creates"). It is reasonable that He would call Himself "I AM," while we call Him "HE WHO IS." This is one possible interpretation of Jehovah. (Remember that our common translation substitutes the word *LORD* in capital letters wherever the four-letter sacred name *JHVH* (i.e., *Jehovah*) appears in Hebrew. It appears only as the four consonants JHVH in Hebrew because that ancient language was *written* without vowels. (IOT 1:75.)

**3:21-22**   The Hebrew word translated "borrow" means "to ask." Evidently the women of the Israelites were to ask the Egyptian women for their jewels, perhaps in payment for favors or work given previously. The King James word "spoil" is the translation of a Hebrew root meaning "empty out." The sentence in Hebrew has no connotation of stealing or of borrowing for temporary use only.

**4:10-12**   The Lord created the heavens and the earth and all things which are in them, including the physical body of man. Thus the Lord can strengthen or alter them according to his divine purposes. Moses evidently needed to be reminded of these things before going back to face Pharaoh and the Egyptians.

**4:13-17**   This is the beginning of the call of Aaron to priesthood responsibility, which call spans several books. (See especially Ex. 7:2; Lev. 8; Num. 3.) Aaron was called directly of God through His prophet, and as the writer of Hebrews declared, "No man taketh this honour unto himself, but he that is called of God, as was Aaron." (Heb. 5:4.)

**4:16**   The prophet is a spokesman for God, and sometimes the Lord provides a spokesman for the prophet also. In the dispensation of the fulness of times, the Lord provided Sidney Rigdon as a spokesman for the Prophet Joseph Smith. (See D&C 100:9.)

**4:21**   The expression "I [the Lord] will harden his [Pharaoh's] heart" should have been translated "Pharaoh will harden his heart against me [the Lord]," according to the Joseph Smith Translation. (See also Ex. 7:3, 13; 9:12; 10:1, 20, 27; 11:10.) Joseph Fielding Smith has written:

The Lord does not harden the hearts of men, they harden their own hearts. In the scriptures where it says the Lord hardened Pharaoh's heart, it is a mistranslation in every case. In the corrected verses of the Inspired Version the Lord said to Moses:

"And Pharaoh will harden his heart, as I said unto thee; and thou shalt multiply my signs, and my wonders, in the land of Egypt." (AGQ 3:136.)

**4:24-27**    The Joseph Smith Translation makes it clear that the Lord's displeasure with Moses on this occasion was because Moses failed to circumcise his son as was required of the covenant people. (See Gen. 17:10-14, 23-27, and 34:15 for background information on circumcision.) Because of his failure to meet this requirement, "Moses was ashamed, and hid his face from the Lord, and said, I have sinned before the Lord." (Ex. 4:26; see also 4:24-25.)

**6:2-3**    The God who spoke unto Moses is Jehovah (of the Old Testament) or Jesus Christ (as he is known in the New Testament). Many biblical scholars and their commentaries have claimed the Lord was not known unto the Hebrews and Israelites by his name Jehovah because of the statement "by my name JEHOVAH was I not known to them." The Joseph Smith Translation clarifies this important point: "I am the Lord God Almighty; the Lord JEHOVAH. And was not my name known unto them?"

The change from a declarative statement to an interrogative alters the entire meaning of the verse, and is fully consistent with the word order and with the Hebrew custom of indicating questions only by raising the voice at the end of the statement.

Joseph Fielding Smith indicated that the God who has worked with man since the fall is Jehovah, or Jesus Christ:

All revelation since the fall has come through Jesus Christ, who is the Jehovah of the Old Testament. In all of the scriptures, where God is mentioned and where he has appeared, it was Jehovah who talked with Abraham, with Noah, Enoch, Moses and all the prophets. He is the God of Israel, the Holy One of Israel; the one who led that nation out of Egyptian bondage, and who gave and fulfilled the Law of Moses. [1 Ne. 19:10; 3 Ne. 11:10, 14; 15:2-9.] The Father has never dealt with man directly and personally since the fall, and he has never appeared except to introduce and bear record of the Son. (DS 1:27.)

**6:8**    The clause "I am the Lord" should read "I the Lord will do it," according to the Joseph Smith Translation.

**7:3**    See commentary for Exodus 4:21.

**7:11**    Some readers have wondered about the source of the power which enabled the "wise men and the sorcerers" and the magicians of Egypt to duplicate some of the feats of Moses and Aaron. Concerning these powers, Joseph Fielding Smith has written:

All down through the ages and in almost all countries, men have exercised great occult and mystical powers, even to the healing of the sick and the performing of miracles. Soothsayers, magicians, and astrologers were found in the courts of ancient kings. They had certain powers by which they divined and solved the monarch's problems, dreams, etc. One of the most striking examples of this is recorded in Exodus, where Pharaoh called "the wise men and the sorcerers" who duplicated some of the miracles the Lord had commanded Moses and Aaron to perform. When Aaron threw down his rod, it became a serpent. The Egyptian magicians threw down their rods, and they also became serpents. . . . Beyond this point the magicians of Egypt could not go. The magicians failed in the days of Joseph to interpret the dream of Pharaoh because it was a dream from the Lord, but Joseph, because he held the priesthood, interpreted it.

. . . It should be remembered that Satan has great knowledge and thereby can exercise authority and to some extent control the elements, when some greater power does not intervene. (AGQ 1:176-78.)

**8:25-27**   The request of Moses that the children of Israel be allowed to go "into the wilderness" to offer their sacrifice so they would not be stoned by the Egyptians was certainly understandable and reasonable. The sacrifices of the Israelites frequently required the killing of animals, and cattle (cows and bulls) were sacred to the Egyptians!

**9:16**   The words "*cause*" and "*in*" are italicized, indicating that their equivalents are not found in the Hebrew. Notice the difference in meaning when these words are deleted: ". . . for this _____ have I raised thee up, for to shew _____ thee my power."

**9:17**   This verse contains the continuation of the words which Moses should say *to Pharaoh*. The Joseph Smith Translation makes this clear: "Therefore speak unto Pharaoh the thing which I command thee, who as yet exalteth himself that he will not let them go."

**10:1**   See the commentary for Exodus 4:21.

**11:8**   The statement "And he went out from Pharaoh in a great anger" seems to indicate that Moses was angry. However, the Joseph Smith Translation puts this sentence in the context of verse 10, which changes the entire meaning: "And Moses and Aaron did all these wonders before Pharaoh, and they went out from Pharaoh, and he was in great anger."

The clause "And he went out from Pharaoh in a great anger" should be deleted from verse 8, according to the Joseph Smith Translation.

**12:8-20**    The unleavened bread is listed here as a reminder of the haste of the Israelites in leaving Egypt. Jewish tradition holds that the unleavened bread is also a symbol of purity, but this claim is not found in the scriptures.

**12:11-27**    The meaning and purpose of the Passover has been explained by Joseph Fielding Smith:

> The term Passover is from the Hebrew word pesach (Greek pascha), to pass by, and from the incident of the angel passing by the homes where the sign of the blood of the lamb was found, the lamb slain and eaten at the feast of the Passover is known as the Paschal lamb. This lamb had to be a male of the first year, and without spot or blemish, which was the requirement in all sacrifices, and not a bone was to be broken. The reason for this is that the sacrifice was typical of the great sacrifice which should be made by Jesus Christ. In commemoration of this passing by of the angel of the Lord and the deliverance of the Israelites from Egypt, the Lord required that this feast should be observed annually in Israel. Moreover, this month (the month of Ahib [Abib], later called Nisan) was to commence their year.
>
> The ceremonies connected with this annual feast were to continue for seven days, beginning on the fourteenth and concluding on the twenty-first day of the month. During that time only unleavened bread should be eaten. (Read Ex. 12; Deut. 16:1-8; and Ezra 6:18-22.) (CHMR 1:130.)

See Part I 40.

**12:12**    The Egyptians had many gods whom they worshipped—gods supposedly inhabiting the heavens, the earth, and the regions beneath the earth. The various plagues brought upon the Egyptians were judgments against one or another of these various gods who controlled the waters, and so on. For example, the plague of darkness (Ex. 10:21-23) was a type of judgment against the most prominent of the Egyptian deities, the sun god *Ra*.

**12:16**    See Part I 32.

**12:17, 24**    The statement of the Lord that the children of Israel should observe an ordinance "for ever" to remind them of their deliverance should not be interpreted to mean they were to observe the Passover feast forever. Much of the symbolism of the "ordinance of the passover" (v. 43) was a foreshadowing of the coming of Jesus Christ, who would deliver people from their sins. Joseph Fielding Smith has written:

> The Feast of the Passover was fulfilled in that form in the crucifixion of Jesus Christ. The Passover was a law given to Israel which was to

continue until Christ, and was to remind the children of Israel of the coming of Christ who would become the sacrificial Lamb. After he was crucified the law was changed by the Savior himself, and from that time forth the law of the sacrament was instituted. We now observe the law of the sacrament instead of the Passover because the Passover was consummated in full by the death of Jesus Christ. It was a custom looking forward to the coming of Christ and his crucifixion and the lamb symbolized his death. (AGQ 5:153-54.)

**12:27** See Part I 40.

**12:33** The statement "We be all dead men" obviously means the Egyptians felt they all would soon be dead if the plagues continued. The Joseph Smith Translation clarifies the meaning: "And the Egyptians . . . said, We have found our first-born all dead; therefore get ye out of the land lest we die also."

**12:35-36** The Hebrew indicates that the Israelites *asked for* (not *borrowed*) the jewels and raiment, and the Egyptians "let them have" (not *lent*) such things as they required. It should be remembered that the Lord earlier had commanded Moses to have the Israelites follow this procedure in order that they would not "go empty" out of Egypt. (See the commentary for Ex. 3:21-22.)

**12:51** The word translated "armies" here and in verse 17 can also be rendered "hosts." The meaning is that the people were numerous and does not necessarily indicate they were armed with weapons.

**13:9** The Bible Dictionary defines a phylactery as a small strip "of parchment inscribed with texts . . . and enclosed in leather cases." The basis for using phylacteries comes from this verse and from the following scriptures: Exodus 13:1-16; Deuteronomy 6:4-9; 11:13-21. The phylactery might be worn on the forehead and also on the left arm near the heart. See Part I 37.

**13:15** See Part I 40.

**14:13-31** The Old Testament miracle of the parting of the sea is verified in the New Testament (Acts 7:36), the Book of Mormon (1 Ne. 4:2; 17:26; Mosiah 7:19; Alma 36:28; Hel. 8:11), and the Doctrine and Covenants (8:3). Believers in the scriptural accounts, which also teach that God created the seas in the beginning, should have no difficulty accepting the literalness of the miracle. Unfortunately, some biblical scholars have tried to explain away the miracle by pointing out that the "sea of reeds" is the meaning of the Hebrew translation rather than the Red Sea, or by claiming that the Israelites invented the story in order to appear mighty in the eyes of their enemies. However, Spencer W. Kimball reaffirmed the literalness of the miracle:

No hope on earth for their liberation! What could save them now? The gloating armed forces of Egypt knew that Israel was trapped. Israel knew it only too well. But Moses, their inspired leader with a supreme faith, knew that God would not have called them on this exodus only to have them destroyed. He knew God would provide the escape. He may not at this moment have known just how, but he trusted. . . .

The mighty warriors pressed on. Hope must have long since died in the breasts of the timid Israelitish souls who knew not faith. Deserts and wilderness and the sea—the uncrossable sea! No boats, no rafts, nor time to construct them! Hopelessness, fear, despair must have gripped their hearts, and then the miracle came. It was born of the faith of their indomitable leader. A cloud hid them from the view of their enemies. A strong east wind blew all the night; the waters were parted; the bed of the sea was dry; and Israel crossed to another world and saw the returning sea envelop and destroy their pursuers. Israel was safe. Faith had been rewarded, and Moses was vindicated. The impossible had happened. An almost superhuman faith had given birth to an unaccountable and mysterious miracle that was to be the theme of the sermons and warnings of Israel and their prophets for centuries. (CR, Oct. 1952, p. 49.)

**16:16, 36** "An omer is the tenth part of an ephah" (dry measurement), which is equal to a bath (liquid measurement), which is about 31.3 liters or 8¼ U.S. gallons. Thus, an omer would be about 3.13 liters or according to *Dummelow's Commentary,* "an omer is a little more than 7 pints. Ten omers make an ephah, which is, roughly, equal to a bushel." (See v. 36.)

**16:23** This verse is combined with Exodus 35:3 to form the basis that no fire is to be lit on the Sabbath day. Thus in many orthodox Jewish homes all of the food to be eaten on the Sabbath is cooked previously. Some of the ultra-orthodox also interpret this injunction to apply to electric lights (the electricity might be generated from turbines requiring fire) and the driving of automobiles (which operate on the principle of internal combustion, which requires a spark). Thus in the Mea Shearim section of modern Jerusalem, no vehicular traffic is allowed on the Sabbath. See Part I 33.

**16:26** See Part I 32.

**16:29** This verse forms the basis of the "Sabbath day's journey" which became the custom among Jewish people. The Bible Dictionary entry indicates "the rabbis, by means of a forced and unnatural interpretation of Ex. 16: 29, fixed this at 2,000 cubits, being the distance between the Ark and the people during the march in the wilderness (Josh. 3:4), and also according to tradition, the distance between the tabernacle and the furthest part of the camp.'' A Sabbath day's journey is thus about 3,000 feet, or 1,000 yards. See Part I 34.

**17:9-12**    The present Bible does not identify further the man named Hur, who assisted Aaron in supporting the hands of Moses. He is mentioned also in connection with Moses and Aaron in Exodus 24:14, when Moses went on top of the mount and left Aaron and Hur with the people. Because of the intimate association of Hur with Moses and Aaron, Jewish tradition holds that Hur was the husband of Miriam and thus brother-in-law of Moses and Aaron.

Harold B. Lee has likened the role of Aaron and Hur to the responsibility of Church members today:

> Here sits today on this stand the man as President of this Church who holds in his hand the rod of the Lord; he is sitting upon the mount, and as long as his hands are upheld by obedience to his direction and his counsel, Israel will prevail against her enemies. But whenever we come to a time when we allow his hands to fall, and we as the Priesthood of the living God fail to uphold his hands, just in that day we may expect our enemies to come upon us and to destroy us. (CR, Apr. 1943, p. 129.)

When Harold B. Lee became a counselor in the First Presidency, he compared the responsibility of the counselors to the modern prophet with the help of Aaron and Hur to Moses:

> I think that is the role that President Tanner and I have to fulfill. The hands of President Smith may grow weary. They may tend to droop at times because of his heavy responsibilities; but as we uphold his hands, and as we lead under his direction, by his side, the gates of hell will not prevail against you and against Israel. Your safety and ours depends upon whether or not we follow the ones whom the Lord has placed to preside over his church. He knows whom he wants to preside over his church, and he will make no mistake. The Lord doesn't do things by accident. He has never done anything accidentally. And I think the scientists and all the philosophers in the world have never discovered or learned anything that God didn't already know. His revelations are more powerful, more meaningful, and have more substance than all the secular learning in the world.
>
> Let's keep our eye on the President of the Church and uphold his hands as President Tanner and I will continue to do. (CR, Oct. 1970, p. 153.)

**18:11**    The Hebrew which has been translated ''for in the thing wherein they dealt proudly he was above them'' more literally reads ''in the manner in which they were proved against them.''

**19:11, 24**   Although the Lord instructed Moses to have the people prepare themselves to come into his presence (v. 11), three days later he counseled Moses, "Let not the priests and the people . . . come up unto the Lord" (v. 24). Evidently the people failed to prepare themselves adequately to see God, although they were privileged to hear his voice, as is made clear in Deuteronomy 4:10-12, 33-36; 5:22-26.

**20:1-26**   For background information on all of the Ten Commandments see *The Ten Commandments Today* published by Deseret Book Company in 1955.

**20:3**   The Hebrew background and possible meanings of the phrase "before me" have been listed by Ellis Rasmussen:

> The phrase "before me" in the familiar translation "Thou shalt have no other gods *before me*" is not from the commonly used Hebrew phrase *lephanai,* but *'al-panai,* which is somewhat more definite and distinct, and is used in the sense of "in front of"—either *to the exclusion* of another as in Deuteronomy 21:16, or *in preference; in addition to,* as in Job 16:14, ("calamity *upon* calamity.") It means "in front of" in a dozen other places in the Old Testament. But whereas this prepositional phrase can be used to mean any of several things, the context is clear as explained above: the worshipper of the Lord is not to make or to adopt any other object to worship. (IOT 1:84.)

Many people who feel they are religious might still be guilty of worshipping "other gods" as explained by Spencer W. Kimball:

> Yet today we worship the gods of wood and stone and metal. Not always are they in the form of a golden calf, but equally real as objects of protection and worship. They are houses, lands, bank accounts, leisure. They are boats, cars, and luxuries. They are bombs and ships and armaments. We bow down to the god of mammon, the god of luxuries, the god of dissipation. (CR, Oct. 1961, p. 33.)

**20:4**   The commandment prohibiting the making of graven images should not be interpreted to mean a person could not make statues, figures, images, motifs, and so on, if these objects were not for the purpose of worship. In fact, the Lord later gives instructions concerning the construction of certain symbolic forms which were to be placed in the Ark of the Covenant (Ex. 25:18-22), embroidered upon the "holy garments" of Aaron (Ex. 26:33-34), used to adorn the tabernacle (Ex. 26:1), or placed in the temple (2 Chr. 3:10-13).

The commandment to worship the Lord was given to Adam and Eve soon after they were cast out of the Garden of Eden (Moses 5:1) and is repeated here as part of the Ten Commandments. Joseph Fielding Smith has explained the almost universal breaking of this commandment:

Idolatry goes back to the earliest period of human history. We know that the inhabitants of the earth were destroyed in the flood for their iniquity. When the Lord made a new start, the teachings of Noah and his sons were soon forgotten by the vast majority of mankind. The worship of idols was soon introduced and became so prevalent that the Lord called Abraham and made covenants with him and his children after him, and Israel became a chosen people. The Lord endeavored to keep them clean and righteous, and therefore cleansed the land of its iniquity including idolatry to make room for Israel. However, not all of the nations with this iniquitous practice were eliminated from the promised land, and they became a plague and a temptation to Israel. . . .

In this wonderful age, which we call an age of remarkable enlightenment, idolatry prevails; not only among those we are in the habit of calling heathens, but in every civilized country on the globe. (AGQ 3:121.)

**20:5**    The Hebrew word translated here as "jealous" could also be translated "zealous." The basic meaning of the Hebrew root is "possessing sensitive and deep feelings." (See also commentary for Ex. 34:14.)

**20:7**    Several ways in which people violate the commandment "Thou shalt not take the name of the Lord thy God in vain" are explained in these statements by President Spencer W. Kimball:

Paul called it filthy communication. In this category of sin could also be foolish talking, profanity, taking the name of the Lord in vain, lewd talking. . . .

As regards profanity or taking the name of the Lord in vain, the names of Deity should be used only in prayer or in dignified address or speech, and certainly never in needless or careless utterance. To use the usual swear words is bad enough—they brand one as crude and careless—but to use profanely any of the names of our Lord is absolutely inexcusable. Should one ever slip in this way he should repent in "sackcloth and ashes," the same as if he had committed any one of the other serious sins. Closely linked to this cursing is being ungodly, irreverent, profane, idolatrous or blasphemous, denying the Holy Ghost, "speaking evil of dignities."

In the category of taking the name of the Lord in vain, we might include the use by unauthorized persons of the name of Deity in performing ordinances. In modern scripture the Lord warned:

"Wherefore, let all men beware how they take my name in their lips—

"For behold, verily I say, that many there be who are under this condemnation, who use the name of the Lord, and use it in vain, having not authority." (D&C 63:61-62.)

Presumptuous and blasphemous are they who purport to baptize, bless, marry, or perform other sacraments in the name of the Lord while in fact lacking his specific authorization. And no one can obtain God's authority from reading the Bible or from just a desire to serve the Lord, no matter how pure his motives. (MF, pp. 54-55.)

When we go to places of entertainment and mingle among people, we are shocked at the blasphemy that seems to be acceptable among them. . . . Except in prayers and proper sermons, we must not use the name of the Lord. Blasphemy used to be a crime punishable by heavy fines. Profanity is the effort of a feeble brain to express itself forcibly. (CR, Oct. 1974, p. 7.)

**20:8-11**    President Spencer W. Kimball has given important advice on the commandment to "remember the sabbath day, to keep it holy":

Remember the Lord said: "Six days shalt thou labor and do all thy work: but the seventh day is the Sabbath of the Lord thy God; in it thou shalt not do any work." You note here the command is two-fold; it is definite that you *shall* labor the six days—no place here for the idler or for loitering on the job or for absenteeism. And equally strong is the command that on the Sabbath "thou shalt not do any work." Even in modern times the command has come again through a modern prophet:

"And on this day thou shalt do none other thing, only let thy food be prepared with singleness of heart." (D&C 59:13.)

It is not enough to refrain from doing the things which would keep the day from being kept holy, but there are some very definite things that we should do to honor the Sabbath. We are required to go to the house of prayer, we are to offer up our sacraments unto the Most High; we are to fast and pray at the proper times; and we are to stand in holy places; we are to rest and to worship.

By resting is not meant the indolent lounging about the home all day or puttering around in the garden, but a consistent attendance at meetings for the worship of the Lord, drinking at the fountain of knowledge and instruction, enjoying the family and finding uplift in music and song. One good but mistaken man I knew claimed that he could get much more out of a good book on Sunday than he could get in attending a sacrament meeting, saying that the sermons were hardly up to his standards.

But I say we do not go to Sabbath meetings to be entertained or amused; we go there to worship the Lord. It is an individual responsibility, and regardless of what is said from the pulpit, if one wishes to worship the Lord in spirit and in truth, he may do so by attending his meetings, partaking of the sacrament, and contemplating the beauties of the Gospel. If the sacrament meeting is a failure to you, you are the one that has failed. No one can worship for you, you must do your own serving of the Lord. (CR, Apr. 1944, p. 145.)

**20:13**    The word translated "kill" means "murder" in the Hebrew. George Albert Smith has explained the seriousness of this sin:

Many people in the world do not seem to realize what a terrible crime it is to take human life. When they become angry, for justifiable reasons as they think, they do not hesitate to destroy human life. Sometimes a life is taken in order that money or property may be seized. And yet there is no crime that a human being can commit that will so far alienate him from the blessings of eternal life in the celestial kingdom as murder. No other crime is equal to it. (CR, Oct. 1932, p. 24.)

Joseph F. Smith has taught that only God, the giver of life, can revoke the commandment "Thou shalt not kill."

It is irrevocable unless He revokes it; you and I can't revoke it; we must not transgress it; it is binding upon us. We should not take away the life we cannot restore or give back. It is an eternal, unchangeable law. (CR, Oct. 1912, p. 10.)

**20:14**　The sin of adultery is one of the most serious on God's list of sins.

This doesn't take much explanation. . . .

All of our children learn from their childhood that they should not commit adultery, which means every kind of adulterous relation. It includes sexual contacts with people who are not husband and wife. . . .

This covers the entire field of sex problems. We train our youth that they should never give their lives to others. They should keep their lives clean and free from immorality until they come to the marriage altar. When they go to the temple, they should be able to greet their new companion, their new spouse, in cleanliness and worthiness.

We teach our married people that the husband and the wife must continue to keep unspotted and free from every kind of immorality and unfaithfulness. The married spouse promises to keep free from unfaithfulness and to keep himself or herself for that spouse and no one else. Men and women are subject to Church courts and to severe penalties of excommunication and to disfellowshipment if they break this important law. Parents are to teach their children that there must be no intimacy in courtship and no unfaithfulness in marriage. . . .

. . . Sexual sins are, next to murder, the most serious of the sins. Sexual immorality is one of the most destructive acts of life for the individual, the family, or the nation. (Spencer W. Kimball, Sao Paulo Area Conference Report, Feb. 1975, p. 4.)

**20:15**　Spencer W. Kimball has repeatedly warned this generation of the evils of stealing. Following are two of his statements:

We are appalled at the reported dishonesty in many communities in our land; that the loss through shoplifting and allied dishonest tricks runs into billions of dollars in this country alone.

The Lord told Adam's posterity and carved it into the stone plates,

"Thou shalt not steal." (Exod. 20:15.) All parents should train their children against this deadly thing which can destroy their characters. Honesty is socially and culturally right. Liars and cheaters are both dishonest and alien to our culture. Dishonesty of all kinds is most reprehensible. "Thou shalt not steal."

We call upon all the . . . members of this church to be honest, full of integrity, pay for what they get, and take only that which they have properly paid for. We must teach our children honor and integrity. (CR, Apr. 1975, p. 6.)

Can anyone truthfully claim that he did not know stealing was wrong? Possessiveness seems to be a basic impulse in humans, but while a child may want other children's toys, he soon comes to know that they are not his. Small thefts grow into larger ones unless the desire is curbed. Parents who "cover up" for their children, excuse them and pay for their misappropriations, miss an important opportunity to teach a lesson and thereby do untold damage to their offspring. If the child is required to return the coin or the pencil or the fruit with an appropriate apology, it is likely that his tendencies to steal will be curbed. But if he is lionized and made a little hero, if his misappropriation is made a joke, he is likely to continue in ever-increasing thefts. Most burglars and hold-up men would not have become so if they had been disciplined early. . . .

This urge to take another's property is exhibited in many forms—theft, bribery, driving hard bargains, evasion of income taxes, extortion, covetousness, greedy court actions, misrepresentations which seek to take something for nothing, and so on. Anyone who practices any such form of dishonesty needs to repent, develop a clear conscience, and be free from fetters, chains, worries, and fears. (MF, pp. 50-51.)

**20:16**    Spencer W. Kimball has listed many warnings in regard to the commandment "Thou shalt not bear false witness against thy neighbor."

The sin of false witness is committed in many ways. Guilty ones are gossipers and bearers of tales, whisperers, those destitute of truth, liars, quarrelers, deceitful persons. Sometimes these weaknesses are thought of as minor, yet they break hearts, destroy reputations and wreck lives. To such offenders, Paul said: [Quoted Eph. 4:31-32.] . . .

Of course, no one sees himself in this category. It is always the other person who gossips, invents tales, slanders, and is double-tongued. But are not we all guilty to some degree and do not all of us need introspection, self-analysis and then repentance? . . .

With the false witness can be classed the flatterer, the insincere, the liar, the gossip. Of such Isaiah wrote: "Wo unto them that call evil good, and good evil, that put darkness for light, and light for darkness, that put bitter for sweet, and sweet for bitter!" (2 Ne. 15:20.) Such things the Lord hates. [Quoted Prov. 6:16-19.] . . .

Lies and gossip which harm reputations are scattered about by the four winds like the seeds of a ripe dandelion held aloft by a child. Neither the seeds nor the gossip can ever be gathered in. The degree and extent of the harm done by the gossip is inestimable. (MF, pp. 52-54.)

**20:17** The first part of the commandment "Thou shalt not covet" is closely associated with the commandment "Thou shalt not commit adultery" as explained by Spencer W. Kimball:

There are those who look with longing eyes, who want and desire and crave these [adulterous] romantic associations. To so desire to possess, to inordinately want and yearn for such, is to *covet*, and the Lord in powerful terms condemns it: "And again I command thee that thou shalt not covet thy neighbor's wife; nor seek thy neighbor's life." (D&C 19:25.)

How powerful!

The seventh and tenth commandments are interwoven into one great command that is awesome in its warning.

To covet that which belongs to another is sin, and that sin begins when hearts begin to entertain a romantic interest in anyone else.

There are many tragedies affecting spouses, children, and loved ones. Even though these "affairs" begin near-innocently, like an octopus the tentacles move gradually to strangle. (FPM, pp. 144-45.)

**20:23** The word "with" should read "unto," according to the Joseph Smith Translation.

**21:2** See the commentary for Deuteronomy 15:1-6 and Part I 35.

**21:20-21** These verses should read as follows, according to the Joseph Smith Translation:

"And if a man smite his servant, or his maid, with a rod, and he die under his hand; he shall surely be put to death.

"Notwithstanding, if he continue a day or two, and recover, he shall not be put to death, for he is his servant."

**22:26** The term "by that the sun goeth down" can be translated "by sundown."

**23:11** See the commentary for Deuteronomy 15:1-6 and Part I 35.

**23:16** The Feast of Pentecost was kept fifty days after the Feast of the Passover. (Lev. 23:16.) This feast is known by several other titles: "the feast of harvest, the firstfruits of thy labours" (Ex. 23:16) and "the feast of weeks" (Deut. 16:10). For further information on this feast, see "Feasts" in the Bible Dictionary (pp. 672-74) and Part I 42.

**23:19** The commandment "Thou shalt not seethe a kid in his mother's milk" warns the Israelites not to participate in the practice of fertility cults of boiling (seething) baby goats (kids) in the cholesterol milk of the mother goat. This practice had evidently been adopted by fertility cultists in the false belief such food would make them more desirous of sensual pleasures.

Throughout the ages, the religious leaders of orthodox Judaism have interpreted this commandment to mean that meat products and dairy products are not to be eaten together. Among orthodox Jews even today the belief is so strong that often different plates, eating utensils, and table coverings are used for meat products than for dairy products, and different pans are used for their cleansing. Sometimes different refrigerators (and in the case of some public eating places, different kitchens!) are required.

In modern Israel, a public eating place must abide by the restrictions associated with the separation of meat products and dairy products in order to be classified as "kosher" ("proper," from *kashrut*) to the Jews.

See Part I 19-23.

**23:24**     The word translated as "quite" means "surely," so the phrase could read "surely break down" their images.

**23:27**     The word "fear" could have been translated as "terror."

**24:1, 9-11**     John Taylor taught that Aaron and the seventy elders of Israel who saw God on this occasion must have held the Melchizedek Priesthood:

By what power did Aaron see God? May we not suppose it was by the power of the Melchizedek Priesthood? . . . It, the Melchizedek, holds the keys of the mysteries of the Kingdom, even the key of the knowledge of God. [D&C 84.] Moses had these keys; but Aaron also saw God, as well as the seventy Elders of Israel, and the people saw his glory and heard his voice. [Ex. 20:22; Deut. 4:36.]

It would seem that Aaron and the seventy Elders of Israel then had the Melchizedek Priesthood, and the Aaronic was about being combined with it, as we have them now. Moses held the keys of the Melchizedek Priesthood, and presided over the whole. Aaron was then in possession of the Melchizedek Priesthood; but another or lesser Priesthood was about to be conferred upon him, which was done soon after. (IP, p. 5.)

The seventy elders of Israel who were given the high honor of seeing God on this occasion (together with Moses, Aaron, Nadab, and Abihu) were evidently in their physical bodies during the manifestation, for the record declares "they saw God, and did eat and drink." (Ex. 24:11.) Other mortal men have seen God while in their physical bodies—e.g., Stephen (Acts 7:55-56) and the brother of Jared (Ether 3:20). Others have beheld Him while they were in the spirit—e.g., John the Revelator (Rev. 1:10) and Joseph Smith and Sidney Rigdon (D&C 76:11). Those mortals who have been privileged to see God while in their bodies must also have been quickened by the Spirit, because the Lord has declared "No man has seen God at any time in the flesh, except quickened by the Spirit of God." (D&C 67:11.)

**25:5** Most scholars feel the shittim tree was a species of acacia. This tree grows to a diameter of three to four feet, and its wood is close-grained, very hard, and orange-brown in color, making it ideal for cabinet work.

**25:31-37** The candlestick or lampstand described here forms the basis of the menorah (seven-branched candelabrum) that became so prominent in Jewish art. See Part I 39.

**27:20** Pure olive oil has been recommended by God for several ordinances and holy purposes. The oil from the olive does not become rancid as do oils derived from animal fat; thus olive oil can be preserved for many years, even in hot climates.

Joseph Fielding Smith has extolled some of the virtues of olive oil:

The olive tree and its golden oil were among the greatest treasures of Israel. . . .

No other kind of oil will do in anointing. It is very apparent that the oil from animal flesh would never do, and there is no other kind of oil that is held so sacredly and is more suited to the anointing than the oil of olive; moreover, the Lord has placed his stamp of approval on it. (AGQ 1:152-53.)

**28:1, 40-43** The purpose of the selection of Aaron and his sons to function in a special relationship to the other tribes of Israel has been explained by Joseph Fielding Smith:

After the children of Israel came out of Egypt and while they were sojourning in the wilderness, Moses received a commandment from the Lord to take Aaron and his sons and ordain them and consecrate them as priests for the people. (Ex. 28.) At that time the males of the entire tribe of Levi were chosen to be the priests instead of the first-born of all the tribes, and Aaron and his sons were given the presidency over the Priesthood thus conferred. Since that time it has been known as the Priesthood of Aaron, including the Levitical Priesthood. The males of the tribe of Levi from one month upwards at the time they were called, numbered 22,000 souls, and they were to be invested with authority from that time forth in Israel. It should be remembered that the Melchizedek Priesthood was withdrawn from the people when Moses was taken away, so that the Aaronic Priesthood remained with the carnal law, or the law of Moses, until the coming of Jesus Christ. In the calling of Aaron and his sons, the Lord made it known that this presiding authority over this Priesthood should be handed down from father to son. This was true also of the Levitical, which is a division of the Aaronic. All who were of the tribe of Levi were entitled to be priests and to officiate in some capacity in this authority. (CHMR 1:63.)

**28:30**    The Urim and Thummim mentioned here are not the same stones which were used by the Prophet Joseph Smith in translating the Book of Mormon. The Lord revealed to Joseph Smith that the Urim and Thummim delivered to him were "given to the brother of Jared upon the mount, when he talked with the Lord face to face." (D&C 17:1; see also Ether 3:23, 28.)

Concerning the Urim and Thummim, Joseph Fielding Smith has written:

> The history concerning the Urim and Thummim, or "Interpreters" as they are called in the Book of Mormon, is not very clear. Abraham had the Urim and Thummim by which he received revelations of the heavenly bodies, as he has recorded in the Book of Abraham. [Abraham 3:1-4.] What became of these after his death we do not know. Aaron also had the Urim and Thummim, and these were, evidently from the reading of the Bible, handed down among the priests of Aaron from generation to generation. [Exodus 28:30; Leviticus 8:8; Numbers 27:21; Deuteronomy 33:8; 1 Samuel 28:6; Ezra 2:63; Nehemiah 7:65.] The Lord gave to the brother of Jared the Urim and Thummim which he brought with him to this continent. These were separate and distinct from the Urim and Thummim had by Abraham and in Israel in the days of Aaron. (AGQ 1:159.)

**30:13**    The value of a shekel varied during different periods of history. By the end of the second century B.C.E. it was the equivalent in weight of 218 grains (15.126 grams).

**32:12, 14**    The Joseph Smith Translation makes it clear that the people, not the Lord, are in need of repentance. (See Gen. 32:14, Bible Appendix, p. 800.)

**32:21-24**    When Moses retold this account later, he mentioned that he had to pray to the Lord to spare Aaron's life on this occasion. (See Deut. 9:20.)

**32:25**    The Hebrew word translated as "naked" can mean "bare," "uncovered" but also means "unruly," "broken loose." It is obvious the Israelites became unruly and riotous under Aaron's brief leadership, and if they also unclothed or bared themselves this would only add to their shame.

**32:35** The Joseph Smith Translation reads: "And the Lord plagued the people, because they worshipped the calf, which Aaron made."

**33:14** Joseph F. Smith has provided the following explanation of the meaning of "God's rest":

The ancient prophets speak of "entering into God's rest"; what does it mean? To my mind, it means entering into the knowledge and love of God, having faith in his purpose and in his plan, to such an extent that we know we are right, and that we are not hunting for something else, we are not disturbed by every wind of doctrine, or by the cunning and craftiness of men who lie in wait to deceive. We know of the doctrine that it is of God, and we do not ask any questions of anybody about it; they are welcome to their opinions, to their ideas and to their vagaries. The man who has reached that degree of faith in God that all doubt and fear have been cast from him, he has entered into "God's rest," and he need not fear the vagaries of men, nor their cunning and craftiness, by which they seek to deceive and mislead him from the truth. I pray that we may all enter into God's rest—rest from doubt, from fear, from apprehension of danger, rest from the religious turmoil of the world; from the cry that is going forth, here and there—lo, here is Christ; lo, there is Christ; lo, he is in the desert, come ye out to meet him. The man who has found God's rest will not be disturbed by these vagaries of men, for the Lord has told him, and does tell us: Go not out to seek them: Go not out to hunt them; for when Christ shall come, he will come with the army of heaven with him in the clouds of glory, and all eyes shall see him. We do not need to be hunting for Christ here or Christ there, or prophets here and prophets there. (GD, p. 58.)

**33:15** John Taylor has applied a meaning to the words of Moses: "If thy presence go not with me, carry us not up hence."

We can only obtain correct knowledge in relation to any of these things from the Almighty. We cannot know how to govern ourselves only by a portion of the wisdom that dwells in the bosom of God; if we do not possess that wisdom we may dispair of ever accomplishing any thing in relation to building up his kingdom. I feel as Moses did when the Lord said "for I will not go up in the midst of thee, for thou art a stiff necked people, lest I consume thee in the way." "And he (Moses) said unto him, if thy presence go not with me, carry us not up hence." So say I, if the Lord does not dictate us we can do nothing of ourselves, we cannot accomplish the purposes of God or build up his kingdom on the earth. (JD 10:280.)

**33:20** The Joseph Smith Translation explains that "no sinful man" can see the face of God and live, but the experience of Moses in these chapters makes it clear that righteous men can see and have seen God. (See Ex. 33:20, Bible Appendix, p. 800.)

Joseph Fielding Smith has provided the following explanation of possible errors in the Bible:

> You quote from Exodus 33:20, "And he said, thou canst not see my face: for there shall no man see me, and live." Yet in the same chapter, Verse 11, it reads thus: "And the Lord spake unto Moses face to face, as a man speaketh unto his friend."
>
> It is to be hoped that you are aware that the Bible has come down to us through many translations and that it has been copied many times; moreover that there is *no* original manuscript of any of the books of the Bible. The scribes in the beginning and through the years had to write every word by hand. Moreover, the original manuscripts were not written as we write today with separate words but in *uncials*, that is to say, the words ran together in this fashion sothatitbecameverydifficultto discover the correct meaning, and errors crept in.
>
> No Bible student today believes that the Bible has come down to us in its perfect and original appearance in the manuscripts. Scribes left out words and phrases, just as we do at times in typing, missing one whole line and thus changing the meaning. Moreover, the scribes added or interpreted according to their own opinions at times. These things are quite generally understood. Therefore we find errors and contradictions in the Bible. (AGQ 2:161-62.)

**33:22-23**    Moses did not see the face of God on this occasion, but he saw God's face at other times as indicated in the Joseph Smith Translation (Ex. 33:23) and Moses 1:2. Concerning the experiences of Moses with the Lord, Ellis Rasmussen has written:

> Encouraged, and having already spoken face-to-face with the Lord "as a man speaketh with his friend," (verse 11), Moses requested the supreme privilege, saying to the Lord: "Show me thy glory!" It was denied him, with a brief reminder, "No man shall see me and live." Moses should not have made such a request, as he had once before received the plain explanation: "No man can behold all my works, except he behold all my glory; and no man can behold all my glory, and afterwards remain in the flesh on the earth." He had, on that occasion, observed that "now mine own eyes have beheld God; but not my natural, but my spiritual eyes, for my natural eyes could not have beheld; for I should have withered and died in his presence; but his glory was upon me; and I beheld his face, for I was transfigured before him." (Moses 1:5, 11.) This, then, was the reason no *man* has seen God: *Man,* meaning mortal, normal, natural man, must be "transfigured" or otherwise specially prepared through the Priesthood of God to be able to behold Him in His glory. (See D&C 84:19-24.) However, a certain privilege was accorded Moses at the time here under consideration (Exodus 33:21-

23), and in "the natural man" he was allowed to see the Lord's departure. (IOT 1:94.)

**34:1-2** Unfortunately these two verses in the King James Version do not provide a full account of the second "tables of stone" provided to Moses by the Lord. The Joseph Smith Translation provides the additional important information:

1. The law as written on the second tablet of stone was not the same as that on the first tablets.

2. The Melchizedek Priesthood was taken away from out of the midst of the Israelites.

3. The law of carnal commandments was written on the second tablets.

(See Ex. 34:1-2, Bible Appendix, p. 800.)

Joseph Fielding Smith has explained some of the results of these changes in the laws to the children of Israel:

> If Israel had remained faithful, they would have had all the blessings and privileges of the Melchizedek Priesthood, but instead they were confined to the scope of the blessings of the Aaronic Priesthood and also became subject to the measures of the Law of Moses, which contained many temporal laws, some of which were severe and drastic in their nature. [Mosiah 13:27-31.] This condition continued until the resurrection of Jesus Christ, when this carnal law was fulfilled and was replaced by the fulness of the gospel. [Gal. 3:19-24; 3 Ne. 9:15-22; 12:18; 15:1-10.] The Aaronic Priesthood did not lose the right to the ministering of angels in the days of restoration when Jesus Christ came to fulfil the law, and this power continues in the Church today, which is fully attested in the words of John. (DS 3:84.)

**34:4** The statement that "he [Moses, according to the Joseph Smith Translation] hewed two tables of stone like unto the first" should not be interpreted to mean the written message on the second tablets was identical to that recorded on the stones which Moses broke. Evidently the second tables of stone were "like unto the first" in the sense they were both hewed out of stone and the writing of the Lord appeared on both.

The Joseph Smith Translation makes it clear that the contents of the second tablets differed greatly from the contents of the first. (See Ex. 34:1-2, Bible Appendix, p. 800.)

**34:7** Something has been left out at the end of this verse and the italicized word "generation" has been added in an attempt to complete the thought. When the statement was first given by the Lord in Exodus 20:5, the concluding portion read "generation of them that hate me."

Joseph F. Smith has explained the justice of this law as stated in its complete form:

Infidels will say to you: "How unjust, how unmerciful, how un-Godlike it is to visit the iniquities of the parents upon the children to the third and fourth generations of them that hate God." How do you see it? This way; and it is strictly in accordance with God's law. The infidel will impart infidelity to his children if he can. The whoremonger will not raise a pure, righteous posterity. He will impart seeds of disease and misery, if not of death and destruction, upon his offspring, which will continue upon his children and descend to his children's children to the third and fourth generation. It is perfectly natural that the children should inherit from their fathers, and if they sow the seeds of corruption, crime and loathsome disease, their children will reap the fruits thereof. Not in accordance with God's wishes for His wish is that men will not sin and therefore will not transmit the consequences of their sin to their children, but that they will keep His commandments, and be free from sin and from entailing the effects of sin upon their offspring; but inasmuch as men will not hearken unto the Lord, but will become a law unto themselves, and will commit sin they will justly reap the consequences of their own iniquity, and will naturally impart its fruits to their children to the third and fourth generation. The laws of nature are the laws of God, who is just; it is not God that inflicts these penalties, they are the effects of disobedience to His law. The results of men's own acts follow them. (CR, Oct. 1912, p. 9.)

**34:14**    The first word translated "Jealous" in this verse should really be "Jehovah" according to the Joseph Smith Translation. The second word translated "jealous" here is from a Hebrew word (*qanah*) with a Semitic root meaning "to become very red" through an emotional response. As indicated in the commentary for Exodus 20:5, the word could have been translated "zealous." The basic idea is that God is not casual or nonchalant about us and our response to his teachings; as a loving and concerned parent, he is quickly and deeply responsive to our actions and attitudes.

**34:21**    See Part I 32.

**34:26**    See the commentary for Exodus 23:19 and Part I 23.

**34:28**    The fact that Moses did not drink water nor eat during his forty days and nights on the mount has prompted some to ask whether or not abstaining from water is part of a proper fast. The following statement provides thoughts on this matter:

The question has been asked as to whether or not it is expected that a person, when fasting, shall abstain from drinking water. In answer thereto, the following statement is made with the approval of the First Presidency:

When fasting, members of the Church are advised to abstain from two meals each Fast Day and to contribute as a donation the amount saved thereby for the support of the worthy poor; also by prayer in connection with fasting to develop spiritual power. No direct instruction is given in the Doctrine and Covenants regarding abstaining from water while fasting. In the Bible there are three references in connection with fasting and abstaining from water. These are: Exodus 34:28 and Deuteronomy 9:9-18, where it states that Moses "did neither eat bread nor drink water"; and Esther 4:16, where Esther asked the Jews to fast for her and to "neither eat nor drink."

The spirit of fasting is the main thing to encourage. Too much stress should not be laid on technical details, but the self denial of food, striving for spiritual strength and donating for the benefit of the poor should constantly be in mind." (Heber J. Grant, Anthony W. Ivins, MFP 5: 307-8.)

**34:29-30** The consonants in the Hebrew word for *shone (KRN)* are the same as those for *horned*. When Jerome translated the Vulgate (a translation from the Hebrew into the Latin), he carried across from the Hebrew the verb *qaran* the idea that the face of Moses was horned when he came off the mount. Thus Michelangelo included horns on this famous statue of Moses.

Other scriptural accounts indicate that spokesmen for God can indeed radiate light. Acts 2:3 indicates that "cloven tongues like as of fire . . . sat upon each of them [the apostles]." Mosiah 13:5 states that when the prophet Abinadi testified before king Noah "the Spirit of the Lord was upon him; and his face shone with exceeding luster, even as Moses' did while in the mount of Sinai, while speaking with the Lord." In this instance the Book of Mormon once again proves to be an inspired commentary and witness for the Bible.

**34:35** The final word, "him," should read "the Lord" according to the Joseph Smith Translation.

**35:2** See Part I 32.

**35:3** See Part I 33.

**35:5** Inasmuch as there are other types of offerings unto the Lord, including the offering of animal sacrifices on altars, the word translated "offering" here might also be read as "contribution."

**35:25** Brigham Young applied the teachings of this verse to the people of his day:

If, instead of our wives and daughters passing their hours in idleness, folding their hands, and rocking themselves in their easy chairs, they would spin a little wool, and a little cotton from our Dixie, or that grown in their own gardens and fields, and make some good warm clothing for the men and boys, and some linsey frocks for the women and girls, they could with propriety be called wise women in Israel. (JD 9:190.)

**38:21**    The term "service of the Levites" refers to some of the functions of the descendants of Levi under the direction of the descendants of Aaron. John Taylor has provided the following explanation of some of these functions:

There were in the days of Moses a tribe of the children of Israel set apart to officiate in some of the lesser duties of the Aaronic priesthood, and their office was called the Levitical priesthood.

Aaron and his sons held the Aaronic priesthood, and the Levites were given unto them to minister unto them to keep his charge, the charge of the congregation, to do the service of the tabernacle, keep the instruments of the tabernacle, and the charge of the children of Israel. . . . They seemed to have been an appendage to the Aaronic priesthood to assist in the service of the tabernacle and other duties. Aaron and his male descendants were selected for the priesthood, the other Levites as assistants, or an appendage.

From the above it would seem—

First.—That the Levites were selected in the place of the firstborn whom the Lord called his own.

Second.—That they were given to Aaron to assist him in the minor or lesser duties of the priesthood; but that Aaron and his sons officiated in the leading offices of the priesthood, and not the Levites.

Third.—That there was a tithing paid to them by the whole house of Israel for their sustenance.

Fourth.—That they paid a tithe of this to Aaron.

Fifth.—That on assuming the higher duties of the priesthood of Aaron, the judgments of God overtook them.

Sixth.—That their priesthood was only an appendage to the Aaronic priesthood, and not that priesthood itself as held by Aaron and his sons. (GK, p. 158.)

**40:34-38**    The glory of the Lord so filled the tabernacle in ancient Israel that even Moses was not able to enter into the tent of the congregation.

The glory of the Lord also filled the first house of the Lord (Kirtland Temple) built in this dispensation, as recorded by Joseph Smith:

Brother George A. Smith arose and began to prophesy, when a noise was heard like the sound of a rushing mighty wind, which filled the Temple, and all the congregation simultaneously arose, being moved upon by an invisible power; many began to speak in tongues and prophesy;

others saw glorious visions; and I beheld the Temple was filled with angels, which fact I declared to the congregation. The people of the neighborhood came running together (hearing an unusual sound within, and seeing a bright light like a pillar of fire resting upon the Temple), and were astonished at what was taking place. This continued until the meeting closed at eleven p.m. (HC 2:428.)

# LEVITICUS

See "Leviticus" in the Bible Dictionary, page 724.

**2:1**   The term "meat offering" in the King James Version would be more understandable today if translated "meal offering." The Hebrew word used is *minhah,* meaning "a gift."

**2:2-3**   Joseph Smith has commented on these verses:

It is a very prevalent opinion that the sacrifices which were offered were entirely consumed. This was not the case; . . . you will observe that the priests took a part as a memorial and offered it up before the Lord, while the remainder was kept for the maintenance of the priests; so that the offerings and sacrifices are not all consumed upon the altar—but the blood is sprinkled, and the fat and certain other portions are consumed. (HC 4:211.)

**5:5**   The Lord here counsels that the sinner should confess his sin. Spencer W. Kimball has provided the following suggestions concerning the confession of sin.

The confession of sin is an important element in repentance. Many offenders have seemed to feel that a few prayers to the Lord were sufficient and they have thus justified themselves in hiding their sins. . . . [Quoted Prov. 28:13; D&C 58:43.] . . .

Especially grave errors such as sexual sins shall be confessed to the bishop as well as to the Lord. There are two remissions that one might wish to have; first, the forgiveness from the Lord, and second, the forgiveness of the Lord's church through its leaders. (FPM, pp. 181-82.)

In regard to the confession of lesser sins, Brigham Young has counseled:

If you have committed a sin that no other person on the earth knows of, and which harms no other one, you have done a wrong and sinned against your God, but keep that within your own bosom, and seek to God and confess there, and get pardon for your sin.

If children have sinned against their parents, or husbands against their wives, or wives against their husbands, let them confess their faults one to another and forgive each other, and there let the confession stop; and then let them ask pardon from their God. Confess your sins to whoever you have sinned against, and let it stop there. If you have committed a sin against the community, confess to them. If you have sinned in your family, confess there. Confess your sins, iniquities, and follies, where that confession belongs. (JD 4:79.)

**5:6** The word translated "trespass" in the King James Version usually comes from a Hebrew word meaning "guilt" or another word meaning "unfaithful" or "treacherous." In contrast, the English word *sin* is usually the translation of a Hebrew word meaning "miss the mark or way," "go wrong."

Some Bible translations consistently use the term *guilt offering* in lieu of the King James *trespass offering*.

**8:33** The term "be at an end" means "are fulfilled."

**10:1-11** It is not clear exactly what caused the death of Nadab and Abihu. Some biblical scholars have suggested that the insertion at this point (vs. 8-11) of instructions against strong drink might indicate that intoxication might have been involved.

**10:1** The Lord has consistently counseled against the use of liquor and strong drinks as indicated in the following biblical references: Leviticus 10:9; Numbers 6:3; Judges 13:4, 14; Proverbs 20:1; 23:21; Ecclesiastes 10:17; Isaiah 5:22; 1 Corinthians 6:10; Galatians 5:21; Ephesians 5:18; 1 Timothy 3:3.

In our own time the Lord has said: "Inasmuch as any man drinketh wine or strong drink among you, behold it is not good . . . strong drinks are not for the belly." (D&C 89:5, 7.)

Spencer W. Kimball has made the following observations concerning the drinking of alcoholic beverages:

> Drinking curses all whom it touches—the seller and the buyer and the consumer. It brings deprivation and sorrow to numerous innocent ones. It is associated with graft, immorality, gambling, fraud, gangsterism, and most other vices. In its wake come wasted money, deprived families, deteriorated bodies, reduced minds, numerous accidents. It has everything against it, nothing for it, yet states sell it and receive revenue from it, and it has become an accepted "normal" part of modern life.
>
> Using this tool of Satan is especially a sin to all Latter-day Saints who know the law of the Word of Wisdom. Given as a Word of Wisdom and not by commandment in 1833, it was declared a commandment in 1851 by a prophet of God. It should be considered in that light and, if violated, repented of as with other sins of major seriousness. The poison, bad enough itself, is secondary to the disobedience of the commands of God. (MF, pp. 55-56.)

**10:13** The term "thy due" might have been translated "thy portion."

**10:20** The idea of the Hebrew term translated here as "content" is that "it was good in his eyes."

**11:1-8** See Part I 19. These verses form the basis of the belief of Jewish people that only the flesh of certain animals should be considered "clean" and consumed. Pork products are not consumed by orthodox Jews because the pig does not "chew the cud" although its foot is parted.

**11:8**    See Part I 30. Also, see the commentaries for Leviticus 21:11 and Deuteronomy 21:22-23.

**11:9-10**    See Part I 20. According to Jewish belief and custom, living things from the sea which do not have scales are not to be consumed. Thus, such items as snails, clams, and shrimp would be prohibited.

**11:13-21**    See Part I 22. The blood must be drained from the meat, before the meat can be consumed, according to the beliefs of orthodox Jews today. These verses form the basis of that belief, together with the scriptures which indicate that blood and blood products are not to be consumed. (See also the commentary for Lev. 17:10-16.)

**12-13**    Ellis Rasmussen has provided the following commentary on the use of the word *leprosy* in these chapters:

> These chapters concern a variety of diseases of the skin; any blemishes, mildew, and mould in cloth or clothing; and even the scaling or crumbling of mortar between the stones of a house, all called by the English word "leprosy." The Hebrew word used denotes a "stroke" or "being stricken." We still use some expressions like that for certain ills or misfortunes.
>
> Note that some forms of such "leprosy" could be cleansed and the person who had it in some cases could become "clean" and acceptable in society again. Such ills as psoriasis may well have been involved. Leprosy proper ("Hansen's Disease") certainly was sometimes involved, and for it there was no cure unless by a miracle.
>
> It is possible that these chapters give us a sample of information provided by revelation which would have helped prevent epidemics of disease from which otherwise they would have had no protection. (IOT 1:103.)

**12:1-8**    The requirement of a "sin offering" by a woman upon the birth of her child should not be interpreted that childbearing itself was a sin. The cleansing or purification procedures may have had something to do with the health and general welfare of the mother. Also it is possible the offering contained some symbolism referring back to the fall of man and woman or anticipating the atonement from the fall.

Verse 8 indicates if the parents are too poor to provide a lamb for the offering they could bring two turtledoves (or pigeons) instead. It is interesting to note that when Mary the mother of Jesus Christ came to Jerusalem for her "purification according to the law of Moses" she offered two young pigeons. (Luke 2:22-24.)

**12:3**   This verse should read "And in the eighth day, the man child shall be circumcised," according to the Joseph Smith Translation.

**12:6-8**   Joseph Fielding Smith has referred to the dove as an "emblem of purity" as used in sacrifice:

> The dove as an emblem of purity was offered in sacrifice in ancient Israel, and perhaps before, by which means certain sins were cleansed. Chief among these was the purifying of mothers after the birth of their children. (AGQ 2:78.)

**16:26**   The word *scapegoat* in modern usage means "a person or thing bearing the blame for others." In the Bible the term is usually understood to refer to "a goat upon whose head are symbolically placed the sins of the people after which he is sent into the wilderness." The Hebrew word *azazel* translated as "scape" has to do with demons or the adversary of the Righteous One.

**16:29-34**   The day of atonement (Yom Kippur) is still observed by Jews throughout the world, although animal sacrifice has not been part of the observance since the destruction of the temple in A.D. 70.

The Lord indicated that the day of atonement should be "in the seventh month, on the tenth day of the month" according to the calendar then in use. Changes in the Jewish calendar have placed Yom Kippur near Rosh Hashanah (literally "head of the year") or New Year's Day, which usually occurs in September or October. See Part I 41.

**17:10-16**   The ritual use of blood at the altar was in sprinkling the worshipper after the sacrifice; evidently this symbolism referred to the atonement which should be made in the future, requiring the shedding of blood.

In these verses, the Lord specifically forbade the eating or drinking of blood; this advice is still good today. Many diseases and ailments can be transmitted through eating or drinking blood.

Orthodox Jews are so careful in the observance of prohibitions concerning blood they will only eat the flesh of clean animals killed in such a way that as much blood as possible is withdrawn from the meat.

Some other religious groups, including Jehovah's Witnesses,

interpret the prohibition to include the placing of the blood of one person into the body of another in any manner whatsoever; such groups do not believe in, nor subscribe to, blood transfusions.

"Jehovah's Witnesses see no difference between being fed blood through the mouth or nose or intravenously . . . The Witnesses would risk 'temporary' death rather than accept a blood transfusion and incur God's disapproval." (*Religions of America,* ed. Leo Rosten, p. 101.)

See also Part I 21-22.

**17:11**    Joseph Fielding Smith has explained why it is necessary for blood to be shed in order for a remission of sins to be accomplished:

> Here is a clear statement that the remission of sins cannot come except by the shedding of blood. In ancient times sacrifices were made by the shedding of the blood of clean animals. This shedding of blood was twofold in its application. It pointed forward to the great sacrifice that was to be made by our Redeemer, and it also became a purifying agency which helped to remind Israel of sin and how to overcome them.
>
> Since it was by the creation of blood that mortality came, it is by the sacrifice of blood that the redemption from death was accomplished, and all creatures freed from Satan's grasp. In no other way could the sacrifice for redemption of the world from death be accomplished. Blood being the agent of mortality, it had to be returned to Satan and to death, whence it came. . . .
>
> No doubt Satan felt that he had accomplished his purpose in bringing death, and therefore the entire posterity of Adam would become subject unto him. The Beloved Son of God was chosen before the foundation of the world to redeem mankind. It had to be a redemption by the shedding of blood; also it had to be by a God, who had power over death, one who could lay down his body by the shedding of his blood, and then take his body up again by the inherent power which was in him. Jesus obtained his blood from his mother Mary; he obtained his power over death from his Father. Therefore he could and did voluntarily surrender himself to his enemies who crucified him by the shedding of his blood. When he arose from the tomb, he was free from blood, and his body had become subject to eternal law henceforth and forever. (AGQ 3:102-4.)

**19:1-37**    The terms "I am the Lord" or "I am the Lord your God" appear at least sixteen times in this one chapter. The phrase not only indicates that the teachings come directly from God (rather than fashioned from the philosophies of man) but also places a "seal of approval" on these admonitions.

**19:3**    The Hebrew word *yareh* translated here as "fear" also means "revere." In fact, this same Hebrew word is translated as "reverence" in verse 30 of this chapter. To "fear" mother, father, and God is to revere them or to stand in awe or reverence of them; the word in this context does not mean you should dread them, nor feel great anxiety or apprehension when near them.

**19:16** The counsel not to "go up and down as a talebearer" applies also in this day, as indicated by Joseph F. Smith:

The "Mormon" creed: "Mind your own business," is a good motto for young people to adopt who wish to succeed, and who wish to make the best use of their time and lives. And when I say young people, it includes as well aged and middle aged men and women.

Let it be remembered that nothing is quite so contemptible as idle gossip. . . .

It is so very much better for a person to strive to develop himself by observing all the good points he can find in others, than to strangle the growth of his better self by cherishing a fault-finding, sullen, and intermeddling spirit. The scriptures support this thought. The great Psalmist says in substance in the fifteenth psalm: "He that backbiteth not with his tongue, nor doeth evil to his neighbor, nor taketh up a reproach against his neighbor, shall abide in the tabernacle of the Lord, and never be moved." To abide in the tabernacle of the Lord is to enjoy his Holy Spirit. Now, he that taketh up a reproach against his neighbor is in great danger of losing the Spirit of the Lord. . . .

The meddler, the gossip, the fault-finder . . . soon ruin their own capacity for observing the better side of human nature; and, not finding it in others, search in vain for its influence in their own souls. (GD, pp. 111-13.)

**19:17-18** Many persons wrongfully assume that the commandment "love thy neighbour as thyself" comes only from the New Testament, but here it appears in the Old Testament, and it is also in the writings of many other religious groups. Verse 34 expounds the principle of loving the stranger "as thyself."

The Lord also counsels not to "hate thy brother in thine heart." In other words, do not cherish or harbor hate, even when righteous rebuke is necessary.

**19:26** See the commentary for Leviticus 17:10-16 and Part I 21.

**19:27** See Part I 24, 25. Certain groups within orthodox Judaism today have interpreted this and similar verses to mean that the razor should not touch the face; thus, such believers grow beards. One of the vows of the Nazarite is that "there shall no razor come upon" the head. (See Num. 6:5; Judg. 13:5; 16:17; 1 Sam. 1:11.)

The statement "Ye shall not round the corners of your head" has been interpreted by some Jewish groups to mean that the hair in front of the earlobes should not be cut. Such believers thus grow ringlets or ear locks. Other scriptures used to substantiate this belief are Leviticus 21:5 and Ezekiel 44:20.

**19:34** Latter-day Saints have also been counseled by Joseph F. Smith to treat the stranger "as one born among you":

> I sometimes hear the Latter-day Saints instructed about the way they should treat strangers; they are told to extend to all men due respect and kindness. You would not be a Latter-day Saint if you did not; you would not manifest the Spirit of the Gospel did you not show them due kindness, and respect; but remember, at the same time, that you do not compromise yourselves. In trying to be kind and courteous to others, we sometimes place ourselves in their power, and as sure as we do, bad men will take advantage of it. (JD 11:313.)

**21:1-4** See Part I 30.

**21:5** See Part I 24, 25.

**21:11** The first clause of this verse reads in the Joseph Smith Translation: "Neither shall he go in to *touch* any dead body." (Italics added.) See Part I 30.

**21:13-15** The Lord's instruction that a priest should "take a wife" was later taught by Paul to include elders and bishops. (Titus 1:5-7.) Evidently the Lord has never required celibacy as a prerequisite to receiving the priesthood.

**22:4-7** See commentary for Leviticus 21:11 and Part I 30.

**22:9** The Joseph Smith Translation adds a "not" at a critical point in this verse: "They shall therefore keep mine ordinance, lest they bear sin for it, and die; therefore, if they profane *not* mine ordinances, I the Lord will sanctify them." (Italics added.)

**23:1-44** The major feasts and sacred seasons discussed in this chapter are the Sabbath (v. 6), Passover and Unleavened Bread (vs. 5-14), Feast of Weeks or Pentecost (vs. 15-22), Feast of Trumpets (vs. 23-25), the Day of Atonement or Yom Kippur (vs. 26-32), and Feast of Booths or Tabernacles (vs. 33-43).

For further information on the Jewish feasts, see "Feasts" in the Bible Dictionary, pp. 672-74. Also, see Part I 40-45.

**23:7-8, 21** See Part I 32.

**23:10-14** See Part I 40.

**23:16** See Part I 42.

**23:26-32** The Jewish people observe their Sabbath from sundown Friday to sundown Saturday. Verse 32 forms the basis of that belief. See also Part I 31.

**23:34** See commentary for 1 Kings 8:54-66 and Part I 43.

**25:8-16, 23-55** The word *jubile* (jubilee) appears only twenty-two times in the Bible, and twenty-one of those usages occur in Leviticus chapters 25 and 27. The word is defined or explained in 25:8-11—it is a sabbath of sabbatical years plus one (that is 7 x 7 plus one), or fifty years. See Part I 36.

**25:20-22** See commentary for Deuteronomy 15:1-6 and Part I 35.

**26:3-46** Spencer W. Kimball has offered several observations on these verses:

The Lord uses the weather sometimes to discipline his people for the violation of his laws. He said to the children of Israel: [Quoted Lev. 26:3-6.]

With the great worry and suffering in the East and threats of drouth here in the West and elsewhere, we asked the people to join in a solemn prayer circle for moisture where needed. Quite immediately our prayers were answered, and we were grateful beyond expression. We are still in need and hope that the Lord may see fit to answer our continued prayers in this matter.

From all around the world we have received letters indicating a general response to the suggestion. From Brisbane, Australia, comes this:

"We received your cable inviting the Saints in Brisbane to join you and the world in a day of fasting and prayer. We share your love and concern for all of our Heavenly Father's children. . . ."

Perhaps the day has come when we should take stock of ourselves and see if we are worthy to ask or if we have been breaking the commandments, making ourselves unworthy of receiving the blessings.

The Lord gave strict commandments: "Ye shall keep my sabbaths, and reverence my sanctuary: I am the Lord." (Lev. 19:30.)

Innumerous times we have quoted this, asking our people not to profane the Sabbath; and yet we see numerous cars lined up at merchandise stores on the Sabbath day, and places of amusement crowded, and we wonder.

Numerous times have we quoted: [Ex. 20:8-11.]

But today numerous of the people of this land spend the Sabbath working, devoting the day to the beaches, to entertainment, to shows, to their weekly purchases. The Lord makes definite promises. He says:

"Then I will give you rain in due season, and the land shall yield her increase, and the trees of the field shall yield their fruit." (Lev. 26:4.)

God does what *he* promises, and many of us continue to defile the Sabbath day. He then continues:

"And your threshing shall reach unto the vintage, and the vintage shall reach unto the sowing time: and ye shall eat your bread to the full, and dwell in your land safely." (Lev. 26:5.)

Those promises are dependable. The Lord says further: [Quoted Lev. 26:12-17, 19-20.]

The Lord goes further and says:

"I will . . . destroy your cattle, and make you few in number; and your high ways shall be desolate." (Lev. 26:22.)

Can you think how the highways could be made desolate? When fuel and power are limited, when there is none to use, when men will walk instead of ride?

Have you ever thought, my good folks, that the matter of peace is in the hands of the Lord who says:

"And I will bring a sword upon you . . ." (Lev. 26:25.)

Would that be difficult? Do you read the papers? Are you acquainted with the hatreds in the world? What guarantee have you for permanent peace?

". . . and ye shall be delivered into the hand of the enemy." (Lev. 26:25.)

Are there enemies who could and would afflict us? Have you thought of that?

"And I will make your cities waste," he says, "and bring your sanctuaries unto desolation. . . .

"Then shall the land enjoy her sabbaths, as long as it lieth desolate, and ye be in your enemies' land; even then shall the land rest, and enjoy her sabbaths.

"As long as it lieth desolate it shall rest; because it did not rest [when it could] in your sabbaths, when ye dwelt upon it." (Lev. 26:31, 34-35.)

Those are difficult and very serious situations, but they are possible.

And the Lord concludes:

"These are the statutes and judgments and laws, which the Lord made between him and the children of Israel in Mount Sinai by the hand of Moses." (Lev. 26:46.)

This applies to you and me. (E, May 1977, pp. 4-5.)

**26:3, 6, 13**    The price of peace is righteousness, according to Spencer W. Kimball:

Peace *is* obtainable, but what *is* the price of *peace?* Let the Lord himself answer: [Quoted Lev. 26:3-12.]

In a word, then, the foundation for peace is righteousness.

The efforts of peace conferences, and the prayers of suffering humanity, may bring an armistice of uncertain length, but peace with totality and permanence can come only when men repent and turn to the Lord. (CR, Oct. 1945, pp. 121-22.)

**26:4-46**    Spencer W. Kimball has reviewed the promises of the Lord as revealed in this significant chapter:

Will we ever turn wholly to God? Fear envelops the world which could be at ease and peace. In God is protection, safety, peace. He has said, "I will fight your battles." But his commitment is on condition of our faithfulness. He promised to the children of Israel:

"I will give you rain in due season,"

The land shall yield her increase and trees their fruit.

Granaries and barns will bulge in seed time and harvest.

Ye shall eat your bread in abundance.

Ye shall dwell in your land safely and none shall make you afraid.

Neither shall the sword go through your land.

And five of you shall chase an hundred, and an hundred of you shall put ten thousand to flight: . . . (See Leviticus 26:4-6, 8.)

*But if you fail to serve me:*

The land will be barren, (perhaps radioactive or dry from drought.)

The trees will be without fruit and the fields without verdure.

There will be rationing and a scarcity of food and hunger sore.

No traffic will jam your desolate highways.

Famine will stalk rudely through your doors and the ogre cannibalism will rob you of your children and your remaining virtues.

There will be pestilence uncontrollable.

Your dead bodies will be piled upon the materialistic things you sought so hard to accumulate and save.

I will give no protection against enemies.

They that hate you shall reign over you.

There will be faintness of heart "and the sound of a shaken leaf" shall chase you into flight and you will fall when none pursueth.

Your power—your supremacy—your price in superiority—will be broken.

Your heaven shall be as iron and your earth as brass. Heaven will not hear your pleadings nor earth bring forth her harvest.

Your strength will be spent in vain as you plow and plant and cultivate.

Your cities will be shambles, your churches in ruins.

Your enemies will be astonished at the barrenness, sterility, desolation of the land they had been told was so choice, so beautiful, so fruitful.

Then shall the land enjoy her Sabbaths under compulsion.

And ye shall have no power to stand before your enemies.

And your people will be scattered among the nations as slaves and bondsmen. You will pay tribute and bondage and fetters shall bind you. (See *Ibid.,* 26:14-43.)

What a bleak prediction! Yet "These are the statutes and judgments and laws, which the Lord made between him and the children of Israel in Mt. Sinai by the hand of Moses." (*Ibid.,* 26:46.) The Israelites failed to heed the warning. They ignored the prophets. They suffered the fulfillment of every dire prophecy.

Do we twentieth century people have reason to think that we can be immune from the same tragic consequences when we ignore the same divine laws? (CR, Oct. 1961, pp. 32-33.)

**27:16-25**    See the commentary for Leviticus 25:8-16, 23-55 and Part I 36.

# NUMBERS

See "Numbers" in the Bible Dictionary, page 739.

**1:20-36** The number of men listed here as twenty years old and over total 603,550, excluding the Levites who were exempt from going to war. (This was a military census to determine the number of possible soldiers.) When children and women are added, the total number probably exceeded three million. Some biblical scholars feel this number is much too large and was purposely inflated by later historians. Other scholars claim the figure is possible and likely accurate in view of the numbers who originally went into Egypt (see Gen. 46:26-27 and the commentary) and the length of time spent there.

The descendants of Judah were most numerous, followed closely by the descendants of Joseph, consisting of the combined totals of Manasseh and Ephraim.

**3:5-51** Joseph Fielding Smith has explained some of the functions of the sons of Levi as outlined in this chapter:

It was the duty of the Levites to take care of [the tabernacle] and keep it in order. They took it apart, carried it and all that pertained to it from place to place as they journeyed in the wilderness, and then set it up again when a new camp was made.

These responsibilities . . . were divided among the descendants of the three sons of Levi, son of Jacob. They were Gershon, Kohath, and Merari. The sons of Gershon had charge of [quoted Num. 3:25-26.] . . .

In a general way the duties and responsibilities of the tabernacle, and of the preparations for sacrifices, were assigned to the descendants of the three sons of Levi. Wagons and oxen were provided for the Gershonites and the Merarites, but the sons of Kohath, "Because the service of the sanctuary belonging unto them was that they should bear upon their shoulders" their burdens—they had no wagons. [Num. 7:3-9.] Not only were the Levites appointed to take care of the tabernacle and all that pertained to it, but other similar duties were assigned to them. They could offer sacrifice, although it was Aaron's place and that of his sons to hold the *keys* of this ministry. . . .

According to this assignment and the instructions given to Moses, the priests (i.e. sons of Aaron) and Levites officiated from the day of their appointment to the days of the coming of Jesus Christ. (DS 3:113-14.)

**3:12, 39-51**   The Lord appointed the male descendants of Levi to perform religious services in place of the firstborn sons of the other tribes of Israel. When the actual census of the Levites and the first-born sons was completed, it was noted that there was an excess of 273 firstborn sons (22,273 as compared with 22,000). The Lord provided that these could be redeemed through a payment of 1,365 shekels, which is equivalent to 5 shekels per firstborn son.

**3:40-45**   Joseph Fielding Smith has offered the following commentary on these verses:

When the Lord took Moses and the Higher Priesthood out of Israel, he established the Aaronic Priesthood with Israel. And the Lord took the males of the tribe of Levi to be the priests to minister for the people. And the Lord said to Moses: [Quoted Num. 3:40-41; 44-45.] From that time forth until the coming of our Lord, the Melchizedek Priesthood, which includes the Patriarchal Priesthood, was taken from the tribes of Israel, the one exception being that the prophets received that Priesthood, but always by special ordination. It was not given generally among the tribes as it is today. (CHMR 2:472.)

**4:3, 47**   The principle contained in the counsel of the Lord that a man should be thirty years of age before beginning his ministry has been followed in other dispensations as indicated by Joseph Fielding Smith:

It is true that the Lord revealed to Moses that the priests of Aaron and Levi were to be men thirty years of age. This custom was followed in Israel down to the days of Paul. Therefore, it was in keeping with the law that Paul instructed Timothy that a deacon should have a wife, for a man thirty years of age holding the priesthood should be married. It was in harmony with this law given to Moses, that John the Baptist waited until he was thirty years of age before entering the ministry, and the same is true of the ministry of our Savior. (AGQ 2:10.)

**6:1-21**   A Nazarite (meaning "separate" or "set apart") could be either male or female and could devote all or part of his or her life to the Lord. Samson, Samuel, and John the Baptist were Nazarites, and Paul evidently took some of their vows on occasion. (See Acts 18:18.)

Jesus Christ was not a Naza*rite*. Rather, he was known as a Naza*rene*, which term had reference to his boyhood hometown, Nazareth.

**8:1-5**   See commentary for Exodus 25:31-37 and Part I 39.

**9:6-8**   Moses sets the example for obtaining answers to religious questions: *Ask the Lord.* The Lord provides the answer for his prophet as he has promised he would do for all who ask in faith. (See James 1:5-6.)

**10:29-36**   Hobab, the father-in-law of Moses, accompanied the Israelites to the promised land and, as is evident from later scriptures, they (as Kenites) obtained an inheritance there. (As examples, see Judg. 1:16; 4:11; 1 Sam. 15:6; 2 Kgs. 10:15; 1 Chr. 2:55.)

The Druze people of the Near East claim to be descendants of the father-in-law of Moses and have largely kept themselves separate from the people among whom they live. Some scholars have speculated that the Druze might be descendants of Hobab.

**11:29**   Brigham Young taught that anyone who is worthy and willing to receive the Spirit of God may be filled with the spirit of prophecy and thus might be called a prophet.

I am like Moses when a messenger came to him saying, "The people are prophesying in their tents." Said Moses, Well, what of that? I would to God that the Lord's people were all prophets! I would to God that they all had revelation! When they receive revelation from heaven the story is told, they know for themselves.

Now, my friends, . . . how do you know anything? Can you be deceived by the eye? You can; you have proved this; you all know that there are men who can deceive the sight of the eye, no matter how closely you observe their movements. Can you be deceived in hearing? Yes; you may hear sounds but not understand their import or whence they come. Can you be deceived by the touch of the finger? You can. The nervous system will not detect everything. What will? The revelations of the Lord Jesus Christ, the spirit of truth will detect everything, and enable all who possess it to understand truth from error, light from darkness, the things of God from the things not of God. It is the only thing that will enable us to understand the Gospel of the Son of God, the will of God, and how we can be saved. Follow it, and it will lead to God, the fountain of light, where the gate will be open, and the mind will be enlightened so that we shall see, know and understand things as they are. (JD 13:336.)

**13:16**   The name *Oshea* means "save"; *Jehoshua* (or Joshua) means "Jehovah is salvation." The name *Jesus* is derived from this same Hebrew root.

**15:38-39**   J. R. Dummelow offers the following commentary on the "fringes in the borders of their garments."

The original form of these is uncertain. Judging from later times, they would be, not ornamental festoons running along the edge of the garment, but tassels attached to each of its four corners by a thread of blue. A religious importance was attached to the wearing of these tassels. They were a visible reminder to the Jews of their obligation to keep the commandments of Jehovah (v. 39). . . . The Jews attached an ever-increasing importance to these symbolical ornaments of dress: cp. Matt. 14:36; 9:20; 23:5. The modern survival is the Jewish *tallith,* or prayer-cloth, consisting of a strip of cloth with fringes on its border, which is thrown over the shoulders during the service in the synagogue. (OVBC, p. 108.)

Many orthodox Jewish men today continue to wear fringes in the border of some of their garments to remind them of certain teachings of the Lord. See also Deuteronomy 22:12 and Part I 26.

The proximity of the statement concerning the "fringes in the borders of their garments" and the statement "that ye may look upon it, and remember all the commandments of the Lord, and do them" suggests a connection between the two. Some Rabbis have pointed out that the numerical value of the letters in the Hebrew word for *fringe* (zizith) is exactly 600. The Rabbis have also identified 613 commandments in the Law. Thus the tassel or fringe was made up of eight threads with five knots for a total of 13 additions, bringing the grand total to 613 which equals the total number of commandments. "In this way each tassel represented the 613 commandments, and the wearing of it was said to be of equal merit with the keeping of the whole law. This is a good example of Rabbinical interpretation and of external scrupulosity." (Dummelow, OVBC, p. 109.)

**16:10**    The Joseph Smith Translation makes it clear that Korah (who rightfully held the Aaronic Priesthood as the son of Levi) sought the *high* priesthood (the Melchizedek Priesthood) held by Moses. Perhaps this was part of the basis of the accusation of the "princes of the assembly" against Moses and Aaron—ye lift "up yourselves above the congregation of the Lord" (v. 3).

**16:22**    God is the "God of the spirits of all flesh" in the sense that he is the father of all of us, as explained by John Taylor:

We are told in the sacred record of truth that [God] is the God and Father of the spirits of all flesh—of all flesh that has lived, that now lives or that will live; and it is proper that we should have just conceptions of our relationship to him, to each other, to the world wherein we live, to those who have existed before us, or to those who shall come after us, that as wise, intelligent beings, under the inspiration of the Almighty, we may be able to conduct our steps so that our pathway in life may be such as to secure the approval of a good conscience and of God, angels and good men; and that whilst we live upon the earth we may fulfil in an honorable manner the measure of our creation, and, obeying our Creator, feel that he is indeed what the Scriptures represent him to be . . . "the God and Father of the spirits of all flesh." (JD 14:357.)

**19:1-22** Bible scholars have speculated much concerning the various symbolisms of the sacrifice of the "red heifer." Some have wondered if the Lord did not choose red (color of blood) and heifer (female, connoting fertility) to emphasize life, inasmuch as the offering was associated with those who touched the dead.

**20:2-12** As great as Moses was (and he was one of the greatest prophets of Israel), he still had his weaknesses. One of these was revealed when he failed to circumcise his son. (See Ex. 4:24-26, especially the Joseph Smith Translation, Bible Appendix, p. 800.) Another was at the water of Meribah where he took the honor unto himself and failed to sanctify the Lord "in the eyes of the children of Israel." Because of this act, Moses was not permitted to lead the children of Israel across the Jordan River into the promised land. (See also Deut. 31:2; 32:51-52.)

Concerning this episode, Spencer W. Kimball has observed:

It seems the Lord calls the weak to serve in high places. Moses was such an one. Though trained in royal courts, he still had limitations and was conscious of them. . . .

Even Moses, like many of us, seemed to let his humility cloak wear thin and threadbare. The wanderers had come to the desert of Zin. . . .

But Moses, undoubtedly annoyed to the limit of human endurance, forgot himself and said to them . . . [Quoted Num. 20:10.]

The Lord was displeased with Moses in assuming to perform the miracle. I can imagine the Lord saying something like this: "*Who,* did you say? Who made the water? Who made the rock? Moses! Who brought the water from the rock?" And He did say . . . [Quoted Num. 20:12.]

"Moses, that was a sad day. You did such a great work in moving Israel from Egypt. You were so patient, generally, with their whims and antagonisms. Oh, Moses, why did you let your humility deteriorate?" (BYUSY, Jan. 1963, p. 7.)

Moses, though one of the greatest . . . said to the continually complaining children of Israel crying for the fleshpots of Egypt: "Hear, now, ye rebels; must *we* fetch you water out of this rock?" (Numbers 20:10.) . . . His reprimand came suddenly and forcefully: [Quoted Num. 20:12.]

Moses had integrity in great measure, but when he had presumptuously taken credit for the Lord's miracle, for a single moment he had forgotten. (BYUSY, Feb. 1964, p. 10.)

**20:7-13**    Some Bible commentaries suggest that Moses was guilty of two trespasses in regard to the incident at the water of Meribah:

1. The Lord told Moses to speak to the rock and it would give forth water; however, Moses smote the rock with the rod, a symbol of divine power.

2. Moses and Aaron took credit for the miracle unto themselves ("Must *we* fetch you water out of this rock?" [Italics added.]) rather than giving the credit to the Lord so the Lord could be sanctified "in the eyes of the children of Israel."

John Taylor has expressed a similar thought concerning this incident:

But Moses did not honor the Lord in that instance as he ought to have done. The Lord felt angry with him, and would not allow him to go into the land of Canaan because he did not sanctify the God of Israel. (JD 26:75.)

**20:24**    The expression that "Aaron shall be gathered unto his people" would suggest that a belief in life after death was definitely prevalent among those people at this time.

**21:2-3**    The question of the possible morality of any war is at least partially answered in these verses and the commentary by Joseph Fielding Smith:

Our question is, however, is there ever a time when war, or the taking up of arms is justified?

Yes, there are such times. There have been many instances when the Lord has justified the taking up of arms and has approved his people in their obedience to such action. When it becomes necessary for a righteous people to take arms against their enemies who are the aggressors, in protection of their lives and in defense of their possessions, the Lord has approved. If you will read the scriptures carefully, you will discover that the Lord commanded his chosen people to prepare for war and even to be the aggressors in the accomplishment of his purposes. Here are a few examples: [Num. 21:2-3; 31:1-3; Deut. 7:1-3.]

All through the Old Testament you will find commandments which were given to Israel to go to war. There were good reasons for this which may be discovered by reading these parts of the Bible. (AGQ 3:50-51.)

**21:4-9**    The miracle of healing associated with the "serpent of brass . . . put . . . upon a pole" has intrigued many generations. The symbol of the American Medical Association (serpent entwined around a pole) derived from this incident.

Jesus used the symbolism to refer to his own resurrection (John 3:14-15), and Book of Mormon prophets also likened the incident to the life-giving resurrection of Jesus Christ. (Hel. 8:14-16; 1 Ne. 17:41.) Some archaeologists who believe in the

Book of Mormon have wondered if the titles for God used by early middle-American cultures (such as Quetzalcoatl, 'bird-serpent') might not have originated when Jesus Christ (whose resurrection was symbolized by the serpent raised up by Moses) appeared to them by descending out of heaven like a bird.

Ellis Rasmussen has provided the following commentary concerning the incident:

> Another complaint again about manna brought punishment in the form of venomous serpents. Escape from death was provided through a little "test" of faith and obedience: Moses made a bronze serpent upon a pole and gave instructions that all who would look up at it should be saved. Another Israelite writer says later that because of the "simplicity" of the cure, the obstinate refused to comply and receive salvation. (Helaman 8:14-16; I Nephi 17:41). Jesus used its symbolism as a type or suggestion of his own being lifted upon a pole that they who would look up to Him in faith and obedience might be saved (John 3:14-15).
>
> It is probably more than coincidental that the serpent-motif became symbolic of both the coming of *death* and of *life* in various cultures, including the Mayan and Aztec. In a sense, a pattern of relationships may exist, that as the serpent in Eden was related to the serpent on a pole, even so was the man in Eden related to the Man on a Cross. Moreover, even as the first death brought also the capacity for reproduction of life, so also the other death (Christ's) brought about resurrection and eternal life. (See I Cor. 15:45-47; see also Hickman, Josiah—*Romance of the Book of Mormon*, 1. 245.) (IOT 1:119.)

**22:1-8**   Balaam came from Pethor, which is located far to the north of Canaan where Abraham once dwelt and is the ancestral home area of Rebekah, Leah, and Rachel.

**22:21-35**   God speaks through any means that serve his divine purposes. Thus a voice and words could come from a bush (as in the case of Moses) or from a donkey (as in the case of Balaam). Also, the same God who created the animal world in the first place could surely enable a donkey to see something (in this case an angel) that might not be perceived by man.

**23:19**   Despite the statement "God is not a man . . . neither the son of man, that he should repent," the Old Testament contains many scriptures indicating that God repented of a particular idea or act. (See as examples Gen. 6:6; Ex. 32:14; Judg. 2:18; 1 Sam. 15:35; 2 Sam. 24:16; Jonah 3:10.) Obviously the translators should have chosen a different word in those situations. The Prophet Joseph Smith suggested possible sources for errors in the Bible:

"I believe the Bible as it read when it came from the pen of the original writers. Ignorant translators, careless transcribers,

or designing and corrupt priests have committed many errors."
(HC 6:57.)

**24:17-19**    The wording and verb tense in these verses, both
in the Hebrew and in the English, indicate it will be sometime in
the future when the "Star out of Jacob" and the "Sceptre" that
"shall rise out of Israel" shall smite Moab.

**27:1-11**    Moses set the example of how to obtain an answer
to a serious problem—ask the Lord in faith. In another example
of direct and continuing revelation, the Lord gave his answer.
Recognition of the rights of girls to inherit the property of their
fathers when there are no sons is extraordinary for this early
period.

A later revelation (Num. 36:1-12) suggested that when such
daughters married they should marry sons of the same tribe so
the father's inheritance would remain within the same tribe.

**27:18-23**    The bestowal of authority by the laying on of
hands has been a practice required by the Lord from the very
beginning. (See as examples D&C 107:44; Gen. 48:17; Ex.
29:10; Lev. 16:21; Acts 6:6; Alma 6:1; JS-H 2:68; A of F 5.)
Through the laying on of hands by one who already has
authority, a person can be ordained and/or set apart to a new
office or position or can receive the right to gifts of the Spirit.
Spencer W. Kimball has noted certain steps which were
followed in the calling and setting apart of Joshua:

> In the call to Joshua, these steps were stressed: The need, the call, the
> laying on of hands with the blessing. There was the revelation as to the need
> since Moses could not go over Jordan and realizing it, pleaded that a
> shepherd be given Israel. . . .
>
> And the blessing gave him power and authority. . . .
>
> The setting apart is an established practice in the Church and men and
> women are "set apart" to special responsibility, in ecclesiastical, quorum,
> and auxiliary positions. All missionaries are set apart and it is remarkable
> how many of them speak often of the authority who officiated and of the
> blessings promised and their fulfilment. (CR, Oct. 1958, pp. 56-57.)

**29:1-40**    It is difficult for many non-Jews, who are not
accustomed to celebrating the many feasts and observing the
numerous offerings and laws, to see the purpose of many of
these regulations. Abinadi, a Book of Mormon prophet, has
given a partial answer:

"Therefore there was a law given them [the Jews], yea, a law
of performances and of ordinances, a law which they were to
observe strictly from day to day, to keep them in remembrance
of God and their duty towards him.

"But . . . all these things were types of things to come."
(Mosiah 13:30-31.)

**31:8**    The death of Balaam did not end the evil influence he
had with the people. As indicated in verse 16, some of the
slaughter recorded in this chapter resulted from "the counsel of
Balaam" that the Midianite women should seduce the Israelite
males.

The reputation of Balaam for evil was continued throughout
the centuries and is even mentioned in New Testament times.
(See 2 Pet. 2:15 and Rev. 2:14.)

**35:1-34**    Although the Levites comprise a *blood* tribe of
Israel, they are not generally considered to be a *land* tribe
because they did not receive a separate land inheritance for their
own. Certain cities among the land inheritances of the other
tribes were designated as cities for the Levites, so the Levites
(who were to perform many religious services) lived among the
people of all the other tribes. As indicated in this chapter, some
of these cities of the Levites were also to serve as cities of refuge.

# DEUTERONOMY

See "Deuteronomy" in the Bible Dictionary, page 656.

**1:37**   In this verse Moses places at least part of the blame for his not being able to enter the promised land upon the wickedness of the people. Numbers 20:7-13 indicates Moses and Aaron were not to enter the promised land because they took the honor unto themselves in calling forth water out of the rock at Meribah and failed to sanctify the Lord in the eyes of the children of Israel. Of course, it *was* the chiding and murmuring of the Israelites that provoked Moses and Aaron to exclaim, "Hear now, ye rebels; must *we* fetch you water out of the rock?" (Num. 20:10, italics added. See also Ex. 17:7; Num. 27:14; Deut. 32:51-52; 33:8.)

**2:30**   The Joseph Smith Translation reads:

"But Sihon king of Heshbon would not let us pass by him; for he hardened his spirit, and made his heart obstinate, that the Lord thy God might deliver him into thy hand, as he hath done this day."

**3:8-17**   Two of the tribes (Reuben and Gad) and one-half of another tribe (Manasseh) had received their inheritance on the east side of the river Jordan. These verses review the boundaries of the respective lands.

**3:23-26**   The fervent plea of Moses for the Lord to allow him to enter the promised land is answered with the rebuke not to mention the matter again. The answer was still no.

**4:2**   Some critics of the true Church have claimed the Book of Mormon cannot be scripture from God because the Apostle John wrote in the last chapter of Revelation, "If any man shall add unto these things, God shall add unto him the plagues that are written in this book." (Rev. 22:18.) It is interesting that Moses placed a similar warning in Deuteronomy 4:2.

Brigham Young has written concerning this principle:

"But if a man should, by the gift of the Holy Ghost, in these days prophesy and write it, would it not be adding to what is already written, and is not that strictly forbidden?" This is a very popular query, and I am disposed to notice it a few moments. . . . [Quoted Deut. 4:2; Prov. 29:5-6; Rev. 22:18-19.]

Where is it intimated in these passages that God would cease or had ceased to give revelation to his children? Those passages were written to guard against the mutilation of the revelations already given, which then existed in manuscript form, and very likely there existed not more than one copy when these words were written. It cannot reasonably be supposed for a moment that the Almighty has sealed his own mouth in silence by the Scriptures quoted, yet they are used in that light by modern Christians. (JD 10:323-24.)

If such quotations [Deut. 4:2; Rev. 22:18] are given with the intent to shut the heavens, and put an end to all new revelation, then the revelations given to Prophets who arose after Moses, and the revelations given to Jesus Christ and his Apostles, including John and his revelation on the Isle of Patmos, all amount to nothing, and are not worthy of our notice. This "sweeping argument," when it is examined, sweeps away rather too much; besides, John's Gospel and his epistle to his brethren were written after he wrote his revelation on the Isle of Patmos, consequently he would destroy his own system; but it sets forth the ignorance and short-sightedness of those who have not the testimony of Jesus, which is the spirit of prophecy. (JD 1:242-43.)

**4:12, 15-16**   This review of some of the events at Sinai suggests at least one reason why the Israelites were not permitted to see God on that occasion (only to hear him)—they would not be tempted to make "graven images" of him.

They were privileged to hear his voice so they would remember the experience more vividly and reverence the Lord, and also so they would teach these things to their descendants (v. 10).

**4:28**   LeGrand Richards has offered the following commentary on this verse:

Today, Israel does not worship gods of "wood and stone" who can "neither see, nor hear, nor eat, nor smell," but they have turned, as has the Christian world, to the worship of a spirit god or spirit essence which is said to be everywhere present in the universe, a god that can no more "see, nor hear, nor eat, nor smell," than could the gods of "wood and stone" to which Moses referred.

This is truly a departure from the worship of the true and living God, the God of Abraham, Isaac and Jacob, with whom Moses communed "face to face as a man speaketh unto his friend." [Exodus 33:9-11.] (IDYK, p. 18.)

**4:31**   Joseph Fielding Smith indicated that fulfillment of several promises of the Lord to Abraham is still in the future:

The inheritance given to Abraham and his posterity was to be an everlasting inheritance. It was given to them for a few years while they were on good behavior and then to be rescinded when their behavior was not good.

It is true, they were driven from their inheritances for their rebellion, but the promise the Lord made to Abraham holds good and whenever the prophets warned them of their dispersion through disobedience they also said that in the latter days when they were repentant they would be gathered again. Moses said: [Quoted Deut. 4:31.]

The promise of Israel's inheritance reaches into eternity when the earth is to be cleansed and made fit for the habitation of the righteous, otherwise the promise to Abraham and Israel would have failed, for, as pointed out by the martyr, Stephen, the Lord gave this land of Palestine to Abraham for him and his posterity forever, and yet in his lifetime Abraham received "not so much as to set his foot on: yet he promised that he would give it to him for a possession, and his seed after him, when as yet he had no child." (Acts 7:5.) (RT, pp. 138-39.)

**5:1-21** Moses reviewed the giving of the Ten Commandments so the people of another generation might "learn . . . keep, and do them." His statement that the covenants of the Lord with the fathers apply also to "us, who are . . . alive this day" reiterates the eternal application of these laws.

**5:21** The two different Hebrew verbs translated as "desire" and "covet" in this sentence have the meanings to "take delight in" and to "yearn for," "long for," "desire."

**6:4-5** These words have been quoted by generations of Jews, and are written on small parchments in the mezuzot placed on the "posts" of their houses (v. 9) and in their phylacteries placed on their foreheads and their left arms (v. 8). In the New Testament the Savior identified the words of verse 5 as the first (foremost) and great commandment (Matt. 22:37; Mark 12:30-32), and in a revelation to Joseph Smith He indicated the commandment to love and serve "the only living and true God" had been on the earth since the beginning and is one of the evidences God is "from everlasting to everlasting the same unchangeable God." (D&C 20:17-19.)

See Part I 37-38.

**6:8** See Part I 37.

**6:9** This verse forms the basis of the use of mezzuzahs (Hebrew *mezzuvot*) by the Jews. These perform essentially the same function on doors and gateposts as phylacteries perform on the forehead and the left arm. Small strips of parchment with biblical texts are placed on the right side of the doorway or gateposts of the homes of orthodox Jews. These may be kissed by the person entering the home, or frequently the person will kiss his fingers and then touch the mezzuzah with his fingers.

Some believing Jews simply touch the mezzuzah when entering, without kissing either the fingers or the mezzuzah itself. See Part I 38.

**7:2-5**    Many people are bothered by God's instructions in these verses because they feel the counsel is in violation of the commandment "Thou shalt not kill." (Ex. 20:13.) Joseph Smith explains this apparent contradiction:

That which is wrong under one circumstance, may be, and often is, right under another.

God said, "Thou shalt not kill;" at another time He said "Thou shalt utterly destroy." This is the principle on which the government of heaven is conducted—by revelation adapted to the circumstances in which the children of the kingdom are placed. Whatever God requires is right, no matter what it is, although we may not see the reason thereof till long after the events transpire. . . .

. . . He never will institute an ordinance or give a commandment to His people that is not calculated in its nature to promote that happiness which He has designed, and which will not end in the greatest amount of good and glory to those who become the recipients of his law and ordinances. (HC 5:135.)

**8:5**    The Lord can and does chasten his children in many ways as indicated in these quotations from the prophets of this dispensation:

Because we will not receive chastisement at the hands of the Prophets and Apostles, the Lord chastiseth us with sickness and death. Let not any man publish his own righteousness, for others can see that for him; sooner let him confess his sins, and then he will be forgiven, and he will bring forth more fruit. When a corrupt man is chastised he gets angry and will not endure it. (Joseph Smith, TPJS, pp. 194-95.)

Though our chastisements are often hard to be borne, those who bear them patiently, willingly, and submissively, will find that they yield the Gospel fruits of righteousness insomuch that they will know how to be Saints indeed.

Chastisement often comes upon the Saints of God on account of the wicked, and that also will redound to the benefit of the humble and faithful. If we receive chastisement for our sins, it will teach us to forsake our sins, and become righteous, for we receive chastisement because there is wickedness among us, and it is permitted to come to prevent our turning from the path of duty, and is always designed for our good. (Brigham Young, JD 3:54.)

It matters not what the minds and feelings of men are, the Lord is determined to raise up a people that will worship Him; and if He has to whip, and scourge, and drive us through a whole generation, He will chastise us until we are willing to submit to righteousness and truth, or until we are like clay in the hands of the potter. The chastisements we have had from time to time have been for our good, and are essential to learn wisdom, and carry us through a school of experience we never could have passed through without. (Wilford Woodruff, JD 2:198.)

In cases where the rebellious exercise repentance, that repentance may be sparked in various ways. Some men come to recognize their sins from introspection while others must be brought to their knees by outside forces. Many, having realized their transgressions, begin their repentance in secrecy. Others must be apprehended and chastised and punished before they begin their transformation. Some even need to be disciplined by forced inactivity, disfellowshipping, or even excommunication before they realize their plight and the need to transform their lives. None of us should resent being reminded of our responsibilities and being called to repent of our sins. The Lord may choose to chasten us in this way or some other, but it is all for our own good. (Spencer W. Kimball, MF, p. 44.)

**9:3-5**   See the commentary for Deuteronomy 7:2-5.

**10:1-2**   According to the Joseph Smith Translation, the word "other" should be inserted between the words "two" and "tables" in verse 1. Also, in verse 2 the following clause should be added after the word "breakest": "save the words of the everlasting covenant of the holy priesthood."

**10:12**   The word *fear* in the King James Version as used in the phrase "fear the Lord" is a classic example of a word in the scripture which does not mean the same today as in the original language. Although several different Hebrew words are translated "fear" in the King James Version, the Hebrew word which is often used to denote a relationship to God is *yare*, which has the basic meaning of "reverence" or "awesome respect."

Joseph Fielding Smith has reviewed some of the meanings of the word:

The Lord is merciful and kind and does not require of those who serve him that they be afraid and tremble before him. There is no delight in his heart in the "fear" of the wicked because of their sins. Most scriptural passages which tell us to "fear the Lord" have no reference to fright.

The word "fear" has more than the one meaning which we so universally use. The scriptural meaning is "to have reverential awe."

When the Lord requires that we "fear" him and keep his commandments, he means that we should pay to him that homage and reverence which we owe to our Eternal Father and his Son Jesus Christ. To fear the Lord is to love him. That is the sense in which the word is used. The Lord is not asking us to be afraid of him, but to draw near unto him, and the greatest of all the commandments is, that we love him. [D&C 45:39; 76:5; Acts 10:34-35; Psalms 111:10; 112:1; Prov. 1:7; Eccl. 12:13.] (DS 1:4-5.)

See the commentary for Leviticus 19:3.

**10:12** The commandment "to serve the Lord thy God with all thy heart and with all thy soul" was identified as the first and great commandment by Jesus Christ when he was on the earth. (See Matt. 22:38.) In the Book of Mormon, King Benjamin taught "When ye are in the service of your fellow beings ye are only in the service of your God." (Mosiah 2:17.) The value of giving service to our fellowmen has been explained by Spencer W. Kimball.

> It is by serving that we learn how to serve. When we are engaged in the service of our fellowmen, not only do our deeds assist them, but we put our own problems in a fresher perspective. When we concern ourselves more with others, there is less time to be concerned with ourselves! In the midst of the miracle of serving, there is the promise of Jesus, that by losing ourselves, we find ourselves!
>
> Not only do we "find" ourselves in terms of acknowledging guidance in our lives, but the more we serve our fellowmen in appropriate ways, the more substance there is to our souls. We become more significant individuals as we serve others. We become more substantive as we serve others—indeed, it is easier to "find" ourselves because there is so much more of us to find! . . .
>
> Sometimes the solution [to a challenge] is not to change our circumstance, but to change our attitude about that circumstance and its difficulties and the opportunities for service. . . .
>
> God does notice us, and he watches over us. But it is usually through another person that he meets our needs. Therefore, it is vital that we serve each other in the Kingdom. The people of the Church need each other's strength, support, and leadership in a community of believers as an enclave of disciples. (MIA June Conference opening address, June 21, 1974, pp. 2-3A; see also CN, June 22, 1974, p. 3.)

**10:17** The idiomatic expression "God of gods" conveys the idea that God is supreme.

**11:10-11** In Egypt the Israelites watered their fields from the waters of the river, but in the promised land they would need to depend upon rain from heaven for moisture for their crops.

**11:18** See Part I 37.

**12:16, 23-25** See the commentary for Leviticus 17:10-16 and Part I 21.

**12:31** Here the Lord specifically forbids the offering of human sacrifice among his covenant people, a practice that had been adopted by some of the people of the nations surrounding Israel.

**13:1-3**   Whenever God works through true prophets upon the earth, the adversary attempts to deceive the people by sending forth false prophets. This was true in both Old Testament and New Testament times as well as in our own day as indicated in the following quotations by true prophets:

It is evident from the Apostles' writings, that many false spirits existed in their day, . . . and that [the Apostles] needed intelligence which God alone could impart to detect false spirits, and to prove what spirits were of God. . . .

The Egyptians were not able to discover the difference between the miracles of Moses and those of the magicians until they came to be tested together; and if Moses had not appeared in their midst, they would unquestionably have thought that the miracles of the magicians were performed through the mighty power of God, for they were great miracles that were performed by them — a supernatural agency was developed, and great power manifested. (Joseph Smith, TPJS, p. 202.)

If a man is called to be a Prophet, and the gift of prophecy is poured upon him, though he afterwards actually defies the power of God and turns away from the holy commandments, that man will continue in his gift and will prophecy lies.

He will make false prophecies, yet he will do it by the spirit of prophecy; he will feel that he is a prophet and can prophecy, but he does it by another spirit and power than that which was given him of the Lord. He uses the gift as much as you and I use ours. (Brigham Young, JD 3:364.)

I tell you that these men who stand up and say that Jesus is not the Christ, that he was a great teacher, but not the Son of God, the Only Begotten of the Father, and thus lead many to deny the power of the resurrection and the divinity of Christ, are taking upon themselves a most terrible responsibility that should cause them to fear and tremble. I could not stand it to know that I had taught an untruth that would lead people to destruction. And when these men realize what they have done and that, not only their own souls have not been saved, but they have been the means of destroying the souls of other men, leading them away from truth and righteousness, I tell you that it shall be hard with them, and their punishment shall be most severe in eternity. (Joseph Fielding Smith, DS 1:33-34.)

**13:1-11**   The warning of the Lord against false prophets and their teachings and the requirement that false prophets should be put to death are consistent with the Savior's admonition that a false teacher should be feared more than a murderer. (See Matt. 10:28.)

Viewed from the perspective of eternity, it is evident why a person should fear a false teacher (who is able to influence him to commit sin and lead him away from salvation) more than a murderer (who is only able to take physical life, which will be restored in the resurrection).

**13:6-10** Joseph Fielding Smith has provided the following commentary on these verses:

> It is no worse to have our Eternal Father command us to go to war and to destroy the lives of the wicked in war, than it is for him to bring fire from heaven to accomplish the same purpose, as he did on the cities of Sodom and Gomorrah; or to destroy cities as he did by earthquake and fire as recorded in the Book of Mormon; or to bring upon the world a flood to cleanse the earth of its wickedness. President John Taylor has given us reasons for the Lord's accomplishment of his purposes in the following words: [Quoted Deut. 13:6-10.]
>
> "Here, then, it is stated, that if brother, son, wife or any one, wish to lead thee from God, thou shalt destroy them; and why? Because in forsaking God, they lose sight of their eternal existence, corrupt themselves, and entail misery on their posterity. Hence it was better to destroy a few individuals, than to entail misery on many. And hence the inhabitants of the old world and of the cities of Sodom and Gomorrah were destroyed, because it was better for them to die, and thus be deprived of their agency, which they abused, then entail so much misery on their posterity, and bring ruin upon millions of unborn persons." (John Taylor, *The Government of God,* p. 53.) (AGQ 3:54-55.)

**14:3-8** See Part I 19.

**14:9-10** See Part I 20.

**14:21** See the commentary for Exodus 23:19 and Part I 22, 23.

**14:22-29** The tithe (one-tenth) could be paid in kind or, if great distances or heavy weights were involved, the material could be sold and the money used to purchase other goods to pay as a tithing. The goods would be used to support the Levites (who were not given a separate land inheritance and who were to dedicate their service to the Lord) and the poor, including "the stranger, and the fatherless, and the widow."

**15:1-6** Every seventh year, Israelites were to forgive the debts of their fellow Israelites, but not necessarily the debts of foreigners. Also, the Israelites were promised that if they observed the commandments of the Lord, they would be so blessed they would not need to borrow money from strangers but would be able to lend money to them.

**15:7-11** The prophets of this dispensation have set the example and taught the responsibility of members of the

Church toward the poor, as indicated in the following statements:

The man who is hungry and destitute has as good a right to my food as any other person, and I should feel as happy in associating with him, if he had a good heart, as with those who have an abundance, or with the princes of the earth. They all are esteemed by me, not according to the wealth and position they hold, but according to the character they have. (Brigham Young, JD 3:245.)

And if there is a widow, or an orphan, or any destitute persons, or any one who has to struggle hard, look after them, and do not try to make paupers of them; but what you do for them, do it in a kind, good feeling, making them to feel and realize that you are their friends. (John Taylor, JD 21:217.)

There are some Christian people in this world who, if a man were poor or hungry, would say, let us pray for him. I would suggest a little different regiment for a person in this condition: rather take him a bag of flour and a little beef or pork, and a little sugar and butter. A few such comforts will do him more good than your prayers. And I would be ashamed to ask the Lord to do something that I would not do myself. Then go to work and help the poor yourselves first, and do all you can for them, and then call upon God to do the balance. (John Taylor, JD 19:340.)

One of the important objects of the Gospel is to benefit the poor temporally as well as spiritually; and, therefore, of all other classes of people, the poor should be the most willing to be directed and governed. The Lord has ever been mindful of his poor; to them, while in their adverse circumstances, he has granted privileges which are withheld from the rich. The fact that the poor had the Gospel preached to them was one of the evidences of Jesus being the Christ, which he himself gave to the disciples of John in answer to the question, "Art thou he that should come, or do we look for another?" The poor have always been an especial charge of the servants of God, in all ages. (Lorenzo Snow, JD 18:300-31.)

**15:23**    See the commentary for Leviticus 17:10-16 and Part I 21.

**16:10**    See Part I 42.

**18:15-18**    The prophecy that a prophet "like unto" Moses would come forth evidently has multiple fulfillments. Earlier as well as later dispensations have had their prophets like unto Moses who talked with the Lord face to face, brought forth new scriptures, and so on, including the Prophet Joseph Smith. Although Jesus Christ was the Son of God and much more than a prophet, he was also a prophet "like unto" Moses. (See Acts 3:19-26, 1 Ne. 22:20-22, and JS-H 2:40.) Concerning this role of Jesus Christ, LeGrand Richards has written:

Who among all the ancient prophets could be likened unto Moses except Jesus Christ? There was a great similarity in their ministries. On this parallel, the following quotation is illuminating:

## MOSES — MESSIAH: A PARALLEL
### 1. Both Knew God Face to Face
*Moses:* [Deut. 34:10]
*Messiah:* [John 6:46]
### 2. The Life of Each Was Sought in Infancy
*Moses:* [Ex. 1:22]
*Messiah:* [Matt. 2]
### 3. Both Had Command Over the Sea
*Moses:* [Ex. 14:21]
*Messiah:* [Matt. 8]
### 4. Both Were Subject to Transfiguration
*Moses:* [Ex. 34:29-33]
*Messiah:* [Matt. 17:2]
### 5. Families of Each Sometimes Opposed Them
*Moses:* [Num. 12:1-2]
*Messiah:* [John 7:5]
### 6. Both Moses and Christ Were Meek
*Moses:* [Num. 12:3]
*Messiah:* [Matt. 11:29]
### 7. Both Rejected the Glory of the World
*Moses:* [Heb. 11:24, 26]
*Messiah:* [Matt. 4:8-11]

Surely Jesus Christ, the Son of God, met all the requirements necessary to justify our accepting Him as the promised prophet like unto Moses. When He came He was rejected by His own, and in this respect He was also like unto Moses, for when Moses went up into the mountain to commune with the Lord, the children of Israel turned away from Moses and made a molten calf from their jewels. (IDYK, pp. 84-86.)

**20:1-9** Those exempted from military service included the newly settled (builders of a new house [v. 5] and the planters of a new vineyard [v. 6]), the newly married (v. 7), and the faint-hearted (v. 8)!

**21:10-14** Obviously a man should have made a captive woman his wife only if she was willing to be submissive to her husband and follow him. Perhaps this submissiveness explains the exception in such instances to the regulation forbidding marriage with peoples other than the chosen group.

**21:12** Among the ultra-orthodox Jewish people today (the Hassidim), the married women continue to shave their heads. When they go out in public, such women often cover their heads with shawls or, in some instances, with wigs and shawls, bandanas, or kerchiefs. See Part I 27.

**21:15**   The statement "If a man have two wives" clearly indicates that polygamy (technically, polygyny) was a commonly accepted practice among the Israelites of that day.

See Part I 12-13.

**21:22-23**   The requirement that the body of a man put to death by hanging must be buried the same day was still in effect in the days of Jesus Christ. (See Matt. 27:57-60; Mark 15:42-47; Luke 23:50-56; and especially John 19:31-42.)

In the modern country of Israel, it is customary for the bodies of the deceased to be buried the very day (within twenty-four hours) death occurs. Memorial services for the deceased are held later.

**22:5**   Men and women have been created for specific purposes, and their roles should not be confused. Here the Lord counsels against the woman wearing anything "which pertaineth unto a man" and also counsels "neither shall a man put on a woman's garment: for all that do so are abomination unto the Lord thy God." This custom is still rigidly followed by many people today. See Part I 28.

**22:12**   See Part I 26.

**24:16**   Joseph Fielding Smith has provided the following commentary on the major principle covered in this verse:

> The millions of souls who have lived on the earth at a time and place when the gospel was not here, due to the transgressions of their fathers, cannot be judged by the standards which the pure gospel proclaims. Many of the people living in the pagan world were intelligent, industrious, honest in their dealings with their fellows, but were unfortunate to be descendants of those who in earlier ages rejected the gospel which had been declared to them, and therefore their descendants were raised in idolatry. The Lord declared through his prophets that the children are not answerable for the sins of their parents. [Quoted Deut. 24:16.]
>
> After the scattering of the people to all parts of the earth, they fell away from the teachings of Noah. Generation after generation came and passed in idolatry. Yet many of these children were otherwise intelligent. They had accepted the worship of images and false gods because of the traditions of their fathers. Among these peoples were many of the Egyptians, the Greeks, the Romans, the Persians, and peoples who had spread out all over the face of the earth. These people were not responsible for their condition. They had followed the teachings of their fathers and lived and died in their ignorance of divine truth taught to Adam, to Noah, and to Abraham. (AGQ 4:75-76.)

**24:16**   The accountability of man for his own actions is one of the basic principles of the gospel of Jesus Christ. God provided for the free agency of man in the very beginning and will continue to bestow this gift as indicated in these statements of his prophets:

Since the day that sin entered into the world men have been held accountable for their own acts, and it has been known upon this earth from the day, at least, that Cain slew his brother Abel. And sin has presented itself in different grades; there are murder, blasphemy, lying, stealing, whoredom, and abominations of many different forms, which have followed man from generation to generation. . . . All the children of men who arrive at the years of accountability are guilty of sin, all being inclined to do evil as the sparks are to fly upwards. (Wilford Woodruff, JD 23:126.)

If there is one principle of the gospel of Jesus Christ that goes directly to the very foundation of justice and righteousness, it is that great and glorious and God-like principle that every man will have to render an account for that which he does, and every man will be rewarded for his works, whether they be good or evil. (Joseph F. Smith, GD, p. 69.)

**25:3**  Under the law, a man could be beaten with "forty stripes" for certain offenses. In order to make certain they kept within the law the Jews usually counted as they beat the person and ended after thirty-nine stripes. (See 2 Cor. 11:24.) At the time of Jesus Christ the beating was often performed in the synagogue upon offenders of the religious law. (See Matt. 10:17 and Acts 26:11.)

A more severe type of beating was scourging, which was frequently inflicted by a whip of different thongs into which iron or other abrasive items were inserted. In later times the Romans used the scourging to prepare the body of a malefactor for crucifixion so that the offender would not suffer too long on the cross. (See Matt. 20:19; Mark 10:34; and Luke 18:33.)

**25:9, 10**  John Taylor has provided the following commentary on the custom of the nearest relative to take the wife of the deceased:

There is another feature of that ancient law which I will mention. It was considered an act of injustice for the nearest relation not to take the wife of the deceased; if he refused to do it, he was obliged to go before the Elders of "Israel, and his brother's wife shall loose his shoe from off his foot, and spit in his face, and shall answer and say, So shall it be done unto the man that will not build up his brother's house; and his name shall be called in Israel, The house of him who hath his shoe loosed." If the restitution of all things is to be brought to pass, there must be a restitution of these things; everything will be put right, and in its proper place. (JD 1:232.)

**28:1-68**  Modern scripture teaches that every blessing is predicated upon obedience to law. (See D&C 130: 20-21.) In this chapter, the Lord recounts the numerous blessings that will come to ancient Israel if they are obedient to his laws (vs. 1-14); then he warns them of the punishments that will come upon them if they are disobedient. Joseph F. Smith has indicated that the same promises and warnings apply to the people in the world today:

> Now, I want to say to you without any hesitancy or fear of successful contradiction, that the words which I have read in your hearing are as applicable to you as they were to the children of Israel. You are modern Israel and they were ancient Israel. The same God spake through His servant Moses that speaks today through His servant Lorenzo Snow. Obedience to the laws of God will produce the same results today that it did anciently. To those who know the history of ancient Israel it is perhaps not necessary for me to say that these words were fulfilled upon Israel. As long as they hearkened to His word, God did prosper them; He did bless their land; He did send them the early and the latter rains; He did multiply them and strengthen them in the land; He did set them on high; He did make them His covenant people, and they became famous throughout the known world. The glory of Solomon reached to the uttermost parts of the earth. . . .
>
> I commend to you the careful reading of the remaining portion of this chapter in Deuteronomy. Time will not permit me to read it, but I would like you to read and contemplate it at your leisure, for there you will find, as if written by eye-witnesses, history of the judgments of God that subsequently fell upon the children of Israel, with an accurate account of the downfall and disintegration of the people. They became a hiss and a byword among the nations of the earth. They were broken asunder, they were carried captive into the various nations of the earth; they served under taskmasters; from that day unto the present they have been under the curse of God through disobedience to His laws, and they will remain under that curse of disobedience so long as they fail to repent of their sins and return not unto the Lord. (CR, Oct. 1899, p. 45.)

**28:1-68**    Some social scientists maintain that people can be motivated more through hope of reward than through fear of punishment, while other social scientists feel the opposite. In this chapter, only fourteen verses (1-14) are used to list the blessings associated with obedience, while fifty-four verses (15-68) list the punishments and evil consequences which result from disobedience to the laws of the Lord.

In this dispensation, the Lord has stated that he delights in blessing those that hear him, but will curse those who hear him not. (D&C 41:1.) In D&C 59, the Lord emphasizes blessings and says relatively little about cursings.

**28:37**    When ancient Israel proved to be disobedient to the commandments of God, they were scattered among the nations of the earth where they became a "proverb, and a byword" exactly as the Lord had indicated. Modern prophets have seen in the scattering of the Jews the fulfillment of the prophecies, but they also indicate that the Jews will be gathered back to their homeland once more, again in fulfillment of prophecies:

The Jews continued, possessing the land of Palestine until after the days of Christ. Then, because of their wickedness and the fact that they had risen up against the Son of God, they too were scattered among the nations of the earth and became a hiss and a byword, and were so to remain until, the Lord says, the times of the gentiles shall be fulfilled. Now the Jews are being gathered again, because the times of the gentiles are coming to their close.

The Lord, through his prophets before Israel was completely scattered, spoke of our day. He spoke of the covenants and how in these latter times he would renew these covenants upon Israel, after Israel had been gathered. [Jer. 31:31-34; 32:36-42; Ezek. 37:24-28; Deut. 4:29-31.] (Joseph Fielding Smith, DS 1:165-66.)

Twenty-three hundred years ago the prophet looking down through the vista of time saw this day. He saw Israel scattered among all nations. He saw them become a hiss and a byword, but added, "Nevertheless, when that *day cometh, . . . that they no more turn aside their hearts against the Holy One of Israel, . . .*"—note he does not say when they accept him as their Redeemer, nor necessarily declare to the world that he was the Messiah to come to their people—the prophet words it most significantly; viz., "*when . . . they no more turn aside their hearts against the Holy One of Israel, then will he remember the covenants which he made to their fathers.*" (I Nephi 19:15.)

Brethren, isn't it a significant thing that today there is a change in the hearts of the descendants of Israel in regard to the Holy One of Israel? (David O. McKay, GSI, p. 67.)

See Part I 80-95, 105-15, 177-91, 193-97, 205-13, 223, 228-32, 239-50.

**28:64-67** Many of the Jewish people were scattered among the nations of the earth as a result of their disobedience to God's commandments, just as the Lord foretold in these verses. However, the scattering has proven to be a blessing to the Gentiles as modern prophets have indicated. Also, the Lord has indicated that he will gather the Jews back home when "they no more turn aside their hearts against the Holy One of Israel." (1 Ne. 19:15; see also as examples Jer. 29:14; 31:10; 32:37; Isa. 54:7; Ezek. 20:41; 36:24; 37:21-28; Micah 4:6.)

How completely and thoroughly have these prophetic words [Deut. 28:25, 64] come to pass! For although the scriptures are filled with examples of the Lord's patience with ancient Israel—how he endured their pettiness, listened to their eternal complaining, recoiled from their filthiness, groaned at their idolatries and their adulteries, and wept at their faithlessness—yet his people finally did reject him through unrighteousness and rebellion. Then, true to the words of his holy prophets, the Lord suffered them to be scattered—first one branch, then another, and another—to the four corners of the earth: "For, lo, I will command, and I will sift the house of Israel among all nations, like as corn is sifted in a sieve." (Amos 9:9.) (Spencer W. Kimball, E, Dec. 1975, p. 2.)

When Israel entered the promised land, the Lord gave them strict commandment that they should serve him and keep his commandments. If they would obey, they were to be greatly blessed and prospered in the land the Lord had given to them. If they should reject his commandments and turn to evil, he would punish them and take them out of the land, and scatter them to all parts of the earth, where they would serve other gods, "which neither thou nor thy fathers have known, even wood and stone." [Deut. 28:64.]

All of this was to come on Israel as a punishment for their wickedness. However, the Lord never punishes his people without turning that punishment into some blessing in the end. The scattering of Israel became a blessing to the Gentile peoples among whom they were dispersed, for the Israelites mixed with the people thus bringing the Gentiles into the benefits of the blessings that had been promised to Abraham and his seed after him. (Joseph Fielding Smith, AGQ 4:38.)

**31:11-12** The importance of reading the scriptures in private and in public has been emphasized by the prophets of this dispensation. Brigham Young has suggested a way to make even ancient scriptures come alive and have special meaning:

Do you read the Scriptures, my brethren and sisters, as though you were writing them a thousand, two thousand, or five thousand years ago? Do you read them as though you stood in the place of the men who wrote them? If you do not feel thus, it is your privilege to do so, that you may be as familiar with the spirit and meaning of the written word of God as you are with your daily walk and conversation, or as you are with your workmen or with your households. You may understand what the Prophets understood and thought—what they designed and planned to bring forth to their brethren for their good. (JD 7:333.)

**32:5** Any people who rebel against the commandments of God might be designated as "a perverse and crooked generation." It is evident here the word *generation* may refer to a state or condition as well as to a time period. Thus, the scriptures refer to an "unbelieving and stiffnecked generation" (D&C 5:8), a "crooked and perverse generation" (Deut. 32:5; D&C 33:2), this "untoward generation" (D&C 36:6), and "evil and adulterous generation" (Matt. 12:39). All of these uses of the word suggest a state or condition rather than a specific period of time.

**32:8-9** Harold B. Lee and Joseph Fielding Smith have provided the following commentaries on these verses:

Now, mind you, this [Deut. 32:8] was said to the children of Israel before they had arrived in the "Promised Land," which was to be the land of their inheritance.

Then note this next verse: "For the Lord's portion is his people; Jacob is the lot of his inheritance." (Deut. 32:9.)

It would seem very clear, then, that those born to the lineage of Jacob, who was later to be called Israel, and his posterity, who were known as the children of Israel, were born into the most illustrious lineage of any of those who came upon the earth as mortal beings.

All these rewards were seemingly promised, or foreordained, before the world was. Surely these matters must have been determined by the kind of lives we had lived in that premortal spirit world. Some may question these assumptions, but at the same time they will accept without any question the belief that each one of us will be judged when we leave this earth according to his or her deeds during our lives here in mortality. Isn't it just as reasonable to believe that what we have received here in this earth [life] was given to each of us according to the merits of our conduct before we came here? (Harold B. Lee, CR, Oct. 1973, pp. 7-8.)

We learn from the word of the Lord to Moses that the Lord selected a place for the children of Israel, even before they were born, thus he indicated the number of spirits who were assigned to become the descendants of Jacob. We may well believe that the Lord also parceled out the surface of the earth for all other peoples. Some of these places were evidently designed for inhabitants who had lost interest in or touch with the plan of salvation. We may well believe that the Lord did not permit the more progressive and more worthy spirits to come to the families of the ungodly and the less progressive peoples of the earth. (Joseph Fielding Smith, AGQ 4:11-12.)

**33:2-3** The word *saints* means "sanctified ones" and was evidently limited to those who had entered into covenant with the Lord and vowed to keep his commandments and observe his ordinances. They all sat down at his feet and everyone received his word.

Joseph Smith taught that the saints of the latter days can also receive great blessings if they prove faithful to the promises made to them, just as the ancient saints received great blessings when they were obedient.

And though we cannot claim these promises which were made to the ancients . . . yet if we are the children of the Most High, and are called with the same calling with which they were called, and embrace the same covenant that they embraced, and are faithful to the testimony of our Lord as they were, we can approach the Father in the name of Christ as they approached Him, and for ourselves obtain the same promises. (TPJS, p. 66.)

**33:5** "King in Jeshurun" means "king in righteousness" or "king of the upright."

**33:6-25** No blessing is pronounced upon Simeon although blessings are provided for all the other sons of Jacob. Perhaps the descendants of Simeon had already been absorbed into the tribe of Judah because of the close proximity of their land inheritances.

It is interesting to note that in the Book of Mormon one *tribe* is evidently absorbed into another. Lehi and Sariah had six sons: Laman, Lemuel, Sam, Nephi, Jacob, and Joseph. All of them married and had seed, including Sam. (See 1 Ne. 16:7 and 2 Ne. 4:11.) Later the descendants of these sons are called by tribal names (Lamanites, Lemuelites, Nephites, Jacobites, Josephites) except for Sam; there are no Samites mentioned by name in the Book of Mormon. Evidently the descendants of Sam were included under the designation *Nephites.*

**33:8-11, 13-17.** The greater blessings appear to be given to Levi and Joseph. Four verses are devoted to the blessing of the descendants of Levi, who because of their priestly inheritance were to officiate at the altars and bless the people. Five verses include the blessing to the descendants of Joseph, who would be "separated" from their brethren in a fruitful land and would help to "push the people together to the ends of the earth." (For additional statements concerning the preeminence of Joseph's blessing through his sons Manasseh and Ephraim, see Gen. 48:15-20; 49:22-26; 1 Chr. 5:1 and any commentaries listed with those references; also see Part I 233-34.)

**33:23** The Hebrew word translated here as "west" is really the word for *sea* and refers to the Sea of Galilee. Isaiah later prophesies that the people who have walked in darkness in the lands of Zebulun and Naphtali shall see "a great light"; this was interpreted by Matthew to refer to the ministry of Jesus Christ in the area of the Sea of Galilee. (Isa. 9:1-2; Matt. 4:14-16.)

**34:5-6** The statements in the Bible concerning the "death" of Moses are confusing, both here and in Jude, verse 9. The Book of Mormon makes it clear that Moses was translated (see Alma 45:19) as was Elijah. (2 Kgs. 2:11; see also D&C 110:13.)

This is also made clear in Joseph Smith Translation Deuteronomy 34:6:

"For the Lord took him unto his fathers, in a valley in the land of Moab, over against Beth-peor; therefore no man knoweth of his sepulcher unto this day."

Josephus claims that when Moses left the children of Israel he was accompanied by "the senate, and Eleazar . . . , and Joshua." After the senate left, Moses "was going to embrace Eleazar and Joshua" and was still talking with them when a cloud stood over him and he disappeared. (*Antiquities of the Jews,* p. 103.) This disappearance on the part of Moses has been compared with the disappearance of Elijah as recorded in 2 Kings 2:11.

Both Moses and Elijah appeared as translated beings on the mount of transfiguration in New Testament times (Matt. 17:3) and as resurrected beings in the Kirtland Temple on April 3, 1836. (D&C 110:11-16.)

# JOSHUA

See "Joshua, Book of" in the Bible Dictionary, page 718.

**1:1-2** Moses did not die a natural death, but was "separated" from his people by being translated ("quickened by the spirit"), as was Elijah. See the commentary for Deuteronomy 34:5-6.

**2:1-22** Rahab's statement "I know that the Lord hath given you the land" (v. 9) reveals her prior knowledge and faith in the Lord as well as her understanding of the futility of opposing his will. Even in New Testament times, the faith, devotion, and good works of Rahab were extolled. (See James 2:25 and Hebrews 11:31.)

Matthew 1:3-6 refers to Rahab, the mother of Boaz, the ancestor of David and thus of Jesus Christ, but it is not certain whether this is the same woman.

**3:4** See Part I 34.

**3:7-17** There may be some relationships and symbolism in the Lord's dividing the waters of the Red Sea as he led the Israelites out of bondage from Egypt and his dividing the waters of the Jordan River as he led the Israelites to promised freedom in the land of Canaan.

**3:15-17; 4:18** A modern prophet has commented on this miracle made possible through faith:

> Israel was later ready to cross into the Promised Land, the productivity and beauty of which could probably be seen from the higher hills. But how to get there? There were no bridges nor ferries across the flooding Jordan. A great prophet, Joshua, received the mind of the Lord and commanded, and another miracle was born of faith. (Spencer W. Kimball, FPM, p. 9.)

**4:1-9** The Lord was the first to suggest the gathering of twelve stones from the spot where the miracle occurred. Although he may also have mentioned some purposes for this, it was Joshua who indicated "these stones shall be for a memorial unto the children of Israel for ever" (v. 7).

It it not clear from the King James Version whether there was one memorial or two erected in honor of the parting of the Jordan. Verses 3, 8, and 20 suggest that the stones were taken *from* the Jordan and made into an altar at Gilgal, while verse 9 indicates Joshua set up twelve stones *in* the midst of the Jordan. The Hebrew of verse 9 could be translated "Joshua lifted up twelve stones" (rather than "set up"); thus there may have been only one memorial.

Such memorials are obviously good visual aids in prompting interest in future generations and teaching them of the goodness of the Lord in the past. Several such memorials exist on Temple Square in Salt Lake City today, commemorating such events as the restoration of the Aaronic Priesthood, the trek of the handcart companies, and the miracle of the seagulls and the crickets. As present day Latter-day Saints look on the memorial built to the seagull (believed to be the only memorial erected to honor a bird), they might well exclaim as did the ancient Israelites, "What mean . . . these stones?" (v. 6).

**5:2-8, 10**   Two customs previously kept by the Israelites were observed again as recorded in these verses: circumcision (vs. 2-8) and the Passover (v. 10). It may be more than coincidental that the Lord prepared the Israelites to go into the land of Canaan at the same time of the year as he had led them from Egypt, as indicated by the keeping of the Passover.

Evidently no circumcisions had been performed during the forty years in the wilderness. The reason for the possible interruption in the observance of this ordinance is not given in our present Bible.

**5:12**   Many readers of the Bible overlook the fact that the miracle of the manna lasted forty years! (See Ex. 16:35.) Perhaps this is because the major references to the miracle appear when it first started. (Ex. 16:1-35.)

The Book of Mormon supports its companion scripture the Bible in teaching of the miracle of the manna. (See 1 Ne. 17:28 and Mosiah 7:19.)

**5:13-15**   Joshua and the armies of the Israelites were not alone when they prepared for battle against Jericho; the captain of "the host of the Lord" (v. 14) was also there with drawn sword.

The statement "the place whereon thou standest" (v. 15) may have referred to (1) an event in the past that occurred there, or (2) the incident occurring to Joshua, or (3) a sacred event to occur in the future. The Savior visited in the area of Jericho several times, healing the blind and performing other miracles. (Matt. 20:29-34; Mark 10:46-52; Luke 18:35-43; 19:1-27.) It was also in the river Jordan which flows near Jericho, where he was baptized. (Matt. 3:13-16.)

**6:25**    Either the account of this conquest was written at a later date, or an editor might have subsequently added a postscript, as the record states Rahab "dwelleth in Israel even unto this day."

**7:6-9**    The lament of Joshua that it would have been better to have left the Israelites on the other side of Jordan than to bring them into Canaan to perish is reminiscent of the earlier murmuring of the Israelites in regard to the fleshpots of Egypt and possible extinction in the wilderness. On both occasions it is not the Lord that causes the difficulties, but the waywardness of the people. The Lord quickly and strongly reminds Joshua of this fact (vs. 10-11).

**7:24-26**    It is unclear whether only Achan was killed for his sin or all the members of his family were executed: "And all Israel stoned *him* with stones, and burned *them* with fire, after they had stoned *them* with stones. And they raised over *him* a great heap of stones." (Italics added.) Obviously Achan perished, but the next pronoun *them* could refer to the possessions, rather than the family, of Achan.

Deuteronomy 24:16 specifically states "neither shall the children be put to death for the [sins of the] fathers."

**8:30-35**    Undoubtedly Joshua followed precisely the earlier instructions of Moses (Deut. 27:11-26) in the performance of this great outdoor pageant, for the record indicates "there was not a word of all that Moses commanded, which Joshua read not before all the congregation of Israel" (v. 35).

Part of the present town of Nablus is located in the small valley between towering Ebal (the mount of cursing) and Gerizim (the mount of blessing).

Mount Gerizim subsequently became the holy mountain for the northern tribes and was still revered as such by the Samaritans at the time Jesus visited there. (John 4:3-42.) The modern Samaritans still celebrate the Passover on top of Mount Gerizim.

**10:12-14**    Surely the Lord who created the heavens and the earth "and all things that in them are" (3 Ne. 9:15) could cause the sun and the moon to stand still (or the earth to stand still so the heavenly bodies would appear to be stationary) as indicated here. (See Hel. 12:13-15.)

Another biblical account even has the sun reversing its direction. (See 2 Kgs. 20:8-11 and Isa. 38:7-8.)

There should be no question concerning the reality of this miracle, although we may not understand the exact manner in which it was accomplished.

The lengthening out of the day prevented the Amorites from regrouping and greatly assisted Joshua and the Israelites in their victory.

**10:13**   See commentary for 2 Samuel 1:18 for information on the book of Jasher.

**11:20**   According to the Joseph Smith Translation, the first clause should read: "For it was of the Lord to destroy them utterly, because they hardened their hearts."

**11:21-22**   The Anakims cut off here are the same "giants" or their descendants who frightened the fellow scouts of Joshua some forty years before. (Num. 13.) On that occasion the report was "And there we saw the giants, the sons of Anak, which come of the giants: and we were in our own sight as grasshoppers, and so we were in their sight." (Num. 13:33.)

Deuteronomy 2:10-11 also refers to the Anakims as "great, and many, and tall . . . giants."

Note here that the Anakims of Gath were not conquered (v. 22). The Bible later tells a brief but dramatic story about a giant from Gath named Goliath. (See 1 Sam. 17:20-51.)

**12:7-24**   The listing here of thirty-one kings who reigned simultaneously in the relatively small area of Canaan (about 50 by 150 miles) indicates there was no strong central government at that time. Rather, the people were largely governed through a series of disunited city-states, probably along family (tribal) lines.

**14:1-15**   The tribes given geographical locations in which to settle were twelve, the same number as the sons of Israel (Jacob). However, the names or titles of the twelve "land" tribes are not identical to those of the twelve "blood" tribes. The "blood" tribes are named after the twelve sons of Jacob: Reuben, Simeon, Levi, Judah, Dan, Naphtali, Gad, Asher, Issachar, Zebulun, Joseph, and Benjamin. The twelve "land" tribes are named after ten of the twelve sons of Jacob, leaving out Levi and Joseph and substituting for them Manasseh and Ephraim.

The Bible is clear as to why the Levites were not given a geographical inheritance—they were the priestly tribe, and had to perform religious services for all the people. (Deut. 18:1-2.)

The Bible is less clear as to why Joseph was not given a geographical inheritance in that area. Most Bible commentaries suggest that Joseph did receive a land inheritance in or near

Canaan, for Joseph's two sons (Manasseh and Ephraim) received such inheritances—the only grandsons of Jacob so honored. The same commentaries usually point out that Joseph, as the eventual birthright son after Reuben's adultery (see Gen. 35:22; 49:4; 1 Chr. 5:1), was entitled to a double portion of Jacob's inheritance, which Joseph received through his two sons. Before his death, Jacob specifically said to Joseph: "I have given to thee one portion above thy brethren." (Gen. 48:22.) These commentaries still do not explain why these land inheritances were not called after the name of Joseph.

A close reading of the blessing given by Jacob to Joseph and to the sons of Joseph may provide at least a partial answer. To Joseph, Jacob said:

"Joseph is a fruitful bough . . . whose branches run over the wall . . .

"The blessings of thy father have prevailed . . . unto the utmost bound of the everlasting hills . . . on the head of Joseph . . . that was separate from his brethren." (Gen. 49:22, 26.)

When "Moses the man of God blessed the children of Israel," he mentioned that the land of Joseph would be blessed "for the precious things of the lasting hills . . . upon the top of the head of him that was separated from his brethren . . . [Joseph] shall push the people together to the ends of the earth." (Deut. 33:1, 13-17.)

To Manasseh and Ephraim, Jacob said: "He [Manasseh] also shall be great: but truly his younger brother [Ephraim] shall be greater than he, and his seed [Ephraim's seed] shall become a multitude of nations." (Gen. 48:19.)

When these blessings are read in the context of the Book of Mormon and the Doctrine and Covenants, it is clear that the land inheritance of Joseph is to be:

1. Separate from his brothers (just as he was separated from them during much of his life on earth).

2. In the land of the everlasting hills (North and South America with their ranges of mountains extending from the north clear to the tip of the south).

3. Where the descendants of his sons could become a "multitude of nations" (in Mexico and Central and South America).

4. Where the priesthood keys of gathering would be restored, enabling Judah and the other remnants of Israel to gather back to the *lands* of their inheritance.

Moroni, after reviewing the history of God's dealings with man as recorded on the brass plates of Laban (essentially the Old Testament), in the record of his own father (the Book of Mormon), and in the record of the Jaredites, was led to exclaim: "The Lord brought a remnant of the seed of Joseph out of the land of Jerusalem, that he might be merciful unto the seed of Joseph that they should perish not. . . .

"Wherefore, the remnant of the house of Joseph shall be built upon this land [North and South America]; and it shall be a land of their inheritance." (Ether 13:7-8.)

Did Moses know when he worked with Joshua in outlining the land of inheritances among the tribes of Israel that Joseph was to receive a land inheritance elsewhere? Of course he did, and Joshua knew also. Thus the land inheritances given to the descendants of Joseph in and around Canaan carried the names of the sons of Joseph (Manasseh and Ephraim), but the land inheritance of Joseph in the Americas will carry his own name and will be a land for the inheritance of his children.

**14:6-15, 15:13-15**    Caleb, the representative of Judah who was sent to scout the land around Arba (Hebron) some forty years before, was rewarded for his faithfulness and positive report by being given, at his request, that very area to conquer! (See Num. 13.) Since the great men (giants) of the Anakims still dwelt there, this request showed the great courage of Caleb.

**20:1-9**    The concept of cities of refuge to help ensure justice was earlier explained by the Lord to Moses with the instruction: "When ye be come over Jordan . . . appoint . . . cities of refuge for you." (Num. 35:10-11; see also Num. 35:6-34; Deut. 4:41-43.)

**22:1-34**    Ellis Rasmussen has provided the following commentary on this chapter:

> After Joshua had blessed the tribes located beyond Jordan and had sent them to their new homes, they built an 'altar'—not for sacrifice nor offerings but as a 'witness' or a memorial monument—so that future generations could always be taught about their relationship with the LORD, and with Israelites west of Jordan. It was to remind them of the true altar of sacrifice at Shiloh where the tabernacle was. Ironically, the tribes of the west saw it from afar and thought it to be an idolatrous altar! Concerned lest the Lord should punish not only the offenders but all Israel (as at Achor in the affair of Achan), they zealously assembled for war against the 'rebels.' Fortunately the princes and the priesthood got together, were able to communicate and clear up the intent and purpose of it all and to avert a war! (IOT 1:146.)

**24:16-18**    An earlier generation had covenanted to serve the Lord, and then failed to keep their promise (Ex. 32:15-35); later generations also failed to serve the Lord. However, the generation that made this promise of faithfulness evidently kept their word as indicated in Judges 2:6-10. Unfortunately the following generation (and many generations thereafter) "knew not the Lord, nor yet the works which he had done for Israel." (Judg. 2:10.)

# JUDGES

See "Judges, Book of" in the Bible Dictionary, pages 719-20.

**1:8, 21**  Although the children of Judah claimed to have "taken" Jerusalem (v. 8), a later entry indicated "the children of Benjamin did not drive out the Jebusites that inhabited Jerusalem" (v. 21). Jerusalem was not completely conquered until the days of David, hundreds of years later.

**1:19**  The defeat of the Israelites on this occasion was probably prompted more by their fright at the sight of the iron chariots than by their lack of manpower. The Hebrew words do not say that the Israelites "could not drive them out," but "there was no driving out."

**2:1-8**  Evidently the message of the angel of the Lord was delivered *before* the death of Joshua, although for some unknown reason it was inserted here rather than in the book which bore Joshua's name.

**2:6-10**  See the commentary for Joshua 24:16-18.

**2:18**  The awkward statement "it repented the Lord because of their groanings by reason of them that oppressed them and vexed them" is difficult to understand. A more literal translation from the Hebrew (but still somewhat difficult to understand) is: "Jehovah took pity because of their groaning from the presence of their oppressors, and of those who crushed them."

The Joseph Smith Translation renders this section of the verse as: "For the Lord hearkened because of their groanings by reason of them that oppressed them and vexed them."

**3:1**  The nations were left to "prove" (test, try) Israel because the Israelites had failed to pass the first test—they had not observed several of the important commandments of the Lord, obedience to which would have enabled him to help them defeat their enemies.

**3:7**  The Hebrew word *Ashtoreth* translated here as "groves" might also be translated as "pillars" or other symbols referring to fertility cult goddesses.

**3:8-11**  The word translated here as "Mesopotamia" does not refer to the great plains between the Tigris and Euphrates rivers. The Hebrew word involved (*naharaim*) means "between the rivers" as does the Greek word *Mesopotamia*. The King James translators erroneously capitalized the *meaning* of the word, thus giving the wrong impression that it refers to the *place* of Mesopotamia.

The name of the place where this king reigned was Aram-Naharaim, or "Aram of the two rivers" (the rivers Orontes and Khabour).

**3:19**    The Hebrew root translated here as "errand" means "word."

**4:4**    The Hebrew root of the word translated here as "judged" also carries the meaning of "governed." Those who served as judges of Israel probably did not hold regular court sessions as the title might suggest; rather they served as governors over the people.

**4:4**    The reference to Deborah as a prophetess does not mean she held the priesthood office or calling of a prophet. Her gift of prophecy would have been essentially the same that is available to every worthy person who has received the gift of the Holy Ghost.

The fact that a good woman was recognized as the spokesperson for the Lord is probably a good indication of the failure of priesthood members to honor their responsibilities.

**5:10**    Another possible translation of the verse from the Hebrew would be: "You who ride on white asses, you who sit on rich carpets, and you who travel on the way, tell of it."

**6:13**    The word *Lord* (with only the first letter capitalized) refers to the angel or messenger and is translated from the Hebrew *adoni*. The word *LORD* (with all letters capitalized) refers to Jehovah (from the Hebrew *JHVH*).

**6:17**    Gideon's request for a sign seems directed toward learning whether or not the messenger has really been sent from the Lord, rather than toward doubting the power of God. As indicated in the Book of Mormon (Alma 30:53) and the Doctrine and Covenants (129:1-9), sometimes the devil deceives people or sends forth his own angels or messengers.

**8:27**    The idiom "Israel went thither a whoring after it" (the ephod or, more probably, an ornament to adorn the priest's ephod) means the Israelites started to look upon it as an idol (false object of worship). Idolatry had been specifically forbidden by the Lord, and anyone guilty of it was unfaithful to the Lord just as a husband would be unfaithful to his wife by following after a woman of ill repute.

**11:29-40**    Jephthah may have been rash in his promise to sacrifice to the Lord the first thing that "cometh forth of the doors" of his house, but he was remembered by prophets centuries later as one who was faithful. (See Heb. 11:32-35.)

Some Bible commentaries suggest that Jephthah did not actually take the life of his daughter. Rather, they say he would not allow her to marry and so she remained a virgin all her life. As she was the only child of Jephthah, her death, whenever it occurred, would mark the end of the family of Jephthah.

A literal translation from the Hebrew of the vow in verses 30 and 31 could read as follows: "If you indeed will give the sons of Ammon into my hand, then it shall be the thing outcoming which comes out from the doors of my house to meet me when I return in peace from the sons of Ammon shall belong to Jehovah, and I will offer it a burnt offering."

Some scholars have pointed out that the last clause in such a translation, "I will offer it [the thing that comes out of the house] a burnt offering" does not necessarily mean the same as "I will offer it *as* a burnt offering."

**12:14** The Hebrew words translated here as "nephews" literally read "sons of sons," (not "sons of brothers"). Thus "grandsons" would be a more correct translation.

**14:17** The Hebrew words translated "she lay sore upon him" could also have been translated "she distressed him."

**15:19** The statement "But God clave an hollow place that was in the jaw" could be translated more literally from the Hebrew as "And God broke open the hollow place which is in Lehi." Although the definite meaning is unclear, the water could have come forth from the *place* called Lehi, which means "jawbone" (see v. 17), rather than from the jawbone itself.

**16:31** The statement that Samson "judged Israel twenty years" is the only reference to such service that might have been given by him.

**17:5** *Teraphim* are household idols. (See "Teraphim," BD, p. 784.)

**17:6** The depth and extent of the apostasy in Israel during this period are manifested in the pathetic expression "in those days there was no king in Israel, but every man did that which was right in his own eyes."

**18:7** The Hebrew meaning of the construction translated "dwelt careless" means "living at ease."

**18:9** The word "still" has been translated from a Hebrew wording meaning "slack," "quiet," or "inactive."

**18:15** The Hebrew translated "and saluted him" could have been translated "and asked for his peace."

# RUTH

See "Ruth" in the Bible Dictionary, page 764.

**1:1-4** The Moabites were Semitic people related to Abraham, the father of the Hebrews; they were descendants of Lot and one of his daughters. (See Gen. 19:30-38.)

**1:14-22** The decision of Ruth to stay with Naomi, and the events that resulted from that decision, affected generations yet unborn and provided Ruth an eternal niche in history. Ruth became the grandmother of King David and an ancestress of Jesus Christ.

In LDS Church history, a somewhat similar decision faced two young widows in Nauvoo, Illinois, in the mid-1840s: Emma Hale Smith, the widow of the martyred Prophet Joseph Smith, and Mary Fielding Smith, the wife of Hyrum Smith. Emma Smith decided to stay in Nauvoo, and most of her descendants have lived their lives outside of the LDS Church. Mary Fielding Smith decided to follow the prophet Brigham Young into the Great Basin. A son (Joseph F. Smith) and a grandson (Joseph Fielding Smith) have served as presidents of the Church, and virtually all of her several hundred descendants are now members.

**2:19** The clause translated "she shewed her mother in law with whom she had wrought, and said" could have been translated "she told her mother-in-law with whom she had worked, and said."

**3-4** The Levirate marriage system provided that a brother (or near kinsman if there were no brothers) of the deceased husband could marry the young widow and, if she were still in child-bearing years, raise up seed unto the deceased husband. (See "Levirate Marriage," BD, p. 724.)

**3:9** The root of the Hebrew word translated "skirt" was translated "wings" in Ruth 2:12. The essential meaning is the same as the English idiom "to take under one's wing," meaning to provide security and protection. In effect, Ruth is proposing marriage to Boaz, and one basis of her proposal is that Boaz is "a near kinsman."

**4:1-10** Ellis Rasmussen has written the following commentary on these verses:

The legal proceedings were duly accomplished. Apparently the writer of the tale did not even bother to find the name of the opportunist kinsman who was only willing to do the duty of a redeemer of his dead kinsman's property until he found that the responsibility of marrying a young widow and raising up a son to the name of the dead was entailed. The first son of such a marriage would be counted the son and heir of the dead husband, and thus, though the "redeemer" paid to get the land back into the possession of the family, it would go to that heir and not increase his own estate.

The word here rendered "redeemer" we translate literally from Hebrew *go'el* and this is its proper translation. It is rendered merely "kinsman" in the King James English translation. The function of a go'el was to make it possible for a widow who had lost home and property to return to her former status and security and to have seed to perpetuate her family.

It is easy to see why the later prophets borrowed this word from the social laws of Israel and used it to describe the functions of Him who would become the Divine Redeemer: Think of what He does to restore us to proper status with God, and to give us future security and eternal "seed."

The socio-economic law involved is found in Deuteronomy 25:5-10. (IOT 1:157.)

# 1 SAMUEL

See "Samuel, Books of" in the Bible Dictionary, page 769.

**1:3** Inasmuch as Elkanah went each year "to sacrifice unto the Lord of hosts in Shiloh," he might well have been of the tribe of Levi. Thus Samuel, if worthy, may have had a right later to perform some of the priestly functions by right of his birth, even without the special vows of his mother and his training with Eli.

Shiloh is the name of a place as well as a title referring to Jesus Christ. (See Gen. 49:10 and associated commentary.) The *place* Shiloh is first mentioned in Joshua 18:1; it was founded when the tabernacle and the ark of the covenant were placed there. (See Josh. 18:1 and Judg. 18:31.)

**1:20** The basic root of the Hebrew name *Samuel* (shmu) can mean either "name" or "heard"; the root *el*, of course, means "God." Thus *Samuel* could either mean "name of God" or "heard of God." In either case, it is an appropriate name, for Hannah asked for a child "of the Lord" and the Lord heard her plea.

The meaning of the Hebrew name *Hannah* is "gracious," and the name remains one of the most popular names for girls in modern Israel. The English name Ann, Anne, or Anna has the same background.

**2:1-10** Ellis Rasmussen has provided the following commentary on the song of Hannah:

Compare Hannah's song of thanksgiving and praise to God with that of Mary (Luke 1:46-55) and to that of Zachariah (Luke 1:68-79). What is the main thing about God and His ways which seems to have impressed all three? Note the usual parallelism and figurative language so characteristic of Hebrew poetry. What is the significance of calling the Lord a "rock"? (Compare such usage of the term in Deuteronomy 32:15, 18, 31 and in I Corinthians 10:1-4. The connotations seem to include the concepts of "firmness" and "security." Similar uses of the term are seen in Psalm 118:22, Matthew 21:42, etc.) Note also that He was called by Hannah "a God of knowledge"; compare that concept of him with the definition of His "glory" in Doctrine and Covenants 93:36.

The term "horn," when used figuratively, usually means "power"; note its use in both the first and the last stich of the poem.

One who was "anointed" of God was a special servant of God, such as a priest or a king. Properly appointed kings in Israel were always anointed with oil as an ordinance to convey authority. The Hebrew word for anointed, as transliterated into English, is *messiah*; eventually it was used in the definite form ("The Messiah") as the title for the anticipated Divine King to come. The Greek word for the same idea was *Christos;* in English, Christ. Does there seem to be a Messianic Hope already in Hannah's words in verse 10? (IOT 1:161.)

**2:12** See "Belial" on page 620 of the Bible Dictionary.

**2:25** The Hebrew term translated "would slay them" might have been translated "desired to put them to death."

**3:1** The word *precious* has the dual meaning of "rare" and "valuable," indicating the heavens had indeed become as brass for these people in their apostasy as the Lord had foretold. (See Deut. 28:23.)

**4:1-22** The depth of the apostasy of the people at this time is evident by their use of sacred objects for selfish and expedient purposes. The ark of the covenant was not intended to be used as a rallying point for the armies of Israel, and it appears the sons of Eli agreed to its use here more in superstitious hope than in real faith.

**6:9-10** The Philistines evidently "loaded the dice" in the test to determine whether or not the God of Israel was involved with the troubles that had come upon them. The milk cows that were to draw the cart with the ark upon it had nursing calves, and the calves were kept at home; evidently the Philistines thought the cows would surely return home to be with their calves rather than continue on to Beth-shemesh.

**6:19** Although the Hebrew words indeed indicate that 50,070 men of Beth-shemesh were smitten, the order of the words suggests that only 70 men were killed and then something else is said about 50 of them. One possible reading is "Jehovah struck seventy among the people, fifty chief men." The accounts in both the Septuagint version of the Bible and the writings of Josephus indicate only seventy men were smitten.

**8:7** Whenever people fail to hearken to the true prophet of God, they fail to hearken to God himself. As the Lord has said in this dispensation, "whether by mine own voice or by the voice of my servants, it is the same." (D&C 1:38.) Thus the Lord said to Samuel: "They [the rebellious people] have not rejected thee, but they have rejected me."

**9:9** The parenthetical observation that the position of prophet in those days was known formerly as the position of seer might indicate (1) the meaning of the word has changed, (2) the function of the prophet has evolved [or devolved] into the function of a seer, or (3) there are somewhat different functions in the calling of a prophet as compared with the calling of a seer.

The inspired commentary of the Bible (known as the Book of Mormon) has again provided the answer.

"A seer is a revelator and a prophet also; and a gift which is greater can no man have, except he should possess the power of God, which no man can; yet a man may have great power given him from God.

"But a seer can know of things which are past, and also of things which are to come." (Mosiah 8:16-17.)

The term *seer* therefore designates a wider and more comprehensive function than the term *prophet*. In other words, a seer is always a prophet, but a prophet might not always be a seer.

The term has been explained by Orson F. Whitney:

> A seer is greater than a prophet. [Mosiah 8:15.] One may be a prophet without being a seer; but a seer is essentially a prophet—if by "prophet" is meant not only a spokesman, but likewise a foreteller. Joseph Smith was both prophet and seer.
>
> A seer is one who sees. But it is not the ordinary sight that is meant. The seeric gift is a supernatural endowment. Joseph was "like unto Moses," and Moses, who saw God face to face, explains how he saw him in these words: "Now mine own eyes have beheld God; but not my natural, but my spiritual eyes; for my natural eyes could not have beheld; for I should have withered and died in his presence; but his glory was upon me; and I beheld his face, for I was transfigured before him." [Moses 1:11.] Such is the testimony of the ancient Seer, as brought to light by the Seer of Latter-days. (SNT, p. 39.)

In The Church of Jesus Christ of Latter-day Saints today, the members of the First Presidency and the Council of the Twelve Apostles are sustained by the members of the Church as "prophets, seers, and revelators."

**8:10-22**   Samuel's woeful prophecies concerning what will happen to the Israelites under kings start to be fulfilled almost immediately after the establishment of the monarchy.

Ellis Rasmussen has provided the following commentary on Samuel's concerns:

> The Lord instructed Samuel to grant them their request even if it be to their detriment. (On the dangers of this sort of exercise of free agency, see D&C 88:64-65.)
>
> Note, by the way, that this speech of Samuel's against the institution of monarchy in Israel was used by George Washington in his rejection of the

proposal that he become a king in the American colonies freed from England by the American Revolutionary War. (IOT 1:164.)

**9:21**   The Hebrew words translated "wherefore then speakest thou so to me" might have been translated "and why have you spoken to me according to this word?" Saul may have been asking Samuel what purpose Samuel had in telling Saul to go up to the high place.

**10:17-25**   Even before the Israelites returned to the promised land, the Lord foretold their eventual desire for a king, and he instructed them as to how the new king should be chosen:

"When thou art come unto the land which the Lord thy God giveth thee, and shalt possess it, and shalt dwell therein, and shalt say, I will set a king over me, like as all the nations that are about me;

"Thou shalt in any wise set him king over thee, whom the Lord thy God shall choose." (Deut. 17:14-15.)

Thus the king selected by the Lord would serve by divine *authority*. Unfortunately some later kings, in Israel and especially elsewhere, came to believe they served by divine *right* and that this right was automatically passed on to their descendants whether or not they were chosen by the Lord.

When the Lord, through Samuel, chose Saul to be king, an assembly of all the tribes was called where Saul could be presented and where the people could sustain the choice (v. 24). Evidently the confirming, sustaining voice of the people was an integral part of the installation of a king, as is also later indicated in the cases of David (2 Sam. 2:1-4; 2 Sam. 5:1-3) and Rehoboam. (1 Kgs. 12:1-20.)

**13:1**   The translated statement "Saul reigned one year" is not found in the Hebrew text. Evidently the original writer of the text intended to give the age of Saul when he first started to reign, but no age is listed. Thus the opening sentence might have been translated "Saul was ( ) years old when he began to reign."

Saul was obviously a young man when he was anointed to become king, but his actual "coronation" as king might not have occurred until many years later. The Bible later indicates that David was also anointed as a boy, but was thirty before becoming king.

**13:8-16**   Saul's assuming of priestly powers through the unauthorized performance of priestly duties cost him and his descendants the privilege of a hereditary monarchy (vs. 13-14).

**13:19-23**    The Philistines evidently held a monopoly in metal work in those days. Their blacksmiths were willing to sharpen agricultural implements for the Israelites, but would not provide them with metal weapons of war. Only Saul and Jonathan had a spear and sword; other soldiers among the Israelites evidently fought with weapons of stone and wood.

**14:45**    The statement "so the people rescued Jonathan" from Saul would indicate the combined will of the people was stronger than the authority of the king during this early period of the monarchy.

**15:32**    The Hebrew word translated "delicately" does not make much sense in this context, even with such possible alternate translations as "daintily" and "cheerfully." The original writer may have meant to convey the idea that Agag was putting on a fake front of optimism and bravado. Agag's statement "Surely the bitterness of death is past" seems to mean "Let's let bygones be bygones." Saul indicates by his subsequent savage handling of the king of the Amalekites that he is not about to be flattered by Agag.

**15:35**    For an explanation of the Hebrew word translated here as "repented," see the commentary for Numbers 23:19.

The Joseph Smith Translation adds a new dimension to this clause: "And the Lord *rent the kingdom* from Saul whom he had made king over Israel." (Italics added.)

**16:7**    Man may deceive his fellowmen, but he cannot deceive the Lord. It would be well if people were willing to have God select all their leaders, for he is able to look through any hypocrisy or sham and perceive real potential. "Man looketh on the outward appearance, but the Lord looketh on the heart."

**16:14-16, 23**    The Joseph Smith Translation makes it clear that the evil spirit was *not* of the Lord.

**17:4-7**    According to the weights and measurements assigned by most biblical scholars, Goliath would have been over nine feet tall, with a "coat of mail" (armor) weighing about 125 pounds and a spear with a head weighing about 15 pounds!

**17:39**    The Hebrew word translated "proved" here could have been translated as "test" or "try." It is even translated as "tempted" in Exodus 17:7 wherein the children of Israel "tempted [tried, tested, proved] the Lord."

**18:18**    The Hebrew that is translated "what is my life" has the essential meaning of "who are my kinfolk."

**18:21**    The Hebrew sentence translated "Wherefore Saul

said to David, Thou shalt this day be my son in law in the one of the twain" might also have been translated "And Saul said to David a second time, You shall be my son-in-law."

**18:23** The Hebrew words translated "Seemeth it to you a light thing to be a king's son in law, seeing that I am a poor man" might have been translated "Is it a light thing in your eyes to be son-in-law to the king; I am a poor man."

**18:27** The word *tale* is older English, meaning tally or number; the idea is that David gave them "all" to the king.

**19:9** The Joseph Smith Translation adds *not* at a critical point in the first clause of this verse: "And the evil spirit which was *not* of the Lord was upon Saul." (Italics added.) This reading is consistent with similar changes in 1 Samuel 16:14, 15, 16 and 18:10.

**21:1-6** The shewbread was changed every sabbath day, and the old loaves were to be eaten by the priests. (See Lev. 24:9.) In this time of emergency, David persuades the priest (Nob) to allow his men to eat the "hallowed" bread, which was contrary to custom.

In New Testament times when the Savior's disciples also unlawfully partook of food on the sabbath in an emergency situation, the Pharisees accused Jesus: "Thy disciples do that which is not lawful to do upon the sabbath day" (Matt. 12:2). Jesus then taught the principle that charity overrides the ritual law by quoting the incident of David and the shewbread. (See Matt. 12:4-9; Mark 2:23-28; Luke 6:1-5.)

**21:9** Evidently the sword of Goliath must have been kept as a memorial of how God can triumph over Israel's enemies.

A similar event occurs in the Book of Mormon; the sword of Laban was retained by the Nephites for hundreds of years. (See 1 Ne. 4:6-19; 2 Ne. 5:14; Jacob 1:10; W of M 1:13; Mosiah 1:16.)

**27:10** The Hebrew words translated "Whither have ye made a road to day?" could have been translated "Have you not attacked today?"

**28:3-20** Ellis Rasmussen has provided the following commentary on the visit of Saul with the witch of En-dor:

Here is the pathetic story of tragic old King Saul as he prepared for his last battle; he could get no guidance from legitimate avenues of communication with the Lord (including the use of the Urim and Thummim), and so turned to diviners, whose activities were against the law of Moses, and who had been banished by Saul himself in better times (cf. Exodus 22:18, Deuteronomy 18:10). Would you think that it was a bonafide revelation from God which he then received through the spiritualist medium? It seems more likely that the medium and her "spirit" communicants deceived Saul into thinking the dead Samuel had responded to his plea! The gloomy prediction was devastating to poor old Saul.

The medium's description of "gods ascended out of the earth" suggests she had a vision of a whole concourse of spirits in this momentous seance. If the forces of evil wished to bring about Saul's final destruction, things were well-calculated to accomplish it. The apparition recalled his rejection and his hopeless situation. (IOT 1:175.)

**28:9**    The following words should be added to the end of this verse, according to the Joseph Smith Translation: "Also, who hath not a familiar spirit."

**28:11-15**    The Joseph Smith Translation makes several changes in these verses. As an example, verse 11 reads:

"Then said the woman, *The word* of whom shall I bring up unto thee? And he said, Bring me up *the word* of Samuel." (Italics added.)

**31:1-6**    Two accounts of the death of Saul are provided in the Bible: 1 Samuel 31:1-6 and 2 Samuel 1:1-10. In the account of 1 Samuel, Saul commits suicide by falling upon his sword. In the account of 2 Samuel, although "Saul leaned upon his spear" (v. 6) it did not cause his death; Saul then asked an Amalekite to kill him, which the Amalekite did. The Amalekite may have fabricated his story in hopes he would receive a reward from David for having killed one he viewed as David's enemy. If that was the hope of the Amalekite, it was in vain. David summarily had the Amalekite killed for destroying "the Lord's anointed."

# 2 SAMUEL

See "Samuel, Books of" in the Bible Dictionary, page 769.

**1:18** The Hebrew wording of this statement in parentheses is incomplete. A possible translation to convey the idea is: "And he said to teach the sons of Judah (the Song of) the Bow. Behold, it is written in the book of Jasher."

No book of Jasher appears in the present Old Testament. The Bible Dictionary mentions that various collections "of the book of Jasher are available today and may be of some worth, but do not appear to be the one spoken of in the Bible." (See "Jasher," BD, p. 710.) The original book of Jasher was evidently prepared about the time of Solomon, and consisted of a collection of "national songs, and stories of deeds of valor." (Ibid.)

The missing book of Jasher is mentioned only twice in the Old Testament: 2 Samuel 1:18 and Joshua 10:13.

**3:2-5** David had only two wives when he first went to Hebron to be made king (2:2), but several additional wives and concubines are listed here.

The Lord has said in modern times, "David . . . received many wives and concubines." (D&C 132:38.)

**3:33** The lament of David could have been translated from the Hebrew "Abner died as the death of a fool?" In other words, his death was vain or purposeless; a great warrior such as Abner should not have been put to death through deceit.

**5:7** This first biblical reference to Zion has been analyzed by Ellis Rasmussen as follows:

It [Zion] seems to have been the fortress of Jerusalem on the lower part of the hill southeast of Moriah's summit. The meaning of the word "Zion" in Hebrew has been much discussed but not yet satisfactorily analyzed. Some earlier uses of the word, however, may be seen in the Pearl of Great Price, Moses 7:18-69, in the Book of Mormon, Alma 13:17-19 and also in the Inspired Revision of the Holy Scriptures by Joseph Smith, and in Genesis 14:18-39 and 24:2-10. It was used as the name of Enoch's city of the "pure in heart" (D&C 97:21). Could the name anciently have been attached also to Melchizedek's city of Salem (later Jerusalem)? In some of the references above it seems so. (IOT 1:183.)

**5:7-8** David was born in Bethlehem, which after his reign as king became known as the "city of David." (See Luke 2:4.)

This title was used in New Testament times by the "angel of the Lord" in announcing the birth of Jesus Christ: "For unto you is born this day in the city of David a Saviour, which is Christ the Lord." (Luke 2:11.)

Jerusalem has also been called "David's city" because of his feat in capturing the city and making it his capital. The city of Jerusalem in David's time was believed to be located to the south of the present walled city of old Jerusalem.

Ellis Rasmussen has provided the following background on Jerusalem:

> David wisely chose as his capital Jerusalem, a city between the northern and southern factions of Israel, but belonging to neither of them, as it was still held by the Canaanite "Jebusites." The manner of conquering the city has been much discussed because of the problematical word rendered "gutter." The word appears most likely to designate a channel or a shaft, as it is similarly used in Mishnaic Hebrew. The shaft running up perpendicularly above a water conduit cut into the rock fifty feet toward the west from Gihon, as discovered by Sir C. Warren in 1867, which would have given people inside the city walls access to water in time of siege, would have made a possible avenue for invaders to enter and open the gates of the city from within. Joab is said to have accomplished that initial entry (1 Chronicles 11:6).
>
> Do you catch the implications of sarcasm in the Jebusites' saying David would have to overcome their "lame and blind"—as if such would have been sufficient to defend the city? David thereafter scathingly referred to *all* the Jebusite defenders as "the lame and the blind" (v. 8). (IOT 1:183.)

**6:6-11**   The dramatic incident of Uzzah's losing his life when he "put forth his hand to the ark of God" (v. 6) not only had an immediate effect on David, but has had a lingering influence on many others over the centuries. The saying "Don't steady the ark" has come to mean "Don't get involved in something in which you have no legitimate business nor authority." The Lord used the term "steady the ark of God" in a revelation to Joseph Smith November 27, 1832. (D&C 85:8.)

**8:1-18**   Hundreds of years before the time of David, the Lord covenanted with Abraham to give his seed a specified area. (See Gen. 13:14-17; 15:18.) Finally, in the days of David the designated lands had either been conquered or the people in the lands were paying tribute to the Israelites.

**19:13**   The expression "God do so to me, and more also" is a form of oath or promise wherein the speaker promises before God to do a certain thing.

In this instance, Amasa might have needed some additional

assurance that David was sincere in making him military leader inasmuch as Amasa had, only shortly before, been leader of the enemy armies.

**19:20**  The term "house of Joseph" is used in place of the term "northern Israel" or "kingdom of Israel." Inasmuch as the word *Israelites* during this period of history could refer either to all the descendants of Jacob or to the citizens of the northern kingdom, sometimes the terms *Joseph* or *Ephraim* are used in order to indicate that only the citizens of the northern kingdom are meant.

**20:3**  Because these wives of David had been taken by his son Absalom while Absalom lived in Jerusalem, (2 Sam. 16:21-23), David could not continue in a connubial status with them.

The Lord had commanded the people through Moses: "The nakedness of thy father's wife shalt thou not uncover: it is thy father's nakedness." (Lev. 18:8.)

**20:8**  "Joab's garment," worn by Amasa on this occasion, may have been a type of military uniform designating a particular rank or position. As the new leader of the armies, Amasa may have felt obliged to wear it.

**21:1-14**  Ellis Rasmussen has written the following commentary on the content of these verses:

This terrible episode must have been done on days of David's spiritual deterioration. The law would not have permitted sons to be put to death for the guilt of a father or a forefather. (Deuteronomy 24:16 is explicit on that; see also Numbers 35:33.) It cannot have been a revelation from the Lord that either required or approved this deed done "to avenge the Gibeonites" —some of whom Saul had slain in spite of the ancient promise of Joshua that they might live in Israel.

It is a pathetic picture to envision the innocent mother of innocent sons guarding their bodies from the birds and beasts; and it is repulsive to read that after all this was done "God was entreated for the land." This is apostate theology, comparable to that of the Canaanite-Baal religions.

The text is somewhat corrupted too, and the name Michal must be a mistake for Merab, for it was Merab who married Adriel. If it is indeed Michal, David's wife and Saul's daughter, who is meant, this is a very bitter ending to their relationships as man and wife. (IOT 1:190.)

**22:1-51**  This same psalm appears in the book of Psalms (number 18) without the introductory verse and with a few changes. The most significant changes in Psalm 18 occur in the verses corresponding to 2 Samuel 22:11, 12, 13, 14, 28, 29, 36, and 50.

The materials in Psalm 18 corresponding to the materials in

2 Samuel 22 usually appear in verses numbered one digit earlier; for example, Psalm 18:3 corresponds to 2 Samuel 22:4.

**23:8-39**    Included in this list of "the mighty men" (heroes, great ones) of David is "Uriah the Hittite" (v. 39), the same Uriah whose wife, Bath-sheba, lay with David and whose life was required by David. (See 11:2-27.)

**24:1-25**    Apostate theology contained in this chapter is discussed in the following commentary by Ellis Rasmussen:

> The Lord is represented as having been angry with Israel and having therefore concocted a plot to get David to do something disapproved so that He would have an excuse to bring punishment! Note that 1 Chronicles 21:1 changes the statement to read that *Satan* moved David to take the offensive census. But in 1 Chronicles 21:17, David is represented as pointing out to the Lord the injustice of his punishing the innocent! The plague is said to have ended when the Lord *repented* and felt it was enough without smiting Jerusalem; nevertheless the threshing-floor of Araunah was purchased by him as a site for an altar, and an offering so that the Lord was "entreated" and the plague was stopped. This is also apostate theology, written according to the understanding of the people of the time, but out of harmony with truths as taught by the prophets. We shall see such concepts and worship practices later evaluated in the writings of Hosea and Isaiah. (IOT 1:191.)

**24:16**    The Joseph Smith Translation makes a significant change in this verse:

"And when the angel stretched out his hand upon Jerusalem to destroy it, the Lord *said unto him,* Stay now thine hand, it is enough; *for the people repented,* and the Lord stayed the hand of the angel, that he destroyed not the people." (Italics added.)

# 1 KINGS

See "Kings, Books of" in the Bible Dictionary, page 721.

**1:5-10**  Adonijah evidently felt he should be the new king by right of his seniority among the sons of David. According to 2 Samuel 3:2-4, Adonijah was the fourth son of David and was preceded only by the following:

Amnon, who seduced his half-sister, Tamar, and was killed in revenge by her brother Absalom (2 Sam. 3:2; 13:1-39; 1 Chr. 3:1).

Chileab (also called Daniel in 1 Chronicles 3:1), who was not mentioned after the account of his birth (2 Sam. 3:3; 1 Chr. 3:1).

Absalom, who killed Amnon, went into exile, and led a revolt against his father during which he was killed by Joab and his men (2 Sam. 3:3; 13:1-39, 1 Chr. 3:2.)

But, as had been determined in the cases of Saul and David, the Lord—not the person—was to select the new king through His prophet.

**1:50**  The horns of the altar were located on each of the four corners. It was customary for people who had killed to seek refuge at the altar of the Lord from any avengers. Deliberate murderers could, even then, be taken from the altar and put to death. (See Ex. 21:14 and "Altar," BD, pp. 606-7.)

**2:1-9**  These final words of David contain a charge to his son Solomon, who is to be the new king. Psalm 72 contains a poetic prayer by David for "the king" Solomon.

Much of David's life was centered on warfare and the shedding of blood, from the days of Goliath to his declining years. Because of this, the Lord declared earlier that David was not to build the temple because he had shed blood. In this regard, it is of interest to note that David's final words on earth as recorded in the Bible are "with blood." (2:9.)

**2:5-6**  David mentions two reasons for wanting the death of Joab: (1) Joab killed Abner; (2) Joab murdered Amasa. Two other acts of Joab may also have influenced David's feelings: (1) Joab was involved in the death of Absalom (2 Sam. 18:5-15); (2) Joab was in alliance with Adonijah when Adonijah sought to become the new king. (1:7.)

**2:10**    Although the record states David was buried *in* "the city of David" (Jerusalem, not Bethlehem—see the commentary for 2 Samuel 5:7-8), he was probably buried outside the walls of the city but in the vicinity; the Israelites usually buried their dead outside the residential areas. Several sites have been honored over the centuries as the possible burial place of David.

**2:13-25**    Custom provided that anyone who received of the harem of the king should be heir to the throne. Whether Adonijah had this fact in mind when he requested Abishag as his wife is not known. Evidently Solomon felt Adonijah had evil purposes in making the request, for he ordered the death of Adonijah.

**3:1**    The Joseph Smith Translation adds an introductory clause and some other key words: "And *the Lord was not pleased with Solomon,* for he made affinity with Pharaoh, king of Egypt, and took Pharaoh's daughter *to wife.*" (Italics added.)

The Hebrew words translated "made affinity with" might have been translated "made a marriage alliance with."

**3:5-15**    Solomon's promise of wisdom and understanding was received from the Lord in a dream.

The statement "I am but a little child: I know not how to go out or come in" (v. 7) has more to do with Solomon's inexperience than his age. The Joseph Smith Translation reads: "And I know not how to lead them, to go out, or come in before them, and I, thy servant, am as a little child." (3:8.)

**3:12-13**    The Lord's statement in verse 12 seems to indicate that Solomon is the most wise and understanding of all the people who ever lived—"there was none like thee before thee, neither after thee shall any arise like unto thee." However, the Joseph Smith Translation makes it clear the Lord is comparing Solomon to the kings of Israel, not to all mankind—"there was none *made king over Israel* like unto thee before thee." (3:12; italics added.)

Verse 13 of the King James Version substantiates the changes in the Joseph Smith Translation—"there shall not be any *among the kings* like unto thee." (Italics added.)

**3:14**    Rather than *commendation* of David, the Joseph Smith Translation refers to *condemnation* of David, with a promise to Solomon if he proves worthy:

"And if thou wilt walk in my ways to keep my statutes, and my commandments, then I will lengthen thy days, *and thou*

*shalt not walk in unrighteousness, as did thy father David."*
(Italics added.)

**3:16-28**   Ellis Rasmussen has commented concerning this well-known story:

> In this best-known story illustrating Solomon's "wisdom," you may think he was simply *fortunate*. Ordinarily neither woman wanting a child would agree to such a shocking and unsatisfying solution as Solomon proposed. Perhaps his wisdom lay in his perceiving that the false claimant *would* be brazen enough to expose herself by agreeing to the dividing of the child! (IOT 1:197.)

**4:5**   The Hebrew words translated "principal officer, and the king's friend" really say in the Hebrew "priest, friend of the king." Whether the word *priest* refers to a priesthood office is not made clear, nor is the precise identity of Zabud's father. The Nathan mentioned may have been the prophet Nathan.

**4:22-25**   Some Bible scholars have estimated that these *daily* provisions would have fed at least 35,000 people. Of course the persons provided for included Solomon's numerous families, the families of court officials and servants, and perhaps the families of military personnel.

**4:32**   Some of the "three thousand proverbs . . . and . . . thousand and five" songs are included in the books of Proverbs and Song of Solomon. Not all of them were inspired of the Lord, of course; in fact, the Lord has revealed that the Song of Solomon was not inspired. (See the commentary for the Song of Solomon.)

**6:1**   The date of the beginning of the temple provides one of the few exact dates in the Old Testament, and then only in relationship to the departure of the children of Israel "out of the land of Egypt." The 480 years might be accounted for approximately as follows: Period in wilderness—40 years; period of Judges (Joshua to Samuel)—356 years; reign of Saul —40 years; reign of David—40 years; period already served by Solomon—4 years.

The major time not accounted for precisely in the Bible is the period of judges. For possible dates of some of the major events, see the chronological tables appearing under the entry "Chronology" in the Bible Dictionary, pp. 635-45.

**6:2-3**   If a cubit is equal to about eighteen inches, as suggested by most Bible scholars, the size of the temple would be ninety feet ("threescore cubits") in length, thirty feet ("twenty cubits") in breadth, and forty–five feet ("thirty cubits") in height. It was not large by today's standards, but was beautifully adorned and lavishly furnished.

**6:7**    The stone for the temple was evidently fashioned right at the quarry so there would be no sound of "hammer nor axe nor any tool of iron heard in the house, while it was in building." This statement may indicate the sense of reverence for the sanctity of the place, and may also suggest that many of the furnishings were prefabricated.

**6:23-25**    The carving of the two large cherubim (each fifteen feet high, with wing spans of fifteen feet) was not in violation of the commandment against engraven idols (or "images," as translated in the King James Version). The cherubim were not to be worshipped, but were for beautification and for representation of heavenly powers. (See Rev. 4:6 and D&C 77:1-4 for the meanings of similar, but not identical, representations; see also "Cherubim," BD, p. 632.)

**7:13-14**    This artisan from Tyre named Hiram should not be confused with the king of Tyre of the same name.

**7:23-26**    Ellis Rasmussen has provided the following commentary on the "molten sea" (brass font) and its possible use:

> The font of bronze placed on the backs of twelve oxen has been calculated to have a possible capacity of 16,000 gallons! According to II Chronicles 4:2-6, it was for the ceremonial "washing of priests." . . . Unfortunately, no record of baptisms in this basin has been found. Recall that the Book of Moses and the Inspired Translation of the Bible mention baptism from Adam's time to that of Enoch. In Genesis 17 of the Inspired Translation it is said that proper baptism had ceased among the apostate peoples at Abraham's time, but in this source no further mention of it is made. . . .
>
> To make so much bronze work possible, no doubt the famous "King Solomon's mines" (recently rediscovered) must have been working to capacity. (IOT 1:200.)

**8:62-64**    Ellis Rasmussen has provided the following commentary on the nature of the sacrifice offered at the dedication of the temple:

> The dedicatory observances concluded with another blessing upon the people by the king and a colossal program of sacrifice of seven days duration. It appears that this was the festival type of "peace offering" such as is described in Leviticus 3 and 7:11 ff., in which the Lord's portion (burned upon the altar) was certain fat portions of the inward parts, about

the kidneys and liver, etc.; the priests received the right shoulder and the brisket, and the remainder was eaten in a feast by the family in whose behalf the animal was sacrificed. It hardly seems likely that the "burnt whole offering" of Leviticus 6:8 ff., or Exodus 29:38-42, or Numbers 28:3 ff., would have been involved. After the seven days' dedication feast, the other feast celebrated would likely have been the festival of Succoth at the time of the year indicated in verse 2 of this chapter. This is a joyful festival to this day throughout Judaism. (It is also called, in English, the Feast of Tabernacles.) (IOT 1:201.)

**10:1** The Hebrew words translated as "hard questions" were translated in Judges 14 as "riddle."

**10:1-13** The exact location of the homeland of the Queen "of Sheba" is in dispute. Some Bible scholars believe it was in Saudi Arabia; others believe it was in Africa. An Ethiopian tradition that the leaders of Ethiopia (including Haile Selassie) were descendants of a son born to Solomon and the Queen of Sheba suggests that Africa was the location of Sheba.

**10:28** The Hebrew of this verse evidently means "from Kue" ("Keveh") and has erroneously been translated "linen yarn." The sentence could have been translated, "And the horses that King Solomon had were brought from Egypt and from Kue; the king's merchants received them from Kue at a price." If the Hebrew word is not intended to designate a place, it might also be translated "in droves."

**11:6** The wording of the Kings James Version and the Joseph Smith Translation are virtually the same, but note how the meaning is greatly altered by changing the order of the clauses! The Joseph Smith Translation reads:

"And Solomon did evil in the sight of the Lord, as David his father, and went not fully after the Lord."

After misinterpreting verse 4, the King James translators evidently decided to arrange the clauses in verse 6 to agree with their interpretation of verse 4.

**11:6-8** Concerning the downfall of Solomon and the sins of David, Ellis Rasmussen has observed:

The fall of Solomon resulted from his system of marrying royal wives from all the countries round about—which policy may well have been for economic and political reasons as well for his "love" of "strange women"! Since he not only tolerated their religions but caused shrines and sacrificial high places to be built for them and "went after" their gods and goddesses himself, it would seem he was seeking power from every imaginable source. . . . Notice that Solomon's violation of the marriage statute (v. 2) led to his breaking the first and second of the Ten Commandments; David's breach of the tenth led to his breaking of the seventh and then the sixth commandments. (IOT 1:202-3.)

**11:33, 38-39**    The Joseph Smith Translation of these verses indicates:

1. Solomon sinned greatly as did David, but Solomon was not repentant and so the Lord could not forgive him.

2. David was blessed by the Lord when he was obedient to the Lord's commandments.

3. Because of the sins of Solomon, the right of reigning over ten of the twelve tribes was taken from him (and his descendants).

4. Because of the sins of David, the descendants of David would be afflicted, "but not for ever."

**13:18**    The present rendering of verse 18 is difficult to understand. The Joseph Smith Translation not only clarifies the situation but also inserts a *not* in a critical place, changing the meaning: "Bring him back with thee into thine house, that he may eat bread and drink water, *that I may prove him*; and he lied *not* unto him." (Italics added.)

**13:26**    The final word of this verse should be *me* (not *him*), according to the Joseph Smith Translation.

**14:8**    The King James Version extols David and condemns Jeroboam. However, the Joseph Smith Translation condemns both:

"And rent the kingdom away from the house of David and gave it thee, *because he kept not my commandments*. But thou hast not been as my servant David, when he followed me with all his heart only to do right in mine eyes."

**15:3-11**    The Joseph Smith Translation makes significant contributions to several of these verses (italics added):

Verse 3: "His [Abijam's] heart was not perfect with the Lord his God, *as the Lord commanded David his father.*"

Verse 5: "Save only in the matter of Uriah the Hittite, *wherein the Lord cursed him.*"

Verse 11: "And Asa did right in the eyes of the Lord, as *he commanded* David his father."

Verse 12: "And he took away the sodomites out of the land and removed all the idols that his fathers had made; *and it pleased the Lord.*"

The statement in verse 5 that David was cursed because of his dealings with Uriah has been reinforced by the Lord in a revelation to Joseph Smith:

"And in none of these things did he [David] sin against me

save in the case of Uriah and his wife; and, therefore he hath fallen from his exaltation.'' (D&C 132:39.)

**16:23-28** Ellis Rasmussen quotes nonbiblical sources concerning the reign and influence of Omri:

And there was still division and violence and bloodshed, for part of the people chose yet another, Tibni, to be king; but the civil war that ensued established Omri. Non-Biblical sources tell more about his eleven years of reign than does the Bible. In addition to his procuring Samaria and building it into a well-fortified capital city for northern Israel, the stone inscription of Mesha, King of Moab, admits that he conquered Moab and exacted tribute all his days. And later inscriptions, such as the annals of Shalmanezer III, designated Israel as the "land of the house of Omri," and its kings were called in that text "sons of Omri" even after his dynasty had been long replaced by another ruling family. Ben Hadad of Syria said his father took certain cities from Omri and forced him to allow free trade in Samaria. (IOT 2:5-6.)

**17:1** This is the first mention of the prophet Elijah ("Jehovah is God") the Tishbite in the Bible. The next three chapters and 2 Kings 1 and 2 are largely devoted to the accomplishments of this great man. It is not certain whether *Tishbite* refers to Elijah's genealogy or to the location of his birth, although some scholars believe it might have reference to the village of Tishbe in the land of Gilead. (For the location of Tishbe, see Map 9 of the Bible, about midpoint between the Sea of Chinnereth (Galilee) and the Salt Sea, just east of the river Jordan.)

**17:1-24** The supernatural powers exhibited by Elijah in this chapter clearly demonstrate that he possessed the power of God. Joseph Fielding Smith taught that the Melchizedek Priesthood held by Elijah was also possessed by other prophets in the Old Testament:

We discover that all the ordinances which could be performed by the Aaronic Priesthood remained with Israel in the dark days of her disobedience. It was necessary, under these conditions, that there be someone with authority to perform ordinances, such as confirmation, for we know that the prophets of old had the gift of the Holy Ghost. [2 Peter 1:21.]

We read in [1] Kings, chapter 17, that power had been given to Elijah to close the heavens that there would be no rain except by his word. He had power given him to bless the widow's oil and meal and to bring down fire from heaven to consume his offering and destroy the false doctrines of the priests of Baal. The fact that Elijah had this great power and authority did not prevent other prophets from also holding some divine authority in the Melchizedek Priesthood which was essential to the faithful in the House of Israel. We should also remember the fact that in the days of the Savior's ministry this authority held by Elijah was bestowed by Elijah, and the authority held by Moses was restored by Moses to Peter, James, and John. (AGQ 4:7-8.)

**17:8-16**    Although most of the Israelites did not recognize Elijah as a prophet, a widow of another land (Zarephath of Zidon) was willing to follow his teachings. In New Testament times, Jesus Christ referred to this event when he was teaching the principle "No prophet is accepted in his own country":

"But I tell you of a truth, many widows were in Israel in the days of Elias [Greek for Elijah], when the heaven was shut up three years and six months, when great famine was throughout all the land;

"But unto none of them was Elias sent, save unto Sarepta, a city of Sidon, unto a woman that was a widow." (Luke 4:24-26.)

**18:21**    The Hebrew word translated "halt" has the meaning of "limping." The idea is that the people have been "vacillating," "skipping back and forth," "staggering" toward one view and then the other. Elijah challenges them to make up their minds.

The people recognized their vacillation on this occasion, and they "answered him not a word."

The stirring challenge of Elijah "if the Lord be God, follow him" is as appropriate today as when first given. John Taylor and Spencer W. Kimball have given their observations concerning this challenge:

Whichever way we decide let us carry out our decisions in good faith, and not have our sign painted on one side in white and on the other black or some other color. But let us feel as the prophet Elijah did on a certain occasion, "If the Lord be God, follow him; but if Baal, then follow him." There was a disposition in ancient Israel to have a part of God and a part of the devil or Baal—an idolatrous god which was worshipped by them. I sometimes think that in some respects we are a good deal like them. Do we believe our religion? Yes. Do we believe in the holy priesthood and that God has restored it to the earth? Yes. Do we believe that God has established his kingdom? Yes. And do we believe that the holy priesthood is under the guidance of the Lord? O, yes; but still we would like a good deal of our own way. (John Taylor, JD 21:54-55.)

The answer to all of our problems—personal, national, and international—has been given to us many times by many prophets, ancient to modern. Why must we grovel in the earth when we could be climbing toward heaven! The path is not obscure. Perhaps it is too simple for us to see. We look to foreign programs, summit conferences, land bases. We depend on fortifications, our gods of stone; upon ships and planes and projectiles, our gods of iron—gods which have no ears, no eyes, no hearts. We pray to them for deliverance and depend upon them for protection. Like the gods of Baal, they could be "talking or pursuing or on a journey or peradventure sleeping" when they are needed most. And like Elijah, we might cry out to our world:

"How long halt ye between two opinions; if the Lord be God, follow him. . . ." (1 Kings 18:21.)

My testimony to you is, the Lord *is* God. He has charted the way, but we do not follow. (Spencer W. Kimball, CR, Apr. 1960, p. 85.)

**18:44-46**   Elijah is so confident that the Lord is about to end the drought he runs ahead of the chariot in order to get off Mount Carmel before the rains come.

The miracle of the termination of the drought is accepted as a literal fact by all faithful Latter-day Saints. The Book of Mormon contains a similar faith-promoting incident when Nephi, the son of Helaman, asked the Lord to cause a famine to stir up the people "in remembrance of the Lord their God." After the people had repented, the Lord responded to Nephi's request to send rain again upon the earth. (Hel. 11:3-18.)

Spencer W. Kimball has indicated such miracles are the result of faith: "It was by and through the faith of Elijah that the drought, which devastated Israel, prolonged for three interminable years, was finally terminated when repentance had come to Israel. . . . "The miracle of faith had again made good the promises of the Lord." (CR, Oct. 1952, p. 50.)

**19:9-10**   Many prophets of God have been required to endure persecution, as explained by John Taylor:

Now, why was it that men that were aiming at an exaltation among the Gods should be so persecuted and cast out by men? For instance I might mention a few of them. I might refer to Job and the kind of trials he passed through; I might talk about Abraham and the trials he was called upon to pass through; I might mention Moses and the trials he had to endure; I might bring to your minds many other prominent men of God, but I will come to Elijah, who was a man that feared God and wrought righteousness. The people had departed from the Lord and trampled under foot His precepts, etc. So much so that Elijah was obliged to flee and hide himself in a cave away from the face of man. . . .

Well, it was a critical position to be in, but it was just as critical for many others who lived in ancient times. And this spirit of murder and persecution still exists. . . .

I merely refer to these things to show that the spirit that actuated men in former times is at work today; irrespective of times, forms of government, places or circumstances. (JD 24:197.)

**19:11-13**    Harold B. Lee has indicated that a person must be sensitive to the Spirit of the Lord to hear the "still small voice" when it speaks:

> Prophets of old learned, as all must know, how to communicate with the Lord by prayer, to talk with and then receive answers in the Lord's own way. . . .
>
> All too often when God speaks in this still, small voice, as he did to Elijah in the cave, it may not be audible to our physical hearing because, like a faulty radio, we may be out of tune with the infinite. (CR, Oct. 1966, p. 115.)

**19:19-21**    The Hebrew seems to indicate that Elijah literally "threw" his mantle (coat) on Elisha.

As indicated in the actions of Elisha, and the much later calling of the apostles by Jesus, true disciples immediately forsake all else and follow the true Master. (See also Matt. 4:18-22; 8:18-22; Luke 9:59-62.)

**22:1-38**    Ellis Rasmussen has provided the following commentary on these verses:

> A difference between the ostensible religion of Ahab and the more reverent faith of Jehoshaphat may be seen in Ahab's seeking and receiving guidance from his 400 court prophets, all of whom reassured him; while Jehoshaphat stood by and made the judicious inquiry, "Is there not here a *prophet of the Lord* besides, that we might inquire of him?" (Emphasis added.)
>
> The true prophet Micaiah's sarcastic repetition of the other prophets' message, followed by the true message of doom to Ahab, is not a serious problem, but his explanation of the Lord's sending a "lying spirit," causing the other prophets to mislead him so that he would go to his doom, is strange theology. (Compare Numbers 23:19 and I Samuel 15:29; also Enos 1:6 and Ether 3:12.) It was apparently either a sarcastic rationale, spoken in disdain, or it has been transmitted wrongly. (It is only when a passage is clearly contrary to true or moral doctrine elsewhere established that one is safe in considering the rejection of a reading, however!)
>
> Note that it must have been by reason of personal worthiness that Jehoshaphat was spared in battle, and that by the influence of the Lord, for it is strange that the enemy would spare *any* opponent, especially a royal one. Directly you will note that they who were looking for Ahab had been told by the King of Syria to fight against no one else. (IOT 2:9.)

# 2 KINGS

See "Kings, Books of" in the Bible Dictionary, page 721.

**1:2, 3, 6, 16**   The only time the Philistine god of Ekron is mentioned by the name *Baal-zebub* is in this chapter. Variations of the name are also used in place of the name of Satan.

In New Testament times the Pharisees challenged the Savior's healing of the "one possessed with a devil, blind, and dumb," by stating: "This fellow [Jesus] doth not cast out devils, but by Beelzebub the prince of the devils." (Matt. 12:22-24.)

The Hebrew meaning of Baal-zebub is "lord of the flies." (See "Beelzebub," BD, p. 620.)

**2:1-18**   This account seems to indicate that Elijah, Elisha, and the "sons of the prophet" knew in advance the exact day when Elijah was to be translated.

Joseph Fielding Smith has likened the "school of the prophets" in this dispensation to the meeting of the sons of the prophets in the days of Elijah:

> The "School of the Prophets" is not something new to this dispensation. In ancient Israel, especially in the days of Samuel, Elijah and Elisha, there was such a school. We read in I Samuel, tenth chapter, that after Samuel had anointed Saul to be king of Israel he met a company of prophets and prophesied with them. In II Kings, chapter two, where we have the account of the translation of Elijah, we are told that a company of the sons of the prophets accompanied Elisha who was determined to follow Elijah. "And fifty men of the sons of the prophets went, and stood in view afar off, and they two (Elijah and Elisha) stood by Jordan," and when Elisha returned to them after the departure of Elijah, these sons of the prophets discovered that the power of Elijah was upon Elisha. (CHMR 1:373.)

**2:9-11**   Ellis Rasmussen has provided the following commentary on (1) Elisha's request for a "double portion" of Elijah's spirit and (2) Elijah's translation:

> Elisha's request for a "double portion" of Elijah's spiritual gift [verse 9] is to be understood in connection with the law of inheritances (Deuteronomy 21:17), which specify that an heir, or birthright son, receive a larger portion of the inheritance than the other children of a man. It is as if Elisha asked to be made Elijah's official "heir," spiritually speaking.

Note also that the mantle of Elijah, which was earlier placed symbolically on Elisha (I Kings 19:19), was now transferred to him. This significant garment has become proverbial in our references to "the mantle of the prophet" falling upon someone.

Concerning Elijah's "translation" to heaven without tasting of death in the ordinary way, and concerning his functions in both the meridian of time and in the fullness of times, there are several allusions in other scriptures. See, for instance, the inquiry about him by Jesus' apostles (Matthew 17:11). In Jesus' reply it is evident not only that the old Prophet was still to be expected to usher in the Messianic age, but also that others, such as John the Baptist, could serve as *forerunners* to important dispensations. (Unfortunately the name spelled "Elijah" in the Old Testament comes through Greek transliteration as "Elias" in the New Testament, and only by context can one tell when the reference is to Elijah, when to any "forerunner," and when to a prophet *named* Elias.) His coming to "plant in the hearts of the children the promises made to the fathers" is spoken of in the Pearl of Great Price, JS-H 1:38-39. This is slightly different from the version of Malachi 4:5-6 as found in the common Old Testament text or as alluded to by the Apostles in the reference above cited in Matthew. Besides some discussion of his future function by the modern Prophet Joseph Smith (in the compilation called *Teachings of the Prophet Joseph Smith* by Joseph Fielding Smith, on pages 335-341), there are numerous references in the Doctrine and Covenants, readily found in its concordance.

Jewish people have honored Elijah with a place left vacant for him at every Passover table for these many centuries, as the anticipated herald of the Messianic kingdom as they understood it from the promise of the prophet Malachi. (IOT 2:10-11.)

**2:9-14** John Taylor has provided the following observations concerning the translation of Elijah and the subsequent designation of Elisha as Elijah's successor:

Elisha, knowing that he had something to do and that he was about to be left alone, and that he might be the better prepared to perform the work before him, requested Elijah to let a double portion of his spirit rest upon him. But could Elijah grant his request? No, he could not. What answer did Elijah make him? He said, thou hast asked a hard thing; nevertheless, if thou seest me when I am taken from thee, it shall be so unto thee; but if not it shall not be so. How did Elijah know that? Because he knew that the Melchizedec Priesthood holds the keys of the mysteries and the revelations of God; and that if he could see him as he ascended, it would be an evidence to him that the Lord had granted his request, although he himself had not power to grant it, Elisha would then know that his prayer was heard. Those other prophets, who knew that Elijah was to be translated, went and stood to view the event afar off; I do not support that they saw anything of Elijah as he was being taken up into heaven. But he was taken up, and Elisha saw the manner in which he went, and cried out,

"My father! my father! the chariot of Israel and the horsemen thereof." And how did he see them? God had conferred upon him that priesthood by which he was enabled to see them. Elijah threw down his mantle as he ascended, which Elisha took up and started off alone, his "head" having been translated. But he had received the answer to his prayer; and approaching the banks of the Jordan, with the mantle that had been left him he smote the waters saying, "Where is the Lord God of Elijah?" And when he did so they parted as they had done at the command of Elijah, and Elisha passed over. And God was with him, manifesting his power through him, as he had done through his predecessor. I speak of this as a certain principle and I speak of it now for the information of you elders, that they did not have then an organized Melchisedec Priesthood, but that if it was conferred upon individuals, they did not have the power to confer it upon others, unless through special command of the Lord. And Elijah knew that if Elisha could see him when he was ascending, that his prayer would be answered: Why? Because the Melchizedec Priesthood holds the keys of the mysteries and the revelations of God. (JD 21:248-49.)

**2:11**    One purpose for the translation of some persons is to allow them to continue to administer to the earth, as explained in this statement by Joseph Fielding Smith:

We learn from modern revelation that there are no angels who administer to this earth but those who do belong or have belonged to it. [D&C 130:5.] Therefore the angels who appeared to Adam and the antediluvian prophets must have been spirits who had not yet tabernacled in the flesh. Since that time messengers coming to give instruction to the prophets could have been spirits of just persons who had lived on the earth or translated beings who had been reserved for that purpose. We may be sure that any messenger coming before the resurrection of Jesus who had a tangible body was a translated being who had lived on the earth and had been translated to become a messenger to men on the earth. Such would be the case evidently in the visitors who came to Abraham and the personage who wrestled with Jacob.

According to the Pearl of Great Price, when Enoch was translated, the inhabitants of the city Zion were also taken and were also translated. How many others have been given this great honor we do not know, but there may have been many of whom we have no record. Prominence has been given to the case of Elijah as well as to Enoch, and the purpose of granting to prophets this great blessing is that they may minister upon the earth. Moreover, the Lord, of necessity, has kept authorized servants on the earth bearing the priesthood from the days of Adam to the present time; in fact, there has never been a moment from the beginning that there were not men on the earth holding the Holy Priesthood. [Moses 5:59.] (AGQ 2:44-45.)

**2:19-22**    The major spring supplying water for modern Jericho is still known as "Elisha's Spring."

**2:23-25**   Ellis Rasmussen has provided the following commentary on these verses:

> The stories of Elisha are mostly tales of his "good-turn" miracles for people, but this initial one is different. He was insulted by youths (Hebrew *na'arim* is "youths" usually, rather than "little children") who challenged him to ascend (as they had perhaps heard that Elijah had ascended), and taunted him with the dishonorable epithet "bald-head." Note that the account does not say the bears *ate* the children, nor even that they *killed* them, but *tore* them. The Hebrew word also means to "lacerate." (IOT 2:11.)

**4:18-37**   The miracle of bringing the dead back to life is mentioned rarely in the Old Testament. Two such instances are:

1 Kings 17:17-24, where Elijah restored to life the widow's son.

2 Kings 4:18-37, where Elisha brought back to life the son of the Shunammite couple.

**5:10-11**   The initial unbelief of Naaman in the way God should demonstrate his power is common to peoples of all ages, as explained in this statement by Spencer W. Kimball:

> Many people of our own day expect that revelations will come only in spectacular vision on Sinais accompanied with lightnings and thunderings. They are not unlike Naaman the Syrian war lord seeking relief from his leprosy. He was dumbfounded when the prophet Elisha ignored his letters of recommendation, his wealth, his position, his prestige, his impressive retinue of servants with chariots. The prophet Elisha merely sent his servant out to meet Naaman with the simple message, "Go and wash in Jordan seven times." (2 Kings 5:10.) The pompous foreign official was angered and bitterly complained: "I thought, He will surely come out to me, and stand, and call on the name of the Lord his God, and strike his hand over the place, and recover the leper." (2 Kings 5:11.) But there were no dramatic histrionics, no spectacular demonstrations, no pomp and show, no glamorous display; and Naaman lost confidence. He did not believe. He was unwilling to accept manifestations from God except in the way he himself prescribed.
>
> Even in our day, many people like him expect if there be revelation it will come with awe-inspiring, earth-shaking display. For many it is hard to accept as revelation those numerous ones in Moses' time, in Joseph's time, and in our own year—those revelations which come to prophets as deep, unassailable impressions settling down on the prophet's mind and heart as dew from heaven or as the dawn dissipates the darkness of night.
>
> The burning bushes, the smoking mountains, the sheets of four-footed beasts, the Cumorahs, and the Kirtlands were realities; but they were the exceptions. The great volume of revelation came to Moses and to Joseph and comes to today's prophet in the less spectacular way—that of deep impressions, without spectacle or glamour or dramatic events.

Always expecting the spectacular, many will miss entirely the constant flow of revealed communication. (Germany Area CR, Aug. 1973, pp. 76-77.)

**6:8-12** Through the power of the Holy Ghost, both ancient and modern prophets have had the power to see and hear what is happening elsewhere; hence, Elisha could know the words which the king of Syria spake "in [his] bedchamber."

Concerning this power, Brigham Young has stated:

When Joseph had a revelation, he had, as it were, the eyes of the Lord. He saw as the Lord sees. How did I know what was going on in Washington? I have known what was going on there all the time, and I know what is going on in other places. I know it by the spirit of God. (WW, p. 415.)

**6:24-33 to 2 Kgs. 7:1-20** This story of war between Israel and Syria is apparently from an earlier time period than the one recounted in 2 Kings 6:8-23. The war account earlier in chapter 6 ended with the words "So the bands of Syria came no more into the land of Israel"; yet in the very next verse the "king of Syria gathered all his host, and went up, and besieged Samaria." It should be remembered that this section of 2 Kings primarily consists of a series of stories that are not necessarily arranged chronologically.

**6:25-33** The Old Testament contains several accounts of people becoming so desperate in times of famine they resort to eating their own relatives. (See Jer. 19:9; Lam. 2:20; 4:10.) Moses had prophesied that this condition would come upon Israel if the people did not live righteously: "And thou shalt eat the fruit of thine own body, the flesh of thy sons and of thy daughters. . . . The tender and delicate women . . . shall eat them [her children] . . . secretly in the siege." (Deut. 28:53, 56-57.)

**7:1-18** Many principles can be learned from the stirring prophecy by Elisha and its startling fulfillment. One obvious lesson is that it is not wise to ridicule the teachings of a prophet.

**13:21** Even after the death and burial of Elisha the Lord restored life through him. As the body of a dead man was lowered into the sepulchre of Elisha "when the man was let down, and touched the bones of Elisha, he [the man] revived, and stood on his feet."

**15:11** The book of Chronicles in the Old Testament is not "the book of the chronicles of the kings of Israel" mentioned here. In fact, virtually nothing is said in Chronicles about the kings of *Israel*; 1 Chronicles and 2 Chronicles are both concerned primarily with the kings of *Judah*.

**15:16**    The savage act of disemboweling pregnant women so both mother and baby died at the same time had been prophesied by Elisha in 2 Kings 8:12.

**16:2-4**    The statement that Ahaz made his son to pass "through the fire, according to the abominations of the heathen" refers to the sacrifices of children to the fire-belching idol, Moloch.

**17:6-23**    This was the famed scattering of the "ten lost tribes of Israel." Verses 12-23 provide a detailed list of the sins of the people of the northern kingdom of Israel "against the Lord their God." (See Part I 48, 54, 79, 120-23, 224.)

**17:24**    The foreigners mentioned in verse 24, and their descendants, eventually intermarried with many of the Israelites who remained in Samaria after the ten tribes were taken into captivity. The offspring of these mixed marriages were the "Samaritans," who were not acceptable to the orthodox of Judah because of their mixed blood.

The scorn of most Jews for the Samaritans was still evident in New Testament times and provided the background for the visit of Jesus with the woman of Samaria at Jacob's well (John 4:3-42) as well as the story of the good Samaritan who proved to be a neighbor to the man who fell among thieves. (Luke 10:25-37.)

**17:41**    The power of example is one of the most effective teaching techniques, as reflected in the statement "as did their fathers, so do they unto this day." Unfortunately during this period of Israel's history the example was bad, for they "served their graven images, both their children and their children's children."

This verse also illustrates the principles behind the Lord's statement that "the iniquity of the fathers" will be visited "upon the children unto the third and fourth generation of them that hate me." (Ex. 20:5.)

**18:4**    Evidently the brass serpent raised up by Moses in the wilderness when the children of Israel were bitten by the fiery serpents (Num. 21:4-9) had been kept as a memorial and was now being used as an idol. Thus Hezekiah has the idol broken "in pieces."

**18:5**    It seems unusual to read *praise* for one of the political leaders, and the statements of commendation used here for Hezekiah are similar to those used centuries earlier for Moses. (See Deut. 34:10.)

**18:9-37** Ellis Rasmussen has provided the following commentary on the Assyrian assault against Judah:

> Ten years later, the Assyrian armies came to Judah and Hezekiah was obliged to resume his payment of tribute. The precious metal given to Assyria has been estimated to have a value today of some $22,800,000. Sennacherib's record on a stone cylinder confirms the amount of gold involved (30 talents), but claims some 800 talents of silver rather than the 300 mentioned by the Bible.
>
> During these crisis times, Isaiah the prophet was warning Judah against depending upon armed opposition or upon aid from Egypt to bring security against Assyria. (See Isaiah, chapters 30, 31.)
>
> It appears that while Sennacherib was involved at Lachish, he sent three of his aids and a host of soldiers to try to persuade the people of Jerusalem to capitulate. The threats, the promises, and the arguments against depending either upon military might or the help of God to break the Assyrians' siege were very persuasive, and had it not been for Isaiah's reassurance, would probably have succeeded. Note that Rabshakeh asserted that (a) the Lord would not help them because they had torn down his altars on the "high places"; (b) the Lord had told Sennacherib to destroy Judah; (c) the Lord could not defend it against the might of Assyria even if He wanted to do so—any more than the gods of other lands had defended them. All of these assertions were either half-truths or bold assumptions, or both. Though there were other attempts to entice and to frighten the people, these were the crucial issues. (See also Isaiah 36.) (IOT 2:62.)

**19:30-31** These intriguing verses evidently refer (1) to a group of Jews ("remnant . . . of the house of Judah") who have either left or will yet leave that area and settle elsewhere and become numerous, and (2) to another remnant of people who shall yet go forth "out of Jerusalem . . . they [shall] escape out of mount Zion."

The Book of Mormon tells of two such groups who fled out of the kingdom of Judah shortly after this period:

1. The people of Mulek—Jews who fled at the very time of the destruction of Jerusalem. Although the wording of the King James Version is not clear, the Hebrew text states this scattering was still in the future from the days of Hezekiah: "And again shall the escaped of the house of Judah that is left [take] root downward and produce fruit upward" (literal translation).

2. The people of Lehi and his colony, mostly of the blood

lineage of Joseph, who fled out of Jerusalem "in the commencement of the first year of the reign of Zedekiah, king of Judah." (1 Ne. 1:4.)

**20:20-21** Unfortunately the Bible provides scant information concerning the feat of Hezekiah's engineers in bringing the waters of the Gihon spring (located outside the walled city) through an underground tunnel to the pool of Siloam (inside the walled city). The account in Chronicles includes only this brief note:

"This same Hezekiah also stopped the upper watercourse of Gihon, and brought it straight down to the west side of the city of David." (2 Chr. 32:30.)

A popular guidebook to modern Israel includes the following information regarding Hezekiah's tunnel:

> In order to protect the water supply from the invading Assyrians, Hezekiah had a 1,777-foot conduit (1,090 feet in a direct line) cut through the solid rock to carry the waters of Gihon Spring to the Pool of Siloam. The Gihon Spring was then covered over from the outside. It was probably completed just before Sennacherib besieged Jerusalem, but after Sargon had captured Samaria in 721 B.C.
>
> Workmen began on each end and accomplished a remarkable engineering feat to meet in the middle within 4 feet of each other. The tunnel averages 6 feet high. In 1880 a boy discovered the *Siloam Inscription* 5 feet from the floor and 19 feet from the Siloam end of the tunnel. The inscription told of "the meeting of workmen." The stone is located in the Archaeological Museum at Istanbul. The inscription in early Hebrew script said: "The completing of the piercing through. While the stone cutters were swinging their axes, each toward his fellow, and while there were yet three cubits to be pierced through, there was heard the voice of a man . . . then ran the waters from the spring to the pool for twelve hundred cubits, and a hundred cubits was the height of the rock above the head of the stone cutters." (DWB, p. 279.)

**21:3** The Hebrew word *Asherah* translated as "grove," has reference to a fertility goddess who was supposedly the wife of Baal. Some English translations use the word *shrine* for this Hebrew word, since shrines and pillars were usually erected in the groves where fertility rites were practiced.

**22:14** Huldah "the prophetess" is mentioned in two biblical references: 2 Kings 22:14 and 2 Chronicles 34:22. She was also mentioned by Wilford Woodruff on January 1, 1877, as part of the dedication of the St. George Temple: "May the society [Relief Society] influence the daughters of Zion to deeds of virtue, holiness, righteousness, and truth. May the blessings of Sarah, Huldah, Hannah, Anna, and Mary, the ancient prophetess, and of the holy women rest upon them.'' (WW, p. 492.)

The Hebrew words translated "in the college" have also been translated "in the second part" or "in the second quarter."

**23:2** The record does not make clear exactly what prophets were present on this occasion. Jeremiah, Habakkuk, and Zephaniah all lived about this time.

**23:27** LeGrand Richards has commented concerning the prophecy in this verse:

This prophecy, as history recounts, was literally fulfilled.

Israel was divided into two kingdoms, Judah and Israel, about 975 B.C. The Kingdom of Israel was overthrown and taken into captivity in the days of Shalmaneser, king of Assyria, and Hoshea, king of Israel about 721 B.C. It is supposed that early in their captivity they made their escape, the main body going northward into unknown lands. Since then they have been known as the "lost tribes."

About a century later, Nebuchadnezzar, king of Babylon, took Jerusalem and carried the tribe of Judah and part of the tribe of Benjamin to Babylon, where Judah served in captivity for seventy years: [Quoted 2 Chr. 36:19-21.]

After this captivity the Kingdom of Judah was restored to its lands by Cyrus, king of Persia. They rebuilt the city and the temple: [Quoted Ezra 1:1-3, 5.]

This gathering of the House of Judah to their promised land, and the rebuilding of their city and temple under Cyrus, king of Persia, occurred about 538 B.C. They continued to occupy the land from this time on until 70 A.D. when Jerusalem was destroyed and the Jews taken captive under an order issued by Nero and executed by Titus, son of Vespasian. After an insurrection headed by Bar-Cochba, 132-135 A.D., Hadrian completely razed to the ground the remains of Jerusalem left by Titus, and erected in its place a Gentile city, with the title Aelia Capitolina. Jews were forbidden to enter this city on pain of death, and the name of Jerusalem was not revived until the time of Constantine. (IDYK, pp. 19-20.) (See Part I 56, 58, 174-76, 239.)

**23:29-30** A much more detailed account of the death of Josiah is contained in 2 Chronicles 35:20-27.

**24:1** Babylonia replaced Egypt as the real ruler of the land "from the river of Egypt [at Wadi El Arish] unto the river Euphrates" (v. 7). (To locate the present site of Wadi El Arish, see "Brook of Egypt" on Map 3, grid C3.) The Babylonian king, Nebuchadnezzar, captured Jerusalem (v. 10); had "all the treasures of the house of the Lord" carried to Babylon (v. 13); carried the royal family into captivity, together with the "mighty of the land" (v. 15); and appointed a new puppet king whose name had been Mattaniah ("God's gift") but was then changed to Zedekiah—"God is (my) righteousness" (v. 17).

Within a year of Zedekiah's "coronation," Lehi and his family left Jerusalem (1 Ne. 1:4), and eleven years later Jerusalem was destroyed through a return visit of Nebuchadnezzar. (2 Kgs. 24:18; 25:1-5.)

**25:7** The biblical account states that Nebuchadnezzar "slew the sons of Zedekiah before his eyes," so most scholars assume *all* the sons of Zedekiah were killed. The Book of Mormon, however, states "the sons of Zedekiah were . . . slain, all except it were Mulek" (Hel. 8:21).

Several explanations of this apparent discrepancy have been offered:

1. The account in the Bible does not necessarily indicate that all the sons of Zedekiah were killed.

2. Mulek may have been a baby with his mother, and therefore was not killed as he posed no particular threat to the Babylonians at that time.

3. Perhaps Mulek was not even born yet. Zedekiah was then only thirty-two years old (2 Kgs. 24:18; 25:2, 7), and undoubtedly his wife was still of child-bearing age.

LeGrand Richards has offered the following commentary on Helaman 8:21:

> It will thus be seen that one of the sons of Zedekiah escaped and he and his people were led to the land of America. This seems to have been about 588 B.C., or twelve years after Lehi and his family left Jerusalem. It seems that the people of Mulek did not keep records but after a sojourn in the land of America for approximately 400 years, the Nephites discovered them, and the two peoples were united under king Mosiah of the people of Nephi. [Quoted Omni 1:15-16, 19.] (IDYK, p. 36.)

Ezekiel had prophesied earlier (Ezek. 12:13) that Zedekiah would be taken to Babylon but would not *see* it. This verse records the fulfillment of that prophecy.

**25:9** Although the temple was burned, it was not completely destroyed and was later rebuilt under the direction of Zerubbabel, Ezra, and others. (See Ezra 1-10.)

**25:21** This is the first major scattering of the Jews since they returned from Egypt. Many of them returned to their homeland after seventy years when Cyrus conquered Babylonia.

They were scattered for the second time by the Romans around 70 A.D. Thus, the present gathering of Judah to the land of their inheritance is the "second time" the Lord has "set his hand" to recover "his people." (See 2 Ne. 6:14; 21:11; 25:17; 29:1; Jacob 6:2 and Part I 56-57, 174.)

# 1 CHRONICLES

See "Chronicles" in the Bible Dictionary, page 635.

**3:1** The son mentioned here by the name *Daniel* was called *Chileab* in 2 Samuel 3:3. Evidently this son died at an early age, as he is not mentioned later, including when possible successors to David are discussed.

**5:1-2** Although Reuben was the initial birthright son of Jacob as the firstborn son of the first wife (Leah), he lost the birthright when he committed adultery with one of his father's concubines (Bilhah). According to the custom of primogeniture (the law of the "first born"), the birthright then went to the firstborn son of the second wife (Joseph, the son of Rachel). Although Joseph was the eleventh son of Jacob in order of birth, he was second in line so far as the birthright was concerned.

In the next generation, Ephraim received the birthright. When Joseph died Ephraim therefore became the birthright son of the house of Israel.

References on each of these major points are listed below.

1. The law of the birthright. (Gen. 43:33; 48:22; Ex. 13:12-15; 22:29; Num. 3:45; Luke 2:22-23.)

2. Birthright son (usually eldest son of firstborn son of first wife) to receive double portion of father's inheritance. (Deut. 21:17.)

3. Reuben as the firstborn son of the first wife. (Gen. 29:32; 35:23; 46:8; 49:3.)

4. Reuben commits adultery with Bilhah, losing right to the birthright. (Gen. 35:22.)

5. Joseph as the firstborn son of the second wife. (Gen. 30:22-24; 35-24.)

6. Joseph as the birthright son after the sin of Reuben. (Gen. 48:22; 49:22-26; 1 Chr. 5:1-2.)

7. Joseph to receive greater blessings than his brethren. (Gen. 49:22-26; Deut. 33:13-17.)

8. Ephraim as the birthright son of Joseph—and thus of Israel upon Joseph's death. (Gen. 48:1-20.)

See also Part I 9-16, 233-34.

**11:22**    These chapters correspond essentially to the materials in 2 Samuel.

**13:5-14; 15:1-3, 14-15, 25-29; 16:1**    These references are primarily concerned with the final travels of the ark of the covenant as it is brought into Jerusalem. The Lord commanded Moses to build the ark during the period of the exodus. (Ex. 25.) Its usual resting place was in the holy of holies in the tabernacle.

The ark led the way across the river Jordan (Josh. 3:3-13) and was mentioned later during the conquest of Jericho. (Josh. 6.) It was kept some time at Gilgal (Josh 9:6; 10:43) and Shiloh. (Josh. 18:1; 1 Sam. 3:3.) Then it was captured by the Philistines in the days of Eli (1 Sam. 4:10-11), who soon sent it to Beth-shemesh (1 Sam. 6:20-7:2) from whence it was taken to Kirjath-jearim. Then David had it brought as far as Perez-uzzah (2 Sam. 6; 1 Chr. 13:11) and finally to Jerusalem. At Jerusalem it was first placed in a tent (1 Chr. 16:1) and then in the holy of holies when Solomon completed the temple. (1 Kgs. 8:1-8.) It is not definitely known what eventually happened to the ark of the covenant. One tradition is that Jeremiah had it taken somewhere for safety. Most scholars believe it must have been destroyed when the Babylonians captured Jerusalem and "burnt the house of the Lord." (2 Kgs. 25:9.)

**17:1-15**    Although David wanted to build the temple so the ark of the covenant could have a more permanent resting place (it was then "under curtains," or in a tent [v. 1]), the Lord forbade him, saying the temple would be built by David's son.

**22:1-10**    The Lord had previously told David (through the prophet Nathan) that he was not to build the temple because it was to be built by David's son. (See 1 Chr. 17:1-15.) Here the Lord explains why David is not to build the temple—"because thou hast shed much blood upon the earth in my sight."

**28:11-19**    Although David was forbidden of the Lord to build the temple (1 Chr. 17:1-15; 22:1-10), the Lord revealed the pattern of the temple "by the spirit" (v. 12). Here David reveals the pattern to Solomon "in writing by his hand" (v. 19).

# 2 CHRONICLES

See "Chronicles" in the Bible Dictionary, page 635.

**1-9** These chapters are similar to 1 Kings 1-11.

**2:4** The last sentence of this verse reads as follows in the Joseph Smith Translation: "And this ordinance shall be kept in Israel for ever."

**7:22** According to the Joseph Smith Translation the words "all this" should be deleted from the last clause of this verse.

**13:5** The "covenant of salt" mentioned in this verse refers to the use of salt in connection with sacrifice. (See Lev. 2:13.) Even much later, in the Arab world it became customary for a person to use the expression "there is salt between us" to indicate the existence of a bond that would guarantee hospitality, protection, and assistance if necessary.

**13:22** A "prophet" and "seer" named Iddo lived at this particular time and kept a record of the major historical events of the period. Some of the key references pertaining to this prophet and his writings are:

2 Chronicles 9:29: "Now the rest of the acts of Solomon, first and last, are they not written . . . in the visions of Iddo the seer against Jeroboam the son of Nebat?"

2 Chronicles 12:15: "Now the acts of Rehoboam, first and last, are they not written in the book . . . of Iddo the seer concerning genealogies?"

2 Chronicles 13:22: "And the rest of the acts of Abijah, and his ways, and his sayings, are written in the story of the prophet Iddo."

Unfortunately the record of Iddo is not in our present Old Testament; it is one of the missing books of the Bible. (See "Lost Books," BD, pp. 725-26.)

Also the Bible does not make it exactly clear which of the men named Iddo mentioned in the Bible is this "prophet" and "seer." One possibility is the Iddo mentioned by Ezra: "And I sent them with commandment unto Iddo the chief at the place Casiphia, and I told them what they should say unto Iddo, and to his brethren the Nethinims, at the place Casiphia, that they should bring unto us ministers for the house of our God." (Ezra 8:17.)

Nehemiah also mentions a "priest and Levite" named Iddo who returned from Babylon with Zerubbabel (Neh. 12:4, 16), but again it is not clear whether this is the "prophet" Iddo.

The prophet Zechariah was a grandson of the prophet Iddo, as revealed in these words that also provide a date for the calling of Zechariah and a general time period of Iddo, his grandfather: "In the eighth month, in the second year of Darius, came the word of the Lord unto Zechariah, the son of Berechiah, the son of Iddo the prophet." (Zech 1:1; see also 1:7.)

**15:1-15**  During this period of general apostasy and almost constant warfare, a prophet named Oded and later his son Azariah led a reform movement. Asa, the king of Judah, supported the efforts of these prophets and destroyed the idols out of some sections of the land and "renewed the altar of the Lord, that was before the porch of the Lord" (v. 8).

Asa also "*gathered* all Judah and Benjamin, and *the strangers with them out of Ephraim and Manasseh,* and out of Simeon: for they fell to him out of Israel in abundance, when they saw that the Lord his God was with him" (v. 9; italics added).

Thus the kingdom of Judah (the citizens of which later became known as Jews) consisted not only of descendants of Judah but also descendants of Benjamin, Ephraim, Manasseh, and Simeon.

This scripture is of particular interest to Latter-day Saints, for the Book of Mormon claims that hundreds of years later—even after the ten tribes comprising the northern kingdom had been taken captive and dispersed—descendants of Ephraim and Manasseh were living in Jerusalem. The two major families that fled Jerusalem about 600 B.C. and eventually were led to the lands now known as the Americas were headed by Lehi, who was a descendant of Manasseh (Alma 10:3) and Ishmael, who was a descendant of Ephraim. (Erastus Snow, JD 23:184-85.) It is possible that the progenitors of Lehi and Ishmael were among those who migrated to the kingdom of Judah (and thus to Jerusalem) in 941 B.C. in the days of Asa.

**16:1**  The date here is evidently in error. Perhaps it should read "In the six and thirtieth year since the beginning of the reign of *Jeroboam*" rather than the reign of Asa.

**18:20**  According to the Joseph Smith Translation, the first sentence of this verse should read: "Then there came out a *lying* spirit, and stood before *them*, and said, I will entice him." (Italics added.)

**20:6**  The Joseph Smith Translation reads as follows: "And said, O Lord God of our fathers, thou God who art in heaven; and rulest over all the kingdoms of the heathen; and in thy hand thou hast power and might, so that none is able to withstand thee."

**20:11**  The Joseph Smith Translation adds a *not* at a significant point in this verse: "Behold, they reward us *not*, but have come to cast us out of thy possession, which thou hast given us to inherit." (Italics added.)

**20:17**  The first clause of this verse reads as follows in the Joseph Smith Translation: "Ye shall not *go* to fight in this *day*." (Italics added.)

**21-28**  The parallel history for this period is found in 2 Kings 9-17.

**21:12-5**  This writing probably came from Elisha rather than Elijah inasmuch as Elijah was translated some thirteen years before this episode.

**21:20**  The Hebrew words describing the death of Jehoahaz ("he departed *without being desired*" [italics added]) literally read "without desire." The meaning might be that Jehoahaz may have lost his desire for life because of his "incurable disease" (v. 18), or the construction may be an idiom meaning "the people did not regret his passing."

**22:2**  The Joseph Smith Translation indicates that this verse should begin "Two and twenty years old," as does 2 Kings 8:26. Ahaziah could not very well have been forty-two years old when he began to reign, since his father had died that very year and was only forty years old at the time of his death. (See 2 Chr. 21:20.)

**24:22**  According to the Joseph Smith Translation, the last clause of this verse should read: "The Lord look upon *me*, and require *me*." (Italics added.)

**29:1-2**  How refreshing (and relatively rare) to read about a king who "did that which was right in the sight of the Lord."

**32-36**  These chapters have much of the same information as contained in 2 Kings 18-25.

The fall of Jerusalem is also related in Jeremiah 39-41 and 52.

Nearly half of the book of Ezekiel contains warnings to Judah before Judah was overthrown by Babylon.

The books of Daniel, Nahum, Habakkuk, and Zephaniah pertain to this same time period.

**32:30**  For information concerning Hezekiah's tunnel, see the commentary for 2 Kings 20:20-21.

**32:32**  Unfortunately at least one of the books listed here (the book of the kings of Judah and Israel) is not in our present Old Testament. Also it is not clear whether the second book (the vision of Isaiah) is part of the book of Isaiah; if so, it is probably chapters 36 through 39, for only in these chapters does Isaiah mention in detail "the acts of Hezekiah and his goodness."

**34:16**  The Joseph Smith Translation reads: "And Shaphan carried the book to the king, and brought the word of the king back again, saying, All that was committed to thy servants, they do."

**35:1-6**  The ark of the covenant had been placed in the holy of holies when Solomon's temple was completed (1 Kgs. 8:1-8), but evidently it had been removed by Manasseh (2 Chr. 33:1 10, especially v. 7) and was being reinstated by Josiah. (See the commentary for 1 Chr. 13:5-14; also see "Ark of the Covenant," BD, pp. 613-14.)

**35:20-27**  It is not clear why Josiah decided to go "out against" Necho, king of Egypt, to battle. Obviously Josiah was not very happy about the Egyptian armies marching through his land on the way to Carchemish, but the major opponent of the Egyptians in this war was Babylonia, not the kingdom of Judah.

Josiah was one of the very few righteous kings of Judah. Little wonder "all Judah and Jerusalem mourned" for him, and the prophet Jeremiah also "lamented for Josiah."

A brief account of Josiah's death is also found in 2 Kings 23:29-30.

**36:5-8**  Because of the rapid turnover in kings during this period and also because several kings had more than one name, it is sometimes hard to understand the relationship of one king to the others. The following summary might help:

Josiah: This good king ruled for thirty-one years; he held the great Passover in the eighteenth year of his reign (2 Chr. 35:1-19); he was killed near Megiddo in a battle with Necho, king of Egypt. (2 Chr. 35:20-25.)

Jehoahaz, son of Josiah: The people made him king at age twenty-three, but he ruled for only three months before he was deposed by the Egyptians and carried into Egypt; the Egyptians replaced Jehoahaz with his brother Jehoiakim, who was also called Eliakim. (2 Chr. 36:1-4.)

Jehoiakim (Eliakim), brother of Jehoahaz and thus son of Josiah: He was named as the successor to Jehoahaz by the Egyptians; he reigned eleven years and was taken into captivity when the Babylonians first conquered Jerusalem, wresting it from the control of the Egyptians. (2 Chr. 36:5.)

Jehoiachin, son of Jehoiakim (Eliakim) and thus grandson of Josiah: He started to reign at eight years of age but only reigned "three months and ten days" before the Babylonians took him captive into Babylon and replaced him on the throne with Zedekiah. (2 Chr. 36:9.)

Zedekiah, the brother of Jehoiachin and thus a son of Jehoiakim and a grandson of Josiah: He began to reign when he was twenty-one years old and reigned for eleven years before Babylonia conquered Jerusalem for the second time and took Zedekiah captive into Babylon. This ended the reign of the kings of Judah. (2 Chr. 36:10-11.)

**36:11-21**    Bible scholars disagree as to the exact year Jerusalem was destroyed by Nebuchadnezzar and the kingdom of Judah came to an end. Many of the scholars agree the date was around 587 B.C., which is the date listed for the "capture of Jerusalem" in the chronology in the Bible Dictionary (p. 639).

Some Latter-day Saints place the date of the destruction of Jerusalem at 589 B.C., rather than 587 B.C. Their reasoning is as follows:

1. Lehi left Jerusalem in "the first year of Zedekiah, king of Judah." (1 Ne. 1:4.) The date of Lehi's departure from Jerusalem in the Christian calendar was 600 years before the birth of Christ. Thus, Zedekiah started to reign in 600 B.C.

2. Jerusalem was destroyed and the kingdom of Judah came to a close in the eleventh year of the reign of Zedekiah. Thus, the kingdom of Judah came to an end in 589 B.C.

**36:22-23** and Ezra 1:1-3    Notice that these references are virtually identical. See the commentary for Ezra 1:1 for a possible explanation.

**35-36** and 2 Kings 23-25 contain most of the facts and dates concerning this period, but Jeremiah (1:1-3; 21:1-14; 39:1-7) also contains vital and interesting information.

# EZRA

See "Ezra" in the Bible Dictionary, page 669.

**1:1**  One explanation that the first three verses of Ezra are essentially the same as the last two verses of 2 Chronicles is that an editor wanted to show continuity between the two books. The book of Ezra has not always followed 2 Chronicles in the Hebrew scriptures, and this repetition might indicate an editor's preference for the present arrangement.

**1:1**  Jeremiah was not the only prophet who foretold the eventual destruction of Babylonia and the return of at least some of the exiled Jews to their homeland. (See Jer. 25:12-14.) Isaiah also prophesied Babylon's downfall (see Isa. 13:1-22; 48:14) and even foretold, over one hundred years before the event, the name of the king who would defeat the Babylonians —Cyrus, the king of Persia. (See Isa. 44:28; 45:1-4.)

**1:8**  The name *Shesh-bazzar* (possibly Persian "fire-worshipper") occurs only four times in the Bible—all in the book of Ezra. (1:8, 11; 5:14, 16.) Some scholars believe *Shesh-bazzar* is simply another name for *Zerub-babel* ("born in Babylon"), since both of them were of royal blood ("princes of Judah"), had Babylonian names, and were prominent in the return of the exiles. The Septuagint version of the Bible, however, distinguishes between them, showing that they were probably two different people. (1 Esdras 6:18.)

**2:61-62**  On November 27, 1832, the Lord specifically mentioned these verses of Ezra to Joseph Smith in regard to the apostasy of priesthood members in the latter days. Such "shall not find an inheritance among the saints of the Most High; Therefore, it shall be done unto them as unto the children of the priest, as will be found recorded in the second chapter and sixty-first and second verses of Ezra." (D&C 85:11-12.)

**2:61-63**  A group of the "children of the priests" was not able to prove their lineage and thus was unable to establish their rightful claim to the priesthood. They were then considered to be "as polluted" and were dropped from the priesthood. If the time should come when their lineage could be proven through a priest with "the Urim and Thummim," then, and not until then, they could eat of "the most holy things."

The Book of Mormon indicates that a person who is entitled

to use the Urim and Thummim (or "holy interpreters") can learn things of the past—"things which are not known shall be made known by them, and also things shall be made known by them which otherwise could not be known." (Mosiah 8:17.)

**2:64-65** Nehemiah 7:66-69 also provides a list of the returning exiles. Although the totals of Ezra do not agree precisely with those of Nehemiah, they are strikingly similar.

|  | **Ezra** | **Nehemiah** |
| --- | --- | --- |
| Number in the "whole congregation" | 42,360 | 42,360 |
| Number of servants | 7,337 | 7,365 |
| Number of "singing men and women" | 200 | 245 |

**3:8-13** The Levites were particularly interested in rebuilding the temple, for they would soon be offering sacrifices there again. Some of the older "priests and Levites and chief of the fathers" could remember the temple erected by Solomon, and they had mixed feelings on the occasion—they "wept with a loud voice" when they remembered what had been destroyed, but "shouted aloud for joy" at the prospects of a new temple.

**4:1-7** The "adversaries of Judah and Benjamin" are the part-Israelitish people living in the lands of Samaria (hence, *Samaritans*), where the peoples of the ten northern tribes had previously lived. The Israelites who had remained in the area at the time of the Assyrian captivity (about 722 B.C.) intermarried with the foreigners who moved in. These mixed-blooded peoples were not considered to be pure Israelites by the returning exiles and were not allowed to assist in the rebuilding of the temple.

The Samaritans then became bitter enemies to the Jews (seventy years of the enmity are accounted for in Ezra 4:5-6), which was still evident in New Testament times. (See John 4:1-42.)

See the commentary for 2 Kings 17:24.

**5:1** The prophets Haggai and Zechariah were prophesying "in Judah and Jerusalem" at this time. The Old Testament books named after these prophets provide important historical information concerning this period.

**6:1-12** When Darius found the decree of Cyrus providing for the rebuilding of the temple, he wanted to maintain the honor of Persia and thus vigorously supported the project. He even ordered the death of those who opposed the work, suggesting that scaffolds be built from the timbers of their houses and that they "be hanged thereon."

**6:15-22**   Now the temple was functional again and many of the feasts and festivals were reemphasized.

**7:1-26**   Although the entire book was named after Ezra, the first time he is mentioned in the book is 7:1. A listing of his genealogy (vs. 1-5) proves he is a descendant of Aaron and thus entitled to the priesthood. Throughout the rest of the book, Ezra is referred to by such titles as "the priest, the scribe, even a scribe of the words of the commandments of the Lord" (v. 11); the title *prophet* is not used for Ezra.

The letter from King Artaxerxes gives permission to Ezra "to set magistrates and judges, which may judge all the people that are beyond the river"; Ezra thus held some civil power over the people to go with his priestly authority.

**9:1-10**   When Ezra arrived in Jerusalem, he was greatly dismayed to learn that the people were not observing many of the commandments given by the Lord through Moses. He was particularly incensed to discover that the people of Israel (and the *priests* and the *Levites*!) had intermarried ("the holy seed have mingled themselves") with the local people and were "doing according to [the] abominations . . . of the Canaanites, the Hittites, the Perizzites, the Jebusites, the Ammonites, the Moabites, the Egyptians, and the Amorites." Marriage with these exact groups had been specifically forbidden by the Lord. (See Ex. 23:20-33; Deut. 7:1-6.)

It is little wonder when Ezra observed these things he rent his garment and mantle, and at the time of the evening sacrifice he promised the Lord he would do what he could to remove these evils (vs. 6-15).

**10:1-12, 18, 44**   "All the congregation" agreed to separate themselves "from the people of the land, and from [their] strange [foreign] wives," and the list of the offenders included "sons of priests" (vs. 18-22), "Levites" (v. 23), "the singers" (v. 24), and "[others] of Israel" (vs. 25-43).

# NEHEMIAH

See "Nehemiah" in the Bible Dictionary, page 738.

**1:1-4**   At least the beginning of this book reads as though it were taken from the personal diary of Nehemiah ("God has consoled"). This particular Nehemiah is mentioned only in this book (other persons named Nehemiah are mentioned in Ezra 2:2 [Neh. 7:7]; and Neh. 3:16), where the following information is provided concerning him:

He was reared in Persia (1:1).

His record begins about 445 B.C. (1:1).

He was the king's cupbearer (1:11), which was a position of considerable trust and responsibility. (Nehemiah is never mentioned as a prophet nor a priest.)

He heard from fellow Jews that the walls of Jerusalem had broken down and the gates been burned (1:2-3) and desired to do something about it, fasting and asking God for directions and help (1:4-11).

He asked for and received the help of King Artaxerxes, including letters from the king to "the governors beyond the river" (2:1-9).

He journeyed to Jerusalem, scouted out the city, recommended the rebuilding of the city walls, and won the support of the local Jewish leaders. He was opposed by non-Jewish governors, particularly Sanballat the Horonite and Tobiah the Ammonite (2:9-20; 3:1-32; 4:1-3).

He organized the builders of the wall and trained them to fight against their oppressors by working with one hand and holding a weapon in the other (4:4-18). The Israelitish workers responded by working long days ("from the rising of the sun till the stars appeared"), even sleeping in their clothes "saving that every one put them off for washing" (4:19-23).

He was appointed governor of the land (5:15) and instituted many reforms, including the restoration of lands taken for lack of payment of interest (5:1-13).

Despite the opposition and deception of Sanballat and Tobiah, he completed the walls of the cities (6:1-19), appointed others to guard them (7:1-4), and joined with Ezra and the Levites in teaching the people (8:1-12) and reemphasizing the feasts and festivals (8:13-18).

He preached tithing (13:10-14), brought about sabbath reforms (13:15-22), and enforced the laws prohibiting the marriage of Israelites with strangers [foreigners] (13:23-31).

Although other reforms and religious activities are mentioned in this book, it is not clear which of these were carried out primarily because of the teachings and efforts of Nehemiah. Enough good works of his are mentioned, however, that hopefully his closing prayer was answered: "Remember me, O my God, for good" (13:31).

**2:1** The wording of another biblical version suggests that the king had several cupbearers who were rotated in service, and it was now Nehemiah's turn to serve. If this is indeed the beginning of a new time of service for Nehemiah, it would help explain why the king had not observed Nehemiah's sadness during the four months that had elapsed since Nehemiah had received the discouraging news concerning Jerusalem. (See Neh. 1:1.)

**4:1-3** Apparently the Jews did not have a reputation among their neighbors as being great artisans or builders. Evidently the Jews had made no earlier attempts to rebuild the walls of their capital city since they had been destroyed some seventy years before when Nebuchadnezzar in his siege had "burnt the house of the Lord, and . . . brake down the walls of Jerusalem round about." (2 Kgs. 25:9-10.) The scorn of the non-Israelitish opponents is reflected in Sanballat's referral to "these feeble Jews" and Tobiah's deprecating appraisal, "Even that which they build, if a fox go up, he shall even break down their stone wall."

**4:13-23** The adversary and the people over whom he has influence consistently oppose the work of those who attempt to build constructively and in righteousness. In Nehemiah's time, the builders worked "every one [with] his sword girded by his side"—"every one with one of his hands wrought in the work, and with the other hand held a weapon."

In this dispensation, during the construction of the temple at Kirtland "the threats of the mob . . . [caused] the brethren to be constantly on the lookout, and those who labored on the temple were engaged at night watching to protect the walls they had laid during the day." (HC 2:2.)

**5:1-13** Some of those engaged in rebuilding the walls of Jerusalem had been forced to borrow money on their "lands, vineyards, and houses" in order to survive. Unable to repay the money and the interest owed, they had been forced to give up their daughters (and in some instances their sons) as bond servants. Nehemiah "rebuked the nobles and the rulers" because of this system and ordered them to restore the lands and to require no more usury (interest).

The collection of usury for loans to their own people had been specifically forbidden by the Lord since the days of Moses: "If thou lend money to any of my people that is poor by thee, thou shalt not be to him as an usurer, neither shalt thou lay upon him usury." (Ex. 22:25.)

**6:11**  The Joseph Smith Translation of this verse reads: "And I said, Should such a man as I flee? and who is mine enemy, that such a man as I would go into the temple to save his life? I will not go in."

**7:5, 6-73**  Nehemiah "found" a list of Israelite exiles who first returned from Babylonia (v. 5), and this list is presented in the remainder of the chapter. The figures in Nehemiah 7:6-73 are essentially the same as those in Ezra 2:1-70, but when they vary the Joseph Smith Translation agrees with the figures in Ezra. Following is a list of the figures that vary—first the figure for Nehemiah and then the figure from Ezra and the Joseph Smith Translation:

| Nehemiah | Ezra |
|---|---|
| 652 (v. 10) | 775 |
| 2,818 (v. 11) | 2,812 |
| 845 (v. 13) | 945 |
| 648 (v. 15) | 642 |
| 628 (v. 16) | 623 |
| 2,322 (v. 17) | 1,222 |
| 667 (v. 18) | 666 |
| 2,067 (v. 19) | 2,056 |
| 655 (v. 20) | 454 |
| 328 (v. 22) | 223 |
| 324 (v. 23) | 323 |
| 123 (v. 32) | 223 |
| 721 (v. 37) | 725 |
| 3,930 (v. 38) | 3,630 |
| 148 (v. 44) | 128 |
| 138 (v. 45) | 139 |
| 642 (v. 62) | 652 |

**7:65, 70**  The *Tirshatha* ("governor") mentioned here is evidently Nehemiah himself. (See also Neh. 5:14; 8:9.) For information concerning this reference to the Urim and Thummim, see the commentary for Ezra 2:61-63.

**7:66-69**   See the commentary for Ezra 2:64-65.

**8:1-5, 8**   Ellis Rasmussen has provided the following commentary on these verses:

A grand assembly was once again called (as in Samuel's day) for the reading of the Law—as Moses had commanded they should periodically do. Ezra was the priestly leader.

Tradition says that Ezra gathered up all of the sacred writings—the Torah, the Prophets, and the other Writings. The Talmud even asserts that those books which were missing he rewrote! However true that may be, it is quite certain that this was the period of collection and primary "determination" of the great Hebrew literature that has come down to us, plus much that has not been passed on down.

It is likely also that this was the time of the beginning of the oral translation of Scriptures from the literary Hebrew into the common language of the people. For some it would have entailed a paraphrasing of the literature in the vernacular; for some it would have required translation into the spoken Aramaic that was becoming the *lingua franca* of the Near East of the time. This would be the beginning of the *Targums* (Hebrew: *Targumim,* meaning "translations"). They were oral at first; then written portions of the Targumim were permitted, and finally whole translations appear to have been sanctioned—not until the early centuries A.D., however. (IOT 2:108.)

**9:21**   This miracle is seldom mentioned but is nevertheless extraordinary. For forty years in the wilderness the clothes of the children of Israel "waxed not old, and their feet swelled not." The Lord had reminded the children of Israel of this miracle just before they entered the promised land. (See Deut. 29:5; see also 8:4.)

**10:29**   The first part of the verse reads as follows in the Joseph Smith Translation: "They clave to their brethren, their nobles, and entered into an oath, that a curse should come upon them if they did not walk in God's law."

**11:1-2**   As indicated in Nehemiah 7:4, the land area of the walled city of Jerusalem was relatively large, but the population was relatively small: "Now the city was large and great: but the people were few therein, and the houses were not builded." Thus, the Israelites living outside the city walls were required "to bring one of ten to dwell in Jerusalem the holy city" to help defend it. Some, however, did not wait to be conscripted, but moved into the city on their own: "And the people blessed all the men, that *willingly* offered themselves to dwell at Jerusalem." (Italics added.)

**13:15-22**   When Nehemiah forbade the selling of merchandise on the sabbath day within the city of Jerusalem, the merchants readily set up shop outside the city ("without Jerusalem"). They only did this "once or twice" before Nehemiah threatened to "lay hands" on them. "From that time forth came they no more on the sabbath."

In modern Israel virtually all stores, gasoline stations, pharmacies, bus and railroad stations, movie houses, and so on are closed on the sabbath—from sundown on Friday to sundown on Saturday.

See Part I 31-36.

# ESTHER

See "Esther, Book of" in the Bible Dictionary, page 667.

**1:1** *Ahasuerus* is the English translation of the Hebrew name for the Persian ruler. The English translation of the Greek version of the same name is *Xerxes*. The dates of this king are 486-465 B.C. according to the Chronological Tables in the Bible Dictionary, p. 640.

**1-10** The book of Esther contains no references to God, Providence, or prayer, although it does mention fasting (4:16) and hints of a belief in foreordination (4:14).

At least fragments from all the books of the Old Testament have been discovered among the Dead Sea Scrolls except for the book of Esther. The fact that Esther does not contain the word *God* may be a reason why the book (or even portions from it) was not discovered among the Dead Sea Scrolls. The writers of the scrolls believed it was necessary to preserve everything that had the name *God* written upon it.

**3:1-6** Mordecai's refusal to bow before Haman and do "him reverence" was in keeping with the first and portions of the second commandments: "Thou shalt have no other gods before me. . . . Thou shalt not bow down thyself to them, nor serve them." (Ex. 20:3, 5.) Apparently there was nothing personal against Haman in Mordecai's behavior, although Haman was filled with "wrath and . . . sought to destroy all the Jews."

**3:13** Haman wanted to make certain all the Jews were permanently removed from the land! The orders are very specific and thorough—the people are "to destroy, to kill, and to cause to perish, all Jews, both young and old, little children and women, in one day."

**4:15-16** The principles of faith and willingness to sacrifice demonstrated so clearly in the story of Esther should also be observed by the Saints today, according to Lorenzo Snow:

In many instances of a similar nature where the destruction of the people of God seemed imminent, and there appeared no way of escape, suddenly there arose something or another that had been prepared for their salvation to avert the impending destruction. We find this in the case of the Israelites when led by Moses. When they came to the Red Sea and the

Egyptian army in their rear threatened their destruction, there seemed no way of escape, but at the very moment when deliverance was required, behold, it appeared and they were delivered. So it has been and so it ever will be with us. Notwithstanding our difficulties may appear very great, yet there will be means provided for our escape if we ourselves perform the duties incumbent upon us as the children of God. But it may become necessary in the future—and this is the point I wish to make—for some of the Saints to act the part of Esther, the queen, and be willing to sacrifice anything and everything that is required at their hands for the purpose of working out the deliverance of the Latter-day Saints. . . .

But it is our business to step forward as did Esther, and be willing to risk all for the salvation of the people. In undertaking her task, Esther said, "If I perish, I perish." Here is a lesson for our sisters. But the people of God will not perish. There will always be a ram caught in the thicket for their deliverance. (JD 23:290, 293.)

**5:14**   The extreme height of the gallows (fifty cubits, or seventy-five feet) is probably a reflection of the extreme hatred of Haman and his family for Mordecai.

**8:3-17**   The earlier order to kill the Jews could not be rescinded because it had been "written in the king's name, and sealed with the king's ring" (v. 8). Now a new letter is sent out, written in the name of the king and "sealed . . . with the king's ring" authorizing the Jews to defend themselves. Not only did many of the Persians and the Medes decide it was the better part of valor not to assault the Jews under these conditions, but "many of the people of the land became Jews" (v. 17).

**9:1-10**   Ellis Rasmussen has provided a brief commentary on the battle that ensued between the Jews and their enemies:

It should be noted that the carnage that ensued was not, as some commentators have said, a show of bloodthirsty vengeance by the Jews. Under the circumstances it was the result of an inevitable conflict, as there were naturally some who were sympathetic with Haman and antagonistic to the Jews who would follow the first edict; on the other hand those among the officers, deputies, rulers, etc., who knew of the vindicating order and of the trend to favor the Jews, opportunely would fight in their behalf. (IOT 2:117-18.)

**9:10, 16**   The same Hebrew word translated "spoil" in verse 10 is translated "prey" in verse 16.

**9:20-32**   The festival of Purim is still observed annually by Jews throughout the world on "the fourteenth . . . and the fifteenth day" "of the month Adar." (See "Feast of Purim," BD, p. 673, and Part I 44.)

# JOB

See "Job, Book of" in the Bible Dictionary, pages 713-14.

Interpretations to the book of Job have been so varied and extreme that it has been claimed that Job has suffered more from the hands of the critics than he ever did from the hands of Satan.

Many critics of the Bible have suggested that Job is a mythological character. In modern times, however, the Lord has verified that Job existed as a real person. To an inquiring Joseph Smith, the Lord replied: "Thou art not yet as Job; thy friends do not contend against thee, neither charge thee with transgression, as they did Job." (D&C 121:10.)

Several other scriptures are also concerned with the themes of the suffering of the righteous and the prosperity of the wicked. (See Jer. 12, 20, 26, 32; Hab. 1; Mal. 3; Alma 14; D&C 121, 122.)

Several statements from Job have been quoted extensively both on and off stage. Some of the more widely quoted statements are:

1:21    Naked came I out of my mother's womb, and naked shall I return thither: the Lord gave, and the Lord hath taken away; blessed be the name of the Lord.

2:4     All that a man hath will he give for his life.

2:10    Shall we receive good at the hand of God, and shall we not receive evil?

5:7     Yet man is born unto trouble, as the sparks fly upward.

5:17    Happy is the man whom God correcteth: therefore despise not thou the chastening of the Almighty.

7:1     Is there not an appointed time to man upon earth?

10:21   Before I go whence I shall not return, even to the land of darkness and the shadow of death.

11:7-8  Canst thou by searching find out God? canst thou find out the Almighty unto perfection? It is as high as heaven; what canst thou do? deeper than hell; what canst thou know?

14:1-2    Man that is born of a woman is of few days, and full of trouble. He cometh forth like a flower, and is cut down: he fleeth also as a shadow, and continueth not.

14:14    If a man die, shall he live again? all the days of my appointed time will I wait, till my change come.

19:25-
27    For I know that my redeemer liveth, and that he shall stand at the latter day upon the earth: And though after my skin worms destroy this body, yet in my flesh shall I see God: Whom I shall see for myself, and mine eyes shall behold, and not another; though my reins be consumed within me.

21:17    How oft is the candle of the wicked put out! and how oft cometh their destruction upon them! God distributeth sorrows in his anger.

28:28    And unto man he said, Behold, the fear of the Lord, that is wisdom; and to depart from evil is understanding.

31:35    Oh . . . that mine adversary had written a book.

32:8    But there is a spirit in man: and the inspiration of the Almighty giveth them understanding.

38:4-7    Where wast thou when I laid the foundations of the earth? declare, if thou hast understanding. Who hath laid the measures thereof, if thou knowest? or who hath stretched the line upon it? Whereupon are the foundations thereof fastened? or who laid the corner stone thereof; when the morning stars sang together, and all the sons of God shouted for joy?

38:36    Who hath put wisdom in the inward parts? or who hath given understanding to the heart?

40:2    Shall he that contendeth with the Almighty instruct him? he that reproveth God, let him answer it.

40:7    Gird up thy loins now like a man: I will demand of thee, and declare thou unto me.

**2:10**    If God has the power to bestow blessings upon his people, then he also has the power to cease giving those blessings, which would result in deprivation or relative punishment. Job reflects this principle in his rhetorical question directed toward his wife: "What? shall we receive good at the hand of God, and shall we not receive evil?"

**5:17** God does not pamper those he would make strong, as is indicated in the story of Job and the lives of many other righteous persons.

Tribulation is the heritage of the righteous. It was never intended that those who serve the Lord in faithful obedience to covenants should find a rosy path to eternity. Persecution has been the reward of righteousness. Hatred of those who love the world is usually made manifest against that which is good. (Joseph Fielding Smith, CHMR 1:308.)

**9:2-10** At least as long ago as Abraham, some people on the earth knew a great deal about heavenly bodies. (See Abraham 3:1-18.) Evidently Job was one of these, as indicated by Joseph Fielding Smith:

It is a foolish notion to think that the ancient inhabitants of the earth were ignorant of the heavenly bodies. They were acquainted with many of the constellations and the movements of the planets and sang about them. . . . Moreover, we read in the words of Job, that he was *evidently* an astronomer, at least was well acquainted with the stars: In his defense against the accusations of his tormentors he said: [Job 9:2-3, 5-10.]

From these passages written anciently we learn that the people of the Lord from the beginning knew the nature of this earth, the course it is pursuing which is the same that has been covered by other worlds throughout the eternities. They were not ignorant of the planets circling our sun in their established courses.

It was not until a later age, when men had fully departed from the teachings of the prophets, that mankind lost touch with the heavens and began to look upon the earth as the great center around which everything revolved. (AGQ 4:118-19.)

**19:25** The term "latter day" in this verse refers to the time of the Second Coming, according to LeGrand Richards:

What Job was given to know was that his Redeemer would stand upon the earth at the latter day and that in his flesh, though it had been destroyed by the worms, he would see God, his Redeemer. This, of course, has reference to Christ's second coming. (IDYK, p. 104.)

**19:25-27** The strong testimony of Job concerning the resurrection has strengthened many others, as explained by Spencer W. Kimball.

The question asked by Job has been asked by millions who have stood at the open bier of a loved one: "If a man die, shall he live again?" (Job 14:14.)

And the question has been answered acceptably to numerous of them as a great, sweet peace settles down upon them like the dews of heaven. And innumerable times hearts that were weary in agonizing suffering have felt the kiss of that peace which knows not understanding.

And when a deep tranquility of soul has brought a new warm assurance to minds that were troubled and hearts that were torn, those numerous could repeat with beloved Job: [Quoted Job 19:25-27.]

Job had expressed the wish that his testimony could be printed in books and cut into stone for the generations following him to read. His wish was granted, for peace has come into many souls as they have read his strong testimony. (CR, Apr. 1969, pp. 30-31.)

John Taylor taught that Job's knowledge of and faith in the resurrection were proof that he understood the gospel of Jesus Christ:

"Though he slay me, yet will I trust in him." And why? Because he had the everlasting gospel. What! Job had the Gospel? Yes, to be sure he had. How do I know? Because the Gospel brings life and immortality to light; and he had a knowledge of that. And hence he says, "For I know that my Redeemer liveth, and that he shall stand at the latter day upon the earth." (JD 20:306.)

**19:26-27**    Brigham Young has offered the following commentary concerning Job's testimony of the literalness of the resurrection:

You see life in human beings and in the growing vegetation, and when that spirit of life departs, another condition of life at once begins to operate upon the organization which remains. By way of illustration I will quote one passage from the book of Job, who in his afflictions was visited by several friends, and after he had concluded that they were all miserable comforters, he exclaimed, "Though worms destroy this body, yet in my flesh shall I see God." To make this passage clearer to your comprehension, I will paraphrase it, though my spirit leave my body, and though worms destroy its present organization, yet in the morning of the resurrection I shall behold the face of my Saviour, in this same tabernacle; that is my understanding of the idea so briefly expressed by Job. (JD 3:277.)

**32:8**    Things of the Spirit are understood only through inspiration from the Almighty, as explained in these statements:

If the Lord does not speak from heaven, and touch the eyes of their understanding by His Spirit, who can instruct or guide them to good? who can give them words of eternal life? It is not in the power of man to do it; but when the Lord gives His Spirit to a person, or to a people, they can then hear, believe, and be instructed. An Elder of Israel may preach the principles of the Gospel, from first to last, as they were taught to him, to a congregation ignorant of them; but if he does not do it under the influence of the Spirit of the Lord, he cannot enlighten that congregation on those principles, it is impossible. Job said that "There is a spirit in man, and the inspiration of the Almighty giveth them understanding." Unless we enjoy that understanding in this probation, we cannot grow or increase, we cannot be made acquainted with the principles of truth and righteousness so as to become exalted. (Brigham Young, JD 1:2-3.)

The Scriptures tell us that there is a spirit in man, and that the inspiration of the Almighty giveth it understanding. It is upon this principle that we become acquainted with the truth, and the power of the Gospel which we have received. The principles of eternal life are manifested unto us by the inspiration of the Holy Ghost; for that Spirit rests upon us—it influences our minds; and if we watch those teachings, having within us the right feeling, we shall comprehend things clearly as they are. (Wilford Woodruff, JD 9:56-57.)

According to Joseph F. Smith, the interaction of the spirit of man with the inspiration of the Almighty distinguishes man from the "brute creation":

I read a Scripture something like this: that "there is a spirit in man." Now, if that should stop here, there would not be perhaps anything very remarkable about man; for the spirit of man knoweth only the things of man, and the things of God are discerned by the Spirit of God. But while there is a spirit in man, it is further stated that "the inspiration of the Almighty giveth it understanding." There is not a man born into the world but has a portion of the Spirit of God, and it is that Spirit of God which gives to his spirit understanding. Without this, he would be but an animal like the rest of the brute creation, without understanding, without judgment, without skill, without ability, except to eat and to drink like the brute beast. But inasmuch as the Spirit of God giveth all men understanding, he is enlightened above the brute beast. He is made in the image of God Himself, so that he can reason, reflect, pray, exercise faith; he can use his energies for the accomplishment of the desires of his heart, and inasmuch as he puts forth his efforts in the proper direction, then he is entitled to an increased portion of the Spirit of the Almighty to inspire him to increased intelligence, to increased prosperity and happiness in the world; but in proportion as he prostitutes his energies for evil, the inspiration of the Almighty is withdrawn from him, until he becomes so dark and so benighted, that so far as his knowledge of God is concerned, so far as the future or hopes of eternal life are concerned, he is quite as ignorant as a dumb brute. (JD 25:53-54.)

# PSALMS

See "Psalms" in the Bible Dictionary, pages 754-55.

The Book of Psalms is one of the most frequently quoted Old Testament books by New Testament writers. The Bible Dictionary contains a list of quotations from the Old Testament found in the New Testament (pp. 756-59). Sixty-four quotations are listed from Psalms, the most from any Old Testament book. It would be educational to read each of these quotations directly in Psalms and then see how each is used in New Testament quotations.

Some of the better known quotations from Psalms are:

1:1, 3   Blessed is the man that walketh not in the counsel of the ungodly, nor standeth in the way of sinners, nor sitteth in the seat of the scornful. . . . he shall be like a tree planted by the rivers of water, that bringeth forth his fruit in his season; his leaf also shall not wither; and whatsoever he doeth shall prosper.

8:4-5   What is man, that thou art mindful of him? and the son of man, that thou visitest him? For thou hast made him a little lower than the angels, and hast crowned him with glory and honour.

14:1   The fool hath said in his heart, There is no God.

18:2   The Lord is my rock, and my fortress, and my deliverer; my God, my strength, in whom I will trust; my buckler, and the horn of my salvation, and my high tower.

19:1   The heavens declare the glory of God; and the firmament sheweth his handywork.

19:14   Let the words of my mouth, and the meditation of my heart, be acceptable in thy sight, O Lord, my strength, and my redeemer.

23:1-6   (This is probably the best known of all the psalms, and should be read in its entirety.)

24:1   The earth is the Lord's, and the fulness thereof; the world, and they that dwell therein.

24:3-4 Who shall ascend into the hill of the Lord? or who shall stand in his holy place? He that hath clean hands, and a pure heart; who hath not lifted up his soul unto vanity, nor sworn deceitfully.

27:1 The Lord is my light and my salvation; whom shall I fear? the Lord is the strength of my life; of whom shall I be afraid?

27:14 Wait on the Lord: be of good courage, and he shall strengthen thine heart: wait, I say, on the Lord.

37:11 But the meek shall inherit the earth; and shall delight themselves in the abundance of peace.

40:4 Blessed is that man that maketh the Lord his trust, and respecteth not the proud, nor such as turn aside to lies.

49:16-17 Be not thou afraid when one is made rich, when the glory of his house is increased; For when he dieth he shall carry nothing away: his glory shall not descend after him.

103:17 But the mercy of the Lord is from everlasting to everlasting upon them that fear him, and his righteousness unto children's children.

118:8 It is better to trust in the Lord than to put confidence in man.

126:6 He that goeth forth and weepeth, bearing precious seed, shall doubtless come again with rejoicing, bringing his sheaves with him.

127:1 Except the Lord build the house, they labour in vain that build it: except the Lord keep the city, the watchman waketh but in vain.

127:3,5 Lo, children are an heritage of the Lord: and the fruit of the womb is his reward. . . . Happy is the man that hath his quiver full of them.

133:1 Behold, how good and how pleasant it is for brethren to dwell together in unity!

137:5-6 If I forget thee, O Jerusalem, let my right hand forget her cunning. If I do not remember thee, let my tongue cleave to the roof of my mouth; if I prefer not Jerusalem above my chief joy.

**139:7-8** Whither shall I go from thy spirit? or whither shall I flee from thy presence? If I ascend up into heaven, thou art there: if I make my bed in hell, behold, thou art there.

**145:8**  The Lord is gracious, and full of compassion; slow to anger, and of great mercy.

**10:6-7, 10**  These three verses read as follows in the Joseph Smith Translation:

"For he hath said in his heart, I shall not be moved; never in adversity.

"His mouth is full of cursing and deceit; and his heart is full of fraud; and under his tongue is mischief and vanity. . . .

"He croucheth to the strong ones, and humbleth himself, that the poor may fall by his devices."

**11:1-5**  The Joseph Smith Translation makes several significant changes in the first five verses of this psalm. (See Ps. 11:1-5, Bible Appendix, p. 800.)

**14:1-7**  All the verses of this psalm are changed in the Joseph Smith Translation. (See Ps. 14:1-7, Bible Appendix, p. 801.)

**17:1-15**  This entire psalm should be compared with the Joseph Smith Translation. As examples, note the changes in verses 1 and 14:

1. Give me right words, O Lord; speak, and thy servant shall hear thee; attend unto my cry, and give ear unto my prayer. I come not unto thee out of feigned lips.

14. Deliver my soul from the wicked by thy sword; from men by thy strong hand. Yea, O Lord, from men of the world; for their portion is in their life, and whose belly thou fillest with thy good things; they are full of children, and they die and leave the rest of their inheritance to their babes.

**18:1-50**  This psalm was also included in 2 Samuel 22. (See the commentary for 2 Sam. 22.)

**22:2**  The word translated here as "hearest" could have been translated "answerest" according to both the Hebrew and the Joseph Smith Translation.

**22:12**  The two words translated here as "bulls" should have been translated "armies," according to the Joseph Smith Translation.

**22:16**  Concerning this verse, LeGrand Richards has written:

That they pierced the hands and feet of the Christ is a well recorded fact of history. The prophets in declaring the second coming of the Messiah indicated that He would present the wounds that He received in the house of His friends as evidence that He was the promised Messiah whom they had rejected. [Quoted Zech. 12:10 and 13:6.] (IDYK, p. 87.)

**24:7-10** See these verses on p. 801 in the Appendix of the Bible for clarification.

**27:13** The Joseph Smith Translation renders this verse as: "Unless I had believed to see the goodness of the Lord in the land of the living, thou wouldst deliver my soul into hell."

**30:12** The clause "to the end that my glory may sing praise to thee" is worded in the Joseph Smith Translation, "To the end that my soul may give *glory to thy name.*" (Italics added.)

**32:3** The Joseph Smith Translation reads as follows: "When I kept silence, my spirit failed within me; when I opened my mouth, my bones waxed old through my speaking all the day long."

**33:4** The first clause reads in the Joseph Smith Translation, "For the word of the Lord is given to the upright."

**36:1-6** The Joseph Smith Translation makes several significant changes in the first six verses. Verse 1 reads: "The wicked, who live in transgression, saith in their hearts, There is no condemnation; for there is no fear of God before their eyes."

**38:7** The word "disease" should read "distress" according to the Joseph Smith Translation.

**39:9** The word "it" should be changed to "chasten me" according to the Joseph Smith Translation.

**42:2-3** The Joseph Smith Translation renders these verses as follows:

"My soul thirsteth for to see God, for to see the living God; when shall I come and appear before thee, O God?

"My tears have been poured out unto thee day and night, while mine enemies continually say unto me, Where is thy God?"

**46:5-6** These verses read as follows in the Joseph Smith Translation:

"*For Zion shall come,* and God *shall be* in the midst of her; she shall not be moved; God shall help her right early.

"The heathen *shall be* enraged, and their kingdoms *shall be* moved, and the Lord shall utter his voice, and the earth *shall be* melted." (Italics added.)

**46:8** The Joseph Smith Translation indicates that these events are in the future: "Come, behold the works of the Lord,

what desolations he *shall make* in the earth *in the latter days.*''
(Italics added.)

**49:7-9** The Joseph Smith Translation makes significant changes in sentence structure and content:

"None can by any means redeem his brother.

"Nor give to God a ransom for him that he should still live for ever, that it ceaseth not for ever to see corruption.

"For the redemption of their souls is through God, and precious.''

**50:1-5** Joseph Smith has provided the following commentary on these verses:

> It is . . . the concurrent testimony of all the Prophets, that this gathering together of all the Saints, must take place before the Lord comes to "take vengeance upon the ungodly," and "to be glorified and admired by all those who obey the Gospel." The fiftieth Psalm, from the first to the fifth verse inclusive, describes the glory and majesty of that event. (HC 4:272.)

**53:5-7** The Joseph Smith Translation reorganizes these verses and makes several significant changes:

> There is none that doeth good, no not one. They were in great fear, for God hath scattered the bones of him that encampeth against him.
>
> O Lord, thou hast put to shame those who have said in their hearts there was no fear, because thou hast despised them.
>
> Oh that Zion were come, the salvation of Israel; for out of Zion shall they be judged, when God bringeth back the captivity of his people. And Jacob shall rejoice; Israel shall be glad.

**56:3** This verse reads in the Joseph Smith Translation: "What! am I afraid? I will trust in thee.''

**82:2** The Joseph Smith Translation reads: "How long will ye *suffer them to* judge unjustly?'' (Italics added.)

**90:13** The Joseph Smith Translation reads:

"Return us, O Lord. How long wilt thou hide thy face from thy servants? and let them repent of all their hard speeches they have spoken concerning thee.''

**94:3** The essential meaning of the lament "Lord, how long shall the wicked . . . triumph?'' was repeated in this dispensation by Joseph Smith when he cried to the Lord:

"O God, where art thou? . . . How long shall thy hand be stayed, and thine eye, yea thy pure eye, behold from the eternal heavens the wrongs of thy people . . . before thine heart shall be softened toward them, and thy bowels be moved with compassion toward them?'' (D&C 121:1-3.)

**102:18** The word "created" should read "gathered" according to the Joseph Smith Translation.

**102:21** Joseph Smith has commented:

"The city of Zion spoken of by David, in the one hundred and second Psalm, will be built upon the land of America." (HC 1:315.)

**104:1** The word "honour" should read "power" according to the Joseph Smith Translation.

**106:45** The word "repented" should read "spared his people" according to the Joseph Smith Translation.

**110:4** The statement "Thou art a priest for ever after the order of Melchizedek" refers to an office in the Melchizedek Priesthood, and has been used by the Lord several times in this dispensation. (See D&C 68:19; 76:57; 107:1-4; 124:123.)

**112:8** The words "his desire" should read "judgment executed," according to the Joseph Smith Translation.

**119:20** The Joseph Smith Translation reads: "My heart breaketh, for my soul longeth after thy judgments at all times."

**124:1-3** The Joseph Smith Translation equivalent reads: "Now may Israel say, If the Lord was not on our side when men rose up against us, then they had swallowed us up quick when their wrath was kindled against us."

**135:21** The Joseph Smith Translation reads: "Blessed be the Lord out of Zion; Blessed be the Lord out of Jerusalem. Praise ye the Lord."

**137:1-6** Spencer W. Kimball has commented concerning these verses:

Can one ever forget the tribulations of the tribes of Israel as the foreign nations came upon them and despoiled their cities and their country, ravished their women, blinded their king and took them captive to serve as slaves? Their temple was defiled, their sacred vessels expropriated, their national identity terminated. We read with sad hearts of the song of regret and anguish and loneliness sung by the Jewish survivors:[Psalm 137:1-6.] (MF, p. 136.)

# PROVERBS

See "Proverbs, Book of" in the Bible Dictionary, page 754.

The book of Proverbs contains a number of "wise sayings" from various authors and periods of time. Most of them have been attributed to Solomon.

Successive chapters of Proverbs are not necessarily related to each other; in fact, many of the "wise sayings" even in successive verses are not related. Alternate readings from the Hebrew and other sources are included where needed in the Bible text.

Some of the better known quotations from Proverbs are:

1:7    The fear of the Lord is the beginning of knowledge: but fools despise wisdom and instruction.

3:5-6    Trust in the Lord with all thine heart; and lean not unto thine own understanding. In all thy ways acknowledge him, and he shall direct thy paths.

3:11-12 Despise not the chastening of the Lord; neither be weary of his correction: For whom the Lord loveth he correcteth.

3:13-14 Happy is the man that findeth wisdom, and the man that getteth understanding. For the merchandise of it is better than the merchandise of silver, and the gain thereof than fine gold.

4:7    Wisdom is the principal thing; therefore get wisdom: and with all thy getting get understanding.

6:6    Go to the ant, thou sluggard; consider her ways, and be wise.

6:16-19 These six things doth the Lord hate: yea, seven are an abomination unto him: A proud look, a lying tongue, and hands that shed innocent blood, An heart that deviseth wicked imaginations, feet that be swift in running to mischief, A false witness that speaketh lies, and he that soweth discord among brethren.

10:1    A wise son maketh a glad father: but a foolish son is the heaviness of his mother.

11:1    A false balance is abomination to the Lord: but a just weight is his delight.

12:1    Whoso loveth instruction loveth knowledge: but he that hateth reproof is brutish.

13:24    He that spareth his rod hateth his son: but he that loveth him chasteneth him betimes.

14:34    Righteousness exalteth a nation: but sin is a reproach to any people.

15:1    A soft answer turneth away wrath: but grievous words stir up anger.

15:32    He that refuseth instruction despiseth his own soul: but he that heareth reproof getteth understanding.

16:18    Pride goeth before destruction, and an haughty spirit before a fall.

16:32    He that is slow to anger is better than the mighty; and he that ruleth his spirit than he that taketh a city.

17:15    He that justifieth the wicked, and he that condemneth the just, even they both are abomination to the Lord.

17:17    A friend loveth at all times, and a brother is born for adversity.

17:28    Even a fool, when he holdeth his peace, is counted wise: and he that shutteth his lips is esteemed a man of understanding.

20:1    Wine is a mocker, strong drink is raging: and whosoever is deceived thereby is not wise.

20:13    Love not sleep, lest thou come to poverty; open thine eyes, and thou shalt be satisfied with bread.

21:23    Whoso keepeth his mouth and his tongue keepeth his soul from troubles.

22:1    A good name is rather to be chosen than great riches, and loving favour rather than silver and gold.

22:6    Train up a child in the way he should go: and when he is old, he will not depart from it.

25:19    Confidence in an unfaithful man in time of trouble is like a broken tooth, and a foot out of joint.

25:21-
22    If thine enemy be hungry, give him bread to eat; and if he be thirsty, give him water to drink: For thou shalt heap coals of fire upon his head, and the Lord shall reward thee.

25:25    As cold waters to a thirsty soul, so is good news from a far country.

26:12    Seest thou a man wise in his own conceit? there is more hope of a fool than of him.

26:20-
21    Where no wood is, there the fire goeth out: so where there is no talebearer, the strife ceaseth. As coals are to burning coals, and wood to fire; so is a contentious man to kindle strife.

27:1-2    Boast not thyself of to morrow; for thou knowest not what a day may bring forth. Let another man praise thee, and not thine own mouth; a stranger, and not thine own lips.

27:10    Thine own friend, and thy father's friend, forsake not; neither go into thy brother's house in the day of thy calamity: for better is a neighbour that is near than a brother far off.

28:1    The wicked flee when no man pursueth: but the righteous are bold as a lion.

29:2    When the righteous are in authority, the people rejoice: but when the wicked beareth rule, the people mourn.

29:18    Where there is no vision, the people perish.

30:18-
19    There be three things which are too wonderful for me, yea, four which I know not: The way of an eagle in the air; the way of a serpent upon a rock; the way of a ship in the midst of the sea; and the way of a man with a maid.

31:10    Who can find a virtuous woman? for her price is far above rubies.

**28:20**    Concerning those who "haste to be rich," Spencer W. Kimball has written:

Are there not many who are hasting to be rich? Is money taken in on the Sabbath, when it is unnecessary, unclean money? Some must work on the Sabbath. If it is not their fault, then of course there is no blame. But men and women who deliberately develop Sunday business programs to increase their holdings, I feel sorry for them. (FPM, p. 238.)

# ECCLESIASTES

See "Ecclesiastes" in the Bible Dictionary, page 659.

Some of the better known quotations from Ecclesiastes are:

1:7    All the rivers run into the sea; yet the sea is not full.

1:9    There is no new thing under the sun.

1:18    For in much wisdom is much grief: and he that increaseth knowledge increaseth sorrow.

3:1-8    To every thing there is a season, and a time to every purpose under the heaven. . . . (Read this passage in its entirety.)

5:12    The sleep of a labouring man is sweet, whether he eat little or much: but the abundance of the rich will not suffer him to sleep.

9:4    A living dog is better than a dead lion.

11:1    Cast thy bread upon the waters: for thou shalt find it after many days.

And finally one quotation that perhaps is only a personal choice at the moment:

12:12    Of making many books there is no end; and much study is a weariness of the flesh.

**1:1**    The Hebrew word for *preacher (koheleth)* comes from a root meaning "to gather," "to call together." Bible scholars disagree as to why the author of this book chose to identify himself by this designation. Some suggest he is "gathering together" some major principles of life.

It is also unknown whether or not Solomon was the actual writer of these words; someone else could have written them and then ascribed them to Solomon to gain great readership and influence.

**1:2**    Ellis Rasmussen has provided the following background on the Hebrew word translated here as "vanity":

The introductory statement presents the author's observation that all things tend to be cyclically transient and repetitive. The word "vanity" means basically "emptiness" and "uselessness" combined with the idea of transitoriness; it translates here the Hebrew word *hevel,* which is a mere breath, a puff, a whiff that is here and gone. The word may be seen translated in its basic sense in Job 7:16: "for my days are a breath"; see also Proverbs 13:11, "wealth vanisheth more swiftly than a breath." Similar usage may be seen in Proverbs 21:6; 31:30; Psalm 39:6, and in Ecclesiastes it is so used in 1:14; 2:11, 17, 23; 4:4, 8; 5:9; 6:9, and in 11:10. The meaning seems always to be, in the context of this book, that which is evanescent, ephemeral, transitory, and in general not enduring. (IOT 2:133.)

**1:9** The statement "there is no new thing under the sun" means the same as "there is no new thing on earth."

**3:1-15** The writer has noted there are opposites in all things, and most people experience both aspects of opposites at one time or another in their lives. The statement may or may not reflect a belief in predestination or a form of foreordination.

**3:2** Spencer W. Kimball has observed concerning the statement that there is "a time to die":

Just as Ecclesiastes (3:2) says, I am confident that there is a time to die, but I believe also that many people die before "their time" because they are careless, abuse their bodies, take unnecessary chances, or expose themselves to hazards, accidents, and sickness.

Of the antediluvians, we read:

"Hast thou marked the old way which wicked men have trodden?

"Which were cut down out of time, whose foundation was overflown with a flood." (Job 22:15-16.)

In Ecclesiastes 7:17 we find this statement:

"Be not over much wicked, neither be thou foolish: why shouldest thou die before thy time?"

I believe we may die prematurely. . . . (FPM, pp. 103-4.)

**12:7** The Preacher has hinted several times before that man is a dual creature—part of earth and part of a more eternal nature. (See 2:11, 9:5.) Here he expresses the truth that "the spirit shall return unto God who gave it." The word *return* in the English and its equivalent in Hebrew both suggest going back to something that was before.

Harold B. Lee has commented on this verse:

So the Old Testament prophets declared with respect to death: "Then shall the dust [meaning our mortal bodies] return to the earth as it was: and the spirit shall return unto God who gave it." (Ecclesiastes 12:7.)

Obviously we could not return to a place where we had never been, so we are talking about death as a process as miraculous as birth, by which we return to "our Father who art in heaven," as the Master taught His disciples to pray. (SHP, pp. 8-9.)

**12:11**    "Goad" suggests action (see footnote in the Bible), while "nails fastened" suggests permanency or fixing in place. Words are indeed wise if they fix truths firmly in our minds and yet motivate us to righteous action.

**12:13-14**    These summary words help to bring everything back in perspective and are "the conclusion of the whole matter." After everything else is said and done, all we need to know is that we should "fear [revere] God, and keep his commandments." One good and perhaps sufficient reason is given for this in the final verse: "For God shall bring every work into judgment, with every secret thing, whether it be good, or whether it be evil."

# SONG OF SOLOMON

See "Song of Solomon" in the Bible Dictionary, page 776.

The Prophet Joseph Smith indicated that the Song of Solomon is not an inspired book (introduction to "Song of Solomon" in the Joseph Smith Translation), and this book does not appear in the Joseph Smith Translation.

B. F. Cummings has left the following interesting account concerning the statement by Joseph Smith:

One day in June, 1909, while I was laboring as a missionary in Independence, Mo., and editing *Liahona, The Elders' Journal*, Mr. Frederick M. Smith, one of the first presidency of the Reorganized church, called me up over the telephone and invited me to come to his office, saying he had something to show me which would interest me. . . . I immediately went to the office . . . and on entering was pleasantly received. On a large office table [was] . . . the manuscript of the inspired revision of the Bible. . . . It was of foolscap paper and made a package three or four inches thick. It bore evidence of having been written at different times and by different scribes. Most of it had been written on paper that had never been cut through the center as a writer would do now-a-days. A quarter or a half a quire of paper, folded in the center in the old-fashioned way, was stitched through the "saddle" or fold, and thus fastened in the form of a book. Sometimes stocking yarn had been used for stitching. Some of these quarter or half quires were enclosed in covers made of a newspaper. Part of a newspaper thus used contained an advertisement dated, 1838. In those days news print paper was far more durable than it is now.

I was permitted to handle the manuscript and scan its pages, but of course anything like a critical examination of it was out of the question within the time at my disposal. As I was turning its leaves I came to a page on which was written in a bold hand and large letters, bolder and larger than the rest of the writing on that page, this sentence, which, unless memory is at fault, I here reproduce verbatim:

"*The Song of Solomon is not inspired writing.*" (IE, Feb. 1915, p. 388-89.)

# ISAIAH

See "Isaiah" in the Bible Dictionary, page 707.

**1-66** The resurrected Jesus Christ emphasized the importance of the writings of Isaiah when He counseled the Nephites. (See 3 Ne. 23:1-3.)

**1:18** The statement "though your sins be as scarlet, they shall be as white as snow" has frequently been misinterpreted, according to Joseph Fielding Smith:

> This quotation from Isaiah [1:18] is quite generally misunderstood. It is clear from a careful reading of this first chapter in Isaiah, that this remark had no reference to individuals at all, but to the House of Israel. The first verse states clearly this prophecy is what Isaiah saw concerning Judah and Jerusalem, and in succeeding verses we have the following: [Isaiah 1:4, 7-9, 17.]
>
> The promise now follows. If you, a rebellious nation, will repent and turn again unto the Lord, your sins, "though as scarlet, they shall be as snow; though they be red like crimson, they shall be as wool." [Isaiah 1:18.] So, we see, this is not an individual promise, but one to a rebellious nation. No matter how many prophets the Lord sent to Israel and Judah, and how many times he pleaded with them, all through their history they were rebellious.
>
> Here we find a promise that if they would return to the Lord, their past sins would be forgotten, and he would again receive them as his people and bless them abundantly, and they should continue to be his covenant people. So we see that this passage does not apply to individuals and individual sins.
>
> If you will read through Isaiah, Jeremiah, and others of the prophets, you will discover that Israel and Judah did not repent; they were finally driven from their cherished land and have suffered through the ages for their iniquities. (AGQ 2:179-80.)

**1:21** The Old Testament prophets often compared the spiritual relation between God and his people to a betrothal or marriage; apostasy, through idolatry or other sin, was likened to harlotry or unfaithfulness on the part of the marriage partner. (See also Jer. 3:1-20; Ezek. 16, 23; Hosea 2.)

**1:21-31** The writings of Isaiah are considered difficult to understand by many people. However, Nephi, a Book of Mormon prophet, testifies that "the words of Isaiah . . . are plain unto all those that are filled with the spirit of prophecy . . . Yea, and my soul delighteth in the words of Isaiah." (2 Ne. 25:4-5.)

**1:29-30**  The "oaks" or terebinth trees mentioned here are common in the eastern Mediterranean area and are used either as decorative windbreaks and sunshields or to yield a resin from which turpentine is derived.

**2-14**  Nephi, a Book of Mormon prophet, quoted all of these chapters from Isaiah, and they are now in the Book of Mormon—2 Nephi chapters 12 through 24. Nephi then provides an inspired commentary for six chapters (2 Ne. 25-30) on the meaning of the teachings of Isaiah. Every serious student of Isaiah should study carefully these chapters from the Book of Mormon.

**2:2**  This prophecy clearly has to do with the gathering of Israel in the last days. Some LDS students of the scriptures have noted the possibility of dual fulfillment: (1) the temple built in Salt Lake City which has been the center of the gathering of the dispersed of Israel for over one hundred years, and (2) the temple yet to be built in Jerusalem, Israel, which is in the tops of the mountains of Judea.

Joseph Fielding Smith has observed:

> This prediction [Isa. 2:2] has been literally fulfilled. Thousands of people have come to the valleys of these mountains from all lands and climes, proclaiming these words of Isaiah and Micah, and here they have found the word of the Lord and have entered into the covenants, in the house of the Lord which the prophets said would be offered them that they might walk in his ways. No other place on the earth is there to be found a place which fits this description and unto which the people are gathering. (RT, p. 143.)

See also Part I 86, 112.

**2:2-4**  Micah 4:1-3 is nearly identical with these verses from Isaiah. The terms *Zion* and *Jerusalem* refer to two separate, distinct places "in the last days" according to Joseph Fielding Smith:

> There are many references which point clearly to the fact that Zion and Jerusalem are two separate and distinct places. This is true of the prophecy in Isaiah so frequently quoted. [Quoted Isa. 2:2-3.]
>
> We have lived to see this partly fulfilled. There are to be two great capitals. One Jerusalem of old and the other the City of Zion, or New Jerusalem. The latter is to be on this continent. The one will be the Lord's headquarters for the people of Judah and Israel his companions; the other for Joseph and his companions on the Western Hemisphere, which was

given to Joseph and his seed after him as an everlasting inheritance. (CHMR 1:412.)

See the commentaries for Micah 4:1-2 and Joel 2:32 and Part I 95, 132-33.

**2:5**    The Joseph Smith Translation adds to this verse the clause: "for ye have all gone astray, every one to his wicked ways."

**2:9**    The Joseph Smith Translation makes a significant change in this verse: "And the mean man boweth *not* down, and the great man humbleth himself *not*; therefore forgive them not." (Italics added.)

**2:12, 14-15**    The Joseph Smith Translation renders these verses as follows:

"For the day of the Lord of hosts soon cometh upon all nations; yea, upon every one; yea, upon the proud and lofty, and upon every one who is lifted up, and he shall be brought low.

"And upon all the high mountains, and upon all the hills, and upon all the nations which are lifted up;

"And upon every people, and upon every high tower, and upon every fenced wall."

**2:16**    This verse is quoted differently in the Book of Mormon and various versions of the Bible, as indicated by Sidney B. Sperry:

In 2 Nephi 12:16 (cf. Isaiah 2:16) the Book of Mormon has a reading of remarkable interest. It prefixes a phrase of eight words not found in the Hebrew or King James versions. Since the ancient Septuagint (Greek) version concurs with the added phrase in the Book of Mormon, let us exhibit the readings of the Book of Mormon (B.M.), the King James Version (K.J.), and the Septuagint (LXX) as follows:

B.M.    And upon all the ships of the sea,
K. J.    _____
LXX    And upon ever ship of the sea,

      and upon all the ships of Tarshish.
      And upon all the ships of Tarshish,

      _____

      and upon all pleasant pictures.
      and upon all pleasant pictures.
      and upon every display of fine ships.

The Book of Mormon suggests that the original text of this verse contained three phrases, all of which commenced with the same opening words, "and upon all." By a common accident, the original Hebrew (and hence the King James) text lost the first phrase, which was, however, preserved by the Septuagint. The latter lost the second phrase, and seems to have corrupted the third phrase. The Book of Mormon preserved all three phrases. (*Our Book of Mormon,* pp. 172-73.)

**2:20** A possible interpretation of this verse has been suggested by Joseph Fielding Smith:

We have frequently quoted these verses [Isa. 2:1-5], but we have failed to study the verses which follow, and they all have to do with our present day. One significant thing in it is that the Lord says we would throw our idols of gold and silver which men worship in these days, to the moles and the bats, and we have nearly done this, have we not? You do not have much gold and did not the Government take it and bury it? This is close to giving it to bats and moles. (ST, pp. 56-57.)

**2:20** When Isaiah uses the phrase "in that day," it almost always pertains to the last days (see v. 2) or to the dispensation of the fullness of times. (See also the commentary for Isa. 19:18-25.)

**2:21** The King James statement "for fear of the Lord, and for the glory of his majesty" is translated in the Joseph Smith Translation as "for the fear of the Lord shall come upon them, and the majesty of the Lord shall smite them."

**3:5** The clause "the child shall behave himself proudly against the ancient" is an apt description of one of the causes of communication gaps between generations.

**3:16-26** Joseph Fielding Smith believed these verses apply primarily to women of the latter days:

Today it is a common sight, even on the streets of the cities of the Latter-day Saints, to see women dressed in pants and suits similar to those worn by men. We are forced to declare that this is not a lovely sight. Moreover, it is also frequently the case at parties and places of entertainment that women are arrayed in what I think they call full or party dress, thus exposing a part of the body which should be sacred and not exposed.

The Prophet Isaiah without question saw our day, for he speaks of the daughters of Zion who, in the latter days, would be guilty of all kinds of improprieties in their dress. I will not quote what he said, but if any are curious enough and wish to read it you will find it in the third chapter of Isaiah, verses sixteen to the end.

Now, my good brethren and sisters, I am making a plea for modesty and chastity and for the members of the Church, male and female alike, to be chaste, clean in their lives, and obedient to the covenants and commandments the Lord has given us. (CR, Apr. 1964, p. 108.)

**4** The footnotes in the Bible are very helpful in understanding this chapter of Isaiah.

**4:1** In a Semitic society, the greatest disgrace for a woman was to be barren. Here Isaiah describes a time in the latter days when women will support themselves financially, but they will seek a husband who will make it possible for them to achieve the honor of motherhood and thus take away their "reproach."

**5:10** The seriousness of the desolation in the fields is demonstrated by the terms used in verse 10. Ordinarily, a farmer would hope to get a thirty, sixty, or even a hundred-fold increase from the seed he planted. But instead he would only get one tenth back because one homer of seed (equal to ten ephahs) would only yield one ephah of harvest. This is a type of "reverse tithing" that results from unfaithfulness.

**5:11, 22** Isaiah includes several warnings in his writings concerning the evils of "strong drink," including the contents of these two verses.

See the commentary for Leviticus 10:1.

**5:20** When a person claims that a certain thing is not a sin when he knows it is sinful, he is calling "evil good." He may do this in order to gain popularity with sinful people or to excuse his own weakness. Concerning such people, Spencer W. Kimball has written:

Woe unto those who wrest the scriptures to interpret them to cover their weaknesses. . . .

Many of the modern terms for sin were not used in the scriptures and in olden days, and some people, therefore, excuse their contaminations because the age-old transgressions were not identified with modern terms. But, if one reads the scriptures carefully, all sins are denounced there in every shade of error. . . .

Surely, every soul who has reached the age of accountability, and especially those who have received the Holy Ghost after baptism, knows the difference; but so often we hear what we want to hear and we see what we want to see. There is a definite war against the soul when evil is perpetrated. And I challenge any normal baptized person who says he did not know he was doing wrong. There is no compatibility between sin and righteousness, between guilt and peace. (BYUSY, Jan. 1965, p. 7.)

**5:26-29** A modern "prophet, seer, and revelator," LeGrand Richards, has interpreted these verses to refer to modern trains or planes and the use of these forms of transportation by LDS missionaries going out into their fields of labor:

In fixing the time of the great gathering, Isaiah seemed to indicate that it would take place in the day of the railroad train and the airplane. [Quoted Isa. 5:26-29.]

Since there were neither trains nor airplanes in that day, Isaiah could hardly have mentioned them by name. However, he seems to have described them in unmistakable words. How better could "their horses' hoofs be counted like flint, and their wheels like a whirlwind" than in the modern train? How better could "their roaring . . . be like a lion" than in the roar of the airplane? Trains and airplanes do not stop for night. Therefore, was not Isaiah justified in saying: "none shall slumber nor sleep; neither shall the girdle of their loins be loosed, nor the latchet of their shoes be broken"? With this manner of transportation the Lord can really "hiss unto them from the end of the earth," that "they shall come with speed swiftly." Indicating that Isaiah must have foreseen the airplane, he stated: "Who are these that fly as a cloud, and as the doves to their windows?" [Isaiah 60:8.] (IDYK, p. 182.)

**6:1-5** "In the mouth of two or three witnesses shall every word be established." (2 Cor. 13:1.) The fact that Isaiah had a personal vision and witness of the Redeemer is testified by Nephi, a Book of Mormon prophet: "Isaiah . . . verily saw my Redeemer, even as I have seen him. And my brother, Jacob, also has seen him as I have seen him; . . . Wherefore, by the words of three, God hath said, I will establish my word. Nevertheless, God sendeth more witnesses, and he proveth all his words." (2 Ne. 11:2-3.)

Careful study of Isaiah indicates that he knew a great deal concerning the coming of Jesus Christ and his mission, including the following:

1. Isaiah knew many of the titles of Christ including the title "Immanuel." (See Isa. 7:14; 9:6.)

2. Isaiah knew the Messiah would be born of a virgin. (See Isa. 7:14; see also Matt. 1:23 and John 1:14.)

3. Isaiah knew the Messiah would be a direct descendant of David. (See Isa. 11:1, 10; see also D&C 113:2.)

4. Isaiah knew the Messiah would be preceded by a special messenger. (See Isa. 40:3; see also Matt. 3:3 and John 1:23.)

5. Isaiah knew the Messiah would reside in territories originally occupied by Zebulun and Naphtali. (See Isa. 9:1-2; see also Matt. 4:14.)

6. Isaiah had personally seen the Messiah and referred to him as the Redeemer (twelve times) and as the Savior (eight times.) (See Isa. 6:1-5; see also 2 Ne. 11:2.)

7. Isaiah knew a great deal concerning the mission of Christ and devoted an entire chapter to this subject. (See Isa. 53.)

8. Isaiah knew of the Second Coming of the Messiah. (See Isa. 24.)

9. Isaiah knew of the Messiah's missionary work to the dead. (See Isa. 24:22; 61:1-2; see also 1 Pet. 3:18-20, 1 Pet. 4:6, and D&C 138.)

**6:9-10**    The Joseph Smith Translation of these verses reads: "And he said, Go, and tell this people, Hear ye indeed, but they understood not; and see ye indeed, but they perceived not.

"Make the heart of this people fat, and make their ears heavy, and shut their eyes; lest they see with their eyes, and hear with their ears, and understand with their heart, and convert, and be healed."

**6:9-13**    The subjects contained in these verses are indicated in the chapter headings of the Bible: Isaiah "prophesies of the rejection by the Jews of Christ's teachings—A remnant shall return."

**7:14**    This is one of the most famous of the Messianic prophecies of Isaiah: "Behold, a virgin shall conceive, and bear a son, and shall call his name Immanuel."

Unfortunately (and erroneously) some modern translations render this verse "a young maiden" rather than "a virgin." Such a change is not justified by the text and destroys the meaning of the statement. How could a young maiden having a child be "a sign" that would help convince the Jews of the coming of their Messiah?

See Part I 64.

**8:1-4**    The date of this prophecy concerning the capture of the northern kingdom by "the king of Assyria" can be determined quite closely because the newly-born son (Maher-shalal-hash-baz, "to speed to the spoil") would not even be old enough to speak before the captivity was to take place. This capture of the ten tribes comprising the kingdom of Israel is usually dated 722 B.C.

**8:5-7**    Isaiah prophesied that Assyria would also invade much of the territory of Judah while capturing the northern kingdom.

**9:1-2**    The heading of this chapter in the Bible says that "Isaiah speaks Messianically." When Jesus Christ came on the earth he was indeed reared in "the land of Zebulun and the land of Naphtali" (where Nazareth and Capernaum are located) "beyond Jordan, in Galilee" as prophesied by Isaiah. (See

Matt. 4:14-16.) Then the people in that area who had "walked in darkness" would see "a great light" who is the Light and Life of the world—Jesus Christ.

See Part I 64.

**9:3**    The Joseph Smith Translation indicates that the word "not" should be deleted from the King James text.

**9:6**    Because of his several visions, Isaiah knew a great deal about the birth, life, mission, and titles of Jesus Christ, even though Isaiah lived some 700 years before Christ was born on the earth. Some Bible scholars who do not believe in the principle of revelation and the spirit of prophecy question whether Isaiah could really have known these things in such detail. That the titles in these verses actually do apply to Jesus Christ is substantiated and explained by Joseph Fielding Smith:

> These titles, and the sayings that Jesus was the Creator and all things were made by him, have proved to be a stumbling block to some who are not well informed. The question arises, "How could he, if he had not body and flesh and bones, before he was born of Mary, accomplish these things as a spirit?" Jesus had no body of flesh and bones until he was born at Bethlehem. This he fully explained to the brother of Jared. The answer to this question is simply that he did these wonderful works because of the glory his Father had given him before he was born (John 17:5-24) and because at that time he was God. (CHMR 1:168.)

See Part I 59-74.

**9:17**    The King James phrase, "every one is a hypocrite," is changed in the Joseph Smith Translation to "every one of them is a hypocrite."

**10**    The first portion of this chapter prophesies of the coming destruction of Assyria, and the last part compares this destruction to what will happen to the wicked in the last days.

**10:23**    The statement "shall make a consumption, even determined" could have been translated from the Hebrew "shall make a full end, as ordained."

**11:1-16**    This chapter of Isaiah was quoted by the angel Moroni when he first appeared to the Prophet Joseph Smith on September 21, 1823. Moroni stated that the chapter "was about to be fulfilled." (JS-H 1:40.)

**11:1-2**    The chapter heading in the Bible says that the "stem of Jesse" who is to judge in righteousness is Jesus Christ.

**11:1-10**    Joseph Smith was once asked a series of questions concerning the contents of these verses. The questions and his inspired answers are in D&C 113:1-6:

Who is the Stem of Jesse spoken of in the 1st, 2d, 3d, 4th, and 5th verses of the 11th chapter of Isaiah?

Verily thus saith the Lord: It is Christ.

What is the rod spoken of in the first verse of the 11th chapter of Isaiah, that should come of the Stem of Jesse?

Behold, thus saith the Lord: It is a servant in the hands of Christ, who is partly a descendant of Jesse as well as of Ephraim, or of the house of Joseph, on whom there is laid much power.

What is the root of Jesse spoken of in the 10th verse of the 11th chapter?

Behold, thus saith the Lord, it is a descendant of Jesse, as well as of Joseph, unto whom rightly belongs the priesthood, and the keys of the kingdom, for an ensign, and for the gathering of my people in the last days.

**11:6-9** Isaiah and other prophets have indicated that during the Millennium enmity will cease between beast and beast, between man and beast, and between man and man. See Part I 100, 155-65.

**11:10-13** LeGrand Richards has provided the following commentary on these verses:

From this prophecy we learn:

*First:* That the Lord would establish an ensign *among the Gentiles.*

*Second:* That the Lord would set his hand again *the second time* to recover the remnant of His people.

*Third:* It will be noted that when the Lord would set His hand "*the second time*" to gather Israel, it would be twofold in nature: (1) That He would "*assemble the outcasts of Israel,* and *gather together the dispersed of Judah.*" (2) That this great movement would have its inception among the Gentiles, the Kingdom of Israel or Ephraim.

*Fourth:* That "The envy also of Ephraim shall depart, and the adversaries of Judah shall be cut off: Ephraim shall not envy Judah, and Judah shall not vex Ephraim." (IDYK, pp. 153-54.)

**12:2** The phrase "God is my salvation!" is actually a play on Isaiah's own given name, as his name has this exact meaning and uses the same Hebrew root.

**13:1-22** Chapter 13 prophesies the type of destruction that will come upon Babylon and then likens it to the destruction of the wicked at the time of the Second Coming. The pattern of the chapter is similar to chapter 10, which prophesied Assyria's destruction.

Concerning the Lord's power to prophesy such events as the forthcoming destruction of Babylon, LeGrand Richards has written:

The Prophet Mormon gave us to understand that all the promises of the Lord would be fulfilled:

"For the eternal purposes of the Lord shall roll on, *until all his promises shall be fulfilled."* (Mormon 8:22.)

In a revelation to the Prophet Joseph Smith given at Hiram, Ohio, February 16, 1832, the Lord gave the prophet to understand that "his purposes fail not:" [Quoted D&C 76:1-4.]

In light of these declarations, it is not difficult to understand how the Prophet Isaiah could declare, one hundred and seventy years in advance, the destruction of the great city Babylon, the greatest city in all the world at that time, and declare in positive terms that it should never be rebuilt. (See Isaiah 13:19-22.) And it never has been rebuilt. (IDYK, p. 211.)

**13:3** The Joseph Smith Translation has significantly clarified this verse: "I have commanded my sanctified ones, I have also called my mighty ones, for mine anger is not upon them that rejoice in my highness."

**13:15** The Joseph Smith Translation clarifies the meaning of this verse: "Every one that is proud shall be thrust through; and every one that is joined to the wicked shall fall by the sword."

**13:22** The Joseph Smith Translation adds the following statement at the end of the King James verse: "for I will destroy her speedily; yea, for I will be merciful unto my people, but the wicked shall perish."

**14:1-3** That Isaiah's prophecies concerning the gathering of Israel in the last days included the promise they should never "be scattered again" is verified by Nephi, a Book of Mormon prophet:

"I spake unto them [his brethren] concerning the restoration of the Jews in the latter days.

"And I did rehearse unto them the words of Isaiah, who spake concerning the restoration of the Jews, or of the house of Israel; and after they were restored they should no more be confounded, neither should they be scattered again." (1 Ne. 15:19-20.)

**14:2** The words in italics are added in the Joseph Smith Translation:

"And the people shall take them, and bring them to their place: *yea, from far, unto the end of the earth, and they shall return to their land of promise,* and the house of Israel shall possess them in the land of the Lord."

**14:3-4** In the Joseph Smith Translation both of these verses contain the phrase "in that day," indicating that these events pertain to the last days.

**14:12-17** The "Lucifer" referred to in these verses also

has other titles such as "devil," "Satan," "the adversary," "the evil one," "the liar from the beginning," and "perdition." (See "Devil," BD, p. 656; "Lucifer," BD, p. 726.)

*Lucifer* is apparently the title or name of the personage in the pre-earthly existence who is now referred to as Satan or the devil. The fact that Isaiah refers to Lucifer and his role in the pre-earthly existence seems to indicate that the Old Testament prophets were acquainted with the doctrine of a pre-earthly existence. It may be that Isaiah and others of the ancient prophets had access to the writings of Moses that are not in our present Old Testament but which were revealed anew to the Prophet Joseph Smith in December 1830. These writings of Moses include the following statement concerning Lucifer and his role in the pre-earthly councils:

> Wherefore, because that Satan rebelled against me, and sought to destroy the agency of man, which I, the Lord God, had given him, and also, that I should give unto him mine own power; by the power of mine Only Begotten, I caused that he should be cast down;
>
> And he became Satan, yea, even the devil, the father of all lies, to deceive and to blind men, and to lead them captive at his will, even as many as would not hearken unto my voice. (Moses 4:3-4.)

Joseph Fielding Smith has provided the following commentary on Lucifer:

> Satan was denied the privilege of receiving a body of flesh and bones, the blessing of mortality and the resurrection, because of his rebellion. There must have been a time in the eternity past when he was considered faithful and great honors had been bestowed upon him, for he was known as Lucifer, which is interpreted as "light-bearer." It is written of him in Isaiah. [14:12-17.]
>
> Lucifer sought to dethrone our Eternal Father and rebelled against the plan for our redemption from the grave. For this rebellion he was cast out with those who followed him, and from that time henceforth he has been the enemy of every mortal man. (AGQ 2:170.)

**14:19** The King James clause "and as the raiment of those that are slain" appears in the Joseph Smith Translation as "and the remnant of those that are slain."

**17:1** Isaiah continues with his prophecies of the coming destruction of cities and countries. He had already prophesied the destruction of Assyria (10:5) and Babylon (13:1-5). Now the destruction of Damascus is foretold (17:1).

**18:1** The identification of the "land shadowing with wings" has been provided by Joseph Fielding Smith:

I will read from the 18th chapter of Isaiah because this has to do with this latter-day work. . . . The way it begins in the King James version is: "Woe to the land shadowing with wings, which is beyond the rivers of Ethiopia." This is a mistranslation. In the Catholic Bible it reads: "Ah, land of the whirring of wings, beyond the rivers of Cush," and in Smith and Goodspeed's translation it reads: "Ah! Land of the buzzing of wings, which lies beyond the rivers of Ethiopia." The chapter shows clearly that no woe was intended, but rather a greeting, as indicated in these other translations. A correct translation would be, "Hail to the land in the shape of wings." Now, do you know of any land in the shape of wings? Think of your map. About twenty-five years ago one of the current magazines printed on the cover the American continents in the shape of wings, with the body of the bird between. . . . Does not this hemisphere take the shape of wings; the spread out wings of a bird? (ST, p. 51.)

**18:2**    Joseph Fielding Smith has indicated: "the word 'bulrushes' is . . . wrong. The meaning is vessels of speed." (ST, p. 51.)

**18:2-3**    The "ambassadors" or "swift messengers" in verse 2 are missionaries of the true Church, according to Joseph Fielding Smith:

This chapter is clearly a reference to the sending forth of the missionaries to the nations of the earth to gather again this people who are scattered and peeled. The ensign has been lifted upon the mountains, and the work of gathering has been going on for over one hundred years. No one understands this chapter, but the Latter-day Saints, and we can see how it is being fulfilled. (ST, p. 54-55.)

America was discovered because the Lord willed it. The gospel was restored in America, rather than in some other land, because the Lord willed it. This is the land "shadowing with wings" spoken of by Isaiah that today is sending ambassadors by the sea to a nation scattered and peeled, which at one time was terrible in the beginning. (Isa. 18:1-2.) Now that nation is being gathered, and once again they shall be in favor with the Lord. (CR, Apr. 1966, p. 14.)

This interpretation suggests that the "ensign on the mountain" in verse 3 is the gospel of Jesus Christ.

**19:1-10**    These verses concerning the "burden" (message) to Egypt have been subject to various interpretations. Some scholars believe the statement "the Egyptians [will fight] against the Egyptians" refers to the struggles for power among many of the Egyptian leaders. Scholars disagree as to whether "the river" referred to in verse 5 is the Nile (whose flow has been altered by the construction of the high dam at Aswan) or the "river of Egypt" that is usually interpreted to be an ancient stream near Wadi El Arish which "dried up" long ago.

**19:18-25**    The term "in that day" (verses 18, 19, 21, 23, and 24) is frequently used by Isaiah to refer to the period of the last days. If this is the meaning here, the contents of some of these verses are still to be fulfilled. (See the commentary for Isa. 2:20.)

**20:1-6**    The contents of this brief chapter evidently refer to the time of the captivity of the northern tribes by the Assyrians. See Part I 54, 120-23, 173, 224, 235-36.

**21:2-12**    In discussing the "grievous vision" described by Isaiah, President Harold B. Lee recalled similar words from the apostle Paul:

This vision [Isa. 21] pictures in our minds a watchman upon a tower, placed there by the Lord in the courtyard below, keeping watch for the approach of a possible enemy, which would be perceived by clouds of dust or other evidences. As he reported hour by hour what he could see, here in the vision you have the Lord asking the watchman, "what of the night, what of the night"; and the watchman said, "the morning cometh, and also the night; if ye will inquire, inquire ye."

This vision of Isaiah recalls the descriptive words of the apostle Paul as he wrote to the Ephesians: "For we wrestle not against flesh and blood, but against principalities, against powers, against the rulers of the darkness of this world, against spiritual wickedness in high places. Wherefore take unto you the whole armour of God, that ye may be able to withstand in the evil day, and having done all, to stand." (Ephesians 6:12-13.) (Germany Area CR, 1973, p. 67.)

**21:11**    Harold B. Lee has provided the following modern application on the meaning of the expression "Watchman, what of the night?"

In a revelation to the Prophet Joseph Smith the Lord said that Satan drew after him a third part of the spirits whom God created, and that they with Satan became the force in the world to try to destroy the work of righteousness. That power was spoken of by Isaiah in a vision which he received which he called a grievous vision, in which it was said: "Set a watchman on the tower to tell what he seeth and report the coming of horsemen and chariots," but a voice spoke out of Mount Seir saying, "Watchman, what of the night." (See Isaiah 21:6-11.) "Watchman, what of the night," suggesting that, more to be feared than the enemies that could be perceived with the physical senses or could be seen by physical eyes were the powers of darkness that came unseen by physical eyes. . . .

Using words that are common to modern warfare, we might say that there are in the world today fifth columnists who are seeking to infiltrate the defenses of every one of us, and when we lower those defenses, we open avenues to an invasion of our souls. There are carefully charted on the maps of the opposition the weak spots in every one of us. They are known to the forces of evil, and just the moment we lower the defense of any one of those ports, that becomes the D Day of our invasion, and our souls are in danger.

The experiences and the examples of many cases recited in testimonies in this and other dispensations of the gospel seem clearly to indicate that whenever we allow ourselves to become doubtful, bitter in our souls, melancholy, and otherwise downcast, or despondent, we open avenues to the forces which are ready to take us in a snare just the moment these weaknesses are discovered in us. (CR, Oct. 1949, p. 56.)

**22:2** The first clause could have been translated "Crashings fill the noisy city, the joyous city."

**22:20-25** The chapter heading in the Bible indicates that the essential message of these verses is that the "Messiah shall hold the key of the house of David, inherit glory, and be fastened as a nail in a sure place."

**24:2** The word *priest* as used in this verse does not necessarily refer to an office in the priesthood, as Spencer W. Kimball has explained:

The term *priest* is here used to denote all religious leaders of any faith. . . . From among the discordant voices we are shocked at those of many priests who encourage the defilement of men and wink at the eroding trends and who deny the omniscience of God. Certainly these men should be holding firm, yet some yield to popular clamor. (CR, Apr. 1971, p. 9.)

**26:2** Some modern students of the scriptures have suggested that "the righteous nation which keepeth the truth" is the United States of America, which provided the basis of religious freedom necessary for the restoration of the true Church in the last days.

**26:19** This statement clearly teaches of the resurrection of the Lord (Jehovah) and of all mankind. Concerning this verse, B. H. Roberts has written:

This is Jehovah speaking! "Thy dead men," O Israel, "shall live"—the resurrection of the dead proclaimed! *Together with Jehovah's dead body shall they arise!* Jehovah, then, is to have a "body"! He is to become "*dead*," and to "arise," Jehovah is to dwell with men in the flesh, to be "Immanuel," to live with men, to die, to arise from the dead, and the dead men of Israel to rise with him! (*Rasha, the Jew*, p. 16.)

Harold B. Lee has also emphasized the teaching of this verse:

The question of every man is: "If a man die, shall he live again?" And it is answered by the certainty of the word of God: "Thy dead men shall live, together with my dead body shall they arise." (Isaiah 26:19.) (*Ye Are the Light of the World,* p. 235.)

**27:6, 12**    The children of Israel (Jacob) will "blossom and bud, and fill the face of the world with fruit . . . [and] shall be gathered one by one."

**28:1-29**    The headings and the explanatory footnotes of this chapter shed considerable light on the meanings of these verses.

**28:10**    Similar instructions were given by the Lord to the prophet Nephi as recorded in the Book of Mormon. (See 2 Ne. 28:30.)

**29:1-8**    The Joseph Smith Translation makes several significant changes in these verses. See Isaiah 29:1-8, Bible Appendix, page 801.

**29:4**    Several modern prophets, seers, and revelators have identified this verse with the coming forth of the Book of Mormon. LeGrand Richards has written:

> Isaiah saw the downfall of Ariel, or Jerusalem, at a time far in the future, "add ye year to year," or approximately 170 years before Jerusalem was destroyed as prophesied by Lehi. Then he seems to have been carried away in vision to witness a similar destruction of the cities of Joseph, "and it shall be unto me as Ariel." Then he describes how they would be besieged and forts would be raised against them. They would be brought down and would speak "out of the ground." Their speech would be low "out of the dust." Now, obviously, the only way a dead people could speak "out of the ground" or "out of the dust" would be by the written word which was accomplished through the "Stick of Joseph." Truly it has a familiar spirit, for it contains the words of the Nephite and Lamanite prophets of God. (IDYK, p. 38.)

**29:9**    The Joseph Smith Translation indicates that this verse is addressed to "all ye that do iniquity."

**29:10**    The Joseph Smith Translation indicates that the Lord did not close the eyes of the people, but "behold, ye have closed your eyes."

**29:10-13**    The Joseph Smith Translation adds thirteen significant verses to the King James text, relating in detail the taking of the "words of the book" to the "one that is learned."

According to the Prophet Joseph Smith, this prophecy of Isaiah was fulfilled in the visit of Martin Harris with professor Charles Anthon. (See HC 1:19-20.)

Joseph Fielding Smith has provided the following comments on this visit:

When Martin returned to the Prophet from New York he seemed to be elated. He gave a detailed report of his visit to these noted gentlemen of learning. If Martin went to them with some misgivings in his mind, these were evidently quieted by the report which he received. From that time forth he became enthusiastic over the work the Prophet was doing. . . .

We have reason to believe that Martin Harris was unacquainted with this prophecy. Certainly when he went to Dr. Anthon, he had no thought in his mind in relation to this prediction. How could he know its meaning? Evidently when he returned he was still ignorant of the significance of the event in which he had played such a prominent part. . . . The story of Martin Harris, in connection with its significance in the fulfillment of the words of Isaiah, should impress every member of the Church deeply and reveal to him the marvelous way in which the Lord acts. This is not merely a coincidence, but the actual fulfillment of the predictions. . . .

Let us stop and reflect how Joseph Smith the man "unlearned" according to the Lord's prediction, has confounded the wise and the learned, the professors of science and of religion, and how their theories and doctrines have crumbled before the truth. False teachings have been exposed. The humble have had the Gospel taught to them, while the wise in their own conceit have stood astounded but unrepentant before the onslaughts of this youth against the citadel of their superstitions and false philosophy. We should humbly thank our Father in heaven for the fulfillment of Isaiah's prophecy. (CHMR 1:21-23.)

**29:14** The "marvellous work and a wonder" of the last days definitely includes the translation and publication of the Book of Mormon according to LeGrand Richards:

The bringing forth of the Stick of Joseph [Book of Mormon] which the Lord has done, surely constitutes "a marvelous work and a wonder." It has truly caused "the wisdom of their wise men [to] perish, and the understanding of their prudent men [to] be hid." (Isaiah 29:14.) It is one of the great steps in the unfoldment of the Lord's eternal program looking to the uniting of the two great houses of Israel, Judah and Joseph, since now He has united their records. (IDYK, p. 39.)

Joseph Fielding Smith believed that the missionary program of the Church should also be included:

Surely this prophecy has been fulfilled, to the satisfaction of every Latter-day Saint. When we think of the manner of the coming forth of the Book of Mormon, its influence upon thousands who have come into the Church; the miraculous, but logical, manner in which the Church was restored and its success in the midst of almost universal hatred or opposition, it is something to make us marvel and wonder. Then again, when we think of the missionary work of the Church; how our young inexperienced men have gone forth to proclaim the Gospel to an unbelieving world and have come off victorious, we must acknowledge that only the guiding hand of the Lord could have accomplished this great work. We have seen the wisdom of the wise perish and the understanding of the prudent, who trust in the world and the traditions of men, come to naught. And so it will and must be. (CHMR 1:23.)

**29:16** The Joseph Smith Translation equivalent of this verse (29:28) begins with the clause: "But behold, I will show unto them, saith the Lord of hosts, that I know all their works."

**29:20** The equivalent verse in the Joseph Smith Translation (29:31) begins: "For, assuredly as the Lord liveth."

**30:14** The imagery of Israel being broken (destroyed and scattered) even as a "potters' vessel that is broken in pieces" was also used by the prophet Jeremiah. (See Jer. 18:1-10; 19:1-15.)

**31:1** In the days of Isaiah, the leaders of Israel were placing their faith in the arm of flesh (Egypt) rather than in the Lord (the Holy One of Israel). During the times of the captivity by both Assyria and Babylonia, the Israelites did not receive any assistance from Egypt.

**33:1-24** The chapter heading in the Bible adds significantly to an understanding of these verses.

**34:4** At least three possible interpretations might explain the phrase "the heavens shall be rolled together as a scroll":

1. The weather phenomena of the last days (D&C 43:25; 133:69) or the manifestations in the skies. (Rev. 6:14; D&C 29:14.)

2. The sealing of the heavens after the completion of one phase or glory of the earth; or the opening of the veil of heaven, indicating a new age. (D&C 77:8; 133:69.)

3. The completion of the work of the telestial world in anticipation of the Millennium and the Second Coming. (D&C 88:95; 101:23.)

**34:5-6** The Hebrew word translated here as "Idumea" is the word for Edom. The Doctrine and Covenants indicates that this word is also used to designate "the world." (See D&C 1:36.)

Joseph Fielding Smith has written:

Now, some Bible commentators, because the name of Idumea, a little country east of the Jordan, is mentioned, have an idea that this had reference to that little country; but the term Idumea is one that the Lord uses to mean the world. You will find it so recorded in Section 1 of the Doctrine and Covenants. He is speaking of the world.

. . . This prophecy had nothing to do with that little country called Idumea but to the nations of the earth. (ST, pp. 150-51.)

**34:16** The second clause reads in the Joseph Smith Translation: "and read the names written therein." The last clause is "my Spirit it hath gathered them."

**35:3** The word "confirm" here means to "firm up."

**35:8** The Joseph Smith Translation adds the words in italics:

"And a highway shall be there; for a way *shall be cast up,* and it shall be called the way of holiness. The unclean shall not pass over upon it; but it shall be cast up for those *who are clean,* and the wayfaring men, though *they are accounted* fools, shall not err therein."

**36:5** The Joseph Smith Translation punctuates the first part of this verse as follows: "I say, thy words are but vain when thou sayest, I have counsel and strength for war."

**36:12-22** The servants of the king of Assyria urged the people of the northern kingdom to surrender to Assyria, rather than to continue to resist in the hope their God would deliver them. Samaria (the northern kingdom of Israel) had already been conquered in the campaign of the Assyrians (v. 19).

**37:7** The word *rumour* as used here does not mean the report will be false or incorrect. The sense of the sentence is that the king of Assyria will hear (receive) news from home that will cause him to return.

**37:32** The "remnant" that went forth "out of Jerusalem" at the time of the Assyrian siege of Jerusalem could have been one of the "graftings" mentioned by the prophet Zenos as recorded in the Book of Mormon. (See Jacob 5:8, 13-14, 20-28.)

The Joseph Smith Translation adds the words in italics: "and they that escape out of *Jerusalem shall come up upon* mount Zion."

**37:36** The Joseph Smith Translation clarifies the last portion: "and when they who were left arose. . ."

**38:16**    The Joseph Smith Translation reads: "Oh Lord, thou who art the life of my spirit, in whom I live; so wilt thou recover me, and make me to live; and in all these things will I praise thee."

**38:17**    The Joseph Smith Translation clarifies the meaning of the first clause: "Behold, I had great bitterness instead of peace."

**40:9**    See the commentary for Isaiah 2:2-4. Joseph Fielding Smith has commented:

These are a few of the passages of scripture which indicate the fact that there are to be two capital cities which will be established when the millennial reign shall come. Zion, the New Jerusalem in America and Jerusalem in Palestine which shall be rebuilt and become a city of magnitude and magnificence. (CHMR 1:412-13.)

**40:15**    In modern times, the Lord has indicated again that he controls the destinies of nations and armies: "Do I not hold the destinies of all the armies of the nations of the earth?" (D&C 117:6.)

**41:8**    Several terms of endearment have been used by the Lord in referring to his servants. The title "my friend" is used by him several times in connection with Abraham. (See 2 Chr. 20:7; James 2:23.) The Lord has also used the term several times in this dispensation to refer to leaders in the Church. (See D&C 84:77; 88:3, 62; 93:45, 51; 94:1; 100:1; 103:1; 104:1; 105:26.)

**41:10**    The term *right hand* has been used by the Lord on several occasions to refer to precedence, authority, or righteousness. Concerning such references to the use of the right hand, Joseph Fielding Smith has written:

"The showing favor to the right hand or side is not something invented by man but was revealed from the heavens in the beginning. To Isaiah the Lord said: [Isaiah 41:10, 13.] . . .

"There are numerous passages in the scriptures referring to the right hand, indicating that it is a symbol of righteousness and was used in the making of covenants." (AGQ 1:156-57.)

See the commentary for Genesis 48:13-19.

**41:18**    LeGrand Richards has commented concerning this verse:

"Rivers in high places" could have reference to the reservoirs built in the canyons to impound the winter run-off of water so it may be used for summer irrigation.

"And fountains in the midst of the valleys." If you have seen some of the flowing wells that have been drilled in some of the dry valleys, you can understand this part of the prophecy. (IDYK, p. 185.)

**42:6-8**   See the commentary for Isaiah 61:1-2.

**42:7**   An inspired commentary on the meaning of such verses as Isaiah 42:7 has recently been added to the Doctrine and Covenants and thus is now accepted as scripture in the Church (see section 138, the Vision of the Redemption of the Dead).

The fact that the gospel of Jesus Christ was taught to the spirits in prison was also mentioned by Peter and commented upon by Joseph Smith:

"He went and preached unto the spirits in prison, which sometimes were disobedient, when once the long suffering of God waited in the days of Noah," [1 Peter 3:19-20]. Here then we have an account of our Savior preaching to the spirits in prison, to spirits that have been imprisoned from the days of Noah; and what did He preach to them? That they were to stay there? Certainly not! . . . Isaiah has it—[Isaiah 42:7]. It is very evident from this that He not only went to preach to them, but to deliver, or bring them out of the prison house. (HC 4:596.)

**42:9**   Often when ancient prophets would speak of future events or prophecies, they would use a verb form sometimes called the "prophetic past tense." That is, they would talk about the future as though the event had already happened. For example, over one hundred years before the birth of Jesus Christ, the prophet Abinadi said: "And now if Christ *had* not come into the world, *speaking of things to come as though they have already come,* there could have been no redemption. And if Christ *had* not risen from the dead . . ." (Mosiah 16:6-7; italics added.) Study Isaiah 42:9 with D&C 93:24 and see why a prophet would talk of the future but be so confident that events would happen that he would talk of them in a "prophetic past tense."

**42:19-23**   The Joseph Smith Translation makes several significant changes in these verses. See Isaiah 42:19-23, Bible Appendix, page 801.

**42:25**   The last portion in the Joseph Smith Translation reads: "And *they* have set them on fire round about, yet *they* know not, and it burned *them,* yet *they* laid it not to heart." (Italics added.)

**43:1-28**   Several significant and appropriate titles of Jehovah the Messiah are used in this chapter, including Lord (vs. 1, 11, 12, 14, 15, 16), God (3, 10, 12), Holy One of Israel (3, 14), Saviour (3, 11), your redeemer (14), your Holy One (15), the creator of Israel (15), and your King (15).

See Part I 74.

**43:13**     The meaning of the clause "who shall let it?" is "who shall reverse it?" or, as the Joseph Smith Translation phrases it, "who shall hinder it?"

**43:19**     LeGrand Richards has provided a possible interpretation for this verse:

> What is this new thing the Lord speaks of through the Prophet Isaiah? Could it not be the great system of "irrigation" which the Lord inspired His servants to teach to His people when they entered the valleys of the mountains? It was irrigation which caused the desert to "rejoice, and blossom as the rose;" to "make a way in the wilderness, and rivers in the desert." The great irrigation canals are larger than many rivers as they flow through the desert, bringing tens of thousands of acres of otherwise arid lands under profitable cultivation. (IDYK, p. 184.)

**43:25**     The Lord "blotted out" the transgressions of men through their repentance and his atonement. In such instances, he has promised that he will remember the sins of man no more. (D&C 58:42.)

**44:6**     The several titles of Jehovah used in this verse (Lord, King of Israel, redeemer, Lord of hosts, the first and the last, and God) also appear numerous times in other scriptures, including the modern scripture, the Doctrine and Covenants. (See the numerous titles listed under the heading "Jesus Christ," Bible Appendix, p. 240; see also Part I 74.)

**44:28**     Although Isaiah lived approximately seven hundred years before Christ, he mentioned by name in this verse (and in 45:1) the exact name of Cyrus, the future king of Persia who conquered the Babylonians around 537 B.C. and allowed the Jewish captives to return home. Bible scholars who question or deny the power of revelation and the spirit of prophecy claim it was not possible for Isaiah, the son of Amoz, to have written these verses. They therefore attempt to credit these and subsequent chapters of Isaiah to a "second" or even a "third" Isaiah living hundreds of years later.

That Isaiah could and did know the name of Cyrus over a hundred years before the birth of Cyrus has been verified and explained by Joseph Fielding Smith:

> The Prophet Joseph Smith once said: "Every man who has a calling to minister to the inhabitants of the world was ordained to that very purpose

in the Grand Council in heaven before this world was. I suppose that I was ordained to this very office in that Grand Council." We read in the Bible that this was the case with Jeremiah [Jeremiah 1:5] and John the Baptist who was called to be the messenger to prepare the way before the Lord. [Malachi 3:1; Luke 1:13.] Nor were these pre-mortal callings confined to the prophets, for in a remarkable prophecy made by Isaiah, the Lord revealed the mission which was assigned Cyrus, king of Persia, over one hundred years before he was born. [Isaiah 44:28; 45:1-3.] (AGQ 5:181.)

**46:11**    The "ravenous bird from the east" refers to Cyrus of Persia and his rapid conquest of the area, according to the footnote of the Bible.

**48:1**    The phrase "the waters of Judah" is amplified by an additional phrase in the Book of Mormon where this chapter is quoted. Although the additional phrase "or out of the waters of baptism" in 1 Nephi 20:1 was not in the original 1830 edition of the Book of Mormon, Joseph Smith allowed it to be included in later editions as an inspired interpretation of the phrase "waters of Judah."

**49:18-26**    As indicated in the chapter heading, "Israel shall be gathered with power in the last days." (For additional information on this important subject, see Part I 78-95, 105-23, 177-97, 205-13, 223, 228-32, 239-50.)

**49:22-23**    Nephi, a Book of Mormon prophet, quoted these two verses of Isaiah to his people and then provided an inspired commentary on the meaning of this prophecy. (See 2 Ne. 6:4-15 and Part I 193-94.)

**49:22**    Orson Pratt has explained the meaning of "my standard":

"[The Standard is] the same as an ensign—an ensign that is to be lifted up upon the mountains, upon a land afar off. It is the standard of the Almighty." (JD 16:85.)

**49:25**    The Joseph Smith Translation adds the words in italics: "For *the mighty God shall deliver his covenant people. For thus saith the Lord,* I will contend with them."

**50:1**    The Joseph Smith Translation begins this verse: "Yea, for thus saith the Lord, Have I put thee away, or have I cast thee off for ever?"

**50:2**    The Joseph Smith Translation makes it clear this message is addressed to "O house of Israel."

**50:6**    Portions of this prophecy were fulfilled in Matthew 26:67 and 27:26. (See "Jesus Christ, Condescension of," TG, p. 244.)

**51:3**   Other scriptures and statements pertaining to the desert blossoming as a rose are found in Part I 82, 195.

**51:20**   The Joseph Smith Translation adds the phrase "save these two" to the introductory statement "Thy sons have fainted."

**52:1**   Joseph Smith was once asked: "What is meant by the command in Isaiah, 52d chapter, 1st verse, which saith: Put on thy strength, O Zion— and what people had Isaiah reference to?" (D&C 113:7.) His inspired answer:

"He had reference to those whom God should call in the last days, who should hold the power of priesthood to bring again Zion, and the redemption of Israel; and to put on her strength is to put on the authority of the priesthood, which she, Zion, has a right to by lineage; also to return to that power which she had lost." (D&C 113:8.)

**52:1**   Nathan Eldon Tanner has explained the meaning of the term "put on thy strength, O Zion":

The Prophet Isaiah foresaw the time in which we are now living, with the development of the priesthood administrative system through the present correlation program. I feel that he had reference to us and that the question and answer exchange referred to by the Prophet Joseph Smith in Section 113 of the Doctrine and Covenants has reference to us now. "What is meant by the command in Isaiah, 52nd chapter, 1st verse, which saith: Put on thy strength, O Zion—and what people had Isaiah reference to?" He said, "He had reference to those whom God should call in the last days, who should hold the power of priesthood to bring again Zion, and the redemption of Israel; and to put on her strength is to put on the authority of the priesthood, which she, Zion, has a right to by lineage."

Priesthood correlation is asking the priesthood member and the priesthood leadership to "Put on the strength of the priesthood," and to assume full responsibility with the "power" at their disposal to build up the Church and, eventually, the Kingdom of God here upon the earth. (Priesthood Correlation Genealogy Committee Training Session, Dec. 1963.)

**52:2**   This verse could have been translated and punctuated as follows: "Shake yourself from the dust; rise up! Sit, Jerusalem! Free yourselves from your neckbands, O captive daughter of Zion."

**52:2**   Another question asked of Joseph Smith was "What are we to understand by Zion loosing herself from the bands of her neck?" (D&C 113:9.) Joseph Smith's answer was:

We are to understand that the scattered remnants are exhorted to return to the Lord from whence they have fallen; which if they do, the promise of the Lord is that he will speak to them, or give them revelation. See the 6th,

7th, and 8th verses. The bands of her neck are the curses of God upon her, or the remnants of Israel in their scattered condition among the Gentiles. (D&C 113:10.)

**52:7-8** These or similar words have been quoted by several prophets, including those of the Old Testament and the Book of Mormon. (See "Missionary Work," TG, pp. 325-26; "Peace," TG, pp. 360-61; "Peacemakers," TG, pp. 361-62.) Abinadi quoted and explained these words to King Noah and his wicked priests. (See Mosiah 12:21-24; 15:11-31.)

**52:8-10** These words of Isaiah were quoted to the Lehites by the resurrected Jesus Christ, with the explanation that these words would be fulfilled *after* "this land [the Americas]" should be given "unto this people [the descendants of the Lehites] . . . for their inheritance." (3 Ne. 16:16-20, italics added.)

In a subsequent meeting with the righteous Lehites, the Savior provided an inspired (and inspiring) commentary on the words of Isaiah. Every serious student of the scriptures should study carefully these teachings of Jesus Christ. (See 3 Ne. 20:11-46 and chapters 21-23.)

**52:8** The last clause, "when the Lord shall bring again Zion" literally reads in the Hebrew, "when Jehovah brings back Zion."

Zion will become a reality only when the people strive and live for it, according to Brigham Young:

It is written [Isaiah 52:8] . . . We talk and read about Zion, we contemplate upon it, and in our imaginations we reach forth to grasp something that is transcendant in heavenly beauty, excellency and glory. But while contemplating the future greatness of Zion, do we realize that we are the pioneers of that future greatness and glory? Do we realize that if we enjoy a Zion in time or in eternity, we must make it for ourselves? (JD 9:282.)

For further information and references pertaining to the building up and redemption of Zion in the latter days, see Part I 124-36.

**52:11** The commandment "be ye clean" is as vital today as it was when recorded by Isaiah, according to President Spencer W. Kimball:

The Lord said, "Be ye clean, that bear the vessels of the Lord." (Isaiah 52:11.) And we must state and restate and call to the attention of our children and their children that chastity and cleanliness are basic in the Church. Parents should teach their children in their home evenings and in all their activities as they rear them that unchastity is a terrible sin, always has been, always will be and that no rationalization by any number of people will ever change it. As long as the stars shine in the heavens and the sun brings warmth to the earth and so long as men and women live upon this earth, there must be this holy standard of chastity and virtue. (Sweden Area CR, 1974, p. 10.)

**52:14** Another possible translation from the Hebrew is: "Just as many were astonished over you—so much was the disfigurement of His appearance away from man, and His form from sons of man."

**52:15** The Joseph Smith Translation replaces the word "sprinkle" with "gather."

**53** A Book of Mormon prophet, Nephi, reaffirms that Isaiah knew a great deal the coming of the Messiah. (See 1 Ne. 19:23.)

Abinadi, a Book of Mormon prophet, quoted this entire chapter to the priests of king Noah and then offered an inspired commentary, relating these teachings to major events in the life of Jesus Christ. (See Mosiah 14-16.)

Bible scholars disagree whether this chapter is speaking of Jesus Christ. Those scholars who claim it would have been impossible for Isaiah to know this much about the life and mission of Jesus Christ some seven hundred years before Christ was born either do not believe in the spirit of prophecy or do not understand it. Joseph Fielding Smith and LeGrand Richards state unequivocally, however, that the chapter does pertain to Christ.

I want to read to you the 53rd chapter of Isaiah. Now *Bible* commentators will tell you that this has nothing to do with the life of Jesus Christ. To them this story is one concerning suffering Israel. I want to tell you that it is a story, a synopsis of the life of our Redeemer, revealed to Isaiah 700 years before the Lord was born. If you have the proper discernment you will discover this. I am going to make some comments on it as I read it. [Quoted Isa. 53:1-2.]

What is the meaning of that? Did not Christ grow up as a tender plant? There was nothing about him to cause people to single him out. In appearance he was like men; and so it is expressed here by the prophet that he had no form or comeliness, that is, he was not so distinctive, so different from others that people would recognize him as the Son of God. He appeared as a mortal man. [Quoted Isa. 53:3-4.]

Was not Christ a man of sorrows? Was he not rejected of men? Was he not acquainted with grief? Did not the people (figuratively) hide their faces from him? Did not the people esteem him not? Surely he knew our griefs and carried our sorrows, but he was thought to be stricken of God and forsaken by him. Did not the people say that? How true all these things are! (Joseph Fielding Smith, DS 1:23-24.)

In the life and mission of Jesus Christ He met every requirement necessary to fulfill all the prophet Isaiah predicted He would do, as herein set forth. [Quoted Isaiah 53.] (LeGrand Richards, IDYK, p. 82.)

**53:4** LeGrand Richards believes that this verse offers proof that there are at least two great Gods (the Father and the Son) referred to in the Old Testament:

The statement that He would bear Israel's griefs, carry their sorrows, and that he would be "smitten of God," indicates that there were two Gods and not one. How could this Redeemer be smitten by Himself? (IDYK, p. 79.)

**53:7** This statement that "he" (the Messiah) will be "as a sheep before her shearers" clearly refers to the time of the crucifixion of Jesus Christ, as is verified by Abinadi, a Book of Mormon prophet. After quoting these words from Isaiah, Abinadi commented: "Yea, even so shall he [the Son of God] be led, crucified, and slain." (Mosiah 15:7.)

**54:1-17** These verses on the gathering of Israel and the establishment of Zion are supplemented by the materials in Part I 75-136.

**54:6** The statement "and a wife of youth, when thou wast refused" could have been translated "even a wife of young men when she is rejected."

**54:10** The term "the mountains shall depart, and the hills be removed" evidently refers to the period in the last days when the Lord's voice out of Zion and Jerusalem will be "as the voice of a great thunder, which shall break down the mountains, and the valleys shall not be found.

"He shall command the great deep, and it shall be driven back into the north countries, and the islands shall become one land;

"And the land of Jerusalem and the land of Zion shall be turned back into their own place, and the earth shall be like as it was in the days before it was divided." (D&C 133:22-24.)

Concerning these events, Joseph Fielding Smith has written:

If one should take a map showing the Western and the Eastern hemispheres, and study them, one would see clearly how today they might be fitted together. Well, that day will come, for, as the earth was divided, so shall it in the restoration be brought back to its original form again, with all the land surface in one place. There are many prophecies in the Bible bearing on this union of continents and islands again. (AGQ 4:23.)

The Joseph Smith Translation replaces "peace" with "people."

See the commentary for Genesis 10:25 concerning the dividing of the earth in the days of Peleg. See also Part I 96, 161 for information on events concerning the earth in the last days.

**54:15** The Joseph Smith Translation adds the words in italics: "they shall surely gather together *against thee.*"

**55:6-7** Joseph Fielding Smith has provided the following commentary on these verses:

If at times we have been requested to seek the help of the Lord in this great struggle which has deluged the world, have we prayed in the true spirit of prayer? What good does it do for us to petition the Lord, if we have no intention of keeping His commandments? Such praying is hollow mockery and an insult before the throne of grace. How dare we presume to expect a favorable answer if such is the case? "Seek ye the Lord while he may be found, call ye upon him while he is near." [Quoted Isa. 55:7.] But is not the Lord always near when we petition Him? Verily no! [D&C 101:7-8.] If we draw near unto Him, He will draw near unto us, and we will not be forsaken; but if we do not draw near to Him, we have no promise that He will answer us in our rebellion. (CR, Apr. 1943, p. 14.)

**56:7** Jesus Christ quoted the phrase "mine house shall be called an house of prayer" in referring to the temple in Jerusalem during his lifetime. (Luke 19:46.)

**57:17** The word "frowardly" here means "returning."

**58:1-7** The origin of the principle of fasting, which is discussed here by Isaiah, is uncertain, although Joseph Fielding Smith believes it must have been taught by God from the days of Adam.

Fasting we may well assume is a religious custom that has come down from the beginning of time, and always associated with prayer. There are numerous customs and practices that were given anciently about which the knowledge became so common that their origin has been lost in antiquity; therefore we cannot give time or place where the first commandment on fasting was given. It was common in the most ancient times, and there are numerous incidents recorded in the Old Testament indicating that it was well established not only among the true worshipers of Deity but also among the heathen nations. All of this indicates the antiquity of fasting, which we may presume was revealed to Adam.

We may obtain the understanding from the writings of Isaiah that fasting and prayer were commanded by the Lord. For their perversion of this doctrine, Isaiah rebukes Israel and endeavors to bring them back to the path of faithful obedience. His words and commandment are as follows: [Isaiah 58:1-7.]

Here Isaiah points out clearly the intent of the fast. It was observed with a contrite spirit, a humbled heart, before the Lord. Evil was to be forsaken, prayer and supplication offered with a covenant to feed the hungry, clothe the naked, and let the oppressed go free. If they would do this, then, said the Lord, "shall thy light break forth as the morning, and thine health shall spring forth speedily: and thy righteousness shall go before thee; the glory of the Lord shall be thy reward." Israel, however, had perverted the fast and thus merited Isaiah's and the Lord's rebuke.

All through the Old Testament we find evidence of the observance of fasting and prayer. (AGQ 1:88-90.)

**59:7**  The eagerness of the Israelites of this period to commit sin ("their feet run to evil, and they make haste to shed innocent blood") was similar to that of the wicked Lehites in the days of Mormon ("they have become strong in their perversion . . . they delight in everything save that which is good." [Moro. 9:19]).

**60:1-22**  Materials related to these events of the last days are found in Part I 124-36, 196-97, 222.

**60:3**  According to Wilford Woodruff, this verse pertains to the last days:

The whole history of this people has been foretold by the prophet Isaiah, thousands of years ago; and it has been a steady growth from the commencement to the present. And will the Lord stop here? No; whether men believe or not, this Zion so often spoken of in holy writ, has got to arise and put on her beautiful garments; these mountain vales have got to be filled with the saints of God and temples reared to his holy name, preparatory to the time when "the Gentiles shall come [to] thy light, and kings to the brightness of thy rising." And this time will come when the nations are fully warned by the preaching of the servant of God, and his judgments commence to be poured out upon the world, in fulfilment of the revelations of St. John. Faith then is what the unbelieving world needs to exercise in God and in his revelations to man; but as I have said, whether we do it or not, our unbelief will never turn the hand of God to the right or the left. (JD 19:359.)

LeGrand Richards believes countries such as Great Britain have helped to fulfill this prophecy:

The Jews will understand how literally this prophecy has been in the course of fulfillment in the establishment of the Nation of Israel, and the help that has been given by the Gentile nations. The part that Great Britain played in the liberation of Palestine from Turkish rule is a matter of history which occurred during World War I, in a remarkable manner. The issuance of the Balfour Declaration on November 2, 1917 had great significance. The text reads:

"His Majesty's Government view with favor the establishment in Palestine of a National Home for the Jewish people, and will use their best endeavors to facilitate the achievement of this object, it being clearly understood that nothing shall be done which may prejudice the civil and religious rights of the existing non-Jewish communities in Palestine or the rights and political status enjoyed by Jews in any other country. (*The Autobiography of Chaim Weizmann,* Trial and Error, Harper and Brothers, publishers, page 208.)'' (IDYK, p. 206.)

See also Part I 196-97, 240-44.

**60:5, 11**   The term "forces of the Gentiles" in these verses could have been translated "wealth of the nations."

**60:8**   LeGrand Richards indicates the development of the airplane has helped fulfill this prophecy:

Clearly, Isaiah was referring to individuals and not to birds. Surely there has never been a time in the history of this world when men flew "as a cloud" or "as the doves to their windows," until our present time since the advent of the airplane. (IDYK, p. 101.)

**61:1-2**   These verses of Isaiah were quoted by Jesus Christ in the synagogue at Nazareth as recorded in Luke 4:16-21. Concerning the meaning of the contents of these verses, Joseph Fielding Smith has written:

These references to the opening of the prison and the proclaiming of liberty to the captives evidently have reference to the dead who had been confined in darkness not knowing their fate. Shortly after the Savior entered his ministry he visited his home town, Nazareth, and upon entering the synagogue the scriptures were placed in his hands. He opened them and read the words of Isaiah, and said to the people: "This day is the scripture fulfilled in your ears." [Luke 4:21.] That is to say, the time had come for the preaching of the gospel and the redemption of both the living and the dead. (AGQ 2:81.)

See Part I 64.

**62:4**   The Joseph Smith Translation replaces "Hephzibah" with "Delightful," and "Beulah" with "Union."

**62:5**   The King James clause "so shall thy sons marry thee" is changed in the Joseph Smith Translation to "so shall thy God marry thee."

**63:1-6**   These verses should be taken literally, according to Joseph Fielding Smith:

Isaiah has pictured this great day when the Lord shall come with his garments, or apparel, red and glorious, to take vengeance on the ungodly. [Isaiah 63:1-6.] This will be a day of mourning to the wicked, but a day of gladness to all who have kept his commandments. Do not let any one think that this is merely figurative language, it is literal, and as surely as we live that day of wrath will come when the cup of iniquity is full. We have received a great many warnings. The great day of the Millennium will come in; the wicked will be consumed and peace and righteousness will dwell upon all the face of the earth for one thousand years. (CHMR 1:191 92.)

See the commentary for Malachi 4:1 and Part I 94, 154, 211.

**63:4** According to John Taylor, the "day of vengeance" will come upon the wicked:

When he comes again he comes to take vengeance on the ungodly and to bring deliverance unto his Saints; [Isaiah 63:4]. It behoves us to be made well aware which class we belong to, that if we are not already among the redeemed we may immediately join that society, that when the Son of God shall come the second time with all the holy angels with him, arrayed in power and great glory to take vengeance on them that know not God and obey not the Gospel, or when he shall come in flaming fire, we shall be among that number who shall be ready to meet him with gladness in our hearts and hail him as our great deliverer and friend. (JD 10:116.)

**64:5** The Joseph Smith Translation reads "Thou meetest him that *worketh* righteousness, and *rejoiceth* him that remembereth thee in thy ways." (Italics added.)

**64:8** Harold B. Lee has commented on the statement, "O Lord, thou art our father; we are the clay, and thou our potter; and we all are the work of thy hand":

I've read that many times, but had not received the full significance until I was down in Old Mexico a few years ago at Telacapaca where they feature the molding of clay into various kinds of pottery. There I saw them take lumps of clay which had been molded, usually by crude, primitive methods, the molder wading in the mud to mix it properly. Then it was put upon a potter's wheel, and there the potter began to fashion the intricate bits of pottery which he was to place on the market. And as we watched, we saw occasionally, because of some defect in the mixing, the necessity for pulling the whole lump of clay apart and throwing it back in to be mixed over again, and sometimes the process had to be done several times before the proper kind of mud was mixed for the potter.

With that in mind, I thought I began to see the meaning of this scripture: "We are as clay in the hands of the potter, and we are all the work of His hands." Yes, we too, have to be tried and tested by poverty, by sickness, by the death of loved ones, by temptation, sometimes by the betrayal of supposed friends, by affluence and riches, by ease and luxury, by false educational ideas, and by the flattery of the world. (BYUSY, Oct. 1956, p. 3.)

**65:1** The Joseph Smith Translation reads: "I am found of them who seek after me, I give unto all them that ask of me; I am not found of them that sought me not, or that inquireth not after me."

**65:11** The terms "that troop" and "that number" refer to the idols Gad and Meni respectively. The clause could have been translated: "who array a table for Fortune and who fill mixed wine for Fate."

**65:17** The following commentaries on this verse have been offered by Joseph Fielding Smith:

That is, the earth as it is now, this mundane earth covered all over its face with wickedness will not be remembered when this change comes. We will be glad to get rid of this condition, and we will not bring it up to mind. Remember, in speaking of the heavens he is not referring to the sidereal heavens. He is speaking of that which pertains to our own earth, the heavens in which the birds fly. . . .

You can see that [Isa. 65:17-20] does not have any reference at all to the earth when it is celestialized. The new heaven and earth have nothing to do at all with this earth as it will be after it dies and is raised in the resurrection to be a celestial body because then there will not be any death at all. It is going to be restored as nearly as possible to what it was in the beginning. This is coming to pass when Christ comes, and that's part of this restoration. (ST, pp. 36-37.)

This new heaven and new earth are our own earth and its heavens renewed to the primitive beauty and condition. This is not the great last change which shall come at the end of the earth, but the change to take place at the coming of Jesus Christ. Moreover, when this change comes all things will be set in order. Enmity between man and man and beast and beast will cease. (RT, p. 23.)

For other materials relating to the changes that will take place in the earth during the latter days, see Part I 97, 154, 161.

**65:20** The Joseph Smith Translation begins with "In those days," indicating that these events will take place during the Millennium after the "new heavens and a new earth" are created.

**66:22** The "new earth" referred to here by Isaiah is the terrestrial earth of the Millenium, according to Joseph Fielding Smith:

When the Lord comes to rule on the earth in his own right, and all kingdoms become subject unto him, and the earth is renewed and again receives its paradisiacal glory, death shall be removed as far as it possibly can be removed before the resurrection, and while mortality remains. During the Millennium the earth will be transformed into a "new earth" with a new heaven, as Isaiah has declared. It will no longer be a telestial earth, but will become a terrestrial earth. Infants will not die until they become old and then death shall be the transition to the immortal from the

25

mortal state in the twinkling of an eye. This day is near at hand, "speaking after the manner of the Lord," and then shall come the time of the entire separation of the wicked from the righteous. (CHMR 1:232-33.)

See also Part I 97, 154, 161.

# JEREMIAH

See "Jeremiah" in the Bible Dictionary, page 711.

**1:1-3**  At least some of the writings of Jeremiah have been preserved on the brass plates of Laban, for they contained "the five books of Moses . . . and also the prophecies of the holy prophets, from the beginning, even down to the commencement of the reign of Zedekiah; and also many prophecies which have been spoken by the mouth of Jeremiah." (1 Ne. 5:11, 13.)

It is difficult to tell from the arrangement of the chapters in the King James Version exactly what portions of the book were written before the reign of Zedekiah and which chapters were written after. One possible listing of the chapters chronologically would be: 1-6, 22, 7-13, 17-18, 26, 19-20, 35, 14-16, 25, 36, 45-46, 23-24, 29, 27, 28, 30-31, 33, 21, 34, 37, 32, 38-44, 47-52.

**1:5**  Many scholars, Jewish and Christian, have concluded from this verse that Jeremiah was foreordained (or destined) to be a prophet before his birth. To some, this also implies a pre-earthly existence for Jeremiah.

The Pearl of Great Price teaches that Abraham was also chosen as a prophet before his birth upon the earth. (Abr. 3:22-23.) Joseph Smith and Wilford Woodruff taught that all prophets and other priesthood leaders are so foreordained:

> Every man who has a calling to minister to the inhabitants of the world was ordained to that very purpose in the Grand Council of heaven before this world was. I suppose that I was ordained to this very office in that Grand Council. (Joseph Smith, HC 6:364.)

Joseph Smith was ordained before he came here, the same as Jeremiah was. . . .

So do I believe with regard to this people, so do I believe with regard to the apostles, the high priests, seventies and the elders of Israel bearing the holy priesthood, I believe they were ordained before they came here; and I believe the God of Israel has raised them up, and has watched over them from their youth, and has carried them through all the scenes of life both seen and unseen, and has prepared them as instruments in his hands to take this kingdom and bear it off. If this be so, what manner of men ought we to be? If anything under the heavens should humble men before the Lord and before one another, it should be the fact that we have been called of God. (Wilford Woodruff, JD 21:317.)

**1:6** The substance of the statement "I cannot speak: for I am a child" is that Jeremiah did not know how to speak the will of God for he was inexperienced and young.

The exact age of Jeremiah when he was called as a prophet is not known; the Hebrew simply refers to him then as "a boy." Other prophets who were called when they were relatively young include Enoch (Moses 6:31), Samuel (1 Sam. 3:1-21), Nephi (1 Ne. 2:19-24), Mormon (Morm. 1:15), and Joseph Smith (JS-H 1:7).

**1:17** Ellis Rasmussen suggests that the idiom "gird up your loins" means "gather up the long robe under the belt or sash and get ready for action." (IOT 2:77.)

**2:13** It was bad enough for the Israelites to forsake Jehovah ("the fountain of living waters"), but they have compounded the sin by worshipping idols ("hewed them out cisterns, broken cisterns, that can hold no water").

Brigham Young maintained that if we do not obey the fountain of living waters today (Jesus Christ), we shall be like the Jews of old.

Unless we believe the Gospel of Christ and obey its ordinances we have no promise of the life to come. If we ever attain to that it will be only by complying with the terms that Jesus has laid down. We cannot build and plan for ourselves; if we do we shall be like the Jews of old, who, as the prophet says, "have hewn out cisterns that will hold no water." We must submit to the ordinances of the house of God. (JD 13:213.)

Sterling W. Sill has taught that through accepting Jesus Christ and his teachings, we can develop a well of living waters within ourselves.

Jesus gave us the best approach for this accomplishment when, on the last day of the passover feast, he stood up and cried, "If any man thirst, let him come unto me, and drink. He that believeth on me, . . . out of his belly shall flow rivers of living water." (John 7:37-38.) That is, our eternal success is not like pouring water into a cistern; rather it is like opening a living spring within ourselves. Through the Prophet Jeremiah the Lord said, [Quoted Jeremiah 2:13]. And Jesus elaborated upon this idea by saying, ". . . unto him that keepeth my commandments I will give the mysteries of my kingdom, and the same shall be in him a well of living water, springing up unto everlasting life." (D&C 63:23.) What a tremendous possibility for us! (CR, Apr. 1968, p. 17.)

**2:20-28** A harlot is not faithful to her husband, and the Israelites were playing the role of a harlot in that they were unfaithful to their husband (Jehovah). The people in the kingdom of Judah have worshipped many idols and false gods ("according to the number of thy cities are thy gods, O Judah"); hence, the Israelites have "played the harlot with many lovers." (Jer. 3:1.)

**3:6-11** By the time of Jeremiah, the ten tribes of the northern kingdom had already been taken captive because of their wickedness. These verses show that people of the kingdom of Judah were committing the same sins which brought about the captivity of the kingdom of Israel. When "backsliding Israel committed adultery I had put her away, and given her a bill of divorce; yet her treacherous sister Judah feared not, but went and played the harlot also."

Judah's grievous sin is that she not only committed whoredoms (by marrying with unworthy people) but she "committed adultery with stones and with stocks" (by worshipping idols of stone and wood).

**3:14** At first glance the following statement seems in error: "I will take you one of a city, and two of a family, and I will bring you to Zion." A city is usually larger than a family, so one might ask, "Shouldn't the verse read 'two of a city and one of a family'?"

The gathering referred to here is the gathering of Israel, and the fact that a person belongs to a particular family (Israel) will have more of an influence on whether or not he will gather than will the place of his residence.

Spencer W. Kimball has provided the following insight on this verse:

> In my youth I used to wonder how the world could be converted to the gospel when it was to go to ". . . one of a city, and two of a family . . ." (Jer. 3:14) but as I came to understand the gospel more clearly, the matter seems quite clear. My grandfather came out of the world only a hundred and forty-four years ago, as one of a family, and today there are possibly eight or ten thousand or more of his direct posterity, most of whom were born in the Church and many of whom are faithful.
>
> "One of a city"—not the world—is to be converted.
>
> I am sure that the veil is thin. My grandfather, being one of a family, searched all his life to get together his genealogical records; and when he died in 1868, he had been unsuccessful in establishing his line back more than the second generation beyond him. I am sure that most of my family

members feel the same as I do—that there was a thin veil between him and the earth after he had gone to the other side and that which he was unable to do as a mortal he perhaps was able to do after he had gone into eternity. After he passed away, the spirit of research took hold of men: his family in the west and two wholly disconnected distant relatives, not members of the Church in the east. For seven years these two men—Morrison and Sharples—unknown to each other and unknown to the members of the family in the west, were gathering genealogy. After seven years they happened to meet and then for three years they worked together. The family feels definitely that the Spirit of Elijah was at work on the other side and that our grandfather had been able to inspire men on this side to search out these records; and as a result, two large volumes are in my possession, with about seventeen thousand names.

". . . one of a city and two of a family . . ." may yet accomplish the great objective. (Regional Representatives' Seminar, Apr. 5, 1976.)

**3:15** The word "pastors" could have been translated "shepherds." It does not refer to a specific calling or office in the priesthood, as is explained by Joseph Fielding Smith:

The dictionary definition of a pastor is a correct one even from our understanding of this term; it is "a Christian minister who has a church or congregation under his official charge." The term pastor does not refer to an order in the priesthood, like deacon, priest, elder, seventy, and so on, but is a general term applied to an officer who presides over a ward, branch in a mission or a stake, and it could even be applied to a president of a stake. There are several references to pastors in the Old Testament, particularly in the Book of Jeremiah. I quote one or two of these showing that this is a general term applied to the priests and teachers in Israel, and not to an order of the priesthood: [Jeremiah 3:15.] (AGO 1:127.)

LeGrand Richard has provided the following commentary on these verses:

From these prophecies it will be seen that Jeremiah realized that as Israel had been "sifted among the nations," the Lord would gather them, not in great multitudes, but "one of a city and two of a family," and that when He should bring them to Zion, He would give them "pastors according to mine heart, which shall feed you with knowledge and understanding." In other words, He would lead them to Zion where He had established His Church and Kingdom, restored His Priesthood, that they may be fed "with knowledge and understanding." (IDYK, p. 176.)

**3:16** Evidently the old ark of the covenant will not have place under the new covenant in effect when Israel has returned and "increased in the land." (See also Jer. 31:31-34.)

**3:18** At least two different major groups will be gathered in the latter days ("in those days")—the house of Judah and the house of Israel. The pronoun "they" in the final clause could mean that Judah and Israel will come together "out of the land of the north." (But they will also come from the east and west and south, from the four corners of the earth. See Ezek. 37:21-28; 1 Ne. 22:25.)

Another possible interpretation is that "they" refers to a third group of people who is specifically to come from "out of the land of the north." The three major gathering groups would then be (1) the house of Judah (descendants of those who lived in the kingdom of Judah); (2) the house of Israel (descendants of those who had been dispersed from the kingdom of Israel), and (3) those who are to come out of the land of the north (descendants of the ten lost tribes).

LeGrand Richards believes all the elements of the house of Israel will be gathered at that time:

> The Prophet Isaiah also speaks [Isa. 11:12-13] of the time when the Lord would establish His Kingdom among men. He indicates they would be brought back together so that a common understanding would exist between them as one nation and one people, even the whole House of Israel. (IDYK, p. 23.)

See Part I 78-95, 105-123, 177-91, 204-19, 223-24, 228-50.

**4:5-7** Some of the prophets of the Book of Mormon were shown in vision the destruction of Jerusalem in the days of Zedekiah and Nebuchadnezzar. (See 2 Ne. 1:4.) One Book of Mormon prophet, Nephi the son of Helaman, specifically mentioned the prophecy of Jeremiah concerning this event: "Jeremiah being that same prophet who testified of the destruction of Jerusalem." (Hel. 8:20.)

**4:10** The Jewish Targums have this verse as follows: "And I said, Receive my supplication, O Lord God; for, behold, the false prophets deceive this people and the inhabitants of Jerusalem, saying 'Ye shall have peace.' "

**4:22** Jeremiah's lament ("my people . . . are wise to do evil, but to do good they have no knowledge") is reminiscent of the lament of Mormon in the Book of Mormon concerning the wicked people of his day when he said, "They delight in everything save that which is good." (Moro. 9:19.)

**4:30** The Hebrew words translated "thou rentest thy face with painting" could have been translated "you enlarge your eyes with paint."

**5:4** Jeremiah's attempt to defend the actions of his people is similar to Moses' defense of the people of his day. Unfortunately both groups of people were sinful and did not sin ignorantly.

**5:6** The word "evenings" should have been translated "deserts" or perhaps "plains" or "wilderness."

**5:13, 31** The words of the false prophets will have no more effect than wind, for their words will not come to pass. A modern idiom meaning about the same thing is "they will be full of hot air." The final responsibility for the apostasy will not rest entirely upon the prophets who "prophesy falsely . . . ; my people love to have it so."

**7:8-11** The worship in the temple had also become corrupted in the day of Jeremiah. When a similar corruption occurred in New Testament times, the Savior referred to Jeremiah 7:11: "It is written, My house shall be called the house of prayer; but ye have made it a den of thieves." (Matt. 21:13.)

**7:15** The "seed of Ephraim" was largely scattered some one hundred years before, as they were part of the ten tribes who were taken into captivity by Assyria.

**10:21** See the commentary for Jeremiah 3:15 on the meaning of "pastor."

**11:7** The Hebrew word translated as "protested unto" could have been translated "admonished."

**11:13** Earlier in Jeremiah the Lord accused the people of Judah of having as many idol gods as they had cities (2:28). Here he accuses the people of Jerusalem of having as many altars to false gods as they have streets.

**12:13** The Hebrew words translated "they have put themselves to pain" could have been translated "they are exhausted" or "they are worn out."

**14:2** The Hebrew words translated "they are black unto the ground" could have been translated more literally "they put on ashes for the land." The idea is that they were mourning for the land.

**14:13-16** Some suggestions are given here to help determine whether or not a prophet is truly sent from God. (See also Isa. 8:19-20.)

**14:22** The Lord has power to cause rain, or to withhold rain from the earth, and he has given this power to his prophets in the past (1 Kgs. 17:1-7; 18:1-2, 41-46; Jer. 3:3; Hel. 11:3-18) and will give it to his prophets in the future (Rev. 11:6). Several scriptures clearly indicate the power of God in this regard. (See Gen. 7:4, 12; Lev. 26:4; Deut. 11:14; 1 Kgs. 8:35; 2 Chr. 6:26; Isa. 5:6; Amos 4:7; Zech. 14:17; Ether 2:24.)

**15:3**  "Four kinds [of doom]" are listed here.

**16:2**  The Lord commands Jeremiah not to marry at that time, for he is not to have "sons or daughters in this place." Then the Lord recounts some of the terrible things that will come upon the "sons and daughters" in that area as a consequence of their extreme wickedness.

**16:14-15**  These verses are repeated in Jeremiah 23:7-8. The miracles performed by the Lord in gathering the various groups of Israel in the last days will even exceed in greatness the miracles performed during the exodus from Egypt in the days of Moses.

In modern times, the Lord has mentioned in greater detail some of the events that will be associated with the return of that portion of Israel from the north countries. (See D&C 133:26-37.)

Joseph Fielding Smith has observed:

Here [D&C 133:26] the Lord says that these people have prophets among them, and Joseph Smith at a conference of the Church held in June, 1831, said: "John the Revelator was then among the ten tribes of Israel who had been led away by Shalmaneser, King of Assyria, to prepare them for their return from their long dispersion." This is the mission given to John portrayed in the symbol of the little book which he was given to eat, in the tenth chapter of Revelation. [See D&C 77:14.] (CHMR 2:36.)

**16:16**  The "fishers" and "hunters" are missionaries, according to LeGrand Richards:

It is evident that the Lord has made bare His arm to fulfill His promise made by the Prophet Jeremiah with respect to the gathering of Israel in the latter days. The prophet indicated that the Lord would send fishers and hunters to "hunt them from every mountain, and from every hill, and out of the holes in the rocks," showing how completely He would fulfill His promise, that after Israel was sifted among the nations, "yet shall not the least grain fall upon the earth." (Amos 9:8-9.)

In the establishment of The Church of Jesus Christ of Latter-day Saints upon the earth in these latter days, the Lord has provided therein a great missionary program, through which a great many male members of the Church give two years or more of their lives, at their own expense, to preach the message of the restored gospel to all the inhabitants of the earth. . . . These are the "fishers" and "hunters" the Lord promised to send. (IDYK, p. 175.)

When Wilford Woodruff was engaged in missionary work, he considered himself to be such a hunter and fisher of men:

One day Elder Hale and I ascended to the top of a high granite rock on South Island for prayer and supplication. We sat down under the shade of a pine tree which grew out of a fissure in the rocks, and Elder Hale read the sixteenth chapter of Jeremiah, where mention is made of the hunters and fishers that God would send in the last days to gather Israel. . . . And what had brought us here? To search out the blood of Ephraim, the honest and meek of the earth, and gather them from these islands, rocks, holes, and caves of the earth unto Zion. (WW, pp. 79-80.)

**17:7-8** The statement that the blessings of a righteous man might be compared to the blessings of "a tree planted by the waters" is found in several scriptures (Ps. 1:3; D&C 97:9) and is the theme of various spiritual songs in America.

The value of water, and of providing reservoirs for the storage of water, was the theme of a major talk by Spencer W. Kimball:

I am grateful to my parents, for they made reservoirs for my brothers, my sisters, and myself. They filled them with prayer habits, study, activities, positive services, and truth and righteousness. Every morning and every night, we knelt at our chairs with backs to the table and prayed, taking turns. When I was married, the habit persisted, and our new family continued the practice.

Some parents are casual or careless or fail to do their duty. These constitute leaks in the dams. The story of Peter with his thumb in the dike may be a myth, but the moral is not a myth. . . .

Abraham built such a reservoir for his son Isaac, and it seemed never to have leaked dry, for we find his son one of the patriarchs and always linked with the God of Abraham, the God of Isaac, and the God of Jacob. And he seems to fit the words of Jeremiah. [Jeremiah 17:8.] (CR, Oct. 1969, pp. 20-21.)

**17:21** See the commentary for Exodus 20:8-11; see also Part I 32.

**18:1-6** The parable of the potter and the clay that was marred has been given several interpretations by biblical scholars. A modern prophet has given help on the correct meaning:

Elder Heber C. Kimball preached at the house of President Joseph Smith, on the parable in the 18th chapter of Jeremiah, of the clay in the hands of the potter, that when it marred in the hands of the potter it was cut off the wheel and then thrown back again into the mill, to go into the next batch, and was a vessel of dishonor; but all clay that formed well in the hands of the potter, and was pliable, was a vessel of honor; and thus it was with the human family, and ever will be: all that are pliable in the hands of God and are obedient to His commands, are vessels of honor, and God will receive them.

President Joseph arose and said—"Brother Kimball has given you a true explanation of the parable." (HC 4:478.)

**20:9**  Jeremiah's statement has probably echoed in the hearts of many missionaries who might be somewhat reluctant to call a wicked world to repentance but who feel compelled to do so: "[The Lord's] word was in mine heart as a burning fire shut up in my bones."

**22:1-30**  The various chapters of Jeremiah are not arranged chronologically. Some scholars believe chapter 22 should be between chapters 6 and 7 if a chronological order were maintained.

**23:1-2**  See the commentary for Jeremiah 3:15 on the meaning of "pastors."

**23:5-6**  These verses are almost identical to Jeremiah 33:14-16. The events discussed here clearly belong to the period of the last days.

**23:5-8**  The chapter heading in the Bible indicates that Jesus Christ is the "King Messiah," the Branch that "shall reign in righteousness." A Book of Mormon prophet, Nephi the son of Helaman, testified at least two decades before Christ of the prophecy of Jeremiah that the Son of God should come: "There have been many prophets that have testified these things . . . Isaiah, and Jeremiah, (Jeremiah being that same prophet who testified of the destruction of Jerusalem) and now we know that Jerusalem was destroyed according to the words of Jeremiah. O then why not the Son of God come, according to his prophecy?" (Hel. 8:19-20.)

**23:7-8**  See the commentary for Jeremiah 16:14-15. Concerning the "King" mentioned here, Joseph Fielding Smith has written:

This King, of course, is Jesus Christ, and he will reign when Judah and Israel are cleansed and restored to their own land, and when the offering of Judah and Jerusalem shall be pleasant unto the Lord, as in the days of old, and as in former times, as spoken of by Malachi. (RT, p. 25.)

**23:23-24**  The Lord is the God of the whole earth; he is, or can be, aware of everything that is going on: "Am I a God at hand . . . and not a God afar off?"

**24:1-10**  The "good figs" in the vision are the Israelites the

Lord has already allowed to be taken captive into Babylon "for their good" (v. 5—these would have included Daniel and his companions). The "bad figs" are king Zedekiah and the wicked Israelites in Jerusalem and "in the land of Egypt." Apparently a "residue" of wicked Jews has already fled into Egypt in an attempt to escape the impending destruction by the Babylonians.

A relatively righteous group of Israelites had also previously left Jerusalem to escape the Babylonian captivity; they were led by the prophet Lehi, and had left Jerusalem "in the commencement of the first year of the reign of Zedekiah, king of Judah." (1 Ne. 1:4.)

**24:2, 8** The same Hebrew word translated "naughty" in verse 2 is translated "evil" in verse 8. The idea is that the figs are bad, not worthy or good enough to be eaten.

**25:12-14** This prophecy of the Lord through Jeremiah was fulfilled when Cyrus became king of Persia and conquered Babylonia.

**26:1, 11** This chapter is definitely out of sequence chronologically since Jehoiakim was king (26:1) *before* Zedekiah (24:8). Jeremiah's life was threatened, and the wicked people exclaimed, "This man is worthy to die." Lehi, the first prophet mentioned in the Book of Mormon, was also preaching in Jerusalem during this general period of time, and his life was also threatened as noted by his son Nephi:

"Lehi . . . went forth among the people [of Jerusalem], and . . . testified of their wickedness and their abominations. . . . And when the Jews heard these things they were angry with him . . . and they also sought his life, that they might take it away." (1 Ne. 1:18-20.)

**26:12-15** True prophets must warn the people of their unrighteousness when commanded to do so by the Lord, regardless of any threat to their personal safety. Jeremiah's stirring testimony and warning in verses 14 and 15 are similar to those of Abinadi, a Book of Mormon prophet, before the wicked king Noah and his evil priests:

"Touch me not, for God shall smite you if ye lay your hands upon me, for I have not delivered the message which the Lord sent me to deliver. . . .

"But I finish my message; and then it matters not whither I go, if it so be that I am saved. But this much I tell you, what you do with me, after this, shall be as a type and a shadow of things which are to come." (Mosiah 13:3, 9-10.)

**26:20-24**   At least one prophet of the Lord had already been put to death because of his testimony of those things which were to come—Urijah (Jer. 26:23), who was killed by king Jehoiakim, being buried in "the graves of the common people."

**29:1-32**   This letter of Jeremiah to the Israelites in exile in Babylonia contains the following advice and prophecies:

1. Build houses, raise families, get along with your neighbors, live as normal a life as possible (vs. 5-7).

2. Do not believe in the false prophets who are among you; two of them (Ahab and Zedekiah) will be killed by Nebuchadnezzar (vs. 8-9, 20-23).

3. In seventy years you will have the opportunity to return to your homeland (vs. 10-14).

4. King Zedekiah and the wicked Israelites now in Jerusalem will be smitten with "the sword, the famine, and the pestilence" and are to be removed from the land among many nations (vs. 15-19).

**30:1-24**   The Lord commands Jeremiah to write his words in a book because he is going to bring his chosen people (both of Israel and of Judah) back "to the land that I gave to their fathers, and they shall possess it" (v. 3). The remainder of this chapter is primarily concerned with prophecies of the Lord concerning what will happen to his people during their period of scattering (the diaspora). Because the record of Jeremiah will be preserved, the people on the earth will understand these prophecies "in the latter days" (v. 24).

**30:3**   At first glance the following statement looks as though the Lord is going to take Israel and Judah captive again: "I will bring again the captivity of my people Israel and Judah." However, the real meaning of this statement is "I will bring again my people Israel and Judah from their captivity."

**30:24**   A more literal translation from the Hebrew for this verse would be: "The fierce anger of Jehovah shall not turn back until he has finished and until he has fulfilled the intentions of his heart. In the latter days you will understand it."

**31:3**   The Hebrew translated here as "the Lord hath appeared of old unto me" could have been translated more literally "Jehovah has appeared to me from far away."

**31:8**   The word "coasts" could have been translated "remote parts."

**31:8**  LeGrand Richards has commented on the word "thither":

Note that Jeremiah does not say that they will return *hither*, or to the place where this prediction was made, but *thither*, or to a distant place. (IDYK, p. 177.)

**31:9**  Joseph eventually received the birthright of Jacob (Israel) and Ephraim received the birthright of Joseph. (See Gen. 48:13-22.) Thus in a real sense Ephraim became the "first-born" of Israel.

Concerning this, LeGrand Richards has written:

Recall that the birthright was taken from Reuben, the firstborn of the twelve sons of Israel, or Jacob, and was given to Joseph, and from him to his sons Ephraim and Manasseh, (1 Chronicles 5:1 2). Thereafter, the Lord regarded Ephraim as his "firstborn." (Jeremiah 31:9.) Therefore, this was to be a gathering of the descendants of Joseph and Ephraim, "to Zion unto the Lord our God." (IDYK, p. 177.)

Joseph Fielding Smith has explained the significance of this:

Ephraim was blessed with the *birthright* in Israel, and in this dispensation he has been called to stand at the *head* to bless the other tribes of Israel. . . .

It is essential in this dispensation that Ephraim stand in his place at the head, exercising the birthright in Israel which was given to him by direct revelation. Therefore, *Ephraim must be gathered to prepare the way,* through the gospel and the priesthood, for the rest of the tribes of Israel when the time comes for them to be gathered to Zion. The great majority of those who have come into the Church are Ephraimites. It is the exception to find one of any other tribe, unless it is of Manasseh. (DS 3:247, 252.)

**31:15**  These words are embroidered in Hebrew on the covering of Rachel's tomb, which is located between modern Jerusalem and Bethlehem.

**31:29-30**  "In those days [the latter days]" the punishments of God will not be delayed unduly; they will come almost immediately.

**31:31-34**  Joseph Smith has made the following observations concerning the covenants between God and His chosen people, the Israelites:

This covenant has never been established with the house of Israel, nor with the house of Judah, for it requires two parties to make a covenant, and those two parties must be agreed, or no covenant can be made.

Christ, in the days of His flesh, proposed to make a covenant with them, but they rejected Him and His proposals, and in consequence thereof, they were broken off, and no covenant was made with them at that time. But their unbelief has not rendered the promise of God of none effect; no, for there was another day limited in David, which was the day of His power; and then His people, Israel, should be a willing people;—and He would write His law in their hearts, and print it in their thoughts; their sins and their iniquities He would remember no more.

Thus after this chosen family had rejected Christ and His proposals, the heralds of salvation said to them, "Lo, we turn unto the Gentiles;" and the Gentiles received the covenant, and were grafted in from whence the chosen family were broken off: but the Gentiles have not continued in the goodness of God, but have departed from the faith that was once delivered to the Saints, and have broken the covenant in which their fathers were established (See Isaiah 24:5); and have become high-minded, and have not feared; therefore, but few of them will be gathered with the chosen family. (HC 1:313-14.)

According to Joseph Fielding Smith, the "new covenant" the Lord will make with Israel in the last days will include the covenants contained in the volume of scripture entitled the Doctrine and Covenants:

"This book [the Doctrine and Covenants] . . . in large measure . . . fulfills the promise of the Lord to his ancient prophets in relation to his covenants which he would make with Israel in the last days." (CHMR 3:65.)

**31:34**    In the last days all those of true Israel, "from the least of them unto the greatest," will "know the Lord." Joseph Fielding Smith has explained this responsibility:

If I may be pardoned for saying it, I think many members of the Church will be condemned for their failure to search for knowledge which is given in clearness in our standard works. When will the time come which was spoken of by the Prophet Jeremiah: [Jeremiah 31:31-34.]

It has always been an astonishment to me that so many members of the Church fail to prepare themselves by study and by faith to know the truth. How many fathers in Israel take time out once a week, or every two weeks, or even once a month, to sit down with the members of their families and have an hour or two in study, reflection, and consideration of the fundamental teachings of the gospel of Jesus Christ? This is a duty which each parent owes to his family. No male member of this Church should be so busy or so completely occupied in this world's affairs that he cannot take out time an evening each week to sit down with his family and teach them and have a discussion on the fundamental principles of the gospel. I often think of the rebuke the Lord gave to Frederick G. Williams and Sidney Rigdon because they had failed to teach their children and bring them up "in light and truth." How many other parents in Israel are worthy of a similar rebuke? (AGQ 5:46-47.)

**32:1** This prophecy was given after the Babylonian siege had already started and just one year before the destruction of Jerusalem.

**32:2-3** The fact that Jeremiah was imprisoned is verified by Nephi, the Book of Mormon writer who lived in Jerusalem at the same time as Jeremiah. Concerning the residents of Jerusalem of about 600 B.C., Nephi wrote: "They have rejected the prophets, and Jeremiah have they cast into prison. And they have sought to take away the life of my father, insomuch that they have driven him out of the land." (1 Ne. 7:14.)

**32:36-44** Although the city of Jerusalem is going to be delivered into the hands of the Babylonians and destroyed, yet in the latter days Israel will be gathered back to that land again and the Lord "will make an everlasting covenant with them . . . that they shall not depart from me" (v. 40).

**33:15-16** See the commentary for Jeremiah 23:5-6.

**34:9** This is the first time the word *Jew* appears in the Old Testament. It is used here in the general sense of "being an Hebrew or an Hebrewess."

The title *Hebrew* was applied to Abraham (Gen. 14:13), and his descendants are known as Hebrews.

The name and title *Israel* was given to Jacob (Gen. 32:28; 35:10), and his descendants are known as Israelites. Inasmuch as Jacob is a descendant of Abraham (he is Abraham's grandson through Isaac), all Israelites (descendants of Jacob) are also Hebrews (descendants of Abraham). But, not all Hebrews (descendants of Abraham) are Israelites (descendants of Jacob).

Now to the next generation after Jacob (Israel). The descendants of Judah are known as Jews. All Jews (descendants of Judah) are Israelites (descendants of Jacob) and are also Hebrews (descendants of Abraham).

Thus, as indicated in this verse, a Jew is also a Hebrew. Although all Jews (descendants of Judah) are Hebrews (descendants of Abraham) not all Hebrews (descendants of Abraham) are Jews (descendants of Judah).

Unfortunately even many of the Jewish people today fail to make this distinction. It is true that the Jews are Israelites, but they are not the *only* Israelites. The descendants of the other eleven sons of Jacob (Reuben, Simeon, Levi, Dan, Naphtali, Gad, Asher, Issachar, Zebulun, Joseph, and Benjamin) are also entitled to be called both Israelites and Hebrews. Also, the Arab peoples, who are also descendants of Abraham, deserve to be called Hebrews.

**36:1-32**    This chapter indicates how scriptures can be restored even though the original copy may be lost or destroyed.

In modern times the Lord revealed to Joseph Smith the writings of John the Revelator, which help to clarify John 21. (See D&C 7.) Also the Lord revealed to Joseph Smith the complete writings of Matthew, which contained the teachings of the Savior to a select group of his apostles during the last week of his life on earth. (See JS-M in the Pearl of Great Price.)

**36:26**    The Hebrew word translated here as though it were the proper name *Hammelech,* literally means "the king." It should probably have been translated according to its basic meaning rather than formed into a name. The statement would then read "Jerahmeel the son of the king." (See also Jer. 38:6.)

**38:5**    The final clause of this verse contains several italicized words, indicating that the equivalent to those words do not appear in the Hebrew text. This rather awkward construction in the King James text could have been translated "for the king cannot do anything against you."

**38:6**    See the commentary for Jeremiah 36:26 on the meaning of the Hebrew *Hammelech.*

**38:7**    The English word *Ebed-melech* is a transliteration of a Hebrew word that literally means "servant of the king." Thus the word could be translated simply as a description of the function of the person or it could be the proper name of the person. The King James translators consider it a proper name. (See also vs. 8, 10, and 12.)

**38:19**    The meaning of the last clause is that Zedekiah is fearful "they" [the Chaldeans] will "mock" ("abuse," "maltreat") him.

**41:10**    The daughters of King Zedekiah survived the destruction of Jerusalem and are last mentioned in the Old Testament as having fled to Egypt. (See Jer. 43:6-7.)

A strong tradition exists among some of the peoples of the British Isles that the daughters of Zedekiah were eventually led to their shores and that some of the British people are their descendants. The Bible neither substantiates nor contradicts this tradition.

**46:27-28**    This promise to gather Israel in the last days will not be completely fulfilled until near the beginning of the Millennium when the Lord "will make a full end of all the nations whither I have driven thee [O Jacob]."

**48:12** The clause translated "I will send unto him wanderers, that shall cause him to wander" could more literally have been translated "I will send pourers to him who shall pour him off."

**48:47** The first sentence of this verse could have been translated: "But I will restore the prisoners of Moab in the latter days [end of the days], says Jehovah."

**49:17** Parley P. Pratt has discussed the fulfillment of this prophecy:

Edom also presents a striking fulness of plain and pointed predictions in the prophets. These predictions were pronounced upon Edom at a time when its soil was very productive and well cultivated, and everywhere abounding in flourishing towns and cities. But now its cities have become heaps of desolate ruins, only inhabited by the cormorant, bittern, and by wild beast, serpents, etc., and its soil has become barren; the Lord has cast upon it the line of confusion, and the stones of emptiness, and it has been waste from generation to generation, in express fulfillment of the word of prophecy.(VW, p. 25.)

**50:17-20** Two separate scatterings and gatherings of the house of Israel are mentioned in these verses:

1. Israel ("the king of Assyria hath devoured him," but the Lord "will bring Israel again to his habitation").

2. Judah ("Nebuchadrezzar king of Babylon hath broken his bones," but "the sins of Judah . . . shall not be found").

For additional information on these two major scatterings and gatherings of Israel, see Part I 54-58, 78-80, 105-19, 177-91, 193-97, 204-19, 223, 228-50.

**50:33-34** The Lord will redeem *both* the "children of Israel" and "the children of Judah."

**51:31** This verse could have been translated: "A runner shall run to meet a runner, and a herald to meet a herald, to announce to the king of Babylon that his city is captured from end to end."

**52:1** The beginning of the reign of Zedekiah also marked the year that Lehi, the great patriarch and prophet of the Book of Mormon, left the city of Jerusalem. Nephi recorded: "For it came to pass in the commencement of the first year of the reign of Zedekiah, king of Judah, (my father, Lehi, having dwelt at

Jerusalem in all his days) . . . my father, Lehi . . . went forth."
(1 Ne. 1:4-5.)

**52:10-11**    Earlier accounts of the capture of Jerusalem and
the blinding of Zedekiah are in 2 Kings 25:1-7 and 2 Chronicles
36:11-20.

# LAMENTATIONS

See "Lamentations, Book of" in the Bible Dictionary, page 722.

**1:19** The last clause, "they sought their meat to relieve their souls," could have been translated "they sought food for them to bring back their life."

**2:14** The clause "have seen for thee false burdens and causes of banishment" could have been translated "have seen false oracles and seductions for you."

**2:18** The word "apple" could have been translated "daughter."

**2:20** The phrase "children of a span long" could have been translated "children of tender care." The idea is that during the siege of Jerusalem by the Babylonians, the scarcity of food became so great some women even ate "their fruit [their own children]."

**3:44** The message of this verse has been given a modern application by Spencer W. Kimball:

Eight lovely children had blessed the temple marriage of a man and woman who in later years were denied a temple recommend. They would not be so dealt with by this young bishop. Why should they be deprived and humiliated? Were they less worthy than others? They argued that this boy-bishop was too strict, too orthodox. Never would they be active, nor enter the door of that Church as long as that bishop presided. They would show him. The history of this family is tragic. The four younger ones were never baptized; the four older ones never were ordained, endowed, nor sealed. No missions were filled by this family. Today the parents are ill at ease, still defiant. They had covered themselves with a cloud, and righteous prayers could not pass through. (CR, Apr. 1955, p. 95.)

**5:21** This woeful lament and plea could have been translated: "Return us to you, O Jehovah, and we shall return; renew our days as of old."

**4:17** Egypt was the nation that "could not save" for which apostate Israel "watched."

# EZEKIEL

See "Ezekiel" in the Bible Dictionary, pages 668-69.

**1:1-3**   Ellis Rasmussen has provided the following commentary on these verses:

There has been a question as to what Ezekiel refers to as the "thirtieth year." Traditional Jewish commentaries say it was the thirtieth year of the jubilee, but do not say when the last jubilee year had occurred. Thirty years from 625 B.C., the beginning of the reign of Nebopolassar, father of Nebuchadnezzar, gives the date 595 B.C. That would be about the same as the fifth year of Jehoiachin's captivity and would be a reasonable interpretation.

The place, the river Chebar, could have been the Euphrates by its Babylonian name—*Naru Kabari*. However, some think it was a canal which connected the Euphrates and the Tigris near their confluence.

We do not have record of any other Hebrew prophets called to the prophetic mission while living *outside* the land of Israel. (IOT 2:84.)

**1:22**   This verse could have been translated: "And a likeness was over the heads of the living creature, an expanse, like the color of awesome crystal, stretched out over their heads from above."

**1:26-28**   This description of Jehovah by Ezekiel has a spirit of reverence and awe similar to the descriptions of other prophets, including Isaiah (Isa. 6:1-8), Moses (Moses 1:9-11), and Joseph Smith (JS-H 1:17).

**3:1-3**   The eating of this "roll of a book" by Ezekiel is similar to a later eating of "a little book" by John the Apostle (Rev. 10:8-11), although the purpose may have been different and certainly the results varied. In the experience of John, the book was "sweet as honey" in his mouth but his "belly was bitter."

Joseph Smith has provided the following explanation concerning John's experience:

"Q. What are we to understand by the little book which was eaten by John . . . ?

"A. It was a mission, and an ordinance, for him to gather the tribes of Israel." (D&C 77:14.)

**3:17-19**   The reminder that Ezekiel is a watchman whose

responsibility is to warn is repeated later in the book of Ezekiel (33:1-9) in greater detail.

Even if a prophet knows the people will not repent as a result of his preaching, he must still warn in order that his garments might be clean from the blood of that generation. (See Jacob 1:18-19.)

The prophet Mormon cautions that even though the people reject the message of missionaries, prophets, or other representatives of God because of their own "hardness, let us labor diligently; for if we should cease to labor, we should be brought under condemnation; for we have a labor to perform whilst in this tabernacle of clay, that we may conquer the enemy of all righteousness, and rest our souls in the kingdom of God." (Moro. 9:6.)

In modern times, Spencer W. Kimball has taught the importance of this principle:

I am sure that Peter and James and Paul found it unpleasant business to constantly be calling people to repentance and warning them of dangers, but they continued unflinchingly. So we, your leaders, must be everlastingly at it; if young people do not understand, then the fault may be partly ours. But, if we make the true way clear to you, then we are blameless. (BYUSY, Jan. 5, 1965, p. 6.)

**3:25-27** The Lord did not always require Ezekiel to preach repentance, for He knew the people would not repent at that time and therefore he would be bringing greater condemnation upon the wicked. However, the Lord promised Ezekiel He would open Ezekiel's mouth and be with him when Ezekiel was sent forth to testify.

The prophet Mormon had a similar experience in regard to the wicked Lehites of his day.

"And I did endeavor to preach unto this people, but my mouth was shut, and I was forbidden that I should preach unto them; for behold they had wilfully rebelled against their God.

". . . I was forbidden to preach unto them, because of the hardness of their hearts." (Morm. 1:16-17.)

**4:6** The last clause could have been translated literally from the Hebrew as follows: "a day for a year; a day for a year I have set it for you."

**4:14** From the days of Moses, the Israelites had been forbidden to eat "of the beast that dieth of itself, and . . . which is torn with beasts." (Lev. 7:24; see also Ex. 22:31.) Ezekiel had been faithful in keeping these commandments.

**5:1-5, 12**    Although Ezekiel was a prophet to the Israelitish exiles in Babylonia, he was permitted to see in vision what would happen to the Israelites who were still around Jerusalem: one-third would die by "pestilence, and with famine," one-third would "fall by the sword," and one-third would be scattered into different parts of the earth ("into all the winds"). This last statement would indicate that the scattering of the people of the kingdom of Judah during this period would not be limited to Babylonia.

The Book of Mormon indicates that some residents of Jerusalem during this period (Lehi, Ishmael, Mulek, and their families and groups) were led across the ocean to the continents now known as the Americas. (See 1 Ne. 2:1-5; 18:1-25; Hel. 6:10; 8:21.)

**5:10**    Similar prophecies concerning cannibalism among Israelites in Jerusalem at the time of the Babylonian siege were recorded in Deuteronomy (28:52-53) and by Jeremiah (19:9).

**11:16-20**    When the Lord gathers Israel from "among the heathen" where they have been scattered, he promises them that he will give them "the land of Israel" and "one heart" and a "new spirit . . . [then] they shall be my people, and I will be their God." See Part I 179-91, 212-13, 240-44.

**12:8-16**    The "burden [message of doom]" to "the prince in Jerusalem [Zedekiah]" includes the baffling information that he should die in the land of Babylon yet should not see that land (v. 13).

The striking way in which this apparent riddle is solved is explained in Jeremiah's account of the capture of Zedekiah (king of Judah) by Nebuchadnezzar (king of Babylon):

Then he [Nebuchadnezzar] put out the eyes of Zedekiah; and the king of Babylon bound him in chains, and carried him to Babylon, and put him in prison till the day of his death. (Jer. 52:11.)

**13:3**    False prophets do not receive visions from God; therefore their purported visions (they "have seen nothing") come from their own minds (they "follow their own spirit").

**14:4-21**    The contemporary prophets Ezekiel (in Babylon) and Jeremiah (in the land of Judah) had come to the same conclusion—the people of the kingdom of Judah were so wicked they would not repent until they had experienced the humbling effects of captivity. (See also Jer. 14:13-16.) Ezekiel claimed that even the presence of "Noah, Daniel, and Job" could not have saved the people (vs. 14, 20), and Jeremiah said the presence of "Moses and Samuel" would not have delivered them (Jer. 15:1). This is the first time Job is mentioned in a prophetic book.

**14:22-23** In the end, the scattering (dispersion) of Israel will prove to be a blessing, for they will finally return to the Lord and accept him. The Lord has purpose in everything he does—"and ye shall know that I have not done without cause all that I have done."

**16:3** Although this generation of Israelites had been born in the promised land ("thy birth and thy nativity is of the land of Canaan"), yet they were still worshipping foreign gods and idols as though they were living in the lands of the heathen ("thy father was an Amorite, and thy mother an Hittite"). This "proverb" is later expanded by Ezekiel (16:44-46).

**16:31-34** The imagery (1) of Israel as a wife who has become a harlot and (2) of the Lord (Jehovah) as a husband who greatly desires his wife to return and be faithful to him is used by several of the Old Testament prophets. (As examples, see also Isa. 1:21; Jer. 3:1-6; Ezek. 16; Hosea 4:15; Micah 1:7.)

**16:44-46** See the commentary for Ezekiel 16:3.

**16:55** The term "Sodom and her daughters" refers to the Moabites and Ammonites, as Lot and his daughters escaped from Sodom and their seed became known as the Moabites and Ammonites. (See Gen. 19:36-38.)

"Samaria and her daughters" refers to the peoples of the northern kingdom of Israel. These had already been taken captive as a group before the days of Ezekiel (2 Kgs. 17:6), although remnants of the northern tribes were to be scattered during the lifetime of Ezekiel. (As examples, the peoples of Lehi, Ishmael, and Mulek mentioned in the Book of Mormon —see 1 Ne. 2:1-5; 18:1-25; Hel. 6:10; 8:21.)

Note that all these groups shall "return to their former estate" during the period of gathering in the last days.

**17:11-13** A careful reading of these verses reveals that there were to be several scatterings of the peoples of Judah at the time of the Babylonian captivity. Some would be taken "to Babylon" (v. 12), which included Zedekiah and those who accompanied him. Also, the Lord "*hath . . . taken* the mighty of the land" (v. 13, italics added), which could be Daniel and his companions who had been taken into Babylon earlier when "all the mighty men of valour, even ten thousand" were taken captive (2 Kgs. 24:11-6). Ezekiel 17:13 seems to refer to a third group involving the "king's seed" (singular) because the Lord had "made a covenant with *him*, and hath taken an oath of *him*." (Italics added.) Orson Pratt believed this statement referred to Mulek, the son of King Zedekiah, who came with a company of exiles to America:

When Zedekiah, king of Judah, was carried away captive into Babylon, the Lord took one of his sons, whose name was Mulek, with a company of those who would hearken unto His words, and brought them over the ocean, and planted them in America. This was done in fulfillment of the 22nd and 23rd verses of the seventeenth chapter of Ezekiel, which read thus: [Quoted Ezek. 17:11-13.] By reading this chapter, it will be seen that the Jews were the "high cedar," that Zedekiah the king was the "highest branch," that the "tender one" cropped off from the top of his young twigs, was one of his sons, whom the Lord brought out and planted him and his company upon the choice land of America, which He had given unto a remnant of the tribe of Joseph for an inheritance, in fulfillment of the blessing of Jacob and Moses upon the head of that tribe. [See Gen. 48-49; Deut. 43.] (Orson Pratt's Works, pp. 280-81.)

**17:15** The Lord had warned Zedekiah through Jeremiah not to form a military alliance with Egypt. (Jer. 43:1-13.) Zedekiah disregarded this counsel, however, and incurred the results of his disobedience.

**17:22** Some LDS scholars have suggested that the "tender one" taken from "the highest branch of the high cedar . . . the top of his young twigs" who was to be planted "upon an high mountain and eminent" was Mulek, the son of Zedekiah. Mulek would not have been very old when his father was taken into captivity, for his father was only thirty-two years of age at the time. Also, any elder sons of Zedekiah would undoubtedly have been killed when Nebuchadnezzar "slew the sons of Zedekiah." (2 Kgs. 25:7.) Another possibility is that Mulek was not yet born at the moment of the destruction of Jerusalem, for undoubtedly Zedekiah's wife was still of child-bearing years.

See the commentary for 2 Kings 25:7.

**18:2** Spencer W. Kimball has likened this verse to a modern situation:

There is the man who resisted release from positions in the Church. He knew positions were temporary trusts, but he criticized the presiding leader who had released him, complaining that proper recognition had not been given; the time had not been propitious; it had been a reflection upon his effectiveness. He bitterly built up a case for himself, absented himself from his meetings, and justified himself in his resultant estrangement. His children partook of his frustrations, and his children's children. In later life he "came to himself," and on the brink of the grave made an about-face. His family would not effect the transformation which now he would give his life to have them make. How selfish! Haughty pride induces eating sour grapes, and innocent ones have their teeth set on edge. "It is hard for thee to kick against the pricks." . . .

. . . Sour grapes! Such unhappy food! (IE, June 1955, p. 426.)

**18:14-30**  The scriptures teach there is an opposite in all things. Thus, if the sinner who repents can have all his sins removed, then the person who commits a sin should expect all his former sins to return. One possibility cannot exist without the possibility of the other.

**20:10-26**  According to Joseph Fielding Smith, it is as important for members of the Church to keep the Sabbath day holy as it was for the people of ancient Israel:

Those are the words of the Lord to Ezekiel. [Ezek. 20:10-26.] Notwithstanding all their backsliding and their wickedness and their violation of his commandments, the Lord still pleaded with them; and in the days of Ezekiel, after the greatest number of the tribes of Israel had been carried off because of their rebellion, the Lord pleaded with those who still remained to keep his sabbaths, to walk in his statutes—and even then they refused. Yet he said if they would do these things, it was a covenant with him, and by keeping that covenant he would bless them.

Now, this is the law to the Church today just as it was the law to ancient Israel, and some of our people get rather disturbed because they feel that observing the Sabbath day curtails their activities. (CR, Apr. 1957, p. 61.)

**20:33-43**  The Lord will fully expect Israel to be obedient to his commandments when he gathers them back to the land and brings them "into the bond of the covenant" (v. 37). When the chosen people recognize they have been disobedient to the Lord during the centuries, they will "lothe" themselves in their "own sight" (v. 43).

The Savior has described the feelings of the descendants in those days:

"And then shall they [the Jews] weep because of their iniquities; then shall they lament because they persecuted their king [the Messiah]." (D&C 45:53.)

**21:5, 27**  The terminology that the Lord will draw a sword "out of [its] sheath" and it shall not be returned "any more" to the sheath "until he come whose right it is" was used by Brigham Young in recounting an experience of Joseph Smith and Oliver Cowdery:

Oliver Cowdery went with the Prophet Joseph when he deposited these plates. Joseph did not translate all of the plates; there was a portion of them sealed, which you can learn from the Book of Doctrine and Covenants. When Joseph got the plates, the angel instructed him to carry them back to the hill Cumorah, which he did. Oliver says that when Joseph and Oliver went there, the hill opened, and they walked into a cave, in which there was a large and spacious room. He says he did not think, at the time, whether they had the light of the sun or artificial light; but that it was just as light as day. They laid the plates on a table; it was a large table that stood in the room. Under this table there was a pile of plates as much as two feet high, and there were altogether in this room more plates than probably many wagon loads; they were piled up in the corners and along the walls. The first time they went there the sword of Laban hung upon the wall; but when they went again it had been taken down and laid upon the table across the gold plates; it was unsheathed, and on it was written these words: "This sword will never be sheathed again until the kingdoms of this world become the kingdom of our God and his Christ." (JD 19:38.)

**24:15-18**   If the contents of chapter 24 all pertain to the same day, the wife of Ezekiel died the very day the "king of Babylon [Nebuchadnezzar]" started his siege against Jerusalem. (Compare Ezek. 24:1-2, 18 with 2 Kgs. 25:1-2.) Ezekiel was commanded by the Lord not to mourn the passing of his wife ("the desire of thine eyes") as an example to the Israelites that they were not to mourn unduly their temporary state of siege and captivity.

The Lord promised Israel through his prophets Jeremiah (Jer. 25:12; 2 Chr. 36:21) and Zechariah (Zech. 1:12; 7:5) that if they endured the captivity well he would deliver them in about seventy years. (See also Dan. 9:2, 24.)

**33:1-9**   See the commentary for Ezekiel 3:17-19.

**33:10-20**   See the commentary for Ezekiel 18:14-30.

**33:17**   This verse could have been translated: "Yet the sons of your people say, The way of the Lord is not fair. But they [and] their way is not fair."

**34:1-10**   One reason for the apostasy of ancient Israel is that the so-called religious leaders ("the shepherds") did not set a good example for the people ("the flock"), did not "feed [teach]" them, and allowed them to follow the pagan ways of their neighbors ("they were scattered, because there is no shepherd"). Thus, Jehovah states: "I am against the shepherds; and I will require my flock at their hand."

Undoubtedly some of the strong statements of the Lord against "the shepherds" were deleted during the periods when "the shepherds" had control of the scriptures. For example, the

Book of Mormon account of Isaiah 49 indicates that this chapter originally began with the following thought: "Hearken, O ye house of Israel, all ye that are broken off and are driven out, *because of the wickedness of the pastors of my people.*" (1 Ne. 21:1; italics added.)

After the record of Isaiah had gone through the hands of "the shepherds," however, the above statement was deleted. Evidently this is one instance of a change in the Bible that came as a result of "designing and corrupt priests." (See TPJS, p. 327.)

**34:23-24** The Lord gave several statements to his prophets anciently concerning a shepherd named David whom he would raise up in the last days to feed his flock. "And I the Lord will be their God, and my servant David a prince among them." (See Jer. 23:5; 30:9; 33:15-26; Ps. 89:3-4; Isa. 55:3-4; Ezek. 34:24; 37:22-25.)

Prophets of this dispensation have also spoken and prophesied concerning the spiritual giant named David who will come forth in the last days to be a blessing to gathered Judah.

Just three months before his martyrdom, the Prophet Joseph Smith taught concerning this David: "The throne and kingdom of David is to be taken from him and given to another by the name of David in the last days, raised up out of his lineage." (TPJS, p. 339.)

**34:29** The first clause could have been translated more literally "And I will raise up for them a planting place of name." Evidently most scholars who prepare cross-referencing systems agree with the idea of the more literal translation, for this verse is usually cross-referenced to Isaiah 61:3, which reads "that they might be called trees of righteousness, the planting of the Lord, that he might be glorified."

The King James wording would suggest the possibility that a new plant might be developed in modern Israel that would become famous ("of renown"), that would help remove the threat of famine in the land, and would help the reputation of Israel in foreign lands.

**36:24-27** One of the conditions among gathered Judah in the last days after being gathered "out of all countries . . . into your own land" is that the people will have "a new spirit."

**36:33-38** Another condition of the land of Israel after the return of the descendants of Judah will be that the "desolate land" will "become like the garden of Eden."

Orson Hyde, in dedicating the land of Israel for the return of the Jewish people, pled with the Lord:

"Grant, therefore, O Lord . . . to remove the barrenness and sterility of this land, and let springs of living water break forth to water its thirsty soil. Let the vine and olive produce in their strength, and the fig-tree bloom and flourish. Let the land become abundantly fruitful . . . let it again flow with plenty. . . . Let the flocks and the herds greatly increase and multiply upon the mountains and the hills." (HC 4:457.)

See Part I 82, 195.

**37:1-14** The bringing back of apostate Israel ("very dry . . . bones") into covenant Israel with the Lord again is likened in these verses to the resurrection from the dead.

". . . These bones are the whole house of Israel: behold, they say, Our bones are dried, and our hope is lost. . . .

". . . O my people, I will open your graves, and cause you to come up out of your graves, and bring you into the land of Israel." (Ezek. 37:11-12.) John Taylor has provided the following commentary on these verses:

"The Lord said unto Abram, after that Lot was separated from him, Lift up now thine eyes, and look from the place where thou art northward, and southward, and eastward, and westward; for all the land which thou seest, to thee will I give it, and to thy seed for ever." [Genesis 13:14, 15.] What did Stephen say, generations afterwards? That God "gave him none inheritance in it, no, not so much as to set his foot on; yet he promised that he would give it to him for a possession, and to his seed after him, when as yet he had no child." [Acts 7:5.] Ezekiel's vision of the dry bones explains this seeming contradiction. The Lord said to him, "Son of man, can these bones live? . . ." [Ezekiel 37:3.] Who are they? We are told, in the same chapter, they are the whole house of Israel, and that they shall come out of their graves, bone come to its bone, and sinew to sinew, and flesh come upon them, and they shall become a living army before God, and they shall inherit the land which was given to them and their fathers before them. The measuring line shall again go forth upon those lands, and mark out the possessions belonging to the tribes of Israel. (JD 1:226.)

**37:15-19** Several prophets and leaders of the Church in this dispensation have interpreted the "stick of Joseph" to be the Book of Mormon and the "stick of Judah" to be the Bible. Although both the Book of Mormon and the Bible are incomplete at the present time, they are undoubtedly the best examples of these two "sticks [records]" now available to the people.

Concerning the meaning of these terms, LeGrand Richards has written:

In ancient times, in addition to keeping records on metal plates, it was the custom to write upon parchment, which was then rolled upon sticks for preservation. Thus when Ezekiel was commanded by the Lord to "take thee one stick and write upon it, For Judah . . . then take another stick and write upon it, For Joseph, the stick of Ephraim," in our present day language it was the equivalent of commanding the prophet to write one record for Judah and a separate one for Joseph.

It is evident that when this commandment was given to Ezekiel, the Lord did not anticipate that all His promises made to Abraham, Isaac and Jacob, and to the twelve sons of Jacob, would be recorded in the record of Judah. Recall that at the time this command was given, the house of Joseph had already departed northward into unknown lands, where they had been for some one hundred twenty years. Nevertheless, the Lord wanted all Israel to know that there would be two records kept, one "For Judah, and for the children of Israel his companions," and the other "For Joseph, the stick of Ephraim, and for all the house of Israel his companions." The Lord made it plain that in His own due time He would "make them one stick, and they shall be one in mine hand."

Therefore, the earnest seeker after truth should realize that he cannot expect to have all the record of the Lord's hand-dealings with His children if he has but one of these records. Since we have had the record of Judah with us always, we must inquire, "Where is the record of Joseph?" (IDYK, pp. 26-27.)

**37:19** This verse refers to "the stick of Joseph, which is in the hand of Ephraim." In Doctrine and Covenants 27:5 the Lord refers to "Moroni, whom I have sent unto you to reveal the Book of Mormon . . . to whom I have committed the keys of the record of the stick of Ephraim."

John Taylor, Joseph Fielding Smith, and Parley P. Pratt have explained further the significance of the "stick of Ephraim":

It is one of those sticks that Ezekiel saw should be written upon, even the stick of Joseph which should be written for Ephraim, and be united with the stick of Judah, and become one stick—one in prophecy, one in revelation, one in doctrine, one in ordinances, one in unfolding the purposes and designs of God, and in leading mankind to a knowledge of the truth, as it was to be introduced in "the times of the restitution of all things spoken of by all the holy Prophets since the world began." (John Taylor, JD 10:126.)

Now if you will carefully analyze this verse, you will discover that it positively states that this "stick" which is the "stick of Joseph," thus covering both tribes, is "in the hand of Ephraim." The record, after its presentation to the Prophet Joseph Smith, was placed in the hand of Ephraim, for Joseph Smith was of Ephraim.

There is no reason for us to attempt a reconciliation. The Book of Mormon is as much the stick of Ephraim as it is of Manasseh, because both Ephraim and Manasseh were the sons of Joseph. The record of Joseph is now in the hand of Ephraim. So far as the fulfilment of the prophecy is concerned, it becomes the record of Ephraim, for the Latter-day Saints are, in the main, of Ephraim. (Joseph Fielding Smith, AGQ 3:198.)

Now, nothing can be more plain than the above prophecy: [Ezek. 37] there is presented two writings, the one to Ephraim, the other of Judah: that of Ephraim is to be brought forth by the Lord, and put up with that of Judah, and they are to become one in their testimony, and grow together in this manner, in order to bring about the gathering of Israel. (Parley P. Pratt, VW, p. 94.)

Elder Richards then provides the answer to his question: it is the Book of Mormon.

**37:21-22**    After the time of the judges (which lasted about 330 years) and of the united kingdom (which lasted about 120 years), the tribes of the house divided into two groups: (1) the northern kingdom (the kingdom of Israel) which was ruled over by descendants of Joseph, with headquarters for some time in Samaria, and (2) the southern kingdom (the kingdom of Judah) which was ruled over by descendants of Judah, with headquarters in Jerusalem.

In the last days, however, when the tribes of Israel will be gathered "on every side" and brought "into their own land," there will be only "one nation" and one leader over them all.

LeGrand Richards has provided the following commentary on Ezekiel 37:22:

How could the Lord make a more positive promise that He would bring these two kingdoms together "and they shall be no more two nations"? This promise should cause the descendants of Judah (the Kingdom of Judah) and the descendants of Joseph (the Kingdom of Israel) to realize that until the two kingdoms are brought together that neither can look for the complete fulfillment of the promises of the Lord unto their fathers, Abraham, Isaac and Jacob. (IDYK, p. 22.)

**37:22-25**    See the commentary for Ezekiel 34:23-24 concerning this David.

**37:22, 26-27**    The covenant with Israel is to be "everlasting"; thus revelation and new scripture must continue, according to Joseph Fielding Smith:

It is clear from this and like predictions by Isaiah, Jeremiah and other prophets, that the Lord never intended that the heavens should be sealed. It is a fallacy that the canon of scripture is full and that since the days of the apostles in the Meridian of Time the Lord decreed that there should be no more revelation or scripture. How can the Lord make a covenant with Israel that will be everlasting without an opening of the heavens and a personal visitation or by divine revelation? (RT, pp. 26-27.)

**37:26-28** "Sanctuary" and "tabernacle" have reference to the temple (house of the Lord) that will be erected in Jerusalem in the last days. It will "sanctify Israel" and "be in the midst of them for evermore."

Joseph Fielding Smith has observed concerning these verses:

Through the prophets of old, the Lord has made great promises both to Israel, and the Jews, and concerning Jerusalem and its temple. Jerusalem when Christ comes, is to be a holy city again. Another temple will be built and Israel will be cleansed from all his sins.

Ezekiel prophesied of the gathering of Israel and the building of the temple in Jerusalem after Israel has been gathered and cleansed. In that day the Lord will make an everlasting covenant with them, [Quoted Ezekiel 37:26-28.] After giving the account of the great battle of Gog and Magog and the destruction of the wicked, he gives a detailed description of the glorious temple which shall be built as this sanctuary. (CHMR 2:171.)

**38-39** Parley P. Pratt has offered an explanation of the battle of Gog:

Chapters 38 and 39 present us with a view of many nations united under one great head, whom the Lord is pleased to call Gog; and being mounted on horseback, and armed with all sorts of armor, they come up against the mountains of Israel, as a cloud to cover the land; their object is to take a prey, to take away silver and gold, and cattle, and goods in great abundance.

This is an event which is to transpire after the return of the Jews and the rebuilding of Jerusalem; while the towns and the land of Judea are without walls, having neither bars nor gates. But while they are at the point to swallow up the Jews, and lay waste their country, behold, the Lord's fury comes up in his face, a mighty earthquake is the result, insomuch that the fishes of the sea, and the fowls of the air, and all the creeping things, and all men upon the face of the earth shall shake at his presence, and every wall shall fall to the ground, and every man's sword shall be turned against his neighbor in this army, and the Lord shall rain upon him, and upon his bands, and upon the many people that are with him an overflowing rain, great hailstones, fire and brimstone. And thus he will magnify himself and sanctify himself, in the eyes of many nations, and they shall know that he is the Lord; thus they shall fall upon the open field, upon the mountains of Israel, even Gog and all his army, horses and horsemen; and the Jews shall go forth and father the weapons of war such as hand staves, spears, shields, bows and arrows; and these weapons shall last the cities of Israel seven years for fuel, so that they shall cut no wood out of the forest, for they shall burn the weapons with the fire; and they shall spoil those that spoiled them; and rob those that robbed them, and they shall gather gold and silver, and apparel, in great abundance.

At this time the fowls of the air and the beasts of the field shall have a great feast; yea, they are to eat fat until they be full, and drink blood until they be drunken. They are to eat the flesh of captains, and kings, and mighty men, and all men of war. But the Jews will have a very serious duty to perform, which will take no less than seven months; namely, the burying of their enemies. They will select a place on the east side of the sea, called the Valley of the Passengers, and there shall they bury Gog and all his multitude, and they shall call it the valley of Hamon Gog. And the scent shall go forth, insomuch that it shall stop the noses of the passengers; thus shall they cleanse the land. (VW, pp. 45-46.)

See the commentaries for Ezekiel 38:1-23 and Joel 2:1-11.
See Part I 86, 112.

**38:1-23**    The battle described here of Gog and Magog against Israel will be "in the latter days" (vs. 8, 16) after the people of Israel have gathered back to their land and "dwelleth safely" (v. 14). In the Doctrine and Covenants the Lord reaffirms that the destructions "spoken by the mouth of Ezekiel the prophet" (29:21) will occur "*before* this great day [the second coming of Christ in power and great glory] shall come." (D&C 29:14.)

A second battle of Gog and Magog against the covenant people of the Lord will occur *after* the Millennium, according to the Lord as revealed to John the Apostle. (Rev. 20:8.)

For further information on these two great battles, see the commentaries for Ezekiel 38-39 and Joel 2:1-11; also Part I 90, 113, 206-13.

**38:14-23**    In September 1830 the Lord referred to this prophecy of Ezekiel and said that it will all be fulfilled "for abominations shall not reign." (D&C 29:21.)

**40-43**    The temple described in these chapters is to be built in Jerusalem in the last days, according to Joseph Fielding Smith:

After the Jews have repented and received the Gospel, having acknowledged Jesus Christ as their Redeemer, the temple in Jerusalem will be built according to the prophecy of Ezekiel. The description of this grand edifice is recorded in chapters 40-43. The glory of the Lord will rest upon it and those who officiate in it will be sanctified, holding the divine authority which was given to their fathers. Then will come the true and lawful division of the land, not only for Judah, but for all the tribes of Israel who are to return. (ST, pp. 238-39.)

**43:1-4** Ezekiel likened his vision of the Lord coming to the temple to his earlier visions of Jehovah "by the river Chebar." (See Ezek. 1:3; 3:23; 10:15, 20.)

For further information on this temple, see Part I 86, 112.

**44:20** See Part I 25.

**47:1-5** One of the miracles associated with the return of the Jewish people to Israel is the springing forth of a river from under the foundation of the temple. The Lord revealed this event to Joel (3:18), Zechariah (14:8), and John the Apostle (Rev. 22:1).

The following verses (Ezek. 47:6-8) mention that the waters of the Dead Sea "shall be healed." The sequence and proximity of these verses would seem to indicate that the rising of the river on the temple mount will be at least one of the causes of the healing of the Dead Sea.

See Part I 87-88.

**47:6-12** Another miracle of the last days when Judah returns home is that the waters of the Dead Sea "shall be healed" at least to the extent that "fish of the great sea" can live therein.

At the present time the Dead Sea is approximately 27 percent salt, while the normal seas of the earth are about 5 percent. Although not all the areas around the Dead Sea will be healed ("the marishes thereof shall not be healed; they shall be given to salt"), the sea itself will support fish life, and on the banks of the river "shall grow all trees for meat [food] . . . and the leaf thereof for medicine."

See Part I 87-88.

**47:13-23; 48:1-35** The division of the land among the twelve tribes of Israel in the last days will correspond roughly to the division determined in the days of Moses and Joshua. (Josh. 13-21.)

The term "Joseph shall have two portions" (v. 13) reflects the custom that the birthright son should have a double portion of his father's inheritance. (See the commentary for 1 Chr. 5:1-2; see also Part I 11.)

When specific names are assigned to the lands, however, no land in ancient Canaan is identified by the name "Joseph." Rather, two lands are identified by the names of Joseph's two sons, Manasseh and Ephraim. (See Part I 53.)

**48:30-34**    The names assigned to the gates of the city are the names of the twelve sons of Jacob (Israel). Levi and Joseph are both rightfully listed here.

# DANIEL

See "Daniel" and "Daniel, Book of" in the Bible Dictionary, pages 652-53.

**1:1** The events listed here indicate that Daniel and his friends were taken captive into Babylon about twenty years before the destruction of Jerusalem by Nebuchadnezzar in the eleventh year of the reign of Zedekiah.

**1:3-4** "Children" could have been translated "youth" or "young men." Some of the young men who were taken captive were of royal bloodlines ("of the king's seed"). Whether or not Daniel was of royal blood is not known; his genealogy is not given.

**1:6-7** The meanings of the old and the new names of Daniel and his three friends are as follows:

Daniel ("God is my judge") became Belteshazzar ("O protect his life").

Hananiah ("Jehovah is gracious") became Shadrach (meaning uncertain).

Mishael ("Who is what God is?") became Meshach (meaning uncertain).

Azariah ("God is my help") became Abednego ("a servant of Nego").

**1:10** The last part of this verse could have been translated: "For why should he see your faces worse looking than the boys who are of your age? Then you would forfeit my head to the king."

**1:17** God blessed Daniel and his three friends, who observed sound eating habits with "knowledge and skill in all learning and wisdom: and Daniel had understanding in all visions and dreams."

The Lord has promised those who keep his health laws (the Word of Wisdom) in the latter days that they "shall find wisdom and great treasures of knowledge, even hidden treasures." (D&C 89:19.)

Spencer W. Kimball sees a direct correlation between Daniel's adherence to the laws of health and the additional spiritual powers he received later:

The gospel was Daniel's life. The Word of Wisdom was vital to him. In the king's court, he could be little criticized, but even for a ruler he would not drink the king's wine nor gorge himself with meat and rich foods. His moderation and his purity of faith brought him health and wisdom and knowledge and skill and understanding, and his faith linked him closely to his Father in heaven, and revelations came to him as often as required. His revealing of the dreams of the king and the interpretations thereof brought him honor and acclaim and gifts and high position such as many men would sell their souls to get. "But Daniel sat in the gate of the King" (Daniel 2:49) and reminded him of his transgression. (Mexico Area CR, 1972, p. 31.)

**2:4-5**    Ellis Rasmussen has provided the following commentary on these verses:

Note the language mentioned in verse 4; after this verse in the Hebrew Bible, it changes from the Hebrew language to the Aramaic ("Syriac") language. The text returns to Hebrew again in chapter 8. No one knows now the reason for this bilingual composition.

In verse 5 the phrase "is gone from me" should probably read "is *certain* with me," as the Persian word *azda* ("sure") is used. Note in verse 9 that the king makes the point that he knows what he dreamt; therefore if the interpreters can tell him the dream, he will know that *they* know what they are talking about and he will know whether he can have confidence in their interpretation or not! (IOT 2:92.)

**2:8**    The last clause could have been translated "the thing [word] is assured from me." This translation would also suggest that the king remembered his dream. (See the commentary for Dan. 2:4-5.)

**2:28**    Daniel attributed the power of seership to God, as did Joseph when he was asked to interpret the dream of Pharoah. (See Gen. 41:16.)

Spencer W. Kimball has commented concerning Daniel's modesty:

He [Daniel] then made known through proper channels that he would reveal the dream and the interpretation thereof, and the great king asked the direct question if he, Daniel, could really do so; to which he answered that the wise men, the astrologers, the magicians and the soothsayers would not be able to ever reveal the dream nor its interpretations: [Daniel 2:28, 29].

Daniel modestly disclaimed any wisdom but gave credit to the Lord, and then gave in detail the dream with the interpretation. (BYUSY, Nov. 11, 1959, p. 4.)

**2:31-44**    Spencer W. Kimball has offered the following commentary on these verses:

This is a revelation concerning the history of the world, when one world power would supersede another until there would be numerous smaller kingdoms to share the control of the earth.

And it was in the days of these kings that power would not be given to men, but the God of heaven would set up a kingdom — the kingdom of God upon the earth, which should never be destroyed nor left to other people. (CR, Apr. 1976, p. 10.)

**2:44** The kingdom of God established in the latter days will stand forever and will "break in pieces and consume all these kingdoms" in the sense that it shall replace all other forms of government at the beginning of the Millennium.

Concerning this kingdom, Brigham Young has stated:

The Lord God Almighty has set up a kingdom that will sway the sceptre of power and authority over all the kingdoms of the world, and will never be destroyed, it is the kingdom that Daniel saw and wrote of. It may be considered treason to say that the kingdom which that Prophet foretold is actually set up; *that* we cannot help, but we know it is so, and call upon the nations to believe our testimony. The kingdom will continue to increase, to grow, to spread and prosper more and more. Every time its enemies undertake to overthrow it, it will become more extensive and powerful; instead of its decreasing, it will continue to increase, it will spread the more, become more wonderful and conspicuous to the nations, until it fills the whole earth. (JD 1:202-3.)

Wilford Woodruff has added:

And I will say, in the name of Jesus Christ, the Son of the living God, that "Mormonism" will live and prosper, Zion will flourish, and the Kingdom of God will stand in power and glory and dominion as Daniel saw it, when this nation is broken to pieces as a potter's vessel and laid in the dust, and brought to judgment, or God never spoke by my mouth. (WW, pp. 508-9.)

**2:45** In this day the keys of the priesthood have been likened to the stone that "was cut out of the mountain without hands."

"The keys of the kingdom of God are committed unto man on the earth, and from thence shall the gospel roll forth unto the ends of the earth, as the stone which is cut out of the mountain without hands shall roll forth, until it has filled the whole earth." (D&C 65:2.)

**2:49** The term "Daniel sat in the gate of the king" means that he was aware of everything that was brought before the king; in other words, he became a counselor and confidant to the king.

**3:1**  The golden image would have been approximately ninety feet high and nine feet wide!

**3:17-19**  The courageous stand of the three young Israelites ("we will not serve thy gods, nor worship the golden image which thou hast set up") inspired the following commentaries by Spencer W. Kimball:

Neither the cunning of the deceivers, the conspiring, cunning tricksters, nor the fear of the king and what he could do to them, dissuaded the three courageous young men from their true path of rightness. When the pre-arranged sounds of the cornet, flute, harp and other instruments reverberated through the area and the masses of men and women everywhere filled their homes and the streets with kneeling worshippers of the huge golden image, three men refused to insult their true God. They prayed to God, and when confronted by the raging and furious emperor king, they courageously answered in the face of what could be certain death: [Daniel 3:17-18.]

Though they did not know the will of God, though they did not know for sure if the Lord would save them, it mattered not. Right was right and their faith sustained them. . . . They emerged safely from the furnace heated to seven times its usual temperature. (BYUSY, Feb. 1964, pp. 18-19.)

There were the three Hebrews who prayed to the living God in spite of the laws to the contrary. Their answer was not contingent upon the Lord performing a miracle. They were content to do right and let the consequence follow, be it rescue or death. . . .

*Integrity!* The promises of eternal life from God supersede all promises of men to greatness, comfort, immunities.

As these brave men were threatened, they did not know that Shakespeare, long centuries later, was to say:

"There is no terror in your threats: for I am armed so strong in honesty that they pass by me as the idle wind, which I respect not." (*Julius Caesar,* act 4, scene 3.)

Integrity in man should bring inner peace, sureness of purpose, and security in action. Lack of integrity brings disunity, fear, sorrow, unsureness. (Mexico Area CR, 1972, pp. 31-32.)

**3:25**  Even Nebuchadnezzar, the pagan worshiper of idols, had no difficulty believing that the "Son of God" could have the appearance of a man.

**3:29**  This statement by Nebuchadnezzar should not be construed to mean that he was instantly and permanently converted to Jehovah. As a worshiper of many gods, Nebuchadnezzar simply wanted to make certain his people did not offend this god who could deliver men unharmed from a "burning fiery furnace."

**5:2** The word "father" probably should have been "grandfather."

**5:5** An earlier leader (the brother of Jared) had also had the experience of seeing "part of the hand" of a divine messenger. (See Ether 3:6.)

**5:11** Daniel was sought as the possible interpreter of the writing upon the wall, for "the spirit of the holy gods" was with him. Spencer W. Kimball recalls others who have shared this gift:

This was a message from another world. Daniel interpreted the solemn warning. . . .

Radioed programs came in great numbers through the ages, faithfully interpreted by the Jeremiahs, the Ezekiels, and the Daniels; by the Nephis, the Moronis, the Benjamins; by the Peters, the Pauls, and the Joseph Smiths. (CR, Apr. 1962, p. 3.)

**5:17** True prophets do not accept salaries, gifts, or bribes in doing the work of the Lord. In refusing the proffered gifts of the king ("let thy gifts be to thyself"), Daniel was following a pattern set by Elisha in refusing the gifts of Naaman. (See 2 Kgs. 5:16.)

**5:23** Spencer W. Kimball has provided the following commentaries on the teachings of this verse:

O mortal men, deaf and blind! Can we not read the past? For thousands of years, have plowshares been beaten into swords and pruning hooks into spears, yet war persists. Ever since Belshazzar saw the finger writing upon the wall of his palace, the warning reappears. It seems to restate with great forcefulness, Daniel's indictment of an unhumble people:

". . . Blessed be the name of God. . . . he removeth kings, and setteth up kings." (Dan. 5:26-27, 22-23; 2:20-21.)

The answer to all of our problems—personal, national, and international—has been given to us many times by many prophets, ancient to modern. Why must we grovel in the earth when we could be climbing toward heaven! The path is not obscure. Perhaps it is too simple for us to see. We look to foreign programs, summit conferences, land bases. We depend on fortifications, our gods of stone; upon ships and planes and projectiles, our gods of iron—gods which have no ears, no eyes, no hearts. (CR, Apr. 1960, p. 85.)

Few men have ever knowingly and deliberately chosen to reject God and his blessings. Rather, we learn from the scriptures that because the exercise of faith has always appeared to be more difficult than relying on things more immediately at hand, carnal man has tended to transfer his trust in God to material things. Therefore, in all ages when men have fallen under the power of Satan and lost the faith, they have put in its place a hope in the "arm of flesh" and in "gods of silver, and gold, of brass, iron, wood, and stone, which see not, nor hear, nor know" (Dan. 5:23)—that is, in idols. This I find to be a dominant theme in the Old Testament. Whatever thing a man sets his heart and his trust in most is his god; and if his god doesn't also happen to be the true and living God of Israel, that man is laboring in idolatry. (E, June 1976, p. 4.)

**5:31**   Concerning the capture of Babylon, Spencer W. Kimball has observed:

The prophets pleaded for repentance. But why should Babylon worry? Was not Babylon the ruler of nations? . . .

Was not this city impregnable? Who could scale its walls? Who could crash its gates? But the monster of sin came. Though impenetrable the walls, and numerous the armed defenders, yet all must fall and crumble as sin makes impotent, weak, and fat the people who become slaves to it. (CR, Oct. 1945, pp. 123-24.)

George Albert Smith has commented concerning the downfall and death of Belshazzar:

The king and others felt perfectly secure, feeling that with food and provisions, and a river of water running through the city, not anything could come in to disturb them, and yet on that wall were written the words which, when interpreted, read, "You have been weighed in the balance and found wanting, and your kingdom will be divided among the Medes and the Persians." At that very hour "my servant Cyrus" had diverted the river that went through the city from its channel and his army entered under the wall, which wall was so high that it could not be scaled or destroyed with any means or weapons that they had, and so wide that several chariots could ride abreast on the top. (CR, Oct. 1948, p. 183.)

**6:3**   The "excellent spirit" that was evident in Daniel was undoubtedly the result of the influence of the Holy Ghost. Pharaoh had detected a similar excellent spirit in faithful Joseph, and when he was considering selecting Joseph as his major governor, the Pharaoh exclaimed: "Can we find such a one as this is, a man in whom the Spirit of God is?" (Gen. 41:38.)

**6:4-24**   The powers and wiles of the earth cannot have power over a person of integrity such as Daniel, according to Spencer W. Kimball:

These vicious men conspired to destroy Daniel. Their clever trick would end his dominion. Knowing the faith and the habits of Daniel, they could not fail. Preying upon the pride and vanity of the emperor, his conceit, his egotism, they persuaded him to sign an unbreakable law—a law which forbade anyone in the ensuing thirty days asking any petition of anyone but Belshazzar. The penalty was to be consigned to the den of lions. Belshazzar signed the decree, not knowing it was leveled at his friend. This unalterable law of the Medes and Persians would have been terrifying to any man, but the faithful Daniel did not flinch. Was there any question what he should do? He could save his life by abandoning his prayers to the Living God. What was he to do? A man of integrity could not fail. Daniel was the soul of integrity. (BYUSY, Feb. 1964, p. 17.)

**6:24**   The last clause, "or ever they came at the bottom of the den," could have been translated "before they came to the lower part of the den."

**6:26**   Darius, in accepting "the God of Daniel" as one of the gods acceptable to the Chaldeans (Babylonians), is following the example of Nebuchadnezzar, who accepted the "God of Shadrach, Meshach, and Abed-nego." (See Dan. 3:29.) In neither case are there indications of real conversion on the part of the kings.

**7:1-28**   This chapter is a "flashback" and is out of sequence chronologically. The four beasts and the countries represented by them have been identified by most scholars as follows: Lion—Babylon; Bear—Persia; Leopard—Greece; Diverse beast—Rome.

Concerning the use of beasts to represent kingdoms, Joseph Smith has stated:

When God made use of the figure of a beast in visions to the prophets He did it to represent those kingdoms which had degenerated and become corrupt, savage and beast-like in their dispositions, even the degenerate kingdoms of the wicked world; but He never made use of the figure of a beast nor any of the brute kind to represent His kingdom.

Daniel says (ch. 7, v. 16) when he saw the vision of the four beasts, "I came near unto one of them that stood by, and asked him the truth of all this," the angel interpreted the vision to Daniel; but we find, by the interpretation that the figures of beasts had no allusion to the kingdom of God. You there see that the beasts are spoken of to represent the kingdoms of the world, the inhabitants whereof were beastly and abominable characters; they were murderers, corrupt, carnivorous, and brutal in their dispositions. The lion, the bear, the leopard, and the ten-horned beast represented the kingdoms of the world, says Daniel. . . .

There is a grand difference and distinction between the visions and figures spoken of by the ancient prophets, and those spoken of in the revelations of John. The things which John saw had no allusion to the scenes of the days of Adam, Enoch, Abraham or Jesus, only so far as is plainly represented by John, and clearly set forth by him. John saw that only which was lying in futurity and which was shortly to come to pass. (HC 5:341-42.)

**7:9-14**  On May 19, 1838, the Lord revealed to Joseph Smith that the name of the place where this conference shall take place is "Adam-ondi-Ahman, because . . . it is the place where Adam shall come to visit his people, or the Ancient of Days shall sit, as spoken of by Daniel the prophet." (D&C 116:1.)

**7:13**  The coming of the "Son of man" in the "clouds of heaven" will be at the time of the Second Coming, according to LeGrand Richards:

Christ's coming in the "clouds of heaven" to which Daniel referred was to be at a much later date than "when a child is born" to which Isaiah referred. There was no kingdom prepared for Him when He was born of the virgin Mary. But when He shall come in the "clouds of heaven," the kingdom will already have been prepared for Him. Unless a kingdom is prepared how can it be given to Him? (IDYK, p. 98.)

For further information on this important event, see Part I 93, 114-15, 210.

**7:13,22**  The "Ancient of days" mentioned in these verses is father Adam, as is clarified in the following quotations by Joseph Smith:

Daniel in his seventh chapter speaks of the Ancient of Days; he means the oldest man, our Father Adam, Michael, he will call his children together and hold a council with them to prepare them for the coming of the Son of Man. He (Adam) is the father of the human family, and presides over the spirits of all men, and all that have had the keys must stand before him in this grand council. This may take place before some of us leave this stage of action. The Son of Man stands before him, and there is given him glory and dominion. Adam delivers up his stewardship to Christ, that which was delivered to him as holding the keys of the universe, but retains his standing as head of the human family.

. . . He (Adam) is the head, and was told to multiply. The keys were first given to him, and by him to others. He will have to give an account of his stewardship, and they to him. (HC 3:386-87.)

In the afternoon I went up the river about half a mile to Wight's Ferry . . . for the purpose of selecting and laying claim to a city plat near said ferry in Daviess County, which the brethren called "Spring Hill," but by the mouth of the Lord it was named Adam-ondi-Ahman, because, said He, it is the place where Adam shall come to visit his people, or the Ancient of Days shall sit, as spoken of by Daniel the Prophet. (HC 3:35.)

See the commentary for Daniel 10:13, 21.

**7:21-22**    Joseph Smith made the following observation concerning these verses:

The "Horn" made war with the Saints and overcame them, until the Ancient of Days came; judgment was given to the Saints of the Most High from the Ancient of Days; the time came that the Saints possessed the Kingdom. This not only makes us ministers here, but in eternity. (HC 3:389.)

Joseph Fielding Smith made it clear that the "saints" mentioned by Daniel are the members of the Church today:

Daniel and John each saw the opposition the little horn made against the Church of Jesus Christ of Latter-day Saints. This opposition will continue until the grand council is held at Adam-ondi-Ahman. This "little horn" (Dan. 7:20-22; Rev. 13) is making a renewed and determined effort today to destroy the Church. The Lord has decreed otherwise and while its power will last until Michael comes and the Son of Man receives his rightful place, this great power will endure. It must, however, fall, and according to the scriptures its end will come rather suddenly. (D&C 29:21; 1 Ne. 13:1-9; Rev., chapters 17-18.) (CHMR 4:44.)

**7:27**    See the commentaries for Daniel 2:44 and 7:21-22.

**8:1-27**    This chapter follows chapter 7 by two years, but both of them chronologically precede chapters 5 and 6.

Scholars believe the ram (vs. 3-4) represents the Medes and the Persians, while the "he goat" (v. 5) represents Greece.

Parley P. Pratt has provided an interpretation of this vision:

In this vision we have first presented the Medes and Persians, as they were to exist until they were conquered by Alexander the great. Now, it is a fact well known that this empire waxed exceedingly great for some time after the death of Daniel, pushing its conquests westward, northward, and southward, so that none could stand before it; until Alexander, the king of Grecia, came from the west, with a small army of chosen men, and attacked the Persians upon the banks of the river, and plunging his horse in, and his army following, they crossed, and attacked the Persians, who stood to oppose them on the bank, with many times their number; but, notwithstanding their number, and their advantage of the ground, they were totally routed, and the Grecians proceeded to over-run and subdue the country, beating the Persians in a number of pitched battles, until they were entirely subdued.

It is also well known that Alexander, the King of Greece, went forth from nation to nation, subduing the world before him, until, having conquered the world, he died at Babylon, at the age of thirty-two years. And thus, when he had waxed strong, the great horn was broken, and for it came up four notable ones towards the four winds of heaven. His kingdom was divided among four of his generals, who never attained unto his power.

Now, in the latter time of their kingdom, when the transgression of the Jewish nation was come to the full, the Roman power destroyed the Jewish nation, took Jerusalem, caused the daily sacrifice to cease, and not only that but afterwards destroyed the mighty and holy people, that is, the apostles and Primitive Christians, who were slain by the authorities of Rome. (VW, p. 26.)

**8:23**   This verse could have been translated: "And in the latter time of their kingdom, when the transgressors have come to the full, a king, strong of face, and skilled at intrigues, shall stand up."

**9:21-22**   Gabriel, who appeared unto Daniel and "informed . . . and talked with" him, is Noah, as explained in this statement by Joseph Smith:

He [Adam] is Michael the Archangel, spoken of in the Scriptures. Then to Noah, who is Gabriel; he stands next in authority to Adam in the Priesthood; he was called of God to this office, and was the father of all living in his day, and to him was given the dominion. These men held keys first on earth, and then in heaven. (HC 3:386.)

See the commentary for Daniel 10:13, 21.

**9:25-26**   Although the term *Messiah* is frequently used by Jewish people to refer to "the Anointed One," the word appears only twice in the entire English version of the Old Testament: Daniel 9:25-26. The Greek form of the same word, *Messias,* appears only twice in the entire English version of the New Testament: John 1:41 and 4:25. The "Anointed One" of Jewish hope and expectation (the Messiah) is the same person as the "Anointed One" of Christian faith and practice (Jesus the Christ, which literally means Jesus the Messiah).

**10:1-21**   Most scholars believe this is a prophecy of the conquest of Persia by Alexander the Great.

**10:2-15**   Spencer W. Kimball has provided the following comments on these verses:

Daniel was worried so much so that he mourned for three weeks and took no pleasant bread nor meat nor wine. Then came his vision which he alone saw: [Quoted Daniel 10:8-10, 15.]

. . . The pattern was established, the chart made, the blue-print drawn. Under special need, at special times, under proper circumstances, God reveals himself to men who are prepared for such manifestations. And since God is the same yesterday, today, and forever, the heavens cannot be closed except as men lock them against themselves with disbelief. (CR, Apr. 1964, p. 97.)

**10:7**   A person must be attuned to the Spirit of God in order to receive revelation, according to Spencer W. Kimball:

Every moment of every day, there are numerous programs on the air. We hear very few, relatively, for we are engrossed in our day's duties, but with powerful beaming broadcasting stations, we could hear any of the programs if we are tuned in.

For thousands of years there have been constant broadcasts from heaven of vital messages of guidance and timely warnings, and there has been a certain constancy in the broadcasts from the most powerful station. Throughout all those centuries there have been times when there were prophets who tuned in and rebroadcasted to the people. The messages have never ceased.

One such message came to Daniel in the presence of others, and he who was on the proper frequency said: "And I Daniel alone saw the vision: for the men that were with me saw not the vision." (Dan. 10:7.) (CR, Apr. 1970, p. 121.)

**10:13, 21**   According to Joseph Fielding Smith, the Michael referred to in these verses is Adam, and Noah is the Gabriel mentioned in Daniel 8:16:

The fact that Adam and Noah, long after they were dead, appeared to Daniel as Michael and Gabriel [Daniel 10:13, 21; 8:16] and to Zacharias and Mary [Luke 1:11-19, 26-31] is evidence that they had received the fulness of blessings that entitled them to stand in the presence of God. (AGQ 1:49.)

See the commentaries for Daniel 7:13, 22 and 9:21-22.

**11:1-45**   If chapter 10 is indeed concerned with the conquest of Persia by Alexander the Great, as believed by most scholars, then chapter 11 foretells the division of Alexander's empire into two parts—the north headed by Seleucus and the south headed by Ptolemy.

**11:8**   This verse could have been translated: "And he will also bring their gods with their casted images, with vessels of their possessions, silver and gold, into exile [to] Egypt. And he shall stand from the king of the north."

**11:14**   The clause "the robbers of thy people shall exalt themselves to establish the vision" could have been translated "the sons of the violent ones of your people shall lift up to establish [the] vision."

**11:31; 12:1**   The "abomination of desolation" mentioned here by Daniel is quoted by the Savior himself as a sign of great destruction in and about Jerusalem. (Matt. 24:15; Mark 13:14; JS-M 1:12, 32.)

**12:1**   The Michael mentioned in this verse has been identified as Adam by Joseph Smith. (See the commentary for Dan. 7:13, 22.)

**12:4**   Joseph Fielding Smith and Spencer W. Kimball have provided the following commentaries on this verse:

Among the signs of the last days was an increase of learning. Daniel was commanded to [Daniel 12:4.] Are not the people "running to and fro" today as they never did before in the history of the world? Go to the Bureau of Information and ask there how many tourists visit Temple Square each year. Make inquiry at the various national parks, at the bus, railroad, and steamship companies; learn how many are running to Europe, Asia, and all parts of the earth.

Are we not, most of us, running to and fro in our automobiles seeking pleasure? Is not knowledge increased? Was there ever a time in the history of the world when so much knowledge was poured out upon the people? But sad to say, the words of Paul are true—the people are "ever learning and never able to come to the knowledge of the truth." (2 Tim. 3:7.)

Have you ever tried to associate the outpouring of knowledge, the great discoveries and inventions during the past 136 years, with the restoration of the gospel? Do you not think there is some connection? It is not because we are more intelligent than our fathers that we have received this knowledge, but because God has willed it so in our generation! Yet men take the honor unto themselves and fail to recognize the hand of the Almighty in these things. (Joseph Fielding Smith, CR, Apr. 1966, pp. 13-14.)

Nineteenth century theologians thought they saw the fulfillment of these predictions in the coming of the steam engine, the sewing machine, the motor car. What they saw was but the dim beginnings of the most spectacular increase of knowledge since men first dwelt upon the earth. Could they emerge from their graves today and behold a giant rocket in flight, a manmade satellite in orbit, and moving pictures of the moon or Mars appearing on a TV set, a famous choir in South Dakota singing to much of the earth through the satellite off in space, they would recognize in all these and numerous other space-age marvels a fulfillment far beyond their expectations but nonetheless valid for all of that.

The works of God are endless. We stand in awe as we see some of the evidences of increased knowledge and we tingle and tingle and tingle. (Spencer W. Kimball, talk given at the dedication of the Language Training Mission, Provo, Utah, Sept. 1976, p. 5.)

**12:5-13**  These verses have been subject to various interpretations by scholars and students of the scriptures. In reviewing and analyzing these interpretations in the various printed commentaries, it would be well to remember the admonition of Peter:

"Knowing this first, that no prophecy of the scripture is of any private interpretation. [Or, as the Joseph Smith Translation phrases it, "no prophecy of the scriptures is given of any private will of man."]

"For the prophecy came not in old time by the will of man: but holy men of God spake as they were moved by the Holy Ghost." (2 Pet. 1:20-21.)

**12:10**   Parley P. Pratt has commented on the statement: "None of the wicked shall understand": "Who are more wicked than the wilfully blind leaders of the blind, who tell us we cannot understand the scriptures?" (VW, p. 48.)

# HOSEA

See "Hosea" in the Bible Dictionary, page 705.

**1:2**   Ellis Rasmussen has written the following commentary on this verse:

> The strange symbolic marriage and family of Hosea parallels the strange covenant relationship of wayward Israel with the LORD. It is the prophet's way of telling of his call from the Lord. Whether the "woman of unfaithfulness" was that way when he took her to wife, or whether she became that way later, no one knows. We do know that Israel was once faithful to God, but became unfaithful later. (IOT 2:31.)

**1:4-9**   The possible symbolic meanings of the names of Hosea's three children have been discussed by Ellis Rasmussen:

> The name of the first child, *Jezreel,* recalls the valley of former King Jehu's bloody purge, and anticipates Israel's overthrow in that strategic valley, next to the pass at Megiddo (N.T. "Armageddon"), famed for crucial battles past and future. "Jezreel" means "God shall sow"—i.e. scatter abroad. It doubtless alludes to the overthrow and scattering of Israel.

> The name of the second child, *Lo-ruhamah,* warned that no mercy from God would overthrow His justice and save northern Israel; the ten tribes would be utterly taken away, and only Judah would be spared.

> The name of the third child, *Lo-ammi,* "Not-my-people," is like a lament over the broken covenant relationship. But the prophecy immediately follows that someday Israel and Judah shall again be gathered together and it shall yet be said unto them "Ye are the sons of the living God." (IOT 2:31-32.)

**3:1**   The Hebrew words translated as "flagons of wine" could have been translated more literally as "raisin cakes of grapes." Such cakes were used during some of the fertility cult rites during that period.

**3:5**   Hosea redeems his unfaithful wife (with "fifteen pieces of silver" which was half the price of a slave [Ex. 21:32; Zech. 11:12]), requiring only that she would not "play the harlot" again but would be faithful to him from that time forth. In somewhat the same way, "in the latter days" the wayward children of Israel will return to their true God and recognize David (or a descendant of David—the Messiah) as their king.

**4:2**   This verse could have been translated: "Lying and

swearing, and killing and stealing, and doing adultery increase; and blood touches against blood.''

**4:12-14**   The evidences of Israel's apostasy are idolatry (vs. 12-13) and adultery (vs. 13-14).

**5:3, 5**   The terms *Ephraim* and *Israel* are used rather consistently in these chapters to refer to the northern kingdom of Israel, whereas *Judah* refers to the southern kingdom of Judah.

**6:6**   Sacrifice and "burnt offerings" are simply outward symbols of more important things. The Lord prefers mercy and a knowledge of him over the performance of the rituals.

**6:7**   The Hebrew word *Adam* can also mean *man*. In the context of this verse, the proper name of the first man, Adam, probably should have been translated "man" rather than "men."

**8:12**   Parley P. Pratt has provided the following commentary on this verse:

> We are to prove that God revealed himself to the seed of Joseph or Ephraim—their location we have already proved—dwelling in America. For this we quote Hosea 8:12; speaking of Ephraim, he says by the spirit of prophecy, "I have written to him the great things of my law, but they were counted as a strange thing." This is proof positive, and needs no comment, that the great truths of heaven were revealed unto Ephraim, and were counted as a strange thing. (VW, p. 93.)

**9:1**   This verse could have been translated: "O Israel, do not rejoice for joy, like the peoples. For you have gone lusting away from your God. You have loved a harlot's hire on every threshing floor."

**11:1**   According to Matthew 2:14-15, this verse contains one of the many prophecies of the coming of the Messiah found in the Old Testament. The last clause is translated in the New Testament: "Out of Egypt have I called my son."

**11:10**   Parley P. Pratt believed this verse refers to the descendants of Ephraim in modern-day America:

> Again, one of the prophets says, in speaking of Ephraim, "When the Lord shall roar, the children of Ephraim shall tremble from the west." Now let us sum up these sayings, [Gen. 49:22-24, 26; Hosea 11:10.] and what have we gained? First, that Ephraim was to grow into a multitude of nations in the midst of the earth; second, Joseph was to be greatly blessed in a large inheritance, as far off as America; third, this was to be on the west of Egypt or Jerusalem.
>
> Now, let the world search from pole to pole, and they will not find a multitude of nations in the midst of the earth who can possibly have sprung

from Ephraim unless they find them in America; for the midst of all other parts of the earth is inhabited by mixed races, who have sprung from various sources; while here an almost boundless country was selected from the rest of the world, and inhabited by a race of men, evidently of the same origin, although as evidently divided into many nations.

Now, the scriptures cannot be broken; therefore, these scriptures must apply to America, for the plainest of reasons, they can apply to no other place. (VW, p. 93.)

**13:3**    Brigham Young has drawn the following lessons from this verse:

If mankind could know the object God has in their creation, and what they might obtain by doing right and by applying to the source and fountain of wisdom of information, how quickly they would turn away from every ungodly action and custom. But as the Prophet says, [Quoted Hosea 4:17]. Instead of seeking unto the Lord for wisdom, they seek unto vain philosophy and the deceit and traditions of men, which are after the rudiments of the world and not after Christ. They are led by their own imaginations and by the dictates of their selfish will, which will lead them in the end to miss the object of their pursuit. Were you to inquire of the leading men of the world—of kings, rulers, philosophers and wise men—the end or result of their pursuits, they cannot tell you. This I believe; and I think it is quite evident, according to what I have witnessed. (JD 10:209.)

**13:4**    Jehovah of the Old Testament, who delivered Israel from the land of Egypt, is also Jesus Christ of the New Testament. As stated here, "there is no saviour beside me."

**13:14**    The statement "repentance shall be hid from mine eyes" refers to a time after the resurrection when evidently there is no suspended judgment.

**13:14**    Two types of death were introduced by the fall of Adam and Eve: (1) physical death, which was the result of the law broken in the Garden of Eden and which is symbolized by the grave, and (2) spiritual death, which is spiritual alienation from God, coming upon Adam and Eve during the process of their breaking the law and which is symbolized by death (separation from God). Through his atonement, Jesus Christ ransoms all mankind from the grave by providing for the resurrection of all; he also redeems all those from spiritual death who will repent of their sins and return to him. "O death, I will be thy plagues; O grave, I will be thy destruction."

See the commentary for Genesis 2:17.

**14:1**    When a person sins, he goes away from God. Thus, when a person *returns* to God, he *repents* to God. A Hebrew word frequently translated "repent" has the basic meaning of returning.

See the commentary for Numbers 23:19.

**14:9** The word "fall" could have been translated "stumble." The basic meaning of this verse is "The wise shall understand the things of God, and the prudent shall know them; the ways of God are right, and the saints [holy ones] shall walk in his ways, but the transgressors shall stumble in them."

# JOEL

See "Joel" in the Bible Dictionary, page 714

**1:4** The four "insects" mentioned here are really four stages in the developmental life cycle of one insect, the locust. This verse could have been translated:

"That which the cutting locust has left, the swarming locust has eaten. And that which the swarming locust has left, the young locust has eaten. And that which the young locust has left, the stripping locust has eaten."

Ellis Rasmussen has prepared the following commentary on this verse:

What will happen according to verse 4 which according to verses 2 and 3 never had happened to the land (or Israel) before? If an 8th Century Jewish Karaite commentator is right—one Jepheth ben Ali—the four insect plagues symbolize four historic invasions. Supposedly they would be the Assyrian, the Babylonian, the Macedonian-Syrian, and the Roman. Do the invasions also seem to be alluded to in the four invitations to lament starting with verses 4, 8, 12, and 15? (IOT 2:35.)

**2:1-3** This great army described by Joel is evidently the army of Gog mentioned in Ezekiel 38 and Revelation 20.

See the commentaries for Joel 2:1-11 and Ezekiel 38:1-23; see also Part I 90, 113, 206-13.

**2:1-11** Two great armies that will eventually meet and fight each other in "the day of the Lord" can be identified in these verses: (1) the "great people and *a strong*" who leave "behind them a desolate wilderness" (vs. 2-10), and (2) the army of the Lord "and who can abide it?" (v. 11).

Concerning these armies, Joseph Fielding Smith has written:

Here we have a great, terrible army, marching with unbroken ranks and crushing everything before it, finding the garden like Eden before them, leaving the wilderness behind, causing mourning, causing suffering; and so the prophet raises the warning voice, and that voice is to us, . . . that we might turn unto the Lord and rend our hearts. . . . And then . . . the Lord says that He will take that great army in hand, that He also has an army. His army is terrible, just as terrible as the other army, and He will take things in hand. When I say the other army, the Lord's army, do not get an idea He is thinking about England or the United States. He is not. He is not thinking about any earthly army. The Lord's army is not an earthly army, but He has a terrible army; and when that army marches, it will put an end to other armies, no matter how terrible they may be; and so He says in these closing words I have read to you that He would do this thing. He would drive this terrible northern army into the wilderness, barren and desolate, with his face towards the east sea and his hinder part towards the utmost sea. He would do that, and then He would bless His people—having references, of course, to Israel. (ST, pp. 160-61.)

See the commentaries for Ezekiel 38:1-23 and chapters 38-39; see also Part I 90, 113, 206-13.

**2:13** The descriptive clause "rend your heart, and not your garments" refers to the custom practiced at least since the days of Jacob of tearing clothes during times of sorrow, grief, or despair. (Gen. 37:34.) The Lord is here counseling men to come before him with a broken heart and a contrite spirit rather than with torn clothing.

They used to rend their garments and sit in sack cloth when they were repentant. So the Lord says, "Rend your heart and not your garments." Humble yourselves. Prepare yourselves, oh Israel, that you may receive My blessings, that you might be protected from this condition that is going to come. (Joseph Fielding Smith, ST, p. 160.)

**2:28** A similar promise was made by the Lord through Isaiah (44:3), Ezekiel (39:29), and Zechariah (12:10).

Joseph Fielding Smith has provided the following commentary on this verse:

Moroni has proclaimed that any honest seeker after truth who diligently asks of the Lord, will receive a manifestation of the truth through the Holy Ghost. But once the Holy Ghost has given that manifestation, then the person has no further claim for further manifestations, until he has complied with the law. Now, IF the world cannot receive this gift, then we must conclude that the enlightenment that comes to men in the world—and such enlightenment has come on many occasions—it must be from some other source. When, therefore, the Lord said through Joel, that he would pour out his spirit on all flesh it was not the Holy Ghost that was to be given to ALL, only to a few, for, remember, the world cannot receive this Spirit.

On the other hand, the Spirit of Christ (sometimes called the Light of Christ, and Spirit of truth, or Spirit of Jesus Christ) is a spirit that is given to EVERY MAN, no matter who he is or what is his belief. (AGQ 5:134-35.)

The statement "I will pour out my spirit upon all flesh" does not refer to the bestowal of the Holy Ghost, according to Joseph Fielding Smith:

This does not have reference to the bestowal of the Holy Ghost, but to the Spirit of Christ, or Light of Truth, which we are informed is given to "every man that cometh into the world." The predictions are made that through the inspiration of this Spirit, wonderful things are to be accomplished in the latter days. (ST, p. 180.)

**2:28-32**    Joseph Smith mentioned that these verses were quoted to him by the angel Moroni on September 21, 1823, with the commentary "that this was not yet fulfilled, but was soon to be. And he further stated that the fulness of the Gentiles was soon to come in." (JS-H 1:41.)

**2:32**    Three different aspects of the gathering might be identified in these words. There shall be deliverance (1) in mount Zion, (2) in Jerusalem, and (3) in "the remnant whom the Lord shall call."

Joseph Fielding Smith has differentiated between "Zion" and "Jerusalem":

There are to be two capital cities which will be established when the millennial reign shall come. Zion, the New Jerusalem in America and Jerusalem in Palestine which shall be rebuilt and become a city of magnitude and magnificence. (CHMR 2:172.)

See the commentary for Isaiah 2:2-4; see also Part I 95, 132-33.

**3:1**    The wording makes it absolutely clear the Lord is talking about the last days just preceding the second coming of the Messiah—"in those days, and in that time" when he will bring Judah and Jerusalem forth from their captivity. The last clause could have been translated "when I will bring again the exiles of Judah and Jerusalem."

**3:10**    During this time of preparation for war, plowshares will be beaten into swords. During the time of peace which will follow after the beginning of the millennial reign of the Messiah, the opposite will be done—swords will then be beaten into plowshares, as the Lord revealed through his prophets Isaiah (2:4) and Micah (4:3).

See Part I 100, 155-65.

**3:12-14**    The "valley of decision" in verse 14 is evidently the same place as the valley identified specifically as Jehoshaphat ("valley of Jehovah's judgment") in verse 12.

**3:15-16**    The darkening of the sun, moon, and stars will likely be a natural result of the great amounts of dust which will be sent into the atmosphere during the great earthquake when "the heavens and the earth shall shake."

**3:17**    The holy status of Jerusalem after the great battle has been clarified in the 1845 Proclamation of the Twelve Apostles. (See Part I 212-13.)

**3:18**    The fountain that shall come forth "of the house of the Lord" is evidently the same one discussed in detail in Ezekiel 47:1-12. See the commentary for Ezekiel 47:1-5; see also Part I 87.

# AMOS

See "Amos" in the Bible Dictionary, pages 607-8.

**1:1**  Amos was of the southern part of the kingdom of Judah.

The Hebrew word *chazah,* translated here as "saw," refers to "prophetic vision."

**1:3, 6, 9, 11, 13 and 2:1**  The statement repeated in all these verses ("for three transgressions . . . and for four") means that these nations are overflowing with sin or, as the Lord has said in this dispensation, "the cup of their iniquity is full." (D&C 101:11.)

**2:12**  One of the vows of the Nazarite was "He shall separate himself from wine and strong drink, and shall drink no vinegar of wine, or vinegar of strong drink, neither shall he drink any liquor." (Num. 6:3.)

**3:6**  The clause "Shall there be evil in a city, and the Lord hath not done it" could have been translated "Is there calamity in a city, has Jehovah not even done [it]?" The basic meaning is that God is aware of all evil and calamities. The Joseph Smith Translation replaces "done" with "known."

Brigham Young has discussed this principle.

Is there anything that passes with the children of men that the Lord does not control to his glory? That is what the Lord wants every man and woman to understand. If there is good, the Lord is there to dictate it. If there is power, has he not power over all the power there is upon the face of the earth? If there is evil, if there is sorrow, if there is trouble, if there are trials for his people, is he not there to dictate those sorrows and troubles? All that passes upon the earth is under his eye; he dictates in the affairs of nations. If a mighty king and kingdom are raised up upon any portion of the earth, the Lord has done it. And when a mighty nation crumbles in its power, the Lord has touched their pride and strength. He raises and casts down; he dictates in the light and in the darkness, at his pleasure; he makes the thick darkness his chariot and rides upon the clouds; and he is also the brightness of the sun. We have the privilege of learning that God dictates, controls, and manages all to his own glory. (JD 6:145-46.)

Is there an evil thing upon the earth that he does not fully understand? There is not. [See Ps. 139.] The Lord understands the evil and the good; why should we not likewise understand them? We should. Why? To know how to choose the good and refuse the evil; which we cannot do, unless we understand the evil as well as the good. I do not wish to convey the idea that it is necessary to commit evil in order to obtain this knowledge. (JD 9:242-43.)

**3:7** This is one of the most widely quoted verses from the writings of Amos.

Joseph Smith taught that this principle has been operating on the earth since the beginning:

According to the testimony of the Scriptures in all ages of the world, whenever God was about to bring a judgment upon the world or accomplish any great work, the first thing he did was to raise up a Prophet, and reveal unto him the secret, and send him to warn the people, so that they may be left without excuse. This was the case in the days of Noah and Lot. God was about to bring judgments upon the people, and he raised up those Prophets who warned the people of it: yet they gave no heed to them, but rejected their testimony; and the judgments came upon the people, so that they were destroyed, while the Prophets were saved by pursuing the course marked out by the Lord. (HC 6:23.)

George Albert Smith stated that this principle operated to help bring forth the United States and also the Church:

I believe that all down through the ages, as recorded in holy writ, the Lord has vindicated that statement. [Amos 3:7.] The preparation for the ushering in of the Gospel of Jesus Christ in this latter dispensation was indicated in the reign of Nebuchadnezzar, and repeated again in the days of the Apostles, and then the foundation was laid for the organization of the government of the United States by men and women who believed in the divine mission of Jesus Christ. The stage was not set hastily; it was preparing through hundreds of years. We who live in this marvelous age may look back and see that throughout the centuries our Heavenly Father has fulfilled his promises to his children, and the people or nation that has observed the laws of God and honored his commandments has been blessed; while those who have been recreant to their opportunity have suffered calamity and in many cases entire destruction. Our Heavenly Father prepared the way for the coming of the Gospel of Jesus Christ, which was to precede the second coming of our Lord. (CR, Apr. 1930, p. 65.)

Another prophet in our day, Spencer W. Kimball, has taught that this principle is always in force; furthermore, each individual is entitled to receive guidance from the Lord based on personal righteousness:

This postulation to the prophet Amos [3:7] has come down from antiquity. . . .

. . . Many people of our own day expect that revelations will come only in spectacular vision on Sinais accompanied with lightnings and thunderings. . . .

. . . For many it is hard to accept as revelation those numerous ones in Moses' time, in Joseph's time, and in our own year—those revelations which come to prophets as deep, unassailable impressions settling down on the prophet's mind and heart as dew from heaven or as the dawn dissipates the darkness of night.

The burning bushes, the smoking mountains, the sheets of four-footed beasts, the Cumorahs, and the Kirtlands were realities; but they were the exceptions. The great volume of revelation came to Moses and to Joseph and comes to today's prophet in the less spectacular way—that of deep impressions, without spectacle or glamour or dramatic events.

Always expecting the spectacular, many will miss entirely the constant flow of revealed communication.

When in a Thursday temple meeting, after sacred prayer and fasting, important decisions are made: new missions and new stakes created, new patterns and policies initiated, a new temple approved, new officials called to fill vital vacancies in leadership; the information is often taken for granted and possibly thought of as mere human calculations. But to those who sit in the intimate circles and hear the solemn prayers of the prophet and the testimony of this man of God; to those who see the astuteness of his deliberations and the sagacity of his decisions and pronouncements, to them he is verily a prophet. To hear him conclude important new developments with such solemn expressions as "The Lord is pleased," "Our Heavenly Father has spoken" is to know it positively.

From the prophet of the restoration, Joseph Smith, to the prophet of our own year, President Harold B. Lee, the communication line is unbroken, the authority is continuous; the light, brilliant and penetrating, continues to illuminate. The voice of the Lord is a continuous, pleasant sound, a sweet peaceful melody, and a thundering appeal. For nearly a century and a half now there has been no interruption nor stoppage.

When such changes come through the prophet, there is certainty and calm, tranquil assurance; and the peace of heaven settles over the hearts of true believers with a sureness. Great and good men rise to new stature under the mantle of prime authority, and when keys of heaven are closed in their palms, the voice of authority comes from their lips.

Man never stands alone unless his own desires are selfishness, independence, and egotism. Every righteous person may have inspiration in his own limited kingdom. The Lord definitely calls prophets today and reveals his secrets unto them; he did yesterday; he does today, and will do tomorrow—that is the way it is. "Surely the Lord God will do nothing, but he revealeth his secret unto his servants the prophets." (Germany Area CR, 1973, pp. 74-77.)

**3:15** The wicked king Ahab had made an ivory house (1 Kgs. 22:39) which apparently had become a symbol of decadence and wickedness by the days of Amos.

**4:4** Pagan altars had been erected in Bethel and Gilgal where the apostates worshiped their idols.

**4:6** Even though a famine had come upon the land, the people had not repented of their sins.

God sometimes uses famine as a way of encouraging people to return to him, according to Brigham Young:

That individual, neighbourhood, people, or nation that will not acknowledge the hand of God in all things, but will squander their blessings, and thus pour contempt upon his kind favours, will become desolate and be wasted away. So long as any people live up to the best light they have, the Almighty will multiply blessings upon them by blessing the earth and causing it to bring forth in its strength to fill their storehouses with plenty; but if they become fat, and are lofty, and kick against the Lord, and trample his blessings under their feet in reckless wastefulness, he will cause them to inherit barrenness, and he will give them "cleanness of teeth in all their cities, and want of bread in all their places." The Lord needs only to say to his angel, "Pass over the land and take away the elements of wheat," and that crop ceases to be produced. (JD 9:169.)

The Bible Dictionary (p. 647) indicates that the phrase "cleanness of teeth" is "a unique phrase used by Amos to describe conditions of famine."

**5:21** The statement "I will not smell in your solemn assemblies" could have been translated "I will not delight in your solemn assemblies."

**6:1** The "mountain of Samaria" referred to here (see also Amos 3:9; 4:1) is mount Gerizim, where the apostates of the northern tribes had worshiped idols.

Nephi, a Book of Mormon prophet, stated that it is the devil who says, "All is well in Zion; yea, Zion prospereth, all is well—and thus the devil cheateth their souls, and leadeth them away carefully down to hell." (2 Ne. 28:21.)

**8:9-10** Ellis Rasmussen has provided the following commentary on these verses:

It is possible that the eclipse which astronomers now calculate as having occurred on June 15, 763 B.C. was the phenomenon here used as a symbol by Amos of the spiritual darkness and doom coming upon Israel. (IOT 2:31.)

**8:11-12** The "famine in the land" which consists of not "hearing the words of the Lord" occurs whenever a prophet is not upon the earth and also when there is a prophet but the people will not "hear."

Harold B. Lee has stated:

In our day, when grave problems are before the nation and the world, men everywhere are seeking panaceas for the ills that afflict mankind and the answers to world problems that remain unanswered.

The ancient prophets seemed to have foreseen our day of complete frustration, when men would be looking for answers in the wrong places and the solutions to their problems in the wrong way. The prophets foresaw the day when there would be [quoted Amos 8:11-12]. (CR, Oct. 1972, p. 59.)

So far as there being prophets on the earth again, the spiritual famine is ended according to Spencer W. Kimball:

After centuries of spiritual darkness, described by Amos and Jeremiah, we solemnly announce to all the world that the spiritual famine is ended, the spiritual drought is spent, the word of the Lord in its purity and totalness is available to all men. One needs not wander from sea to sea nor from the north to the east, seeking the true gospel as Amos predicted, for the everlasting truth is available. (CR, Apr. 1964, pp. 93-94.)

**9:9**   The word translated here as "sift" has in the Hebrew the basic meaning of "cause to move." Thus, "shake" could be substituted for "sift." The fact that "not the least grain" shall fall upon the earth indicates that they will not be destroyed or allowed to perish, which was also emphasized in verse 8.

**9:10**   The last clause could have been translated "The evil shall not come near or go before us."

**9:13**   The weather in certain areas of Israel is so ideal for agriculture that certain crops can be grown the year around. As soon as a field is harvested, it is plowed and prepared for planting. Thus, "the plowman shall overtake the reaper."

**9:14-15**   The basic meaning of "I will bring again the captivity of my people of Israel" is that the Lord will bring forth his chosen people again *from* captivity. This meaning is made clear in the remainder of the verse and in verse 15.

LeGrand Richards has observed concerning these verses:

The prophets often spoke of the House of Judah and the House of Israel in the same sense as the Prophet Amos in this quotation: "my people of Israel." This prophecy, can only have reference to the latter-day gathering when "they shall no more be pulled up out of their land." (IDYK, p. 204.)

# OBADIAH

See "Obadiah" in the Bible Dictionary, page 739.

**1:1-4** These verses are almost identical to Jeremiah 49:9-10, 14-16. It is not clear who was the originator of these writings; it might even have been an earlier writer whose works were available to both Obadiah and Jeremiah.

**1:1** The Edomites are descendants of Esau, the older twin brother of Jacob. The enmity that began during the days of their forefathers (Gen. 27:41) apparently continued in their descendants.

**1:3** The Edomites were located primarily in the south and east of Judah, in the mountains that were called the mountains of Edom. (See Bible map 1, 3, 5, 6, 7, 8, 9, or 10.) Petra (Sela) was one of the major strongholds of the Edomites. (See Bible map 7 or 10.)

**1:15** The eternal law of consequences will eventually come upon the Edomites. As they have looted Israel (v. 13) the Israelites will eventually possess the lands of the Edomites.

**1:21** Prophets of this dispensation have provided commentaries on this verse:

But how are they to become saviors on Mount Zion? By building their temples, erecting their baptismal fonts, and going forth and receiving all the ordinances, baptisms, confirmations, washings, anointings, ordinations and sealing powers upon their heads, in behalf of all their progenitors who are dead, and redeem them that they may come forth in the first resurrection and be exalted to thrones of glory with them; and herein is the chain that binds the hearts of the fathers to the children, and the children to the fathers, which fulfills the mission of Elijah. (Joseph Smith, HC 6:184.)

It is recorded in the Bible that in the last days the God of heaven will set up a kingdom. Will that kingdom destroy the human family? No: it will save every person that will and can be saved. The doctrines of the Savior reveal and place the believers in possession of principles whereby saviours will come upon Mount Zion to save the house of Esau, which is the Gentile nations, from sin and death,—all except those who have sinned against the Holy Ghost. Men and women will enter into the temples of God, and be, in comparison, pillars there, and officiate year after year for those who have slept thousands of years. (Brigham Young, JD 6:344.)

God is looking upon us, and has called us to be saviors upon Mount Zion. And what does a savior mean? It means a person who saves somebody. Jesus went and preached to the spirits in prison; and he was a savior to that people. When he came to atone for the sins of the world, he was a savior, was he not? Yes. And we are told in the revelations that saviors should stand upon Mount Zion; and the kingdom shall be the Lord's. Would we be saviors if we did not save somebody? I think not. Could we save anyone if we did not build Temples? No, we could not; for God would not accept our offerings and sacrifices. Then we came here to be saviors on Mount Zion, and the kingdom is to be the Lord's. Then what shall we do? We will build Temples. And what then? Administer in them, when we get them done. (John Taylor, JD 22:308.)

# JONAH

See "Jonah" in the Bible Dictionary, page 716.

**1-4** Jonah has the distinction of being mentioned in another book of the Old Testament as well as in two books of the New Testament.

2 Kings 14:25 mentions some of the teachings of "Jonah, the son of Amittai, the prophet, which was of Gath-hepher." Evidently these teachings of Jonah have been lost, for the subject matter mentioned in 2 Kings is not discussed in the present book of Jonah.

In New Testament times the Savior referred to some of the experiences of Jonah (Jonas) in the belly of the whale and also at Nineveh; these statements are recorded in Matthew 12:39-41; 16:4 and Luke 11:29-32.

True believers in the Bible should not have any difficulty believing the story of Jonah. Joseph Fielding Smith has written:

Are we to reject it as being an impossibility and say that the Lord could not prepare a fish, or whale, to swallow Jonah? If Mr. Robert Ripley and some of the others are to be believed, a similar occurrence has taken place—perhaps more than once—within the memory of man now living. Surely the Lord sits in the heavens and laughs at the wisdom of the scoffer, and then on a sudden answers his folly by a repetition of the miracle in dispute, or by the presentation of one still greater.

Is it more of a miracle for the Lord to prepare a fish to carry Jonah to shore that he might fill the mission assigned to him, than it is for the President of the United States to speak in an ordinary tone and be heard, under certain conditions, by all people in all parts of the earth? Honestly, which is the greater miracle?

I believe, as did Mr. William J. Bryan, the story of Jonah. My chief reason for so believing is not in the fact that it is recorded in the *Bible,* or that the incident has been duplicated in our day, but in the fact that *Jesus Christ, our Lord, believed it.* [Matthew 12:39-40.] (DS 2:314.)

**1:2** Spencer W. Kimball has likened this scripture to conditions in the world today:

We have come far in material progress in these centuries. But the sins of the ancients still afflict the hearts of men.

Can we not learn by the experiences of others? Must we also defile our bodies, corrupt our souls, and reap destruction as have peoples and nations before us?

Both sacred scripture and profane history give us the tragic stories of young nations rising in power, then in the luxurious and degenerate years of their glory being replaced by vigorous peoples yet unspoiled by the decay of self-indulgence, political intrigue, and immoral shamelessness.

Long centuries ago the Lord commanded the Prophet Jonah: "Arise, go to Nineveh, that great city, and cry against it; for their wickedness is come up before me." (Jonah 1:2.)

That "great city" was the envy of the ancient world in its magnificence and power. Historians describe it as surrounded by walls one hundred feet high and broad enough that three chariots could drive abreast. Fifteen hundred towers held watchmen to note the approach of enemies.

Jonah arrived, and so powerfully preached repentance that the people reformed their lives, and the promised destruction was averted. But Nineveh turned again to sin. (CR, Oct. 1945, p. 122.)

**1:2** Nineveh was then the capital of Assyria. It was built on the upper Tigris River and was mentioned as early as Genesis 10:11.

**1:3** The exact location of the Tarshish to which Jonah was fleeing is not known, although some scholars believe it was Tartessus in the southwestern part of what is now Spain. It is clear from Jonah's account that Tarshish could be reached most easily by sea and it was not in the direction of Nineveh.

When placed in context, it is easy to understand Jonah's reluctance to go to Nineveh, as it was the capital city of the enemy of Israel.

**1:9** Jonah's reference to himself as a Hebrew indicates that he is a descendant of Abraham.

**1:12** The meaning of the phrase "for my sake" is "because of me."

**1:17** The account in the Old Testament refers to the large sea creature that swallowed Jonah as "a great fish." In the New Testament account, Jesus referred to it as a "whale." (Matt. 12:40.) The Savior also substantiated the claim that Jonah spent "three days and three nights" in the belly of the whale and used this as an analogy of His death and resurrection: "So shall the Son of man be three days and three nights in the heart of the earth."

**2:1-9** These words of Jonah were obviously recorded by him after the episode with "the great fish" was over and after he had returned to Jerusalem and visited the temple (vs. 7-8.) Evidently while Jonah was in the belly of the fish he had promised the Lord certain things if he were safely delivered.

Here he reaffirms that promise: "I will pay that that I have vowed" (v. 9).

**3:3**    The statement "Nineveh was an exceeding great city of three days' journey" means that it took three days to walk *through* the city.

It may be that the land area around the city carried the same name as the city. This custom was followed during a certain period of the Israelites' history (see Nibley, *Lehi in the Desert*, p. 5) and also in Book of Mormon times (see Hel. 5:15; 6:10).

**3:7-8**    Animals not given anything to eat or drink would normally "cry mightily" as indicated here. Herodotus indicates the Persians would clip the hair of some of their animals so that they could participate in mourning. Also, they would even clothe the animals with sackcloth while the animals were fasting, as indicated here in verse 8. (OVBC, p. 577.)

**4:2**    The meaning of the clause that has been translated "repentest thee of the evil" is that God is sorry or feels remorseful when people do evil.

Note the enlightening Bible footnote on this verse. Jonah was "angry" and feeling sorry for himself because he thought now it might be more difficult for the people to accept him as a prophet.

**4:8**    The word "vehement" could have been translated "scorching."

**4:11**    Many of the people in Nineveh had been transgressing the law in ignorance; 120,000 of them were so innocent they didn't even know the difference "between their right hand and their left hand."

# MICAH

See "Micah" in the Bible Dictionary, pages 731-32.

**1:5** The capital of the northern kingdom (kingdom of Israel) was Samaria, while the capital of the southern kingdom (kingdom of Judah) was Jerusalem. These two cities, Samaria and Jerusalem, became symbols for the wickedness of the people, in much the same way as Babylon represented the evils of Babylonia and Nineveh the sins and abominations of Assyria.

**1:7-9** The people of the kingdom of Israel (Samaria) turned to the worship of idols, which unfaithfulness is comparable to "the hire of an harlot." Also her sins are now being imitated by the people of Judah (Jerusalem) so that "her wound is incurable" for the infection has spread.

**2:1-2** People who "work evil upon their beds" spend all night thinking of the evils they can do "when the morning is light" and how they can take advantage of others by coveting fields and oppressing men.

Spencer W. Kimball has provided commentary on these verses:

And to me that means, woe unto them who will rationalize, who will explain away their errors in these matters, who justify their oppressions. Farm hands, domestic help, and unprotected people are often oppressed, when economic circumstances place them in the position where they must accept what is offered or remain unemployed. And we sometimes justify ourselves in underpaying and even boast about it: [Quoted Micah 2:1-2.]

And then there are those of us who require excessive compensation for services and who fail to give "value received" and who give no loyalty with their insufficient and inefficient service.

Scripture writers admonish the employed to obey masters, to please their employers, to work with singleness of heart, to be honest in time spent and service rendered and to avoid purloining.

The Lord knows that we need food, clothes, shelter, and other things. He expects us to earn our living. He commands us to give the necessities to our families. He permits, perhaps, that we may have reasonable luxuries, but not with unclean money. (CR, Oct. 1953, pp. 53-54.)

**2:7** It is difficult to make a literal translation from the Hebrew. A possible translation is: "House of Israel, It is said,

The Spirit of Jacob is limited, if these are His doings. Do not my words do good with the one walking upright?"

**2:11** People are willing to listen to the false prophets who encourage them to continue in their iniquity, but they are not willing to listen and follow the true prophets who warn them to repent of their evil doings.

**3:5-7** Because false prophets cause people to err, true prophets will be taken out of their midst: "the sun shall go down over the prophets, and the day shall be dark over them . . . for there is no answer of God."

Concerning this concept, President Spencer W. Kimball has written:

In the meridian of time, the Son of God, the Light of the World, came and opened the curtains of heaven, and earth and heaven were again in communion.

But when the light of that century went out, the darkness was again impenetrable; the heavens were sealed and the "dark ages" moved in.

I bear witness to the world today that more than a century and a half ago the iron ceiling was shattered; the heavens were once again opened, and since that time revelations have been continuous.

That new day dawned when another soul with passionate yearning prayed for divine guidance. A spot of hidden solitude was found, knees were bent, a heart was humbled, pleadings were voiced, and a light brighter than the noonday sun illuminated the world—the curtain never to be closed again.

A young lad spoken of by some of our brethren today, Joseph Smith, of incomparable faith, broke the spell, shattered the "heavens of iron" and reestablished communication. Heaven kissed the earth, light dissipated the darkness, and God again spoke to man, revealing anew "his secret unto his servants the prophets." (Amos 3:7.) A new prophet was in the land and through him God set up his kingdom, never to be destroyed nor left to another people—a kingdom that will stand forever.

The foreverness of this kingdom and the revelations which it brought into existence are absolute realities. Never again will the sun go down; never again will all men prove totally unworthy of communication with their Maker. Never again will God be hidden from his children on the earth. Revelation is here to remain. (E, May 1977, p. 77.)

**3:11** Some of the sure signs of apostate churches and religious groups are that "the heads thereof judge for reward, and the priests thereof teach for hire, and the prophets thereof divine for money."

Moroni, a Book of Mormon prophet, also identified the love of money and power as an indication of false religion.

"Yea, it [the Book of Mormon] shall come in a day when

the power of God shall be denied, and churches become defiled and be lifted up in the pride of their hearts . . . when there shall be churches built up that shall say: Come unto me, and for your money you shall be forgiven of your sins. O ye wicked and perverse and stiffnecked people, why have ye built up churches unto yourselves to get gain? . . . For behold, ye do love money, and your substance, and your fine apparel, and the adorning of your churches, more than ye love the poor and the needy, the sick and the afflicted." (Morm. 8:28, 32, 37.)

**4:1-2**    These verses are almost identical to Isaiah 2:2-4. (See the commentary for Isa. 2:2-4.) Both of these prophets clearly and definitely taught that these events would occur "in the last days."

Harold B. Lee has provided the following commentaries on these verses:

> Over the years I have begun to observe at least the beginning of the fulfillment of the ancient prophecy of Micah relating to the establishment of the Lord's house in the tops of the mountains. This prophet said, [Micah 4:1.]
>
> The expression "the mountain of the Lord's house," as here indicated, was undoubtedly to be referred to as a place as well as a definition of a righteous people, because we have the Lord in a revelation saying, [D&C 97:21.]
>
> And then the ancient prophet said, [Micah 4:2.]
>
> With the coming of the pioneers to establish the Church in the tops of the mountains, our early leaders declared this to be the beginning of the fulfillment of that prophecy. Orson Pratt, one of the members of the Twelve delivered an oration on that occasion, in which he declared that this was the beginning of the fulfillment of the prophecy that out of Zion should go forth the law and the word of the Lord from Jerusalem. (England Area CR, 1971, p. 138.)
>
> I have often wondered what the scripture meant to say that says, ". . . for the law shall go forth of Zion, and the word of the Lord from Jerusalem." (Micah 4:2.) As I was pondering that one day at the dedicatory services of the Idaho Falls Temple, I heard President George Albert Smith say in the dedicatory prayer:
>
> "We thank thee that thou hast revealed to us that those who gave us our constitutional form of government were men wise in thy sight and that thou didst raise them up for the very purpose of putting forth that sacred document. . . .
>
> "We pray that kings and rulers and the peoples of all nations under heaven may be persuaded of the blessings enjoyed by the people of this land by reason of their freedom under thy guidance and be constrained to adopt similar governmental systems, thus to fulfill the ancient prophecy of

Isaiah that '. . . out of Zion shall go forth the law and the word of the Lord from Jerusalem.' " (*Improvement Era,* October 1945, p. 564.)

If ever there came into my mind, at a time when I needed it, a definition of what a scripture meant, I heard it from the mouth of a prophet when the Idaho Falls Temple was dedicated. (*Ye Are the Light of the World,* pp. 340-41.)

**4:3**    Brigham Young has provided the following commentary on this verse:

If the Christian world would follow the instructions of the New Testament, they would believe the doctrines of the Latter-day Saints: and our swords would be beaten into plough-shares, and our spears into pruning-hooks, and we should hail each other as brethren. All quarrelling upon these plains would come to an end, and all desire to injure each other would cease. The word in each person's mouth would be "Brother, what can I do for you? Have I anything you need, that I can serve you with, which is necessary to administer to your sick wife and children? Are your cattle lost, and shall I help you to find them?" All the weapons of warfare would be buried in the dust, no more to be resurrected, and each man would say, "Come, let us hail each other as brethren, and do each other good instead of evil." (JD 1:245.)

**4:7**    Modern prophets have identified the remnant of Israel that "halted . . . and . . . was cast far off" and was to become "a strong nation" over whom the Lord shall reign in mount Zion. (See Part I 204, 214-19.)

**4:11-13**    The resurrected Jesus Christ quoted these verses to the survivors among the Lehites when he appeared to them. (3 Ne. 20:18-19.) He then placed this event in the context of other events in the last days. (See 3 Ne. 20:12-46 and Part I 90, 94, 113, 206-13.)

**5:2**    This verse from Micah is widely quoted as a "messianic prophecy" of the birth of Jesus Christ. Both Matthew (2:6) and John (7:42) quote Micah 5:2 as one of the many evidences that Old Testament prophets knew a great deal about the birth, life, and mission of the Messiah ("the Anointed One"), Jesus Christ. LeGrand Richards has stated:

It must be more than a coincidence that Jesus Christ, the Son of God, who answers all the requirements of the prophecies, should have been born in "Bethlehem Ephratah." How much better could Micah have described Him who was to be "ruler in Israel?" (IDYK, p. 87.)

**5:8-15**    The "remnant of Jacob" referred to in these verses evidently refers to the descendants of Joseph in America, according to the testimony of the resurrected Jesus Christ. (See 3 Ne. 21:11-29 and Part I 78, 116-19, 204, 214-19, 233-38.)

**5:10-15**    Each of these verses is quoting the Lord: "I will cut off the cities of thy land," "I will execute vengeance in anger and fury," and soon. Is the Lord really the cause of these destructions?

Joseph Fielding Smith has written:

> There are some, even in the Church, unfortunately, who think that such expressions are cruel, and they are not willing to accept them as coming from a "merciful God." However, man brings the punishment upon himself and the judgments of the Almighty are bound to follow. (CHMR 1:144.)

**6:8**    This verse is widely quoted as containing the essentials of true religion.

**6:14**    The statement "thy casting down shall be in the midst of thee" could have been translated "your hunger will be in your midst."

**6:16**    Omri and Ahab were among the most wicked of the kings of Israel. If their "statutes" and "works" continued to be followed, the destruction that would follow would result in desolation and a scattering of the people.

# NAHUM

See "Nahum" in the Bible Dictionary, page 736.

**1:1** The "burden" (message of doom) of Nahum was directed primarily against Assyria and its capital city, Nineveh. Some of the same destructive powers that led to the downfall of Nineveh will also be active in the last days as indicated in the chapter heading.

**1:11** The "wicked counsellor" was counselling "worthlessness" according to the Hebrew. Evidently a "false prophet" had come forth in Assyria, saying the Assyrians would not be defeated in battle. Yet within a short while the Assyrians were "cut down" (v. 12) as prophesied by the Lord through Nahum.

**1:15** Statements similar to the first sentence in this verse are found in several books of the scriptures: "Behold upon the mountains the feet of him that bringeth good tidings, that publisheth peace." (See Isa. 52:7; Rom. 10:15; 1 Ne. 13:37; Mosiah 12:21; 15:14-18; 27:37; 3 Ne. 20:40.)

The resurrected Jesus Christ quoted Isaiah's wording of this thought (Isa. 52:7) and said it would be repeated in Jerusalem in the last days after the Jews have been redeemed. (3 Ne. 20:29-40.)

One of the best explanations of this expression was provided by the prophet Abinadi in the Book of Mormon.

Yea, and are not the prophets, every one that has opened his mouth to prophesy, that has not fallen into transgression, I mean all the holy prophets ever since the world began? I say unto you that they are his seed.

And these are they who have published peace, who have brought good tidings of good, who have published salvation; and said unto Zion: Thy God reigneth!

And O how beautiful upon the mountains were their feet!

And again, how beautiful upon the mountains are the feet of those that are still publishing peace!

And again, how beautiful upon the mountains are the feet of those who shall hereafter publish peace, yea, from this time henceforth and forever! (Mosiah 15:13-17.)

**2:2** This verse could have been translated: "For Jehovah has turned the glory of Jacob, as the glory of Israel. For the plunderers have plundered them, and have destroyed their vine branches.''

**2:6** The opening of the sluice gates of the city moats resulted in the capture of Nineveh by the Babylonians, as prophesied in this verse. Once the city was captured, the palace was "dissolved" (literally "melted" or "destroyed").

Concerning the destruction of Nineveh, Spencer W. Kimball has written:

> In fulfilment, the river overflowed, inundated the walls for miles, the gates were burned, the king and his concubines and his wealth were consumed with the palaces, and the unconquerable city, now made vulnerable by flood and fire, was taken by the invaders while its boasted defenders lay in drunken stupor and lolled in licentiousness. Today the canals of Nineveh are gone, leaving the country a desolate waste. Sheep and cattle seek scanty pasture among the mounds of the once greatest city.
>
> God cannot be mocked! His laws are immutable. True repentance is rewarded by forgiveness but sin brings the sting of death.
>
> Nineveh is not the only instance. Historians are still puzzled regarding the annihilation of the infamous cities of Sodom and Gomorrah. Whatever happened to these peoples, this we know, that swift destruction came to them. Perhaps the Japanese of Hiroshima were no more completely nor quickly destroyed. At least students agree that there was a devastating holocaust which enveloped the cities, leaving the monuments and the people in utter desolation, never to be rediscovered nor rebuilt. (CR, Oct. 1945, pp. 122-23.)

**3:8** Other great and large cities had been destroyed earlier because of their wickedness, including the city of No in Egypt (Hebrew *No Amon,* believed by many scholars to be Thebes which was destroyed in approximately 667 B.C.).

**3:13** Nineveh was captured by diverting the waters of the river which ran under her walls. The Babylonian soldiers were then able to enter the city under the walls and open the huge gates so other Babylonian soldiers could enter. The "gates of thy land" were indeed "set wide open unto" her enemies.

**3:19** This verse reveals that the Assyrians had been extremely wicked and cruel and were not repenting of these evils; thus, their destruction was certain.

# HABAKKUK

See "Habakkuk" in the Bible Dictionary, page 697.

**1:1-6** The "burden" (message of doom) of Habakkuk included the impending invasion of "the Chaldeans [Babylonians], that bitter and hasty nation." The Hebrew word translated "hasty" could have been translated "impetuous."

**1:3-4** One of the problems faced by many of the prophets is that the Lord requires them to preach against wickedness at that moment when the wicked seem to be prospering more than the righteous. This appeared to Habakkuk to be contrary to the principle that happiness results from obedience to law (righteousness), so that he exclaimed, "wrong judgment proceedeth [justice is being perverted]."

The Lord's answer (Hab. 2:2-4) is that at the appointed time or in the end judgment (justice) will surely come; in the meantime the just are to walk by faith.

The punishment (misery) that is the consequence of broken law (sin) does not always come upon the sinner immediately. If it did, then the sinner would soon stop breaking the law for the reason he does not want the punishment to come upon him. The person would then be doing the right thing, but he would be doing it for the wrong reason [to escape the punishment].

Often the major punishment for broken law is delayed in order for the sinner to repent on his own volition. Hopefully, he will stop sinning [breaking the law] because he knows breaking the law is wrong and also because he wants to enjoy the peace and happiness associated with righteousness [obedience to the law]. He is then doing the right thing for the right reasons.

**1:11** This verse could have been translated more literally: "Then he sweeps on as the wind, and transgresses and is guilty, attributing his power to his god." The basic idea is that the Babylonians will be swiftly victorious in their battles against the Israelites; but then the Babylonians will wrongly assume it was the power of their idol god that caused the victory, rather than the unrighteousness of the Israelites.

**1:15** The old English word *angle* (from whence derives *angler*) is used consistently in the King James text as the translation of a Hebrew word meaning "hook."

The word "drag" in this verse could have been translated "fishnet."

**2:1**  The first "watch" in this verse could have been translated "guard."

**2:2**  The writings of Habakkuk were to be easy to understand and read (in other words, "put the words in large type!") so that "he may run" who is reading them.

**2:3-4**  See the commentary for Habakkuk 1:3-4.

**2:4**  If the righteous ("the just") have sufficient faith in the Lord, they will be willing to wait for the "appointed time" of the Lord when blessings will be bestowed upon the righteous and punishments upon the wicked.

The Hebrew word translated here as "faith" could more literally have been translated as "faithfulness"—that is, "steadfastness" or "firmness."

**2:14**  A similar expression was used by Isaiah in expressing a condition that would occur in the last days: "The earth shall be full of the knowledge of the Lord, as the waters cover the sea." (Isa. 11:9.)

**2:15**  Both ancient and current prophets have warned against strong drink and giving your "neighbor drink." Spencer W. Kimball has observed:

Liquor has been used to neutralize the inhibitions and dull the senses of many a young woman so that her virtue might be more easily taken. [Quoted Hab. 2:15.] . . .

. . . It is reported that American citizens spend of the national income two and one half times as much for liquor as on education. . . .

One of the saddest notes in this business is the blasphemy at Christmas time in social home parties, club socials, and staff Christmas parties where drinks are supplied to employees.

Remember Habakkuk: [Quoted Hab. 2:15.] . . .

Drinking is now considered aristocratic in planes, in cafes, hotels, in airport bars—everywhere. Someone said, "The cocktail parlor is but a saloon in petticoats."

What a frightening responsibility to be an advertiser, dispenser, manufacturer who would go into the living rooms of millions of homes and indoctrinate little children's minds till they accepted liquor as part of acceptable social living. For the dollar today, they would corrupt a generation tomorrow. Someone made a survey and found that 67 percent of the films show drinking as the smart and proper thing to do. (CR, Oct. 1967, pp. 31-33.)

**2:18-19**  When the crisis comes, those who have placed their trust in idols will be lost. Their wooden idols will not respond, and their stone idols will not be able to tell them what to do.

**3:2-19**  Habakkuk wanted the Lord to "revive thy work [preserve or give new life to your work]" and then listed some of the great works of the Lord in the past, particularly during the days of Moses and Joshua.

**3:3, 9, 13**  This entire chapter is a prayer of Habakkuk set in poetic form. The word *Selah* is inserted to indicate a break in the reading (chanting) at specified points.

# ZEPHANIAH

See "Zephaniah" in the Bible Dictionary, page 792.

**1:1**  The historical information provided here suggests that Zephaniah may have been contemporary with Jeremiah, Nahum, and Habakkuk. It is not clear where his field of missionary labor was located.

**1:12**  The punishments for wickedness will come upon all, including the complacent ("that are settled on their lees") and those who say, "God is dead" ("The Lord will not do good, neither will he do evil").

**1:14**  The term *great day of the Lord* is usually reserved by the prophets to refer to the last days or the period immediately preceding the second coming of Jesus Christ in power and glory, which indeed would be a "great day" for the righteous. Evidently many of the prophecies of Zephaniah pertain to events in the last days.

**1:18**  The term *fire of his jealousy* used here and in 3:8 indicates the determination or zealousness of the Lord in seeing that justice is administered.

See the commentaries for Exodus 20:5 and 34:14.

**2:1**  "Desired" could have been translated "ashamed." The meaning of the verse is that the proud, unrepentant nation is preparing itself for destruction.

**2:13-15**  The major message of these verses is: Just as the great city of Nineveh will be destroyed ["the rejoicing city that dwelt carelessly" in her pride], so all the wicked will be destroyed and their cities shall become "a desolation."

**3:9**  One of the blessings that will result from the destruction of the wicked is that a "pure language" will be restored which will be spoken by everyone. From the days of Adam until the time of the tower of Babel, a single, universal language was on the earth (the "Adamic language"), patterned after the language of God. Since the confusion of languages at Babel, the people have not served the Lord with either "one consent" or one voice.

Brigham Young has suggested that our current languages

are inadequate, but when one speaks through the gift of the Holy Ghost he can convey the intelligence of God.

Although the language we now speak is as good as any language that has yet come to our knowledge, still it is very meagre, and limited in its range and power, and though it is a good medium at ordinary times, yet it comes very far short of being such a medium, as man needs to convey thoughts, when he is inspired by the power of God, through the gift of the Holy Ghost, and is full of the revelations of Jesus. It is written [Quoted Zeph. 3:8-9]. When a man rises up to speak in the name of the Lord, and is filled with the light, and the intelligence and power which cometh from God, his countenance alone will convey more, to those who are inspired by the same spirit, than can possibly be conveyed, by the words of any language now used by mankind. (JD 10:353.)

**3:16** The Lord is clearly referring to two separate, distinct places here: (1) Jerusalem and (2) Zion. Isaiah also differentiated between the two major cities or locations of the last days when he prophesied: "Out of Zion shall go forth the law, and the word of the Lord from Jerusalem." (Isa. 2:3.)

See the commentaries for Isaiah 2:2-4; Micah 4:1-2; and Joel 2:32; see also Part I 95, 132-33.

**3:19** Apparently two different groups are being referred to here by the Lord: (1) "I will save her that halteth" and (2) "[I will] gather her that was driven out."

The April 6, 1845, proclamation of the Twelve Apostles of The Church of Jesus Christ of Latter-day Saints has identified the group referred to as "her that halteth." (See Part I 204, 214-19.)

# HAGGAI

See "Haggai" in the Bible Dictionary, page 698.

**1:1** Haggai, the prophet, is also mentioned in Ezra 5:1 and 6:14—both times in conjunction with his contemporary prophet, Zechariah.

**2:3** The temple of Solomon had been destroyed some sixty-six years before, so there would be relatively few still living who would have remembered the house of the Lord "in her first glory."

**2:7-9** If the "desire of all nations" refers to the coming of the Messiah ("the Anointed One"—Jesus Christ), then the "latter house [temple]" that would be greater than the former (Solomon's temple) would refer to the temple in existence at the time of Christ.

**2:20-23** Ellis Rasmussen has written the following commentary on these verses:

Although addressed to Zerubbabel of the royal line himself, is it not likely that this should be understood to be a Messianic prophecy of the ultimate King of the royal line of David and Zerubbabel? (Cf. Luke 3:27; Matt. 1:12-13 for mention of Zerubbabel in the genealogy of Jesus.) (IOT 2:102.)

# ZECHARIAH

See "Zechariah" in the Bible Dictionary, pages 791-92.

**1:1** This revelation to Zechariah ("in the eighth month, in the second year of Darius") was received about two months after Haggai received his revelation ("in the second year of Darius the king, in the sixth month, in the first day of the month" [Hag. 1:1]).

**1:17** Two separate cities are referred to in this verse: (1) Zion and (2) Jerusalem.

See the commentaries for Isaiah 2:2-4; Micah 4:1-2; and Joel 2:32; see also Part I 95, 132-33.

**2:10-13** The prophecy in these verses primarily deals with the gathering of Judah (the Jews) to the Holy Land, including Jerusalem. (See Part I 80-95, 105-15, 177-91, 193-97, 205-13, 223, 228-32, 239-50.)

**3:1** The same name translated here as "Joshua" has been translated as "Jeshua" in other references. (As examples, see 2 Chr. 31:15; Ezra 5:2; Neh. 3:19.) Ellis Rasmussen has commented on the significance of this name:

> You may see in this vision of *Joshua* the high priest of the time (called *Jeshua* in Ezra and Nehemiah—e.g. Ezra 5:2) a prophecy of the cleansing or restoration of the Priesthood, and of the coming of the Messiah (the "BRANCH"); also of the purification of Israel in preparation for the Millennium, which seems to be hinted in verse 10. . . .
>
> The name *Jesus* is English spelling of the Latin form of the Greek form of the Hebrew name *Jeshua,* or *Yeshua,* which means "salvation"! (IOT 2:102.)

**4:14** The "two anointed ones, that stand by the Lord of the whole earth" may be the "two witnesses" mentioned by John the Revelator who would be given power of God and would be "standing before the God of the earth." (Rev. 11:3-4.)

The Doctrine and Covenants supplies additional information on the two witnesses mentioned by John.

Q. What is to be understood by the two witnesses, in the eleventh chapter of Revelation?

A.  They are two prophets that are to be raised up to the Jewish nation in the last days, at the time of the restoration, and to prophesy to the Jews after they are gathered and have built the city of Jerusalem in the land of their fathers. (D&C 77:15.)

Joseph Fielding Smith has found meaning in the fact that the two anointed ones are represented by olive trees:

In Revelation 11:4, the Lord speaks of his two witnesses as two olive trees, and in Zechariah 4:11-14 is a similar prophetic parable. So we find through all the prophetic writings that olive trees and olive oil are emblems of sacredness and purity. (AGQ 1:152.)

**6:12-15**    The BRANCH is mentioned in several scriptures pertaining to the last days, including Isaiah 11:1; Jeremiah 23:5; 33:15; and Zechariah 3:8.

**8:3-8**    The Lord has made it very plain through his prophets that Jerusalem will be inhabited in the last days by his covenant people, both by "old men and old women" and by "boys and girls playing in the streets thereof."

**8:9**    The Lord also made it clear through his prophets that a temple will be built in Jerusalem in the last days, prior to his second coming in power and great glory.

**9:9**    This is one of the most widely quoted messianic prophecies of Zechariah. Matthew (21:1-9) and John (12:12-16) both believed this prophecy was fulfilled when Jesus Christ came riding into Jerusalem seated on "the foal of an ass."

Although the full symbolism of the Savior entering the holy city riding on a donkey may not be known, it would have special meaning to the people of his day. Rome held political power in Judea in the days of Jesus, and the symbol of Roman might and power in warfare was the Roman soldier seated on a prancing stallion. The Savior wanted the world to know he was not coming as a man of war; he was coming as a Man of Peace. Thus, he entered the city not on the back of a prancing horse, but seated on the lowly donkey.

Harold B. Lee has provided the following commentary on the triumphal entry of Jesus Christ into Jerusalem:

My text today is taken from the "Hosanna shout" which sounded from the multitude who jubilantly acclaimed Jesus, the lowly Nazarene as he rode triumphantly into Jerusalem from Bethany on a colt which had been borrowed for that occasion. As the animal upon which he rode had been designated in their literature as the "ancient symbol of Jewish royalty" [Zech. 9:9] and their acquaintanceship with the might of His Messianic power impressed the appropriateness of his kingly right to such an entry, they cast their garments before him and cast palm branches and other foliage in His path as though carpeting the way of a king. What might at first have been but the humble testimony of a faithful few, increased into a mighty chorus of voices as the multitude shouted in harmony: "Blessed be the King that cometh in the name of the Lord. Hosanna, to the Son of David."

And then perhaps as they remembered the angels' announcement to the shepherds on the night of His birth, they reverently repeated the theme of the angels' song: "Peace in heaven, and glory in the highest." And again, probably remembering the charge he had given His disciples to carry on after he would be taken from them, and as a supplication for their Master and those who would carry on after His ascension, as well as in the remembrance of the ancient prophets whom they revered, came the expressions of adulation from the multitude: "Blessed is he that cometh in the name of the Lord." (CR, Apr. 1955, p. 17.)

**10:6-9, 12**   Again, two distinct groups are mentioned in regard to the gathering of Israel in the last days: (1) "the house of Judah" and (2) "the house of Joseph." LeGrand Richards has commented concerning this gathering:

> From these scriptures [Zech. 10:6-9, 12] it is evident the Lord had definitely in mind that no matter how Israel would be scattered, He would eventually bring them together again. How could His promises to Abraham be fulfilled without accomplishing this objective.
>
> Zechariah called attention to the fact that "Ephraim shall be like a mighty man . . . and I will sow them among the people . . . and they shall remember me in far countries." This prophecy seems to attach importance to the House of Joseph, and to what their prophets might have to say, as recorded in the Stick of Joseph [Book of Mormon] since Jeremiah definitely states that "In those days the house of Judah shall walk with the house of Israel." (Jeremiah 3:18.) This implies that Israel will point the way to Judah, and that in this accomplishment, the Stick of Joseph would perform a great mission in making plain unto Judah many important matters which they hitherto have not understood. (IDYK, p. 46.)

For further information on the gathering of these two major branches of the house of Israel (Judah and Joseph), see Part I 78-95, 105-19, 177-91, 193-97, 204-19, 223, 228-50.

**10:7-9**   "They of Ephraim," mentioned in verse 7, are part of "the house of Joseph" referred to in verse 6. Ephraim was the son of Joseph (Gen. 41:52), and so naturally those "of Ephraim" would also be "of Joseph."

**11:10**   "Beauty" could have been translated "kindness."

**11:11**   The clause "that waited upon me" could have been translated "who were watching me."

**11:12**   Fulfillment of this messianic prophecy is recorded in Matthew 26:14-15.

**12:6-10; 13:6; 14:1-21**   These verses refer to one of the greatest events in the latter days—the appearance of the Messiah (the resurrected Jesus Christ) to the Jewish people at the Mount of Olives, and the great battle that will take place in that area. The following commentary by Parley P. Pratt indicates the significance of these events:

Zechariah . . . has said, in plain words, that the Lord shall come at the very time of the overthrow of that army, yes, in fact, even while they are in the act of taking Jerusalem, and have already succeeded in taking one-half the city, and spoiling their houses, and ravishing their women.

Then, behold their long-expected Messiah, suddenly appearing, shall stand upon the Mount of Olives, a little east of Jerusalem, to fight against those nations and deliver the Jews. Zechariah says the Mount of Olives shall cleave in twain, from east to west, and one-half of the mountain shall remove to the north, while the other half falls off to the south, suddenly forming a very great valley, into which the Jews shall flee for protection from their enemies as they fled from the earthquake in the days of Uzziah, king of Judah; while the Lord cometh and all the saints with him.

Then will the Jews behold that long, long-expected Messiah, coming in power to their deliverance, as they always looked for him. He will destroy their enemies, and deliver them from trouble at the very time they are in the utmost consternation, and about to be swallowed up by their enemies. But what will be their astonishment when they are about to fall at the feet of their Deliverer, and acknowledge him their Messiah! They discover the wounds which were once made in his hands, feet, and side; and on inquiry, at once recognize Jesus of Nazareth, the King of the Jews, the man so long rejected. (VW, p. 40.)

See also Part I 93-94, 114-115, 210.

**12:8**   Concerning the Lord's promise to "defend the inhabitants of Jerusalem," LeGrand Richards has written:

This clearly has reference to the events which shall precede the second coming of the Messiah, when the Jews shall again be gathered to Jerusalem, for the Lord said: "they shall look upon me whom they have pierced."

Of interest is the following quotation from an article by Arthur U. Michelson which was published in "The Jewish Hope," Issue No. 9, Vol. 22, September, 1950. The article suggests how the Lord may, even now, be fulfilling the prophecy of Zechariah, "In that day shall the Lord defend the inhabitants of Jerusalem . . .":

"On my recent trip to Palestine I saw with my own eyes how God's prophecy is being fulfilled. . . .

"It was marvelous what God did for the Jews, especially in Jerusalem, during the fighting with the Arabs. Though quite a few months had passed since the victory of Israel's army in Israel, they were still talking about what had taken place. Everywhere I went I heard how God had intervened in their behalf, and how He helped them to win the battles. One of the officials told me how much the Jews had to suffer. They had hardly anything with which to resist the heavy attacks of the Arabs, who were well organized and equipped with the latest weapons. Besides, they had neither food nor water because all their supplies were cut off.

"The Arabs, who had a great army in strong position, were determined to destroy the Jews, while the Jews were few in number, without any arms and ammunition. The two or three guns they possessed had to be rushed from one point to another, to give the Arabs the impression they had many of them. The Jews had quite a few tin cans which they beat as they shot the guns, giving the impression of many shots. But as the pressure was too great, they were unable to hold the lines any longer and finally decided to give up the city. At this critical moment God showed them that He was on their side, for He performed one of the greatest miracles that ever happened. The Arabs suddenly threw down their arms and surrendered. When their delegation appeared with the white flag, they asked, 'Where are the three men that led you, and where are all the troops we saw?' The Jews told them that they did not know anything of the three men, for this group was their entire force. *The Arabs said that they saw three persons with long beards and flowing white robes, who warned them not to fight any longer, otherwise they would all be killed.* They became so frightened that they decided to give up. What an encouragement this was for the Jews, who realized that God was fighting for them." (IDYK, pp. 229-30.)

For other materials on how the Lord will help fight the battles of Judah in the last days, see Part I 83, 94.

**12:10**   Ezekiel also prophesied that Jehovah would appear to the descendants of Jacob brought forth out of captivity and would not hide his face "any more from them." (Ezek. 39:25-29.)

The Lord has revealed in modern times an even more detailed account of his appearance in the last days to "the inhabitants of Jerusalem":

"And then shall the Jews look upon me and say: What are these wounds in thine hands and in thy feet?

"Then shall they know that I am the Lord; for I will say unto them: These wounds are the wounds with which I was wounded in the house of my friends. I am he who was lifted up. I am Jesus that was crucified. I am the Son of God.

"And then shall they weep because of their iniquities; then

shall they lament because they persecuted their king.'' (D&C 45:51-53.)

**13:1**    Joseph Fielding Smith believes this verse refers to baptism:

When John the Baptist came from the wilderness crying repentance and baptizing all who came to him, his act did not seem to create any curiosity as if he were introducing some new and strange doctrine. The repentant Jews took it as an essential ordinance well known among them and so it was. According to many Jewish writers baptism was an ordinance in ancient Israel. Here are a few quotations referring to this fact: "Christian baptism is of uncertain origin. . . . Possibly the baptism of Jewish proselytes furnished the model followed by Christian missionaries." [*Encyclopedia of Religion,* edited by Virgilius Ferm, p. 53.]

"John stood forth in the spirit of the prophets of old to preach his baptism of repentance symbolized by cleansing with water." (See Jer. 4:14, Ezek. 36:25, Zech. 13:1.) (AGQ 2:67-68.)

**13:6**    See also the commentary for Zechariah 12:10. Joseph Fielding Smith has observed the following concerning this appearance of the resurrected Messiah to the Jewish people:

The Prophet Zechariah has also prophesied of the Savior's second coming and his appearance to the Jews when they will flee from their enemies and the Mount of Olives shall cleave in twain making a valley in which they shall seek refuge. At that particular time he will appear and they shall say: [Quoted Zechariah 13:6.] Then they will mourn, each family apart, because they had rejected their Lord.

It is true that he also showed these wounds to the Nephites when he visited with them with the same purpose in view, to convince them of his identity, and give to them a witness of his suffering. It can hardly be accepted as a fact that these wounds have remained in his hands, side, and feet all through the centuries from the time of his crucifixion and will remain until his second coming, but they will appear to the Jews as a witness against their fathers and their stubbornness in following the teachings of their fathers. After their weeping and mourning they shall be cleansed. (AGQ 1:45.)

**13:7-9**    The reference in verse 8 to the "two parts" of Israel who shall "die [be separated]" from the land evidently refers (1) to the ten lost tribes of the northern kingdom taken from the land of Israel by the Assyrians (2 Kgs. 17:6), and (2) to the dispersed of Israel led out of the land by the Lord, such as Lehi, Ishmael, and the colony associated with Mulek. (1 Ne. 1:4; 2:1-2; Omni 1:15; Mosiah 25:2; Hel. 8:21.)

The "third" part that "shall be left therein" evidently refers to the descendants of Judah and the citizens of the kingdom of

Judah; these are to be tested "through the fire" and refined "as silver is refined."

**14:1-3**    The battle mentioned here is evidently the battle of Gog mentioned by Ezekiel (38), Joel (3:2), and John the Revelator (Rev. 11; 16:14). See the commentaries for Joel 2:1-11; Ezekiel 38:1-23 and chapters 38-39; see also Part I 90, 94, 113, 206-13.

**14:4-7**    The appearance of the resurrected Jesus Christ (the Messiah) to the Jews at the Mount of Olives in the last days is mentioned several times in both ancient and modern scriptures.

This appearance of the Savior *precedes* his second coming in power and great glory.

See the commentary for Zechariah 12:6-10; see also Part I 93, 114-15, 210.

**14:8**    The "living waters" that shall go out of Jerusalem in the last days are evidently the waters of the river beheld by Ezekiel (47:1-12) and the fountain that "shall come forth of the house of the Lord" seen by Joel (3:18) and John the Revelator (Rev. 22:1).

See the commentary for Ezekiel 47:1-5; see also Part I 87-88.

**14:10**    The clause "it shall be lifted up, and inhabited in her place" could have been translated "Jerusalem shall rise and dwell in her place."

**14:12**    The Lord has warned through his prophets the danger of placing private interpretation on prophecy. (2 Pet. 1:20-21.) Nevertheless it is tempting to point out here the striking similarities between the "plague" that will come upon "all the people that have fought against Jerusalem" and the conditions suffered by the victims of the atomic bombs in Hiroshima and Nagasaki: "their flesh shall consume away"; "their eyes shall consume away in their holes"; "their tongue shall consume away in their mouth."

In September 1830 the Lord described anew one of the plagues of the last days: "Flies . . . shall eat their flesh"; "their flesh shall fall from off their bones, and their eyes from their sockets." (D&C 29:18-19.)

**14:16-19**    Other prophets also prophesied of the lack of rain upon the earth during a certain period of the last days, including John the Revelator. (Rev. 11:6.)

The proclamation of the Twelve Apostles issued in April 1845 contains a reference to this event. See Part I 212-13.

# MALACHI

See "Malachi" in the Bible Dictionary, page 728.

**1-4**   Ellis Rasmussen has provided the following background information on the book of Malachi:

Although no date for the prophecies of Malachi is given, his times are reflected by the above passages. Malachi could have come during and after the days of Ezra and Nehemiah, after the prophets Haggai and Zechariah, and also after the temple had been built. It was evidently a time when some abuses had again appeared. According to scholars and traditions, Malachi was the last of the prophets. You will perhaps be surprised to know that "the Talmud declares that with the death of Haggai, Zechariah and Malachi the Holy Spirit departed from Israel," according to Eli Cashdan, in the Jewish publication, *Soncino Books of the Bible,* Rev. Dr. A. Cohen, ed.; London: The Soncino Press, 1948 (sixth impression 1966), vol. title: *The Twelve Prophets,* p. 254. (IOT 2:110.)

**1:2-3**   Joseph Smith has commented on these verses:

"As it is written, Jacob have I loved, but Esau have I hated." Where is it written? [Malachi 1:1, 2.] When was it written? About 397 years before Christ, and Esau and Jacob were born about 1,773 years before Christ, (according to the computation of time in Scripture margin), so Esau and Jacob lived about 1,376 years before the Lord spoke by Malachi, saying, "Jacob have I loved, but Esau have I hated," as quoted by Paul. This text is often brought forward to prove that God loved Jacob and hated Esau before they were born, or before they had done good or evil; but if God did love one and hate the other before they had done good or evil, He has not seen fit to tell us of it, either in the Old or New Testament, or any other revelation: but this only we learn that 1,376 years after Esau and Jacob were born, God said by Malachi—"Jacob have I loved, and Esau have I hated;" and surely that was time sufficient to prove their works, and ascertain whether they were worthy to be loved or hated.

And why did He love the one and hate the other? For the same reason that He accepted the offering of Abel and rejected Cain's offering. Because Jacob's works had been righteous, and Esau's wicked. (HC 4:262.)

**1:6**   God, our Heavenly Father, is the father and master of all mankind. Thus, all should reverence God and be willing to honor and serve him.

**1:8**   The Lord emphasized to Moses that the animal to be offered in the sacrifice should "be perfect to be accepted; there shall be no blemish therein." (Lev. 22:21.) The Lord also specifically commanded "ye shall not offer [anything] . . . blind, or broken, or maimed." (Lev. 22:22.)

The animal used in the sacrifice was to be perfect ("without spot or blemish") as it was being offered in similitude of the sacrifice of the perfect, sinless Son of God.

When the Israelites in the days of Malachi were offering "blind . . . lame and sick" animals for sacrifice, it not only destroyed the significance of the spotless sacrifice of the Savior, but it was solemn mockery before God.

**1:10** Ellis Rasmussen has provided the following commentary on the first part of this verse:

"This should rather be translated as a wish: 'Oh that there were even one among you that would shut the doors, that ye might not kindle fire on mine altar in vain.' " (IOT 2:110.)

**2:10** As brothers and sisters to each other—sons and daughters of our Heavenly Father—we should love and serve each other as well as honor and serve our Father.

**2:14-16** God and his prophets have always spoken against divorce, except in certain extreme circumstances. Inasmuch as God has commanded that the husband and wife should become as one, divorce is always the result of sin of one type or another.

**3-4** The resurrected Jesus Christ commanded the Book of Mormon prophets to "write the words which the Father had given unto Malachi," which He then gave unto them. (3 Ne. 24:1.) The words then quoted by the Savior were Malachi chapters 3 and 4. (3 Ne. 24:1-18; 25:1-6.)

**3:1** Joseph Fielding Smith believes this prophecy was at least partially fulfilled through the events associated with the dedication of the Kirtland Temple:

Malachi predicted that the Savior would come suddenly to his temple with power and authority. It is customary in the Church for the members to still look forward for the coming of this great day, thinking that it is to be fulfilled when the great temple in the city Zion shall be built; but may it not be the case that this predicted coming has already taken place in this wonderful manifestation in the Kirtland Temple? The Savior came suddenly to this temple. . . . Without any question when the temple in Zion and the temple in Jerusalem are built the Lord will come to them, but his coming to the Kirtland Temple carries great weight and is far more significant than some among us have thought it to be. (CHMR 3:79.)

For other materials pertaining to the prophecy that the Lord will come "suddenly to his temple," see Part I 92.

**3:2-3**    The essential contents of verses 2 and 3 were quoted in an epistle by Joseph Smith September 6, 1842, with the introduction: "Behold, the great day of the Lord is at hand." (D&C 128:24.) Obviously these verses refer to the second coming of Jesus Christ, when he shall come in power and great glory. Joseph Fielding Smith has also emphasized this point:

> Bible interpreters have declared that this was fulfilled in the days of Christ's ministry; but this is not so. It is very evident, notwithstanding the fact that John the Baptist came in the Dispensation of the Meridian of Time, and was the forerunner of Christ, that this prophecy was not fulfilled at that time, but was to be fulfilled at a later day, or in the Dispensation of the Fulness of Times. This prophecy declares that (1) Christ was to come suddenly to his temple; as the messenger of the covenant. (2) He was to be like a refiner's fire, and like fuller's soap, to be a refiner and purifier, to purify the sons of Levi and purge them, that they "may offer unto the Lord, an offering in righteousness." (3) It was to be a day when the offering of Judah and Jerusalem would be pleasant, as in days of old and former years. (4) It was to be a day of judgment and swift witness against the sorcerers and adulterers, false swearers, and those who oppress the widow and the fatherless. Surely these things did not happen in the days of the ministry of our Lord when he dwelt among men. In that day the Levites and the sons of Judah turned against him and brought him to his death; every one abode his coming, and he did not come in that ministry in judgment like a refiner's fire. The sons of Levi were not purged, and they did not offer an offering in righteousness.
>
> No! We must look for a later day for the fulfilment of this prophecy. Much of this prophetic prediction by Malachi is yet future. (AGQ 3:9-10.)

**3:1-3**    When the angel Moroni first appeared to the Prophet Joseph Smith September 21, 1823, he quoted some of the prophecies of the Old Testament. The first scripture quoted by Moroni was "part of the third chapter of Malachi." (JS-H 1:36.) Moroni then quoted "the fourth or last chapter of the same prophecy [Malachi]." (JS-H 1:36.)

Although Joseph Smith did not identify exactly which verses Moroni quoted from Malachi chapter 3, some have thought he probably quoted the introductory verses, since these are concerned with the second coming of Jesus Christ, as are the verses in chapter 4 also quoted by Moroni.

**3:3**    Joseph Smith referred to the "offering in righteousness" of the sons of Levi and then added:

"Let us, therefore, as a church and a people, and as Latter-day Saints, offer unto the Lord an offering in righteousness; and let us present in his holy temple . . . a book containing the records of our dead, which shall be worthy of all acceptation.'' (D&C 128:24.)

Spencer W. Kimball has also indicated that acceptable records are necessary:

We have asked the members of the Church to further the work of turning the hearts of the children to the fathers by getting their own sacred family records in order. These records, including especially the "book containing the records of our dead" (D&C 128:24) are a portion of the "offering in righteousness" referred to by Malachi (3:3) which we are to present in His holy temple, and without which we shall not abide the day of his coming. (Genealogical Society Seminar, BYU, Aug. 1977, pp. 34-35.)

However, this offering will also involve the ordinance of sacrifice, as explained by Joseph Smith:

It will be necessary here to make a few observations on the doctrine set forth in the above quotation [Malachi 3:3], and it is generally supposed that sacrifice was entirely done away when the Great Sacrifice [*i.e.*, the sacrifice of the Lord Jesus] was offered up, and that there will be no necessity for the ordinance of sacrifice in future: but those who assert this are certainly not acquainted with the duties, privileges and authority of the priesthood, or with the Prophets.

The offering of sacrifice has ever been connected and forms a part of the duties of the Priesthood. It began with the Priesthood, and will be continued until after the coming of Christ, from generation to generation. We frequently have mention made of the offering of sacrifice by the servants of the Most High in ancient days, prior to the law of Moses; which ordinances will be continued when the Priesthood is restored with all its authority, power and blessings.

These sacrifices, as well as every ordinance belonging to the Priesthood, will, when the Temple of the Lord shall be built, and the sons of Levi be purified, be fully restored and attended to in all their powers, ramifications, and blessings. This ever did and ever will exist when the powers of the Melchisedic Priesthood are sufficiently manifest; else how can the restitution of all things spoken of by the holy Prophets be brought to pass? It is not to be understood that the law of Moses will be established again with all its rites and variety of ceremonies; this has never been spoken of by the Prophets; but those things which existed prior to Moses' day, namely, sacrifice, will be continued.

It may be asked by some, what necessity for sacrifice, since the Great Sacrifice was offered? In answer to which, if repentance, baptism, and faith existed prior to the days of Christ, what necessity for them since that time? The Priesthood has descended in a regular line from father to son, through their succeeding generations. (HC 4:211-12.)

**3:8** Spencer W. Kimball has provided the following observation on this verse:

No honest man would rob his Lord of tithes and offerings. . . .

Would you steal a dollar from your friend? a tire from your neighbor's car? Would you borrow a widow's insurance money with no intent to pay? Do you rob banks? You are shocked at such suggestions. Then, would you rob your God, your Lord, who has made such generous arrangements with you?

Do you have a right to appropriate the funds of your employer with which to pay your debts, to buy a car, to clothe your family, to feed your children, to build your home?

Would you take from your neighbor's funds to send your children to college or on a mission? Would you help relatives or friends with funds not your own? Some people get their standards mixed, their ideals out of line. Would you take tithes to pay your building fund or ward maintenance contribution? Would you supply gifts to the poor with someone else's money? The Lord's money?

The Lord continues to ask: "Will a man rob God? Yet ye have robbed me." (Malachi 3:8.)

And he has said that "today . . . is a day of sacrifice, and a day for the tithing of my people." (D&C 64:23.)

Does not the law of tithing apply to all the children of men, regardless of church or creed? All who believe the Bible really must believe that this is a law of God. (FPM, pp. 289-90.)

### 3:8-9 Payment of "tithes and offerings" has been an important part of God's plan of growth and progression from the very beginning.

And another great neglect and infringement of the law of God by the children of Israel was in relation to their Tithes and offerings. The law of Tithing was revealed in very early times to the people of God; but they failed to observe it, and the Prophets whom God sent to Israel declared that they had transgressed the laws, changed the ordinances, and broken the everlasting covenant. Covenants were made with Abraham, Isaac and Jacob, but their descendants broke them. They would not observe but they would transgress the laws which God gave unto them, and they continued to do so down to the days of Malachi. The Lord, through this Prophet, declared—"This whole nation have robbed me." I also declare that this whole people, called the Latter-day Saints, are guilty of the same sin—they have robbed the Lord in their Tithes and in their offerings. . . . If the Lord requires one-tenth of my ability to be devoted to building temples, meeting-houses, school-houses, to schooling our children, gathering the poor from the nations of the earth, bringing home the aged, lame, halt and blind, and building houses for them to live in, that they may be comfortable when they reach Zion, and to sustaining the Priesthood, it is not my prerogative to question the authority of the Almighty in this, nor of his servants who have charge of it. If I am required to pay my Tithing, it is my duty to pay it. (Brigham Young, JD 16:111.)

**3:10** Spencer W. Kimball has explained the modern meaning of the clause "that there may be meat in mine house":

We will remember our tithing—one tenth of our increase annually. We quote but one holy scripture on this: [Quoted Malachi 3:10-11.]

This is serious, and we must be faithful and honest in meeting this requirement. "That there may be meat in mine house" indicates the need for funds to meet the costs of building numerous branch and stake buildings, temples, furnishing them, missionary work, institute and seminary work, education work, and all the needs of the Saints. It must be remembered that all the tithing goes back to the people for their benefit.

We must remember also that this is a command of the Lord given thousands of years ago and restated in our own day. Fathers, mothers, youth, and children all should pay their tithing with accuracy and regularity and with a clear conscience. This is expected of the members of the Church. It is the fair way. It is the Lord's way. (Sweden Area CR, 1974, p. 9.)

**4:1** This verse appears in several of the standard works of the Church. Although the essential meaning is the same in the various quotations, some differences of wording exist. Compare the King James text with the following:

For behold, the day cometh that shall burn as an oven, and all the proud, yea, and all that do wickedly shall burn as stubble; for they that come shall burn them, saith the Lord of Hosts, that it shall leave them neither root nor branch. (JS-H 1:37.)

For behold, the day cometh that shall burn as an oven; and all the proud, yea, and all that do wickedly, shall be stubble; and the day that cometh shall burn them up, saith the Lord of Hosts, that it shall leave them neither root nor branch. (3 Ne. 25:1.)

**4:1** Theodore M. Burton has commented on key terms in this verse:

Malachi went on to say they "shall burn as stubble." This means that they shall be destroyed. By whom? Malachi explains, "They that come shall burn them, saith the Lord of Hosts."

. . . But what is meant by the expression "that it shall leave them neither root nor branch"? This expression simply means that wicked and indifferent persons who reject the gospel of Jesus Christ will have no family inheritance or patriarchal lineage—neither root (ancestors or progenitors) nor branch (children or posterity). Such persons cannot be received into the celestial kingdom of glory of resurrected beings, but must be content with a lesser blessing. (CR, Sept. 1967, p. 81.)

**4:1** Joseph Fielding Smith has provided commentary on the clause "the day that cometh shall burn them up":

Again, it is not a figure of speech that is meaningless, or one not to be taken literally when the Lord speaks of the burning. All through the scriptures we have the word of the Lord that at his coming the wicked and the rebellious will be as stubble and will be consumed. Isaiah has so prophecied. Malachi is very definite when he says: [Quoted Mal. 4:1.] Surely the words of the Lord are not to be received lightly or considered meaningless.

We are all commanded to labor "while it is called today." None shall be spared from this burning who "remain in Babylon." Babylon is the world, those who remain in Babylon are those who follow the practices of the world, and who do not accept in their hearts the word of the Lord. (CHMR 2:11.)

**4:5**   Joseph Smith has answered the question, "Why send Elijah?"

Elijah was the last prophet that held the keys of the Priesthood, and who will, before the last dispensation, restore the authority and deliver the keys of the Priesthood, in order that all the ordinances may be attended to in righteousness. It is true that the Savior had authority and power to bestow this blessing; but the sons of Levi were too prejudiced. "And I will send Elijah the prophet before the great and terrible day of the Lord," etc., etc. [Mal. 4:5-6.] Why send Elijah? Because he holds the keys of the authority to administer in all the ordinances of the Priesthood; and without the authority is given, the ordinances could not be administered in righteousness. (HC 4:211.)

**4:5-6**   When Elijah appeared in the Kirtland Temple April 3, 1836, he acknowledged his appearance was in fulfillment of the prophecy "which was spoken . . . by the mouth of Malachi." (D&C 110:14.) He then mentioned one of the purposes of his coming: "To turn the hearts of the fathers to the children, and the children to the fathers, lest the whole earth be smitten with a curse." (D&C 110:15.) Malachi 4:5-6 has been quoted or paraphrased in several other of the standard works of the Church. Compare these with the King James text:

Behold, I will reveal unto you the Priesthood, by the hand of Elijah the prophet, before the coming of the great and dreadful day of the Lord. . . .
And he shall plant in the hearts of the children the promises made to the fathers, and the hearts of the children shall turn to their fathers. If it were not so, the whole earth would be utterly wasted at his coming. (JS-H 1:38-39.)

Behold, I will reveal unto you the Priesthood, by the hand of Elijah the prophet, before the coming of the great and dreadful day of the Lord.
And he shall plant in the hearts of the children the promises made to the fathers, and the hearts of the children shall turn to their fathers.
If it were not so, the whole earth would be utterly wasted at his coming. (D&C 2:1-3.)

Behold, I will send you Elijah the prophet before the coming of the great and dreadful day of the Lord;

And he shall turn the heart of the fathers to the children, and the heart of the children to their fathers, lest I come and smite the earth with a curse. (3 Ne. 25:5-6.)

## The fact this prophecy has been fulfilled has been explained by Joseph Fielding Smith:

We know that this prophecy was fulfilled, for on the third day of April, 1836, Elijah came to Joseph Smith and Oliver Cowdery in the Kirtland Temple and conferred upon them this sealing authority. Since that day the hearts of the children have turned to their fathers, and without doubt the hearts of the fathers have turned to their children, and this influence is felt throughout the world causing the children to search the records of their dead. This fact is so definitely apparent that it cannot be denied. (AGQ 1:50.)

The power which Elijah restored is the power to seal and bind for eternity. It has to do more particularly with the ordinances of the temple and reaches out and embraces the dead as well as the living in its scope. And this is the real significance of the turning of the hearts of the fathers to the children and the hearts of the children to their fathers. This authority provides the means by which the fathers who are dead, and who died without the privilege of the gospel, may receive the ordinances of the gospel vicariously by their children performing them in the temples. The hearts of the children have turned to their dead fathers, and we believe that the hearts of the dead fathers have turned to their children through the preaching of the gospel to the dead. (RT, p. 173.)

## The following commentary on these verses has been provided by Joseph Fielding Smith:

Malachi declared that if the authority held by Elijah was not restored that "the whole earth" would be "smitten with a curse." When the great and dreadful day of the Lord comes, if there had not been restored the sealing power by which the ordinances in the House of the Lord could be performed for both the living and the dead, then the work of the Lord in relation to the salvation of man would fail. The great and dreadful day of the Lord is the day when judgments are poured out upon the wicked and the earth is cleansed of its iniquity. It is not to be a dreadful day to the righteous, but it certainly will be to all that do wickedly, for they will be as stubble and will be burned when the Lord comes in his glory, and they shall be left with "neither root nor branch." (Malachi 4:1.) This sealing power by which family ties are made secure and by which baptism for the dead becomes effective, is absolutely essential and must be exercised, for all those who died without the knowledge of the Gospel and who would have received it if it had been offered them while they were living on the earth before the end of the earth can come. If these keys were not here, then the dreadful day when Christ shall come would be a day of utter confusion, but the Lord, who knows the end from the beginning, revealed this Priesthood so that all who will, whether living or dead, may escape through the ordinances of the Gospel. (CHMR 3:82.)

**4:5-6**  On September 6, 1841, Joseph Smith quoted these verses of Malachi with the introduction "I will give unto you a quotation from one of the prophets, who had his eye fixed on the restoration of the priesthood, the glories to be revealed in the last days, and in an especial manner this most glorious of all subjects belonging to the everlasting gospel, namely, the baptism for the dead." (D&C 128:17.)

**4:6**  Joseph Smith has commented on the significance of this verse:

Now, the word *turn* here should be translated *bind,* or *seal.* But what is the object of this important mission? or how is it to be fulfilled? The keys are to be delivered, the spirit of Elijah is to come, the Gospel to be established, the Saints of God gathered, Zion built up, and the Saints to come up as saviors on Mount Zion.

But how are they to become saviors on Mount Zion? By building their temples, erecting their baptismal fonts, and going forth and receiving all the ordinances, baptisms, confirmations, washings, anointings, ordinations and sealing powers upon their heads, in behalf of all of their progenitors who are dead, and redeem them that they may come forth in the first resurrection and be exalted to thrones of glory with them; and herein is the chain that binds the hearts of the fathers to the children, and the children to the fathers, which fulfills the mission of Elijah. (HC 6:184.)

# APPENDIX
# KEY WORDS AND TERMS
# FROM THE KING JAMES VERSION
# OF THE OLD TESTAMENT

The following alphabetical list of difficult words or terms from the King James Version provides definitions, meanings, or alternate readings. If additional information is readily available on these terms in the entries of the Topical Guide (TG) or Bible Dictionary (BD) or in the commentaries (book, chapter, verse), these will also be indicated.

The King James Version of the Old Testament has been considered the standard for the Protestant world since it was first published in 1611. Today, however, even this traditional text is being closely examined for possible changes and improvements. Some changes are deemed desirable by many persons because of the following:

1. The meanings of many words in the King James Version have changed since the first edition in 1611.

2. Frequently the English word used in the King James text is not the only acceptable word. The translators were obligated to select only one of several acceptable words. The listing of several such acceptable words will help the reader understand the various shades of meaning associated with that particular term.

3. The Old Testament was written originally in Hebrew or a closely related Semitic language. Recent discoveries of ancient Hebrew texts (such as the Dead Sea Scrolls) have increased the scholars' understanding of the Hebrew language. Additional light has also been shed on the meaning of some difficult Hebrew idioms.

The Prophet Joseph Smith stated concerning the Bible: "Our latitude and longitude can be determined in the original Hebrew with far greater accuracy than in the English version. There is a grand distinction between the actual meaning of the prophets and the present translation." (TPJS, pp. 290-91.)

In the preparation of this list of words and terms, the King James text was compared with the earliest Hebrew manuscripts available at the present time. Whenever possible meanings of the Hebrew word or term vary significantly from the English of the King James Version, the additional possible meanings are included in parentheses after the word or term of the King James Version.

Several of the alternate readings in the following list are included as footnotes in the Bible. However, because an alphabetical list of such words is not included in the Bible, and because the alternate readings are seldom listed every time the word is used, this list will hopefully be helpful.

**abase**    humble; see TG "abase"

**abate**    decrease, deduct; see TG "abate"

**abominable**    detestable, unclean; see TG "abominable" and BD "abomination"

**accursed**    forbidden or banned; see TG and BD "accursed"

**adamant**    diamond, any extremely hard substance

**adjure**    charge (as by an oath); see TG "adjure"

**advertise**    tell, inform, notify

**affinity**    allied by marriage, companionship, friendliness

**afflict [your souls]**    humble

**ague**    fever

**albeit**    although, even though

**alien**    sojourner

**amerce**    fine

**ancient and honourable**    elder and man of rank; see TG "ancient"

**ancients**    aged, elders; see TG "ancient"

**angels**    messengers, agent; see TG and BD "angels"

**angle**    fish hook; see commentary for Hab. 1:15

**anything near**    anywhere near

**apothecary**    perfumer (ointment-maker)—similar to a druggist

**aprons**    things to gird about or wrap around the body; see TG "aprons"

**ark**    cabinet, chest, box; see BD "ark of the covenant"

**army**   host; see TG "army"

**[cunning] artificer**   wise man of magic arts, skilled man of craft

**assay**   attempt, try, assess

**assembly**   congregation; see TG "assembly for worship"

**asswage**   subside

**astonied**   astonished; see TG "astonished"

**asunder**   in two, apart; see TG "asunder"

**[as men] averse [from war]**   returning

**avouch**   declare, testify, acknowledge

**[I cannot] away with**   endure

**backsliding**   unruly, apostate; see TG "backsliding"

**badger**   dugong, seal

**bands**   troops, shackles; see TG "band"

**banner**   ensign; see TG "banner"

**banquet [of them]**   revelry

**base [kingdom]**   lowly, humble; see TG "base"

**basest [of men]**   humblest, lowliest; see TG "base"

**battlement [for thy roof]**   railing, parapet

**befall**   happen, come to pass, occur

**before [Jordan]**   on the east of

**be gracious**   show favor

**beguile**   deceive, cheat, defraud; see TG "beguile"

**Belial**   worthlessness, wickedness, ungodliness [when capitalized, often used as a substitute for *Satan*]; see BD "Belial"

**[children of] Belial**   children of worthlessness, of evil affiliation; see BD "Belial"

**bereave [my soul]**   deprive; see TG "bereave"

**bereave [thee]**   deprive of children

**besom [of destruction]**   broom

**bethink themselves**   consider in their heart, recall in their mind, remember, reflect

**betimes**   early, presently, promptly

**blains**   blisters, pustules, swellings

**blameless**   pure; see TG "blameless"

**blasting**   blight, rust, smut

**blemish**   defect; see "without blemish"; see TG "blemish"

**[his] blood [upon me]**   guilt; see TG and BD "blood"

**[flax was] bolled**   in bud, in seed

**[her] bond**   pledge; see TG "bond"

**bondage**   labor, slavery; see TG "bondage, physical"

**bonnets**   caps, headdresses; see TG "bonnet"

**booth**   shelter; see TG "booth"

**booties**   plunder, spoil, prey, loot

**border**   territory, coast; see TG "border"

**borrow**   ask, receive from another as a gift or as by inheritance; see TG "borrow, borrowing"

**botch [of Egypt]**   boils, swollen sores

**bottles**   waterskins, wineskins; see TG "bottle" and BD "bottles"

**bottom**   foundation, base

**bramble**   thistle, thornbush; see TG "bramble"

**brass**   bronze, copper, brass; see TG "brass"

**breaches**   gaps, holes, cracks, broken areas; see TG "breach"

**bread**   food

**breath**   spirit; see TG "breath of life"

**brimstone**   combustible materials such as sulfur and pitch; see TG and BD "brimstone"

**bring again [the captivity]**   turn away, remove, cause the return; see TG "bring, brought"; see commentary for Jer. 30:3

**brook**   wadi, valley

**bruise**   crush, grind; see TG "bruise"

**bruit**   report, rumor; see BD "bruit"

**buckler**   shield; see TG and BD "buckler"

**bullock**   young bull, offspring of cattle, calf, son of the herd, ox

**burden**   a message or prophecy of doom, heavy load, duty or responsibility; see TG "burden"

**burning boil**   inflamed boil

**caldrons**   pans, pots

**candlesticks**   lampstands; see TG and BD "candlestick"

**[gather the] captivity**   captives; see TG "captivity"

**[out of] captivity**   exile; see TG "captivity"

**carcase**   dead body; see TG "carcass"

**[dwell] carelessly**   without care, securely, confidently; see commentary for Judg. 18:7

**carpenters**   craftsmen, artisans, woodworkers; see TG "carpenter"

**castles**   fortifications, towers, citadels

**cattle**   sheep, flock, herd; see TG "cattle"

**caul**   lobe, fold, chamber, diaphragm

**celebrate [your sabbath]**   observe, keep

**censer**   shovel, vessel for burning incense; see TG and BD "censer"

**[we] certify [you]**   inform, declare

**[king's] chapel**   sanctuary; see TG "chapel"

**chapiters**   capitals; headwork; decorative heads of columns

**chapmen**   traders, traveling merchants

**chargers**   basins, platters; see BD "charger"

**chide**   strive with, complain, contend, rebuke

**chase roe**   hunt deer

**chasten thyself**   humble thyself; see TG "chastening"

**cheweth the cud**   brings up the cud; see commentary for Lev. 11:1-8

**[people] chode [with Moses]**   contended, strove, rebuked

**chure**   miser

**churlish**   rude, rough, hard, mean, cruel

**cieled [houses]**   paneled, covered

**clave**   held fast to, split, cut up, adhered

**clean passed**    thoroughly passed

**cleanse [the Levites]**    ritually purify; see TG "cleanse" and BD "clean and unclean"

**[bride out of her] closet**    wedding canopy

**cloths of service**    officiating garments; see TG "clothes"

**coast**    boundary, territory, area, border, land; in Jer. 31:8 "coasts" means "remote parts"

**coat**    tunic, garments, long robe; see TG "coat"

**cockle**    noxious weeds

**coffer**    basket, chest, trunk especially for valuables

**cogitations**    thoughts, meditation

**comeliness**    splendor; see TG "comeliness"

**comfort**    sustain; see TG "comfort"

**compass**    turn, enclose, surround, go around, ledge; see TG and BD "compass"

**compasseth**    encircles, surrounds; see TG "compass"

**concubine**    in Old Testament times, a legal, though second-class, wife; see TG "concubine"

**conduit**    ditch, aqueduct

**coney**    rock badger; see BD "coney"

**confectionary**    perfumer, ointment-maker

**confederacy**    league, agreement, conspiracy

**confound**    mix, confuse, put down; see TG "confound"

**confusion of face**    shame; see TG "confusion"

**congregation**    company, assembly; see TG "congregation"

**consecrate**    set apart, sanctify, ordain; see TG "consecration"

**consider**    look, examine; see TG "consider"

**contemn**    reject, despise, loathe

**convocation**    assembly, meeting; see TG "convocation"

**copper**    brass

**corn**    fodder, kernel, grain, wheat, barley, rye, beans, lentils; see TG and BD "corn"

**cornets**    horns, *shofarim,* trumpets

**cornfloor**  threshing floor

**corrupt**  make low, debase, destroy, consume; see TG "corrupt"

**coulter**  a blade on a plough; see BD "coulter"

**countenance**  face; see TG "countenance"

**couple**  join

**covering**  tent

**covet**  desire, take pleasure in; see TG "covet, covetousness"

**cracknel**  cake, cookie, cracker

**create**  shape, fashion, see TG "creation, create"

**creep**  swarm; see TG "creep, creeping"

**crib**  manger, stall

**crown**  wreath

**crown of the anointing oil**  consecration

**cruse**  dish, bowl

**cumbrance**  troubles, burden

**cunning**  skilled craftsmanship, learning, acquaintance with

**cunning works**  designs, work of a skilled workman

**curious girdle**  skillfully woven fastening band

**curious [works]**  artistic, detailed

**cut off**  excommunicate, withdraw, ostracize; see TG "cut"

**dam**  mother

**daubing**  plaster

**daysman**  arbiter, umpire, mediator

**deal**  measure, apportion, treat, act; see TG "deal, dealt"

**dearth**  famine; see TG "dearth"

**declare**  explain, clarify, expound

**[the great] deep**  a Hebrew idiom for *ocean*; see TG "deep, deeper"

**defence**  shade, protection, fortification; see TG "defense"

**denounce**  declare, proclaim

**[Egypt is] destroyed**  ruined, desolate, laid waste; see TG "destroy"

**diadem**    headdress, mitre

**diamond**    jasper, hard stone

**discomfit**    confuse, scatter, put to flight

**discover**    lay bare, uncover, reveal

**dissemble**    deceive, be false

**[gather them in their] drag**    net

**dragon**    jackal, serpents, see TG and BD "dragon"

**draught house**    outhouse, public latrine

**dress [the earth]**    till, cultivate

**dromedary**    fast steed, swift riding camel; see BD "dromedary"

**drop thy word**    preach

**duke**    chief, vassal prince, tribal chief, leader

**dwell with [me]**    honor, exalt; see TG "dwell"

**dwelt**    resided; see TG "dwell"

**ear his ground**    cultivate his ground; see TG "ear"

**earring upon her face**    ring in her nose

**earth**    land; see TG "earth"

**emerod**    tumor, boil, hemorrhoid; see BD "emerods"

**engines of war**    battering rams; see BD "engines of war"

**environ [us around]**    surround, encircle

**ephod**    special apron, garment for high priest and others; see BD "ephod"

**ere they attain to innocency**    before they become clean

**escheweth**    turn from; see TG "eschew"

**espied**    sought out, watched

**eunuch**    courtier, official, officer; see TG and BD "eunuch"

**evil**    unpleasant, calamity; see TG "evil"

**exalt**    raise; see TG "exalt"

**excellency [of Jacob]**    pride; see TG "excellency"

**[sword of] excellency**    victory, triumph; see TG "excellency"

**face [of the gate]**    front; see TG "face"

**fair [mitre]**    clean, pure

**familiar spirit**   a spirit medium's supposed associate in the spirit world; see TG "familiar"

**fast [by my maidens]**   near, close; see TG "fast, faster"

**fat [shall overflow]**   vat, tub, large vessel

**fear [God; the Lord]**   revere, respect, worship, honor, reverence, awe, regard; see TG and BD "fear"; see commentary for Lev. 19:3; Deut. 10:12

**[I will send my] fear**   terror; see TG "fear"

**fearful in praises**   to be praised with awe; see TG and BD "fear"

**fell away**   deserted

**fenced**   fortified, covered, protected, enclosed

**fens**   marshes

**fields**   open land; see TG "field"

**fiery [serpents]**   poisonous; see TG "fiery" and BD "fiery serpents"

**fillet**   band, thread, cord

**firmament**   expanse; see TG and BD "firmament"

**fir tree**   cypress, conifer; see BD "fir"

**[a] fit [man]**   chosen, appointed; see TG "fit"

**fitches**   spelt [a type of wheat]

**[in the] flags [by the river]**   among the reeds

**flagons [of wine]**   raisin cakes [used in fertility rites]

**flayed**   skinned

**folly**   disgrace, wantonness; see TG "folly"

**foot**   base

**[have] forborn [to fight]**   ceased

**formed thee**   gave you birth; see TG "form"

**former rain**   winter rain; see BD "rain"

**form of his visage**   expression of his countenance; see TG "form"

**fray**   terrify, frighten

**fretting**   malignant, corroding, gnawing

**froward**   perverse, deceitful, crooked; see BD "froward"; in Isa. 57:17 "frowardly" means "returning"

**frying pan**    stewing pan

**furbished**    polished

**garners**    storehouses, granaries

**gates**    cities, towns; see TG and BD "gate"

**[let thy cattle] gender**    breed, beget, produce

**generations**    genealogical lines, posterity, lineage, descent; see TG "generation" and BD "genealogy"

**gentile**    the basic meaning of the Semite word is "nations" or "people," but the English word has come to mean "non" such as "non-Hebrew," "non-Israelite," or "non-Jew" see commentary for Gen. 10:5

**giants**    the Hebrew word is *nephilim* which could be translated "fallen ones"; see TG "giant" and BD "giants"

**gift**    bribe; see TG "gift"

**gin**    trap, bait, lure

**glory**    wealth, honor; see TG "glory"

**goads**    sharp pointed sticks to spur oxen onward; see BD "goads"

**gotten**    made, converted

**gourd**    castor bean plant; see TG and BD "gourd"

**grain of oppression**    profit by extortion

**green withs**    new cords, e.g., fresh or moist sinews from animals

**grief of mind**    bitterness of spirit, great sorrow, mental anguish; see TG "grief"

**groves**    cultic deities, fertility cult goddesses, idolatrous objects associated with fertility cults, pillars, shrines; see TG and BD "grove"; see commentary for 2 Kgs. 21:3

**habergeon**    corselet, coat of mail; see BD "habergeon"

**habitation of dragons**    resorts of jackals; see TG "habitation"

**habitation [of the shepherds]**    pastures; see TG "habitation"

**haft**    handle, hilt of a dagger

**hallow**    sanctify, consecrate, keep holy, dedicate, purify; see TG "hallow, hallowed"

**[her that] halteth**    is lame, crippled; see TG "halt"

**hanging**   screen, curtain

**hap**   chance, good fortune, luck

**haply**   perchance

**harnessed**   equipped for battle, armored; see TG "harness"

**hart**   gazelle, fawn, deer; see BD "hart"

**haunt**   go to, frequent, attend

**hazel**   almond

**heaps**   ruins; see TG "heap"

**heathen**   nations, gentiles; see TG "heathen"

**heave**   elevate, lift up, raise

**heave offering**   contribution; see TG "heave offering"

**help meet**   helper suited to, worthy of, corresponding to; see TG "help"

**hew**   cut; see TG "hew, hewn"

**[stone] hewed in the mountain**   quarry stone; see TG "hew, hewn"

**high heaps**   signposts

**hindermost**   last

**hiss**   whistle, signal, summon; see TG "hiss, hissing"

**hoar hairs**   grey hairs

**holden**   strengthened; see TG "hold, held, holden"

**[into] holds**   strongholds; see TG "hold, held, holden"

**holy flock**   flock consecrated for sacrifices

**holy place**   sanctuary; see BD "holy place"

**hook**   nail

**host**   camp, encampment, army; see TG "host"

**hough**   hock, cut the hamstring of; see BD "hough"

**house [of their fathers]**   family, clan, tribe; see TG and BD "house"

**houses**   households, descendants; see TG and BD "house"

**imputed**   reckoned

**inclosings**   settings

**[in the] increase**   at the harvest; see TG "increase"

**infinite**   without limit; see TG "infinite"

**infirmity**   affliction, malady, physical impairment, imperfection

**[her] infirmity**   menstrual impurity; see TG "infirmity"

**inflamation of the burning**   scar

**iniquity**   guilt; see TG "iniquity"

**instructer**   forger, sharpener

**in the plain of Mamre**   by the terebinths [a small tree] of Mamre

**inventions**   devices, arts, designs

**inward [friend]**   intimate; see TG "inward"

**in ward**   under guard, secret, hidden

**isles**   coasts, continents; see TG "isle" and BD "isles"

**issue [of her blood]**   fountain; see TG "issue"

**jasper**   chrysolite, dark green stone; see BD "jasper"

**jealous**   possessing sensitive and deep feelings, desiring exclusive devotion, zealous; see TG "jealous, jealousy"; see commentary for Ex. 34:14

**[stir up] jealousy**   zeal, ardor; see TG "jealous, jealousy"

**jewels**   royal treasure, see TG "jewel"

**joined affinity**   allied by marriage, yoked together

**judge**   rule; see TG "judge"

**judge not**   do not do justice; see TG "judge"

**judgments**   ordinances, decrees, laws, precepts, justice, equity; see TG "judgment"

**justice**   charity, righteousness; see TG "justice"

**kill**   murder; see TG "kill"

**kin**   relative; see TG "kin"

**kinds**   families, species, races; see TG "kind"

**kine**   cattle, cows; see TG and BD "kine"

**knit together**   united, bind, fastened

**knop**   crown shaped circlets, bud, knob; see BD "knop"

**lace**   ribbon, cord, thread

**latter rain**   spring rain; see BD "rain"

**laugh**   rejoice; see TG "laughter, laugh"

**laver**   wash basin; see BD "laver"

**law**   teaching, doctrine; see TG "law"

**league**   covenant, pact, treaty, agreement; see TG "league"

**lesser cattle**   sheep, goats; see TG "less, lesser"

**lien**   lain; see TG "lie, lay, lain"

**lifted up mine hand**   covenanted; see TG "lift"

**light [off the camel]**   dismount

**light thing**   insignificant thing

**ligure**   opal

**liquors**   vintage, alcohol, any liquid, as milk, juice, etc.; see TG "word of wisdom"

**lodge**   watchman's hut, temporary dwelling, cabin; see TG "lodge"

**[eyes of the] lofty**   haughty

**looketh [southward]**   faces

**LORD**   Jehovah; see TG "Lord" and BD "Christ"

**[casting of] lots**   pebbles; see TG "lot" and BD "lots, casting of"

**lust**   desire, long or yearn for

**lusty**   fat, hardy

**[maketh a man] mad**   foolish; see TG "mad"

**make fat [thy bones]**   strengthen

**manner**   statute, ordinance; see TG "manner"

**mantle**   rug, blanket, covering; see TG "mantle"

**mark [her mouth]**   see, note

**matrix**   womb

**mattock**   an implement for digging and grubbing

**maw**   stomach, liver

**meat**   food, meal; see TG and BD "meat"

**meat offering**   cereal, meal, or flour; see BD "meat offering"

**[it is not] meet**   right, fitting, proper; see BD "meet"

**[mountains] melt**   quake; see TG "melt"

**mercy seat**    see BD "mercy seat"

**mightily [oppressed]**    forcibly, violently; see TG "mightily"

**milch [kine]**    milk

**minister**    attendant, servant; see TG "minister"

**mirth**    rejoicing; see TG "mirth"

**mischief**    evil, misfortune; see TG "mischief"

**mitre**    turban, cap, headdress worn by the high priest

**Molech**    a god of the Moabites, represented by a large statue with a hollow belly, in which a fire could be stoked and into which infants were sometimes thrown to be sacrificed; see BD "Molech"

**mollified**    softened, soothed

**most holy**    holy of holies

**[cast up a] mount**    siegework; see TG "mount"

**murrain**    plague

**nail**    tent peg or pin; see TG "nail"

**naked**    riotous, let loose; see TG "naked"

**neesings**    sneezings

**nether**    lower, below, underneath

**nether parts of the earth**    below the earth, the grave

**Nethinims**    temple servants

**new wine**    grape juice; see TG "wine"

**nitre**    alkali, carbonate of soda

**noisome**    wild, evil

**not ought [of your work]**    none of

**oblation**    contribution, offering; see TG "oblation"

**offering**    sacrifice, contribution; see TG "offering"

**old corn**    grain from previous harvestings

**old men**    elders; see TG "old age"

**oracle**    innermost room of Solomon's temple, inner sanctuary; see TG "oracle"

**oracle of God**    word of God; see TG "oracle"

**order**    arrange; see TG "order"

**organ** flute, pipe; see TG "musical instruments" and BD "organ"

**ouches** settings, plaited work

**ought** any

**over against** opposite, facing, adjoining

**palaces [of Jerusalem]** citadels, great buildings

**pan** griddle

**parlour** upper room, roof, chamber

**pastor** shepherd; see TG "pastor"; see commentary for Jer. 3:15

**pattern** plan; see TG "pattern"

**pavilion** booth, shelter, tent, see TG "pavilion"

**pay tribute** provide labor

**peculiar people** treasured people; see TG "peculiar people" and BD "peculiar"

**[all the] people [around about]** nations

**peradventure** perhaps

**perfect** complete, whole, having integrity; see TG "perfection, perfect, perfectly"

**perpetual** never ending; see TG "perpetual"

**pilled** peeled, stripped

**pine away** decay, waste away

**pine [tree]** ash

**pining sickness** emaciation

**pin** peg

**pit** well, cistern; see TG and BD "pit"

**pitched** set camp, encamped; see TG "pitch"

**pity** concern; see TG "pity"

**plain man** whole, complete, perfect, simple; see TG "plain"

**plaister** daub, plaster

**plead [with me]** contend, quarrel; see TG "plead"

**pleasant [bread]** desirable; see TG "pleasant"

**pluck [it out]** draw; see TG "pluck"

**poll**   cut, trim, cut off hair

**poll**   head

**possess**   dispossess; see TG "possess"

**possessor of heaven**   creator; see TG "possessor"

**post**   runner, messenger

**post**   pillar; see TG "post"

**pourtray**   engrave, portray

**preacher**   gather, call together; see commentary for Eccl. 1:1; see TG "preacher"

**presently**   the first of all, immediately; see BD "presently"

**pressfat**   winevat

**prey**   spoil, booty, plunder; see TG "prey"; see commentary for Esth. 9:10, 16

**prince**   leader, president, head, ruler, official, minister, priest, officer; see TG "prince"

**privily**   secretly, privately; see TG "privily"

**profane**   irreligious, common, pollute; see TG "profane"

**profaned**   dishonored; see TG "profane"

**profaneness**   ungodliness; see TG "profane"

**prove**   try, test; see TG "prove"; see commentary for 1 Sam. 17:39

**provender**   food, fodder

**psaltery**   lyre; see BD "psaltery"

**pulse**   foods made of seeds, grains; see BD "pulse"

**purtenance**   edible inner parts

**put him down**   deposed him

**put to the worse**   smitten

**quenched as tow**   extinguished as smoldering flax; see TG "quench"

**[owner shall be] quit**   clear, innocent

**quit yourself like men**   be men

**railed on**   swooped upon; see TG "rail"

**raiment**   garment, clothing; see TG "raiment"

**raven**   torn flesh, also, a type of bird; see TG "raven"

**rear up**  set up, raise; see TG "rear"

**recompense his trespasses**  restore his guilt; see TG "recompence, recompense"

**reconcile**  make atonement; see TG "reconciliation, reconcile"

**Red Sea**  Reed Sea; see BD "Red Sea"

**refrain [my mouth]**  restrain; see TG "refrain"

**reins [and the heart]**  inward parts, kidneys; see TG and BD "reins"

**remainder**  rest

**[I will] render**  restore; see TG "render"

**rent**  was torn; see TG "rent"

**repent**  relent, change, feel sorry; see TG "repent, repentance" and BD "repentance"

**repented**  to be sorry, moved to pity, have compassion, sighed, felt sorrow, relent; see TG "repent, repentance" and BD "repentance"; see commentary for Num. 23:19.

**replenish**  fill; see TG and BD "replenish"

**reprove**  decide with equity, correct, discipline, call to account; see TG "reproof, reprove"

**rereward**  rear, rearguard, those at the back of the group

**requite**  do, recompense

**requited**  returned

**residue [of Jerusalem]**  remnant; see TG "residue"

**return**  repent, go back, gather; see TG "return"

**reward**  bribe; see TG "reward"

**rie**  spelt [a type of wheat], rye

**[thou shalt rule over him with] rigour**  severity

**rise in obscurity**  shine in the darkness; see TG "rise, rose, risen"

**rising**  swelling

**[on this side of the] river**  the Euphrates river; see TG and BD "river"

**river of Egypt**  Wadi of Egypt—modern Wadi El Arish in northern Sinai; see TG "river" and BD "Egypt, river of"

**roe**  deer

**roebuck**   gazelle

**[home of the] rolls**   books, archives, scrolls; see TG and BD "roll"

**rump**   fat tail

**sacrifice**   offering, offer, self-denial; see TG "sacrifice" and BD "sacrifices"

**saint**   holy one; see TG "saints" and BD "saint"

**salute [our master]**   bless, greet; see TG "salute"

**sanctify**   consecrate, make clean, set apart for holy purposes; see TG "sanctification, sanctify"

**Satan**   the Adversary, Accuser; see TG "Satan" and BD "devil"

**[take no] satisfaction [for the life of a murderer]**   ransom, fine; see TG "satisfy"

**savour**   fragrance, essence

**scall**   scurf, tinea [or other scaly symptoms], scalp disease

**scarlet**   crimson; see TG "scarlet"

**scorpion**   stinging whip; see TG and BD "scorpion"

**scourge**   investigate; make inquiry, flog; see TG "scourge"

**seethe**   cook, boil; see BD "sod"

**seethe therein**   cook them; see BD "sod"

**selvedge**   edge of the juncture, selvage

**separation**   consecration; see TG "separation, separate"

**[her] separation**   menstruation; see TG "separation, separate"

**serve themselves of him**   make him subservient, enslave him, exploit him; see TG "serve"

**servile [work]**   laboring, manual

**settled on their lees**   complacent, indifferent

**sever**   separate, segregate, distinguish between, set apart, cut off; see TG "sever"

**several [city]**   single, individual

**several [house]**   separate

**shew**   show, tell, accomplish for you, declare, reveal; see TG "show, shew"

**shewbread** bread of faces, bread of the Presence; see TG "bread, shewbread" and BD "shewbread"

**shittah tree** acacia; see BD "shittim"

**shittim** acacia; see BD "shittim"

**shoulder** leg; see TG "shoulder"

**silly** naive; see TG "silly"

**similitude** form; see TG "similitude"

**sith** since

**slew** killed; see TG "slay, slew, slain"

**slime [for mortar]** bitumen

**snuffed at it** belittled it

**snuffer** device for extinguishing lamps

**socket** base

**sod** boil; see BD "sod"

**sodden** boiled, cooked

**sodomite** male prostitute, cultic

**sojourner** temporary dweller, alien newcomer, with no inherited rights; see TG "sojourn"

**[battle was] sore** heavy, hard, strong, intense; see TG "sore, sorely"

**sore [evil]** grievous; see TG "sore, sorely"

**sore athirst** very thirsty

**sorrow** travail, pain; see TG "sorrow"

**soul** person; see TG "soul"

**spoil** despoil, make empty; see TG "spoil"

**spoiled** plundered; see TG "spoil"

**spring of the day** dawn

**spue** vomit, spew

**statute of judgment** statutory law; see TG "statute"

**staves** poles; see TG "stave"

**stay** armrest

**stayed** ceased, stopped, withheld

**stayed up** propped up, supported

**stiffnecked**    stubborn

**stock**    wood, idol

**[words have been] stout**    strong, proud, hard, haughty

**strait**    narrow, tight; see TG "strait"

**straiten them**    distress, afflict; see TG "straiten"

**straitly**    strictly

**straitness**    distress; see TG "straiten"

**strange**    unauthorized; see TG "strange"

**strange**    foreign; see TG and BD "stranger"

**stranger**    resident alien, sojourner, alien, proselyte, unauthorized person, foreigner; see TG and BD "stranger"

**strange vanities**    foreign idols; see TG and BD "stranger"

**strengthen**    assist; see TG "strengthen"

**stricken**    smitten; see TG "strike, struck, stricken"

**stricken in age**    advanced; see TG "strike, struck, stricken"

**stripling**    young man; see TG "stripling"

**stumblingblock**    idol; see TG "stumblingblock"

**subtil**    crafty, sly; see TG "subtle, subtile"

**suburbs**    open land surrounding Levite cities

**succour us**    help us, aid us

**such like**    like them

**[will not] suffer [the destroyer]**    allow, permit; see TG and BD "suffer"

**supple [thee]**    cleanse, soothe

**sware**    promise, covenant; see TG "swearing, swear, sware, sworn"

**swear**    oath, covenant, curse; see TG "swearing, swear, sware, sworn"

**sweet calamus**    aromatic calamus

**Syrian tongue**    Aramaic

**tabering**    beating

**tabernacle**    tent, dwelling place; see TG and BD "tabernacle"

**tabernacle of the congregation**    tent of meeting, tent of assembly; see TG and BD "tabernacle"

**taches**   clasps, hooks

**take knowledge**   notice

**tale**   quota, number

**target**   large shield

**tell [the stars]**   count; see TG "tell, told"

**temper [with fine flour]**   moisten, soften

**temple**   palace, great building; see TG and BD "temple"

**tempt**   test, prove, try; see TG and BD "tempt"

**tenon**   pin

**tent**   tabernacle; see TG "tent"

**tents**   camps; see TG "tent"

**[God is] terrible**   feared, revered, awesome; see TG "terrible"

**thresholds [of the gates]**   storehouses

**throughly**   thoroughly

**timbrel**   small hand drum

**tire [her head]**   adorn; see BD "tire"

**tire of thine head**   headdress, turban; see BD "tire"

**Tirshatha**   governor; see BD "Tirshatha"

**token**   sign, symbol; see TG "token"

**tong**   pan

**to wit**   namely

**traffick**   trade, traders, traffic, commerce

**travail**   business, work, occupation; see TG "travail"

**treasure**   storehouse; see TG "treasure"

**treasure city**   storage city, granary; see TG "treasure"

**trespass offering**   guilt offering; see TG "trespass" and BD "sacrifices"

**tributary**   servant, tribute payment

**troop**   caravan

**trumpet**   ram's horn, *shofar* or alarm; see TG "trumpet"

**try**   test; see TG "try, tried"

**turtle**   turtle dove; see BD "turtle"

**two leaved gates**   double doors

**uncircumcised lips**   impaired speech, stammering lips, slow of speech

**under the sun**   on the earth

**unicorn**   wild ox, buffalo, bison; see BD "unicorn"

**unrighteousness**   injustice; see TG "unrighteous, unrighteousness"

**unwittingly**   through ignorance, unknowingly, unintentionally

**usury**   interest, bribe; see TG and BD "usury"

**utter court**   outer court

**vail**   cloak, covering, mantle [a square piece of cloth used as an outer robe]; see TG "veil, vail" and BD "veil"

**vail of the covering**   screening veil; see TG "veil, vail" and BD "veil"

**vain**   empty, idle, worthless, reckless [or violent]; see TG "vain"

**vale**   lowland, foothill area, valley

**vanities of the Gentiles**   worthless idols of the nations; see TG and BD "vanity"

**vanity**   empty, fleeting, unsubstantial, transitoriness, folly; see TG and BD "vanity"; see commentary for Eccl. 1:2

**vestments**   ceremonial robes

**vexation of spirit**   "striving after wind," frustration; see TG "vexation"

**vex**   crush; see TG "vex"

**victuals**   bread, provisions, goods, food, grain, supplies

**vine undressed**   the time of its separation, consecration

**visage**   appearance

**visit**   punish; see TG "visit"

**[remember me, and] visit [me]**   be mindful of; see TG "visit"

**void**   empty, unoccupied

**voluntary**   free; see TG "voluntary"

**wait upon me**   watch for me, in wait for me, serve me; see TG "wait"

**[cities] walled up to heaven**   fortified

**[shall never] want** lack, need; see TG "want" and BD "wanted".

**[kept the] ward** guard, watch

**ware** merchandise

**wash** bathe; see TG "wash, washing"

**waste places** ruins; see TG "waste"

**wax** increase continually, become worn, decay, grow, become, be aroused; see TG "wax"

**waxen great** grown large; see TG "wax"

**waxen old** become old; see TG "wax"

**weary themselves [to commit iniquity]** are impatient; see TG "weary"

**well favoured** good in appearance, handsome

**wen** wart, blemish

**were conversant** went, walked

**whatsoever** all, anyone

**whatsoever parteth** any that divides

**whatsoever soul** any person

**wilily** craftily, with cunning

**wist** knew; see TG "wot, wist"

**wit** know, learn

**witch** one practicing sorcery, one communing with evil spirits, harlot; see TG "witch, witchcraft"

**without blemish** whole, sound, perfect

**[earth was] without form** empty, desolate

**without spot** without blemish, without defect

**without [the sanctuary]** outside

**wonderful [plagues]** extraordinary

**wont** accustomed

**worse liking [than the children]** less healthy; see TG "worse"

**worthies** nobles, leaders; TG "worthiness, worthy"

**wot** know; see TG "wot, wist"

**woundeth** smites, bruises; see TG "wound"

**wrath shall wax hot**    anger shall be aroused; see TG "wrath"

**wreathed**    intertwined

**wreathen chains**    cords

**wroth**    angry

**wrought**    work, does; see TG "wrought"

**wrought folly**    done a foolish thing; see TG "wrought"

# INDEX